Marketing Issues in Modern China

Marketing Issues in Modern China

Edited by

Robert Guang Tian
Dan Trotter
Wong Ming Wong
Camilla Hong Wang

NA

NorthAmerican
Business Press

Atlanta – Seattle – South Florida - Toronto

North American Business Press, Inc
Atlanta, Georgia
Seattle, Washington
South Florida
Toronto, Canada

Marketing Issues in Modern China
Modern China Series
ISBN: 9780988919334
© 2013 All Rights Reserved.

Supported by the Publication Fund of Shantou University

Along with trade books for various business disciplines, the North American Business Press also publishes a variety of academic-peer reviewed journals.

Library of Congress Control Number: 2013932953

Library of Congress
Cataloging in Publication Division
101 Independence Ave., SE
Washington, DC 20540-4320
Printed in theUnited States of America

First Edition:

PREFACE

In today's world market no one would deny the importance of China marketing and no one will ignore the increasingly tight connections between China and the rest of the world. "As China goes, so goes the world" has become almost a common sense shared by the business leaders of the world. China is roaring into the 21st century with the force of a locomotive and its economy has doubled almost every six years. The great changes that have been made by the Chinese people in every aspect not only impact the domestic market in China but also the international economy (Wu, 2009; Yu et al., 2006). In Karl Gerth's recently published book, *As China Goes, So Goes the World* (Gerth, 2010), the famous Harvard Business School Spangler Family Professor William Kirby claims that the changes that define Chinese markets today may transform the world in the future.

More than thirty years ago the economic system of China was a centralized planning system that remained largely closed to international trade, in which the market mechanism played a limited role in the production and consumption process. In the late 1970s and early 1980s, under the leadership of Deng Xiaoping, China launched its economic system reform and open door campaign. It is this campaign that brought China into a market oriented economy, created a rapidly growing for-profit sector, and made China a major player in the global economy. As such the market mechanism has became an important factor in the economic development of China (Tian and Wang, 2003; Tian 2008). Measured on a purchasing power parity (PPP) basis that adjusts for price differences, China in 2009 stood as the second-largest economy in the world after the US, although in per capita terms the country is still lower middle-income (Central Intelligence Agency, 2010; Saxon, 2006).

As the market oriented economic system in China is relatively new to the world, China marketing is even newer to marketers in the world. The new concept of China marketing refers to all the issues pertaining to effective marketing in China by domestic marketers and international marketers alike, issues including, but not limited to, product design and development, pricing strategy, distribution and logistics management, and advertising and promotions. As the market in China evolves and changes, marketing strategy must adapt to the changing environment. There is no doubt that the economic transition in China will definitely affect marketing strategies across a wide range of industries, namely telecommunications, the auto industry, the hospitality industry, the airline industry, textiles, cosmetics, and so on (Alon, 2003; Gerth, 2010).

Marketing in China for us mainly refers to effectively marketing the products and services produced by Chinese domestic marketers to the international market. It covers a large set of subjects, such as how to upgrade products and service to meet international market needs, how to effectively reach target markets and how to position products and services and how to effectively conduct advertising and promotions internationally and cross-culturally. Chinese marketers need to realize the changes that are taking place every day in the world marketplace, and to better market their products and service internationally they must have a better understanding of the international market environment from a cross-cultural perspective (Paliwoda and Ryans, 2008; Terpstra and Sarathy, 2001; Yu et al., 2006).

We all realize that China markets and Chinese consumers are getting attention from marketers and scholars alike. We all agree to the fact that there are many special issues about China markets and Chinese consumers that require multi-disciplinary approaches. We all believe that a bridge should be built to connect world marketers and scholars with Chinese markets and consumers, as well as to connect Chinese marketers and scholars with international markets and consumers. Therefore, it is important that a platform be set up to provide marketers and scholars worldwide with a place to share ideas and exchange information about China and international markets.

This is the reason that we decided to edit this book - to explore the importance of China Marketing and Marketing in China. It is our honor to have this opportunity to serve the community of China marketing scholars and to meet the needs of China marketing scholars for collecting and publishing academic works with strong practical value. It is our duty to build such a platform for our colleagues to share their thoughts, their findings, and their ideas. It is our obligation to promote China marketing and marketing in China as a special field within the discipline of marketing. It is our hope that in the near future China marketing and marketing in China as a special field will be able to draw more and more attention from the academic world and from the business world as well. We are extremely confident about the success of China marketing and marketing in China in the world today as well as tomorrow.

Like most other rewarding endeavors, the experience of editing this book has been a rewarding one, as it has given us the opportunity to appreciate the great strides made in the field of business anthropology. We feel it is auspicious to have collaborated on a subject matter of immense interest to us in an atmosphere of warm collegiality. No flight of fantasy is required to see that this book could not have been created without help from many business acquaintances, friends, and colleagues at many universities, who have provided the editors inspiration, encouragement, and counsel in the realization of this project.

We especially want to sincerely thank those professionals who have contributed early on to this work with their ideas, suggestions, and research activities. Without the resourceful and competent assistance of the authors who made their initial contributions to the *International Journal of China Marketing*, this project would not have attained the expertise it offers academic as well as business readers. Many thanks go to Dr. Baoku Li, Dean of the Marketing Management College at Liaoning Engineering and Technology, for his sponsorship of the *International Journal of China Marketing*.

We would like to express our gratitude to the leadership of the Business School at Shantou University for all the support they gave to us. We would also like to give our thanks to the editorial staff at the North American Business Press, a fine organization with superb personnel. It is a pleasure to have the competent professionals at NABP to support us. Therefore, a special note of genuine appreciation goes to Dr. David Smith, the Editor in Chief of NABP for sharing our vision, for encouraging our efforts, and for having the courage to see this project through to its completion. Finally, we are proud to announce that the publishing of this book has been financially supported by the Shantou University Publishing Foundation.

Robert Guang Tian
Dan Trotter
Wong Ming Wong
Camilla Hong Wang

TABLE OF CONTENTS

Part I: General Issues in China Marketing

Part II: Marketing Mix in China

FOREWORD

CHINA MARKETING AND MARKETING IN CHINA
Feng Ouyang

Dr. Philip Kotler, the famous marketing professor and general advisor of the *International Journal of China Marketing*, indicates in the preface of IJCM Vol. 1 (1) that the Western world has become increasingly worried about China's competition for jobs in the manufacturing industry and for energy resources. He further asserts that Westerners have failed to notice an even more serious fact: China's rapid assimilation of American-style consumer culture, which is revolutionizing the lives of hundreds of millions of Chinese, will have the potential to reshape the world. Therefore to study China marketing and marketing in China is a very important topic in the contemporary marketing world. As a marketing professor in China, I personally hold the same opinion as that of Dr. Kotler concerning consumer issues in modern China. I believe that studies concerning China marketing will become of more interest to and will have more and more relevance for marketers in the whole world.

In today's world nobody doubts the growth and size of the Chinese economy. Even a casual observer of the global market will see that China is among the world's most prominent developing economic regions. China's rapid economic expansion has been widely reported. There is no question that China is poised to become one of the top innovating nations in the near future. At the same time Chinese firms also have evolved during this period in terms of their commitment to the global marketplace. Chinese firms have already taken leadership positions in some industries, and have benefited from government investment in innovation as a bridge to future competitiveness. Therefore, it is important for Chinese firms to become better acquainted with marketing theories and methods in order to market their products more efficiently in both domestic and international markets.

Recent evidence suggests that, some large Western multinationals are transferring senior level executives to China to administer global research and development. These firms understand the importance of getting closer to the Chinese customer and markets, as such, they are eager to know marketing issues in China.

The above phenomena serve as the background for this well edited reference book of *Marketing Issues in Modern China*. The editors of this book collected and adapted research articles most of which were previously published in the *International Journal of China Marketing*. All the editors of this book have had experience in marketing and business in China and in the

USA. The articles they have selected reflect their vision and understanding concerning marketing issues in modern China.

The book is divided into three main sections: (a) general marketing issues in China, (b) marketing mix issues in China, and (c) consumer issues in China. As indicated, the China market today is becoming closely integrated with the global market, and in fact, has become one of the most important parts of the global market. Included in this volume are articles featuring some outstanding Chinese enterprises which have contributed to the world's economy. Covered are such topics as channel management as practiced at Lenovo, the after sales service of Haier, the brand operation of Wahaha, the marketing strategy of Changhong, the implementation of a low cost strategy at Galanz. These marketing strategies are uniquely applicable to the China market. However, even if these well known Chinese enterprises mentioned above are considered to be successful, in some aspects they are still facing some problems with their marketing. For example, these companies have experienced such problems as weakness in data management and in the market segmentation process, building brands, adding value to their services, marketing resource allocation, and promotion strategy.

It is our view that solving these problems depends on judiciously blending the practice of Chinese enterprises and the theoretical research and explorations of scholars. On the one hand, scholars explore theory and make careful analysis in order to enrich the study and teaching of marketing theory, and on the other hand marketing practitioners will provide useful guidance and reference. The close integration of theory and practice, as well as more interaction between industry and the academy, will help propel Chinese enterprises to an ever-brighter future.

We believe that *Marketing Issues in Modern China* will provide a launchpad for future research into China marketing. It will also provide more ideas for Chinese enterprises when they engage in marketing research, and can even guide senior managers in their future practice.

INTRODUCTION

Marketing in modern China has become a profoundly significant enterprise. This is not surprising, given the remarkable growth of the Chinese market economy. A cursory review of statistics published by experts will overwhelm the reader, and convince him of the dynamic energy of the world's soon-to-be number one economy. Here are a few examples. From 1978 to 2010, there has been a tenfold increase of GDP (Kotler, 2010) In the second quarter of 2010, China's economy was valued at $1.33 trillion, ahead of Japan, whose economy was valued at $1.28 trillion. (Kotler, 2010) In terms of land area, China is the third or fourth largest country in the world. In terms of population, China is the most populous country in the world, containing a population nearly five times that of the United States. In terms of the size of its economy, China is the second largest economy in the world (Fisher, 2012). No one, not even casual observers, doubts that China is among the world's most prominent developing economic regions. Some would even argue that when adjustment has been made for purchase power parity, China has even surpassed the United States in terms of purchasing power. Chinese exports to the United States surpassed the $100 billion mark as far back as 2006. China is also a leading destination for Western manufacturing capital, serving as the eighth largest investment destination for United States manufacturers. Hundreds of leading Western companies, from consumer retailers (Starbucks) and frequently-purchased consumer goods (Pepsico) to cars (General Motors) and services (Disney, Federal Express) have in recent years greatly expanded their business commitments in China, marketing a wide variety of manufactured products and services to the increasingly affluent Chinese market (Benedetto, 2012). Not only does Western manufacturing capital invested in China tie China to the rest of the world, but China's economic involvement with the West also links the two areas of the world. China's relationship with Walmart is emblematic of the growing fusion of the economies of the United States and China. In 2003, ten to 13 percent of Chinese exports to the United States ended up on the shelves of Walmart. If Walmart were a nation, there would only be four countries whose exports received from China would rank ahead of Walmart. Walmart's trade with and within China is 1.5% of China's gross domestic product. Eighty percent of factories supplying Walmart are located in China. (Fishman, 2006)

China's economic miracle can not merely be considered as an academic object to be studied. Dealing with China is of vital importance to businesspeople, government officials, and others who want to penetrate the fog surrounding the world's most dynamic economy. Understanding the Chinese economy is not an option, it is a necessity. The editors of this

3

volume present the marketing research articles contained herein in the hope that the reader will gain a feeling for the subtle nuances of Chinese markets and marketers. We hope that any information gleaned will advance understanding, and push back stereotypes, with regard to the People's Republic.

An economy as charged with energy as China's is will inevitably invite scholarly scrutiny. Because China's rise is relatively recent, marketing research published in English is in its infancy, although research into China marketing is increasing. Most China marketing research done to date concerns consumer behavior, and most research has been qualitative, although there is a trend towards quantitative research. The research has been broad in scope, but not extremely deep. Most researchers of the China market writing in English are ethnic Chinese; however, there has been much cooperation between Western researchers and Chinese researchers. Although the top institutions supporting China marketing research are in Hong Kong, most China marketing researchers are not located in Asia, but rather in the West. Giving the vibrant dynamism of the Chinese economy, it is not surprising that the demand for China marketing research has outstripped the supply. (Trotter & Tian 2012)

While marketing in China shares many common features with marketing in the West, China marketing is also unique in several aspects. The first and most obvious difference is that marketing in China employees ideographic characters which do not carry within them a representation of proper pronunciation, whereas Western countries employs alphabetic scripts which represent the sound of a word. This has implications for branding. For example, memories of English brand names tend to be linked to auditory brand identifiers, in contrast to Chinese brand names, which are more closely tied to visual brand identifiers. (Tavassoli & Han, cited in Fisher, 2012) With regard to branding, the fact that China is the most brand-conscious country in the world will increase the relative importance of branding in China as compared to branding in the West. Another difference is the regulatory environment of media in China, which is more restrictive than that of the West. Marketers in China cannot freely market ads satirical of government policy, or use permissive sexual images to promote products.

The price marketers set for their products may be influenced by several factors which set the Chinese market apart from western markets. For example, the relatively lower per capita income in China compared to Western countries will of necessity influence the price assigned to products whose destination is the China market. Distribution channels in China will very probably be influenced by the pervasive and hard-to-understand Chinese practice of *guanxi*, which perhaps will cause participants in a distribution channel to favor relationships over efficiency. The very large rural, relatively-undeveloped areas, populated by speakers of mutually unintelligible dialects, which areas are characterized by culturally closed and conservative ethnic cultures, will affect both distribution channels and advertising appeals. The relatively undeveloped legal structure will affect marketers' efforts to create intellectual property in their brands that can be protected by the courts, as well as competition from a very large number of knock-off *shanzhai* brands.

All of China's economic dynamism has naturally propelled China marketing, and not only China marketing, but China marketing research. Although not extremely deep, China marketing research in English is broad in scope. And although in its infancy, the demand for China marketing research has outstripped the supply. (Trotter and Tian, 2012) This book concerns marketing and marketing research in China, and is designed to help meet the demand for China marketing research, in addition to pointing the way for researchers to forge ahead in this fertile field. The articles contained in this book should contribute to the investigation of one of the world's most important phenomena. They should also help lay the foundation of an emerging China marketing profession, as well as to shrink the shortage of useful marketing research.

All of the articles collected together in this volume were taken from the *International Journal of China Marketing*. As far as is known by the editors of this book, this is the first academic journal in print devoted entirely to marketing in China. The journal was established in the United States in 2010, and was introduced by the renowned marketing scholar Philip Kotler, who has earned the sobriquet "the father of marketing." In the introduction to the inaugural issue, Dr. Kotler suggested that the journal could examine "almost all aspects" of marketing in China. (Kotler, 2010) Some of the marketing aspects, all of which are particularly oriented to China, which contributors to IJCM have researched include the following categories: advertising and promotion, consumer behavior, marketing strategy, and theoretical issues. In commentary provided to introduce the third issue, Geoffrey P. Lantos proclaimed "The notion of a market oriented economy is still brand new in China, while marketing as a field of scholastic study is just in its beginning steps... I feel it is an honor to write this commentary... I sincerely hope the International Journal of China Marketing will continue to deliver the highest quality research in the service of those who wish to understand the world of Chinese marketing better." (Lantos, 2011). The editors of this volume present these articles to the reader in the confident expectation that he will indeed judge the articles to be high quality research, which propels him to a higher level of understanding of the world of China marketing.

Structure of the Book

This volume is divided into three sections. Part I is "General Marketing Issues in China." Part II deals with the "Marketing Mix in China." Part III concerns "Consumer Behavior in China." The following is a short synopsis and sampling of the articles in each section.

Part I: General Marketing Issues in China Part I is a potpourri of marketing issues, ranging the gamut between traditional issues such as cross cultural management, innovation, cluster marketing models, automobile purchase intention, and population aging (all in the context of a Chinese market), to more exotic issues such as marketing by Chinese in a computer-created virtual world to ethnic cultural tourism in China.

Chapter One deals with innovation in China. There are two schools of thought concerning innovation in China, one negative, and one positive. Regardless of whichever school of thought is accurate, there has not yet been a meaningful examination of China's innovation position compared to other countries in the world. The negative school of thought concerning innovation in China believes that China is laggard and unoriginal when it comes to innovation. The positive school of thought, on the other hand, believes that China is becoming increasingly innovative. However, the evidence for that positive evaluation has been derived from micro-level studies of firms and industries. There has as of yet never been a macro-level study at the national level researching China's innovation potential and position. The initial chapter lists the major factors conducive to raising a country's innovation capacity, and then rates China on those factors. Then China is compared with other countries, using those factors as criteria. It made some recommendations which, if adopted, would enhance China's innovative capabilities. Compared with nine other countries in China's geographical region, China was found to rank fifth in the list of ten countries with regard to her overall innovative position. On sub-criteria, China ranked as follows: sixth in innovation inputs, eighth in innovation outputs, sixth in political environment, fifth in regulatory environment, second in research and development, first in infrastructure, fourth in market sophistication, third in business sophistication, and first in turning innovation inputs into outputs (efficiency). Recommendations for China include reforming the educational system in such a way that Chinese education will more greatly encourage creative thinking. In addition, it is suggested that China evolve from a manufacturing- and export-dominated economy into an economy that is more knowledge intensive and more innovative.

Chapter Two examines whether the traditional cluster marketing model, which has been found suitable to apply to industrial clusters, is also suitable to apply to a high-tech cluster. A "cluster" is a "group of interconnected companies, suppliers, related industries, and specialized institutions and associations" located in a particular area. Traditional manufacturing companies located in such clusters have been found to derive from the cluster certain competitive advantages in marketing, including access to current and new markets, synergies in market research, the development of new markets, more market share, better product development, better dissemination of information, the development of distribution channels, and more effective sales promotion. Chapter Two concludes with the proposition that cluster marketing models can indeed be applied to the high-tech industry.

Chapter Three explores marketing performed not in China, but marketing by Chinese in an alternate world. The alternate world is Second Life, which is one of the fastest growing and leading three-dimensional virtual worlds available on the internet. Within this world, participants do what people in the real world do: build and create things, socialize with each other, meet other people, build products and services, and create an online marketing environment. This is more than a game. Real-world revenue can be gained as participants sell their virtual assets for real-world money. Real-world companies such as Nissan, IBM, and Cisco have designed and tested new products and services in Second Life. ABN Amro and Meta Bank have provided services to their virtual customers such as opening accounts, making deposits, and withdrawing virtual funds. Toyota, Dell, Adidas, and IBM have opened virtual stores in Second Life for the purpose of brand awareness. Residents in Second Life's virtual world are running shops, clubs, and recreation sites. Activities such as these provide a huge opportunity for marketing and product testing. Advertisement and brand promotion are key factors in e-marketing activity in Second Life. Second Life's virtual world provides opportunities for real-life businesses to provide an opportunity to engage with customers, suppliers and business partners. This chapter explores opportunities for e-marketing in Second Life, and asks the question "How important is communication in Second Life for online marketing?" Second Life makes these questions important from the view of international marketing, because the residents of Second Life are all from many different countries all over the world. There are no legal barriers obstructing intercourse between people of different nationalities, thus the costs of learning are significantly lowered. Specifically, with regard to China, Chapter Two informs us that a majority of Chinese companies have a presence in Second Life for online marketing and brand promotion.

Chapter Four investigates the oft-discussed prediction of a bursting real estate bubble in China. Scholarly opinion has been divided on the question of whether there will be a crash in housing prices. This chapter uses microeconomic data from the China National Bureau of Statistics in order to investigate the possibility that there is a correlation between certain economic variables and a rise in housing prices. These economic variables were studied: Gross Domestic Product, Gross national income and saving, household consumption and expenditure, social consumption goods, gross domestic saving, and housing sales. It was discovered that these variables were correlated. The overall conclusion drawn was that as the Chinese economy develops, the more housing is sold, and that since Chinese economic variables are continuing to rise, housing sales will rise also, and thus a bursting bubble in the real estate market will not occur. The author recognizes that there are many complicating factors at work in the Chinese real estate market that might moderate the effect of rising economic variables on housing sales – factors such as government policy and regulatory issues, population trends, and different geographical locations. However, the general conclusion is that the real estate market should be growing in the next few years.

Chapter Five is an investigation of the impacts of population aging on the Chinese economy, and its effects on marketing in China in particular. All of the world's populations are aging, but China's aging population is unique because it has the largest aged population in the world. In addition, the rate of aging of China's population is high: the number of people above the age of 60 is increasing at the rate of five percent annually. Furthermore, the transition to an aged society from an adult society took place relatively faster than other countries. For example, it took Sweden forty years to make the transition, and Britain required eighty years. Because of various sociopolitical factors, the Chinese population went through a transition from an adult type of population to an aged population very quickly at a time when the country was not economically affluent. The potential impact of this on China's society and economy is potentially quite significant. For example, as the labor forces ages, it will thus become more inefficient, and, as a result, could affect China's ability to compete in a global market, perhaps making China a net importer of goods and services, rather than a net exporter. In addition, an aging labor force places a greater financial strain on the shrinking pool of younger workers who must support their elders in their old age. Furthermore, an aging labor market will provide opportunities to providers of goods and services to the elderly. The author offers recommendations which, if adopted, might assist China in overcoming any negative impacts brought about by its aging population. These recommendations include suggestions to seek for intensive economic growth, implementing pension reforms, practicing phased retirement, nurturing savings incentives for the younger generation, and making use of China's capital market in order to create financial instruments that can alleviate the risks of growing old.

Chapter Six provides an interesting glimpse into a little-noticed segment of the Chinese economy. In addition to the Han majority, China has 55 ethnic minorities. These ethnic minorities are attracting increased attention as targets of tourist interest. Public media and government tourism agencies often provide information about the various customs, dress, and languages of these ethnic minorities, in an effort to attract tourists. The author does not deal with how better to market these ethnic minorities to the touring public; rather, he focuses on how to protect the interests of the minorities themselves who are being marketed. What are some of the interests which an ethnic minority might want cultivated? Ethnic pride is an example of one such interest. For example, the matrilineal Mosuo ethnic group, located near Lake Lugu near the Yunnan and Sichuan border, have created a Lugu Lake Mosuo Cultural Development Association, which has adopted a statement that prohibits the promotion, marketing, or advertising of Mosuo programs in a light which will present the Mosuo as a "poor, pitiful people." Other interests an ethnic community might want protected include the preservation of the ethnic community and its traditions, or, protection from stress caused by an invasion of tourists. These interests might be violated, for example, by a large influx of tourists, or by the construction of large hotels and other businesses to accommodate those tourists. Such activities might also have unintended effects upon minority musicians and performers, who are used to performing before small crowds.

Chapter Seven examines the perennial tradeoffs of globalization and localization in the context of multinational business management. The subject of study is the Japanese overseas retail group YOWA, which invested in retail stores in Guangdong Province in China. The chief focus was upon the strategies YOWA used in order to localize their business practices in China. In the context of localization, the two most important areas to investigate are how business localize in the area of the consumption market, and in human resources practices. In the field of human resources, core issues include the replacement of expatriates by host country nationals. In particular, in the case of YOWA, not only were Japanese expatriates replaced by local Chinese managers, but in addition, YOWA changed its corporate human resource management strategies in order to adjust to Chinese society. For example, YOWA began to use more local female Chinese workers in a positive fashion. This followed the Chinese pattern, in which local workers in retail chain stores are predominately Chinese. In addition, YOWA changed its parent company policy of using part-time workers as its main labor force to a policy of using predominately full-time workers in China (this occurred primarily due to legal reasons in China). A third change in human resource policy implemented by YOWA was the extensive use of suppliers, who promoted their consigned products in YOWA stores. This was a practice almost unheard of in Japan, but quite common in China. The author not only deals with YOWA's localization practices in the area of human resource management, but in addition, the chapter discusses YOWA's other localization practices in the area of marketing to consumers. YOWA conformed its practices to Chinese practices in location selection, overall image, shopping environment, promotion strategies, merchandise and service standards, and the targeting of customers.

Part II: The Marketing Mix in China Part II of this book concentrates on the marketing mix in China, with special emphasis on promotion and pricing. Issues covered are *shanzhai* branding (weak or fake branding), new product launch execution, price wars, rural Chinese consumer behavior in the purchase of refrigerators, cultural differences in advertising appeals, and information handling styles with regard to advertising.

Chapter Eight deals with *shanzhai* branding. The strict meaning of *shanzhai* is that which has to do with small-scale factories or small family-run workshops. Because so many products made in such enterprises are knock-offs and counterfeits, the word *shanzhai* has taken on connotations of "piracy" and "counterfeit." However, *shanzhai* marketing goes far beyond piracy. Properly speaking, *shanzhai* strategy is an imitation-plus-innovation strategy. This strategy has been applied in China first to products in the mobile phone industry, and finally to the entire gamut of digital products. The strategy is used by small- and medium enterprises in order to accumulate capital which will be used to "de-*shanzhai*," when the enterprise will then be able to make a "big brand" product who pursue this perfectly legitimate strategy have a difficulty in avoiding the popular prejudice that *shanzhai* products are pirated, fake, and shoddy. Despite this popular prejudice, however, *shanzhai* brands have become quite popular in China. One reason is that the low price enables the consumer to enjoy a product similar to a more expensive product which he admires, but cannot afford. Another reason is the "E generation", which is the generation of Chinese consumers who have grown up in the age of networks and electronic media. This E generation, many of whom are products of one-child-only families, when compared with earlier generations of Chinese consumers are more tolerant, more curious, and have a stronger sense of self. These attributes cause Generation E consumers to be less brand loyal, and more interested in product functionality. These Generation E consumers are characterized by contempt for authority, and a dislike for being rule-bound. They care less for brands than previous consumers. All of this makes E Generation consumers attracted to the low-priced, functional, weakly-branded Shanzhai product.

Chapter Nine compares the launch of new products in China with new product launches in the United States. Cross-cultural differences were observed between the two countries in terms of new product performance. We find that the effect of business unit resources on new product performance was significant in the United States, but not significant in China. It is speculated that the reason for the disparity can be traced to the fact that the government in China is more involved in investment, hiring, and performance-target setting, and thus in China the management of a state-owned enterprise may be lacking in resources, but still may be able to launch innovative new products successfully because of government support and investment. A second difference between the United States and China was found in the relationship between business unit resources and the execution of marketing strategy. It was discovered that this relationship was stronger for Chinese businesses. It is speculated that the reason for this is that enterprises with fewer resources (such as those in China) are also relatively inexperienced, and thus have more difficulty in executing marketing strategy. A third difference between the United States and China was discovered in the relationship between channel cooperation and launch timing. This relationship was found to be stronger in China than in the United States. A possible reason for this is that Chinese managers with little experience in making launch timing decisions on their own may be dependent on the expertise of their channel partners to help them launch the new product. A fourth difference between the United States and China was discovered in the relationship between market orientation and marketing strategy execution. This relationship was found to be stronger for United States companies. It is speculated that the reason for this is that market orientation is less important in a centralized economy like China's.

Chapter Ten informs the reader of price wars in China. There are several paradoxes. For example, price wars in the West are often seen as wasteful, useless, and harmless to participants, and yet Chinese firms often relish them, and many of these firms emerge from price wars stronger, bigger, and more profitable. The question arises: do Chinese firms know something about fighting price wars that Western firms do not? To answer this question, the authors analyze two price wars that were fought in China involving the color TV industry and the microwave oven industry in the mid-1990s. Upon analysis, it is concluded that Chinese companies do seem to know something about price wars that Western executives don't know, or have forgotten. Further, the authors explore how Chinese executives decide to start a price war, and when do they decide to start a price war. Also examined is whether it would be profitable to start a price war, and if so, by which firm, in which industry, and under what structural conditions in the marketplace. It was concluded that the elimination of inefficient rivals, and cost reductions due to scale economies produced by the increased volume that followed the price cuts, both made price wars not only reasonable, but profitable as well. In addition, another factor that tends to make price wars in China more profitable than such a war in America, is that in China, there are many more growth industries in unsaturated markets in China, which allows for great increases in volume for a given price cut, thus providing scale economies, and thus making price wars profitable.

Chapter Eleven investigates refrigerator purchase behavior by rural Chinese. It was determined that because Chinese peasants approached the purchase of refrigerators with a different psychology than urban refrigerator consumers, refrigerator markets should segment the market. Furthermore, regional variations were found that differentiated peasants' purchasing behavior. Overall, peasants especially desired cost performance, and they paid great attention to capacity of the refrigerators and the cost to use the refrigerators.

Chapter Twelve is a cross-cultural study that compares the impacts of cultural differences between China and the United States on the impacts of advertising appeals. Hofstede's famous cultural model was used, as was Pollay's model of advertising appeals. The main question investigated was whether advertising appeals adapted to a country's salient cultural values (e.g., individualism for North Americans and collectivism for Chinese) performed better than advertising appeals which took no cognizance of cultural differences. It was discovered that if advertising appeals indeed were sensitive to cultural differences, the Hofstede model was not fine-grained enough to detect which cultural differences would affect which advertising appeals. However, it was also discovered that to advertise in China, it would be best to consider seven particular appeals; namely, effectiveness, safety, tamed, durable, natural, nurturance and succorance. Conversely, advertisers in China should avoid ten particular appeals; namely, casual, distinctiveness, community, status, adventure, dear, family, untamed, magic, and popular.

Chapter Thirteen examines the effect of rational and emotional advertising appeals on Chinese consumers. Not every individual responds to rational advertisements, or emotional ones, in the same fashion. Consumer responses are conditioned by an individual's information processing styles, for example. The authors focus on the possibility that the consumer's information handling style is an important modulating variable affecting the relationship between an advertisement and brand attitude, a modulating variable that affects the direct relationship between need for cognition and preference for affect with brand attitude. Heretofore, little research had been done exploring the effect of an individual's information handling style on preference of advertising appeal. Information handling style can be divided into two kinds: sensing style and intuitive style. Individuals who prefer sensing are more likely to have faith in information that is concrete, tangible, and in the present. On the other hand, an individual who uses an intuitive style of information   processing tends to trust information that is more abstract or theoretical, and that can be remembered by seeking a wider context or pattern. Comparing the two types of information processing styles, an individual who uses a sensing style to handle information will grasp rational advertisements more easily than a consumer who employs an intuitive style. It was discovered that the information handling style of the consumer indeed influenced the relationship between emotional or rational perception of advertising style and attitude towards a brand. For example, intuitive style customers are more sensitive to emotional advertisements, and if they receive more advertisements with emotional appeal, their brand attitude will improve. On the other hand, a sensing style consumer prefers rational advertisement content, and if such is provided to them, this well help improve brand attitude.

Part III: Consumer Behavior in China Part III of this book deals with consumer behavior in China. Four articles describe the shopping behavior of northwest Chinese, customer satisfaction in a Chinese restaurant, consumers' choices in fresh food retail markets, and Chinese consumers of globally branded products.

Chapter Fourteen reminds us that Western marketing and merchandising strategies are likely to fail if not adapted to the Chinese context. Many factors affect the shopping behavior of Chinese consumers, including willingness to take risks, importance of the group and the role of consensus, and the profound role of the family. In addition to differences between China and the West, there are different cultural differences within the various regions of China, brought about by such factors as geographic size of the region, linguistic differences, historical legacy, and economic disparities caused by government policy. The authors study the shopping behavior of Chinese in Lanzhou, one of the most important cities in northwest China. Previous studies of Chinese consumers depict them as mainly functional shoppers as opposed to hedonic shoppers. The authors explore the possibility that shoppers in China's northwest may shop for hedonic reasons. In addition, the chapter attempts to identify criteria which determine store choice among northwest China shoppers. Factors determining store choice include perceptions of product price and quality, service quality, the cost in time and money to shop at a given store, mental stress and other emotional factors, store reputation, store atmosphere, and consumer characteristics. The authors conclude by finding that northwest Chinese consumers do indeed shop for other than functional reasons, such as need for market exploration, social obligations, socialization, self-gratification, diversion from routine, and visual appreciation. In addition, they describe store choice criteria employed by the research sample. Among the several types of stores which the Lanzhou consumers could choose, there were free (street) markets, specialty stores, convenience stores, department stores, and supermarkets. It was discovered that the Lanzhou shoppers interviewed used seven major store choice criteria. Four criteria had reference to the merchandise sought (product quality/trust, price, style, assortment) and three criteria had reference to service (store location, shopping environment, and customer service).

Chapter Fifteen deals not with marketing in China, but rather marketing by Chinese to Americans in America. Specifically, a Chinese restaurant located in the southern part of the United States was put to examination in order to evaluate factors contributing to customer satisfaction in a Chinese restaurant, factors such as reliability, assurance, empathy, cultural awareness, cultural atmosphere, and responsiveness. Customer satisfaction is important, because it a determinant of repeat sales and consumer loyalty. It is an important determinant of product choice and post-purchase attitude. It was discovered that reliability and value were the primary indicators of customer satisfaction. In addition, it was discovered that cultural awareness of ethnic food did not have a positive effect on customer satisfaction, contrary to what was suggested by earlier research investigating this question. Furthermore, it was found that the atmosphere of the restaurant, as reflected in such items as décor and music, had no impact on customer satisfaction. However, it was also discovered that a customer's perception of the restaurant's Chinese organizational culture is correlated with the level of the customer's satisfaction. For example, if a customer perceived that Chinese are possessed of a very strong work ethic, the customer would not attribute any dissatisfying experiences to the fault of the Chinese restaurant. The most surprising finding outlined is the discovery that customer satisfaction was not correlated to knowledge of the ethnic culture associated with the restaurant. Customer's did not expect a "one hour trip to China," and they did not expect to get authentic Chinese food.

Chapter Sixteen investigates the behavior of Chinese consumers who are faced with the choice of buying fresh food in a supermarket or a wet market. The advantages of the supermarket are such that the proportion of Chinese consumers who buy fresh food from supermarkets is increasing year by year. Factors which favor the choice of a wet market is the desire for freshness, time available to shop, knowledge of the safety of the fresh food purchased, consumer age. On the other hand, factors which favor the choice of a supermarket include age of the consumer and the education of the consumer. The younger the consumer is, the more likely that consumer will choose to shop at a supermarket. In addition, the more educated the consumer is, the more likely that consumer will shop at a supermarket. The distance the retail establishment is from the consumer will affect the choice:

the closer the supermarket, the more likely the consumer will choose the supermarket. If the income of the consumer is over 8000 RMB per month, that consumer will pay almost no attention to price, and will pursue high quality food, and convenience and comfort in shopping. On the other hand, the higher price for fresh food in a supermarket will negatively affect shopping frequency for consumers who make less than 8000 RMB per month. The author recommends that supermarkets establish a supply point from which they can directly purchase fresh foods, thus cutting out middlemen, and thus reducing prices. Other recommendations include one that suggests the government strengthen its monitoring and certification processes with regard both to supermarkets and wet markets, in order to insure that the consumer is getting, and knows he is getting, safe, fresh food.

Chapter Seventeen investigated Chinese consumer decision making in relation to ten global brands. Nine constructs were explored to see if they might predict brand purchase intent. These nine constructs were divided into two categories, along with two uncategorized constructs. The first category was "consumer characteristics." This category included four constructs – perceived ethnocentrism, perceived cosmopolitanism, perceived global-local identity, and perceived identification with a global consumer culture. The second category was "belief and attitude formation." This category contained three constructs, namely global brand familiarity, global brand liking, and global brand trust. Two uncategorized constructs were importance of country of origin and exposure to multinational corporation advertising. Of those constructs, brand familiarity, brand liking, and brand trust were the three that were found to be most influential on overall brand purchase intent. The brand purchase intent that was studied was the intent of Chinese consumers to buy foreign brands as opposed to the intent to buy domestic brands. Although brand familiarity, brand liking, and brand trust had the greatest overall impact on the ten brands generally considered, the constructs studied had different impacts on the intention to purchase different global brands. For example, for Colgate, HSBC, and Levi's, trust was the strongest predictor. Surprisingly, identification with global consumer culture and exposure to multinational advertising were not predictors of Chinese consumers' intent to purchase a global brand. The authors finally conclude that Chinese consumers behave very similarly to the consumers in other nations, the likenesses between the two outnumbering the differences. It is suggested that marketers, instead of looking for variance between international consumers, should focus rather on commonalities.

Chapter Eighteen provides an overview of academic marketing research which has investigated marketing in China and which has been published in English. Included in its conclusions are the following propositions: the number of such academic articles are increasing in number and expanding in scope over the first decade of the twenty-first century. General categories into which China marketing research in English can be divided include advertising, consumer behavior, marketing strategy, and marketing theory. The authors not only overview the marketing research being published in English, but they also give insight into the researchers who are doing the research. We are informed that most researchers were ethnic Chinese, although there was much collaboration between Chinese scholars and non-Chinese scholars. Finally, it was discovered that very much research has been done by Hong Kong institutions.

In conclusion, Marketing in Modern China provides the English reader with an excellent overview of the field of marketing in China. The subject matter of the articles contained in this volume range from general issues in marketing, to the marketing mix in China, to consumer behavior in China. The articles have all been published in the double-blind, peer reviewed, SSCI indexed research journal International Journal of China Marketing. The articles are technical enough for the marketing scholar, yet informative enough for the general reader. This book may well be the platform from which a new scholarly enterprise is launched, which endeavors to come to terms with one of the most incredible economic phenomena in all of human history – China.

Robert Guang Tian
Dan Trotter
Wong Ming Wong
Camilla Hong Wang

Part I: General Marketing Issues in China

Chapter One

Innovation Capacity in China: An Analysis in a Global Context

The objective of this study is to identify the position of China's innovation in the world. We discussed the major challenges China faces with respect to the sustainability of her outstanding economic growth. Using a canonical correlation analysis, we examined the major factors that are important to raise a country's innovation capacity, and to evaluate China's innovation level in terms of those innovation-enabling factors. We also compared China's level of innovation with its potential competitors. To address major challenging issues, we make recommendations in regard to China's policy making for enhancing those innovation-enabling factors, hence, improving innovation outputs.

INTRODUCTION

Innovation has long been regarded as an important element in creating sustainable competitive advantage for firms and even societies. Organizations need to innovate in response to changing customer demands and business environments and in order to capitalize on opportunities offered by new technologies (Rowley et al., 2011; Yang et al., 2008; Cheung and Prendergast, 2006). China, as the world's fastest growing economy, has created a huge amount of attention and business interaction with the rest of the world. With globalization and an interconnected business community, the innovation process today is more critical, collaborative, and global than ever.

Prior studies so far have presented two schools of thoughts regarding the subject of innovativeness in China. One stream of literature that has presented a more critical perspective generally suggests Chinese firms have been laggard in being innovative and have largely relied on imitating the innovative ideas and technologies from the West (Swike et al., 2008; Johnson and Weiss, 2008). That stream of literature basically suggests that China is still lacking the propensity towards being proactive and original in innovation. Some literature even criticizes China for lacking both a system and a spirit of innovation (Zhan and Renwei, 2003, cited in Johnson and Weiss, 2008). The other school of thought, on the other hand, presents a relatively positive perspective focusing more on China's increasing capacity of being innovative. However, studies that present that school of thought concentrate mainly on microscopic levels, focusing on either the firm and industry level (Zhang et al., 2003; Ren et al., 2010; Rubera and Kirca, 2012) or the regional and provincial levels (Bai and Li, 2011; Wu, 2011) of innovation. Such a focus has left the subject of innovations from a broader country level unexamined. Research on China's innovation potential, especially its innovation position compared to other countries, therefore, is limited.

Our objective for this current study is to fill in this gap by looking at the position of China's innovation in a world spectrum. We examine the major factors that are important to raise a country's innovation capacity, and then evaluate China's innovation level in terms of those innovation enabling factors. We also compare China's level of innovation with other countries that are China's potential competitors in terms of their future economic development. Finally, we make recommendations based on our analysis to China in regard of her policy making for enhancing those innovation-enabling factors, hence, improving the innovation outputs.

In the following sessions, we first provide a brief review of prior studies exploring the topic of innovation, followed by an account of how previous research has classified different kinds of innovations. We then present the two schools of thoughts in regard to innovation capacity in China. Subsequent to the introduction and background sections is the presentation of the methodology and data analysis we performed using the data extracted from INSEAD. At the end of the paper, we relate our findings in the data analysis to China's own development pattern and make recommendations to China's public administrative authorities.

BACKGROUND

Typologies of Innovation

The New Oxford American dictionary defines innovation as "making changes in something established, especially by introducing new methods." However, the definitions and types of innovation described by different researchers in literature are much more varied. Boer and During (2001, p.84) define innovation as "creation of a new product-market-technology-organization combination". Damanpour (1991, p.676) defined innovation as the "implementation of an idea – whether pertaining to a device, system, process, policy, program, or service – that is new to the organization at the time of adoption". In our study, we adopt the definition used in OECD (2005) and define innovation as "the implantation of a new or significantly improved product (good or service), a new process, a new marketing method, or a new organizational method in business practices, workplace organization, or external relations" (OECD/EC, 2005, also known as the Oslo Manual 2005, cited in Global Innovation Index 2011 by

20

INSEAD). In other words, innovation converts imagination and information into valuable knowledge and subsequently derives different or greater value and delivers significant benefits to individuals or organizations in the form of new or improved products, processes, or services.

An innovation can be new to the world, or new to a sector or market. When it is new to a market, it can be "perceived as new" instead of being totally new. For example, a dish washer may not be an "innovation" for American consumers, however when it is newly introduced to an emerging market where dish washers have never been introduced, it may be regarded as an "innovation" for that specific market. An innovation can be disruptive or dynamic, where the focus is on its impact in addition to novelty. In order to have a clear view of different types of innovation, several typologies of innovation have been conducted in literature (e.g., Zaltman et al., 1973; Rowley et al., 2011). Table 1.1 summarized the major literature regarding the classifications of innovation typology based on Rowley et al.'s (2011) study.

Knight (1967) has identified four types of innovation, namely product and service innovation, production process innovation, organizational structure innovation and people innovation. Product, service, and process innovation have been widely discussed in the literature. People innovation in Knight's (1967) study refers to the changes to people through altering personnel by hiring or dismissing and changes of beliefs or behavior through education. Although people innovation is not as frequently discussed by other researchers, strengthening innovation indeed begins with strengthening people. Innovation calls for more and better educated people, including employees, administrations, researchers, and even customers.

Another type of innovation is Binary Innovations. Binary (pair) types of innovation gained much attention during the 1970s to 1990s. The following three pairs of innovation dichotomies are frequently discussed in literature (e.g., Daft, 1978; Damanpour, 1987; Cooper, 1998): product versus process innovation, technical versus administrative, and radical versus incremental innovation. The product-production dichotomy is related to whether the changes are about the offerings (products/service) or production operation. Product, service, and process innovation are related to technical innovation, while administrative innovations bring changes to the structure or administration of the organizations such as change of compensation system or hiring procedure. The incremental-radical dichotomy is based on the degree of change and dynamics of the innovation. Similar concepts can be found in continuous and discontinuous technological changes (Porter, 1986), incremental vs. breakthrough innovations (Tushman and Anderson, 1986 cited in Innovationzen.com) and conservative vs. radical innovations (Abernathy and Clark, 1985 cited in Innovationzen.com).

21

TABLE 1.1
MAJOR INNOVATION TYPOLOGIES

Authors	Types of innovation	Interpretations
Knight (1967)	4 kinds of innovation: 1. Product or service innovation 2. Production-process innovation 3. Organizational structure innovation 4. People innovation	 changes to product or service offerings changes to production operations as a result of technology advances changes to organization's system such as communications changes to the people within an organization
Binary (pair wise) types of innovation 1970s-1990s (e.g., Daft 1978; Damanpour 1987; cooper 1998)	3 Pairs of innovation are identified: 1. Product vs. process 2. Technical vs. administrative 3. Radical vs. incremental	 product/service vs. production or service operation new products, processes or services vs. organization operation fundamental changes vs. add-on changes
Hovgaard & Hansen (2004)	3 types of innovation: 1. Product innovation 2. Process innovation 3. Business systems innovation	 changes to product or service offerings changes to organizational operations "all of those innovations that do not fall under product or process" (p. 27), such as marketing innovation
Trott (2005)	7 different kinds of innovation: 1. Product innovation 2. Service innovation 3. Process innovation 4. production innovation 5. organizational innovation 6. management innovation 7. commercial/marketing innovation	 changes to product offerings changes to service offerings changes to organizational operations changes to production operation such as just-in-time (JIT) manufacturing changes to organization, such as introducing a new venture division changes to management systems such as TQM (total quality management) changes to marketing; e.g., new sales approach such as Direct Marketing
Bessant and Tidd (2007)	4 categories of innovation 1. product innovation 2. process innovation 3. position innovation 4. paradigm innovation	 changes to product or service offerings changes to organizational operations changes consumers' view or understanding of products changes in the underlying mental models which frame what the organization does (p.13)

Starting from the late 1990s to twenty-first century, researchers have recognized a wider range of innovation types and emphasized the business system and marketing innovations in addition to product, process, and administrative innovation. Hovgaard and Hansen (2004) introduced business system innovation. Trott (2005) proposed the related concept of marketing innovation and Bessant and Tidd (2007) identified position innovation and paradigm innovation. Position innovation is highly related to marketing strategy through communication and branding. The basic approach to position innovation is not to create something new, but to change what is already in the mind of the customer. In other words, a position innovation

22

changes the customer's view or understanding the product (Kim and Mauborgne, 1999). Paradigm innovation, however, is associated with a significant shift in perceptions of what an organization is about and in what ways it comes up with new approaches to deal with situations and its external world. For example, with the launch of iPhone, iPad, and App stores, Apple Inc. is no longer being viewed as just a computer manufacturer. The paradigm of the Apple Inc. is expanded, and Apple is a computer, phone, entertainments, and even educational program provider.

Literature of Innovation in China

During the last few decades, China has maintained an annual growth of over 9%. This outstanding growth has largely been attributed to China's industry modernization. As mentioned earlier, one stream of literature has already shed light on China's innovation outcomes derived from her industry modernization.

Such literature generally consented that China had gained a steady improvement in its innovation inputs, outputs, and innovation efficiency in the past decades. Statistics show that China's investment in R&D (research and development) has increased from $40.5 billion PPP in 2000 to $153.7 billion PPP in 2011(Battelle.org). China's R&D growth over the past 15 years has consistently exceeded 10%. China's growth in R&D has been forecasted to be 11.5% per year while U.S. would maintain an annual growth rate in R&D at about 4.0% for the next 13 years (Battelle.org). Mu and Fan (2011) measured 38 countries' national innovation capacity (NIC) and concluded that China's ranking of NIC among those 38 countries has moved forward from the 28th in 2000 to the 10th in 2008. Johnson and Weiss's (2008) model describes that China has moved from a pure imitation stage (direct copying) to what the authors refer as "incremental innovation stage" (modified offering), and that China is heading towards the radical innovation stage (new to the world offering). They further claim that if China stays in the imitation and incremental innovation stage, she will not be able to further its economic progress for too long. Wu's (2011) study shows that infrastructure development, participation of foreign capital, government spending, development of private sector and increase in human capital all have played a significantly positive role in innovation and economic growth in China.

While gaining significant improvement and successes on her way towards being a country of innovation, China is facing some major challenges according to the literature. First, as the role of Chinese governments at all levels is pivotal in facilitating and boosting innovation in China, the implementation of the central policy for innovation is neither effective nor efficient. Bai and Li (2011) evaluate the efficiency of China's regional innovation system and found that the provincial governments have not effectively carried out their assigned roles. It is suggested that government should provide and secure an innovation-friendly business environment through making courageous policy (such as protective innovation policy) for the promotion of more creative innovations, and a freer market as well.

The second challenge faced by China is the call for educational reforms to develop a more liberal educational system (Johnson and Weiss, 2008). Johnson and Weiss' (2008) conceptual stage model demonstrated the important linkage between creative educations with radical innovation. China needs to provide a more liberal education, in mode and in contents, to the school children in order for them to develop a creative mind. Such a creative mind is instrumental for original and radical innovations.

The third challenge that China's business and government have to face is to transit from the current export based economy to one that is more sustainable; one that is likely to be more knowledge-intensive. According to the State Council document released in the beginning of year 2006, the Medium- and Long-Term Plan for National Science and Technology Development (2006-2020) proposed that China would become an innovation-driven nation by 2020. Chinese government recognizes that the export-led, manufacturing-based pattern of economic development would not be indefinitely sustainable (Dodgson and Xue, 2009; Johnson and Weiss, 2008). The 2008 US subprime credit crisis and the subsequently wide-spreading recession in the States and Europe have caused the demands for Chinese exports to decline (Wu, 2011). Furthermore, the increasingly serious depletion in natural resources, the rising cost of labor and raw materials, and the deterioration of environmental conditions are threats to the sustainability of rapid economic growth in China. Policy-makers should be keen at steering the country towards an alternative growth model that is more knowledge-intensive and high-tech based. The main challenge here is how China's industries can change the business model from one of imitation to one that is truly innovative.

METHODOLOGY

Our objective for this study is two-fold: first, to evaluate China of her relative capacity and capability to be innovative as a nation compared to others; and, second, to identify possible future directions, towards which, China may consider formulating her public policies for the promotion of innovation in the country. We need a research tool that would allow us to develop (a) an objective measurement of the outcomes of a nation's innovativeness, and (b) a parsimonious set of factors that are most critical for a nation to promote innovation. Such a research tool is necessary for the accomplishment of our research objective.

In the following paragraphs of this section, we will first give a brief background of the Global Innovation Index, and then provide a discussion on our data analysis procedure to guide our identification of a parsimonious set of factors that are critical for promoting innovation.

Global Innovation Index

Recognizing innovation's key role of being a major driver for economic growth and prosperity, INSEAD and the World Intellectual Property Organization (WIPO) since 2007 co-publish the yearly Global Innovation Index, a comprehensive study on 125 nations and economic entities with respect to their relative capacity of promoting innovation. A conceptual framework was developed in the GII study seeing each subject nation (or economic entity) as a system converting input required for innovation (the "input pillars") to the innovation output (the "output pillars"). The GII framework consists of altogether seven scales, five for measuring the innovation inputs of a subject nation, and two scales for the measurement of the subject nation's innovation outputs. A total of eighty indicators covering the areas of social, political, intellectual, and economic areas are included in the seven scales. The five input pillars embrace a total of seventy-one indicators to capture the pulses of an economy in these areas: (1) institutions, (2) human capital and research, (3) infrastructure, (4) market sophistication, and (5) business sophistication; while the two output pillars capture innovation performance in two aspects: (1) scientific outputs and (2) creative outputs. Details of all the constructs and subscales that are used by GII are listed in figure 1.1.

In this current study, we use the GII conceptual framework to provide us with a comprehensive set of factors that are relevant in shaping and the development of a nation's innovation. In addition, the framework includes not only the innovation input factors, but also multiple measurements of the innovation outputs as well. The availability of objective output measures provides a reference so that discriminating analysis can be done to single out the more powerful predicting indicators in the five input pillars. Furthermore, GII covers measures from both the more affluent developed nations as well as those that are still emerging. The well representative sample set of 125 nations and economic entities, which account for 93.2% of the world's population and 98.0% of the world's GDP, would allow a more stable analytical result to be derived.

A main reason for narrowing down the number of innovation input factors is that China, like many other emerging states, may not be able to devise a policy that can cover all the deficient areas due to limitations of resources or implementation. Therefore, ranking the various input pillars in terms of their potential impacts on innovation outputs serves a very pragmatic purpose.

FIGURE 1.1
THE CONCEPTUAL FRAMEWORK OF THE GLOBAL INNOVATION INDEX 2011

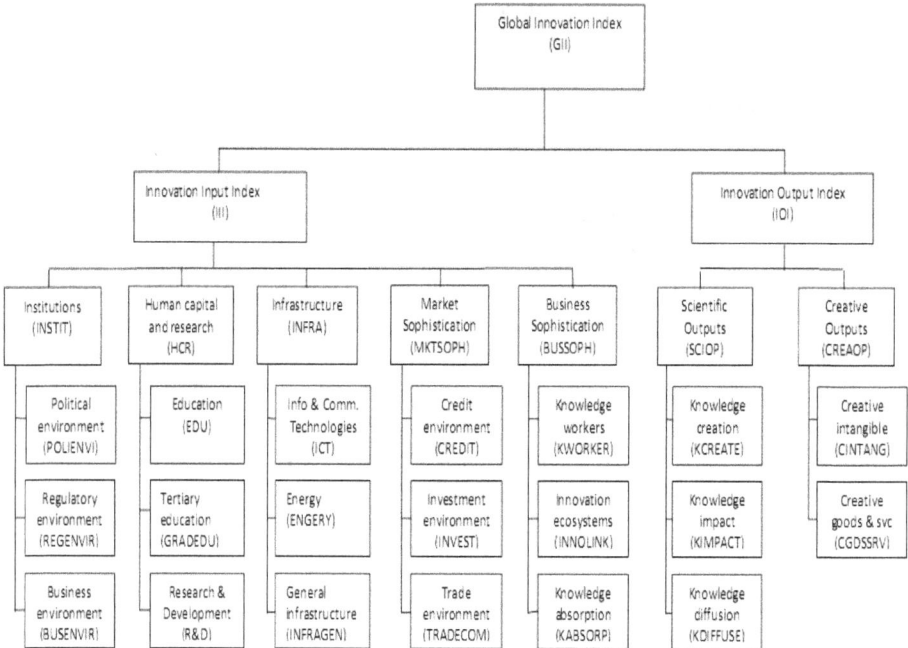

Source: The Global Innovation Index 2011, INSEAD

Data

The quantitative analysis for this current study was based on secondary data obtained from the 2011 Global Innovation Index of INSEAD in Fontainebleau, France. Major data sources for GII were from the World Bank statistic division (World Development Indicators), World Bank, and International Monetary Fund. These sources are considered reliable with uniformed terminology and methodology, and they are frequently used in the business studies (Cavusgil et al., 2004; Sheng and Mullen, 2011). For our study, we used the open-source programming language R to perform 'Web-scraping' to retrieve a data set of 107 measures of 124 countries or economies.

Data Analysis
The objective for the data analysis in the current study is to obtain insights into the interrelationships between the innovation input scales and the innovation output scales. In the current study, we have a set of five metric scales for the innovation inputs as the independent variables and two for the innovation outputs as the criterion variables. Since ordinary regression analysis or stepwise regression analysis handle only a single criterion variable; therefore, these statistical techniques do not provide an accommodation for the multiple criterion variables in our study. As such, we use the canonical correlation analysis method to analyze the data we retrieved from the GII study.

Canonical Correlation Analysis
Canonical correlation analysis (CCA) is a multivariate statistical model aimed at studying the interrelationships among sets of multiple dependent variables and multiple independent variables. It is generally accepted to be the most appropriate and powerful multivariate approach (Hair et. al 1998). CCA develops a number of orthogonal canonical functions that maximize the correlation between the linear composites, also known as canonical variates, which are sets of dependent and independent variables. Each canonical function is actually based on the correlation between two canonical variates, one variate for the dependent variables and another for the independent variables. Those variates are derived to maximize the correlation between them. In addition, CCA generates a number of canonical functions (pairs of canonical variates). The number of functions generated each time is equal to the number of variables in the smaller set of variables.

The CCA Model
In the current study, our objective is to evaluate the strength of the associations among the innovation input scales (the independent variables) and the innovation output scales (the dependent variables). Due to the relatively small data set (only 125 data points), in our preliminary analysis we included only the main scales and left the sub-scales out of the analysis. The set of independent variables includes the five scales: INSTIT, HCR, INFRA, MKTSOPH, and BUSSOPH. The set of dependent variables includes the two innovation output scales of SCIOP and CREAOP.

The designation of the variables includes two metric-dependent and five metric-independent variables. The five variables resulted in a 25:1 ratio of observations to variables, exceeding the guideline of 10 observations per

27

variable. The canonical correlation analysis in our study was restricted to deriving two canonical functions as the dependent variable set contained only two variables, SCIOP and CREAOP. To determine if both canonical functions to include in the interpretation stage, we focused on the level of statistical significance, the practical significance of the canonical correlation, and the redundancy indices for each variate.

TABLE 1.2
MEASURES OF OVERALL MODEL FIT FOR CANONICAL CORRELATION ANALYSIS

Can. Function	F	Canon. Corr.	Sq. Corr	p
1	15.644	0.87	0.75	0.000
2	1.480	0.22	0.05	0.213

The first statistical significance test is for the canonical correlations of each of the two canonical functions. Only the first function was tested to be statistically significant (see Table 1.2). In addition to tests of each canonical function separately, multivariate tests of both functions simultaneously are also performed. The test statistics employed are Pillai's criterion, Hotelling's trace, Wilks' lambda, and Roy's gcr. Table 1.3 also details the multivariate test statistics, which all indicate that the canonical functions, taken collectively, are statistically significant at the .000 level. In addition to statistical significance, the first canonical correlation was of sufficient size to be deemed practically significant. The next step was to perform redundancy analyses on both canonical functions.

TABLE 1.3
MULTIVARIATE TESTS OF SIGNIFICANCE

Test Name	Value	Approx. F	Sig. of F
Pillais	0.79727	15.64391	0.000
Hotellings	3.04232	35.29089	0.000
Wilks	0.23853	24.5122	0.000
Roys	0.74951		

Redundancy Analysis
What the squared canonical correlations (roots) provide is an estimate of the shared variance between the canonical variates rather than

that from the sets of dependent and independent variables (Alpert and Peterson 1972). The interpretation of the canonical correlations can be misleading. This is particularly so when the roots are considerably larger than previously reported bivariate and multiple correlation coefficients. The researcher may be tempted to assume that the canonical analysis has uncovered substantial relationships of conceptual and practical significance (Hair et. al 1998). To overcome this issue, Steward and Love (1968) proposed the calculation of the redundancy index as a summary measure of the ability of a set of independent variables (taken as a set) to explain variation in the dependent variables (taken one at a time).

TABLE 1.4
CALCULATION OF THE REDUNDANCY INDICES FOR THE FIRST CANONICAL FUNCTION

Predictor Variable	Canonical Loading	Sq. Can. Loading	Avg. Sq. Loading	Sq. Can. Corr.	Redundancy Index
INSTIT	0.8185	0.6699			
HCR	0.9008	0.8115			
INFRA	0.9455	0.8940			
MKTSOPH	0.8729	0.7620			
BUSSOPH	0.8794	0.7733			
Predictor Variate		3.9107	**0.7821**	**0.7495**	**0.5862**
Criterion Variable					
SCIOP	0.9285	0.8621			
CREAOP	0.8239	0.6788			
Criterion Variate		1.5409	**0.7705**	**0.7495**	**0.5775**

Interpretation of the Canonical Variates

In the earlier statistical significance tests, it is obvious that only the first of the two functions is statistically significant and thus should be accepted. In Table 1.4 we summarized the computation of the redundancy indices for the independent and dependent variates of the first function.

The redundancy index for the criterion variables is 0.5775. That is, approximately 58% of the variances in the criterion variables can be explained by the predictor variate. As there have not been any generally accepted guidelines to judge what level, above which, a redundancy index is supposed to be acceptable, one needs to make his judgment in accordance to the context of the study. In the current study, as the input and output scales we use are at their aggregate levels, we consider the redundancy indices for both of the dependent and independent variates to be substantial (0.576 and 0.586 respectively).

Since the canonical relationship deemed statistically significant, magnitude of the canonical root and the redundancy indices acceptable, we proceed to making substantive interpretations of the CCA results.

The CCA results are summarized in the Canonical Structure Matrix (Table 1.5). The canonical structure matrix reveals the correlations between each variable and its own variate in the canonical functions. It can be said that these correlations are like the factor loadings of the variables on each discriminant function. It allows the comparison of the variables in terms of their correlations and see how closely a variable is related to each function. Generally, any variable with a correlation of 0.3 or more is considered to be significant.

TABLE 1.5
CANONICAL STRUCTURE MATRIX (CANONICAL LOADING)

Predictor Variable	Canonical Functions	
	1	2
INSTIT	0.8185	0.16702 -
HCR	0.9008	0.26503
INFRA	0.9455	0.2542
MKTSOPH	0.8729	0.1579
BUSSOPH	0.8794	-0.3037
Criterion Variable		
SCIOP	0.9285	-0.3713
CREAOP	0.8239	0.5667

Recall the results of the significance tests in the earlier paragraphs. Since only the first canonical function is statistically significant, we interpret only that canonical function and not the second one. According to the loading of the variables, all of the independent and dependent variables have significant contribution to their correspondent variates in the canonical function. Based on their loading values, we can rank the importance of the independent variables in the following orders: INFRA, HCR, BUSSOPH, MKTSOPH, and INSTIT. That is to say that the infrastructure variable (INFRA) contributes most highly in explaining the variances in the dependent variate in the canonical function. In terms of the dependent variables, it appears that the variances in the scientific outputs variable (SCIOP) are slightly more ready to be explained by the independent variate than the other innovation outputs (CREAOP).

Subscale Level Analysis

In this section, we discuss our performance of the CCA to the GII data set at the sub-scale level. The objective we aim at accomplishing is to develop a more insightful understanding of the dimensions in the five innovation input scales that are actually contributing to the variances in the innovation outputs.

TABLE 1.6
CANONICAL STRUCTURE MATRIX (CANONICAL LOADING)

Predictor Variable	1	2
POLIENVI	**0.7659**	0.3082
REGENVIR	**0.7911**	0.1989
		-
BUSENVIR	0.4496	0.2779
EDU	0.6808	0.1484
		-
GRADEDU	0.6019	0.0775
		-
R&D	**0.8598**	0.1790
ICT	**0.9249**	0.2108
ENGERGY	0.5061	0.2037
INFRAGEN	0.4182	0.0085
CREDIT	**0.8079**	0.1731
		-
INVEST	0.6042	0.1021
TRADECOM	0.5671	0.2805
KWORKER	**0.8208**	0.0217
INNOLINK	0.6093	0.0915
		-
KABSORP	0.6355	0.2854
Criterion Variable		
		-
SCIOP	0.9389	0.3443
CREAOP	0.8072	0.5903

There are three sub-scales for each of the five innovation input scales, altogether fifteen of them in total. Table 1.6 summarizes the structural loadings on the predictor and criterion variables for the two canonical functions. As we have concluded earlier that only the first canonical function would have captured most of the variance; therefore, we interpret only the first canonical function in the sub-scale level CCA.

The shortcoming of increasing the number of variables in our CCA is that the number of cases to variable ratio is relatively low. Therefore, the handling of the result needs to be careful as the result may not be very stable. To facilitate our focusing on uncovering which dimensions in the innovative input scales to be more important, we set the cut-off point at a relatively high level of 0.7. There are six sub-scale variables having a canonical loading of above 0.7. These six variables in a descending order in terms of their loading are: ICT (0.925), R&D (0.86), KWORKER (0.821), CREDIT (0.808), REGENVIR (0.791), and POLIENVI (0.766). The structural loadings on the sub-scale variables are basically consistent with our analysis done at the scale level.

Figure 1.2 graphically depicts the relationships between the independent and dependent variables and their variates. From the sub-scale level analysis, we are informed that the variable having the heaviest loading on the independent variate is the ICT dimension within the INFRA scale. The next heaviest one is R&D (0.86) of the HCR scale. The third heaviest loading is on the knowledge-worker sub-scale (0.82) under the business sophistication scale, followed by CREDIT (0.81) of the market-sophistication scale. For the INSTIT scale, both the regulatory environment (0.79) and political environment (0.77) are particularly important.

The information obtained in the sub-scale analysis is valuable. This additional information allows the researcher an in-depth understanding what particularly within the innovation input scales provide most explanation for the variances in the output scales.

DISCUSSION

In this section, we provide discussions, first, on China's global position within the GII framework; second, on the implications for China in regard of policy making for the promotion of innovation outputs; and, finally, on the contributions and limitations of this study.

FIGURE 1.2
CANONICAL CORRELATION MODEL INTEGRATING THE
SCALE AND SUB-SCALE VARIABLES

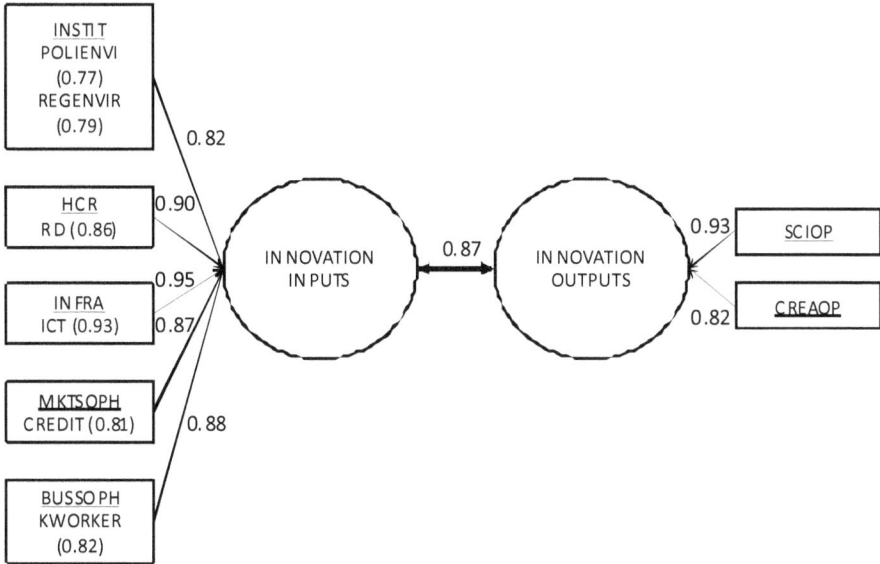

Innovation Position of China

By simple averaging the innovation input and output scales and subscales, GII provides the ranking of the 125 countries in the study in several ways: by the innovation inputs score, by the innovation outputs score, by efficiency of turning the innovation inputs into innovation outputs, and by an overall average score. As our objective for the current study is to identify China's innovation position in relation to other countries within her geographic proximity, we compare China with nine other countries within the region that maintain a close relationship with China due to either economic collaborations or trading. Table 1.7 lists the ten countries and their ranking in four ways.

China ranks sixth both in the innovation inputs (Inputs) comparison and eighth in the innovation outputs (Outputs) comparison. Countries that rank ahead of China are Singapore, Hong Kong, Korea, Japan, and Malaysia while Singapore, Japan, Malaysia, Thailand, Vietnam, India and Philippines are ahead of China in the innovation outputs (Outputs). Unlike China who demonstrated a better performance in the scientific outputs, India and Vietnam instead showed much better performance in the creative outputs (see Table 1.7 and Table 1.8). Such difference may be attributed to the rapid development of the film entertainment industry in India and Vietnam.

TABLE 1.7
GII 2011 RANKING OF SELECTED COUNTRIES

World RANKING				
COUNTRY	INPUT	OUTPUT	EFF	OVERALL
Singapore	1	18	94	3
Hong Kong	2	13	66	4
Korea	17	11	25	16
Japan	18	27	64	20
China	**43**	**14**	**3**	**29**
Malaysia	28	15	77	31
Thailand	48	46	57	48
Vietnam	63	63	20	51
India	87	44	9	62
Philippines	93	84	62	91

Source: Global Innovation Index, 2011

Table 1.8 summarizes the Inputs and Outputs subscale scores for the ten countries. Based on their scores, we computed the relative ranking of these ten countries and summarize it in Table 1.9. For the ICT sub-scale, China ranks the 6th among the ten countries. For the second most significant Inputs sub-scale, R&D, China did relatively better ranking in the fourth position of the ten countries. For the third and fourth most important Inputs sub-scales, KWORKER and CREDIT, China ranks the fifth and the seventh, respectively.

Implications of the Ranking on China's Innovation Policy
Despite the fact that China ranks only the sixth in providing an innovation enabling environment, China ranks first in being efficient in turning innovation inputs into outputs (Efficiency). Countries that rank higher than China in Inputs and Outputs all rank much lower than China in the Efficiency ranking. It is interesting to note that countries that rank second and third are India and Vietnam, respectively (see Table 1.7).

34

TABLE 1.8
INNOVATION INPUTS AND OUTPUTS PERFORMANCE OF SELECTED COUNTRIES IN COMPETING POSITIONS TO CHINA

COUNTRY	INSTIT POLIENVI (6)*	REGENVIR (5)*	HCR R&D (2)*	INFRA ICT (1)*	MRTSOPH CREDIT (4)*	BUSSOPH KWORKER (3)*	Innovation Outputs SCIOP	CREAOP
Singapore	80.00	97.50	60.20	69.00	65.10	87.30	48.90	41.40
Hong Kong	88.60	96.70	32.10	70.20	78.00	65.60	38.10	57.60
Korea	73.90	73.30	58.40	81.00	66.30	57.70	53.70	42.20
Japan	89.20	84.40	65.10	68.80	79.70	82.30	49.80	32.80
China	32.80	53.50	42.30	28.40	49.10	64.80	52.70	40.90
Malaysia	57.50	71.70	26.40	44.20	58.00	69.00	30.40	39.90
Thailand	38.00	67.30	18.50	21.30	44.70	52.70	23.90	39.90
Vietnam	39.20	50.50	17.80	22.10	64.30	26.00	25.30	41.30
India	42.20	56.60	38.80	16.30	38.20	24.40	24.80	40.30
Philippines	32.50	52.90	11.50	22.30	21.00	46.70	22.30	25.70

* The number in the parentheses represents the ranked importance of the sub-scale in terms of its structural loading in the canonical function.

TABLE 1.9
INNOVATION INPUTS AND OUTPUTS PERFORMANCE RANKING OF SELECTED COUNTRIES IN COMPETING POSITION WITH CHINA

COUNTRY	INSTIT POLIENVI (6)*	REGENVIR (5)*	HCR R&D (2)*	INFRA ICT (1)*	MRTSOPH CREDIT (4)*	BUSSOPH KWORKER (3)*	Innovation Output SCIOP	CREAOP
Singapore	3.00	1.00	2.00	3.00	4.00	1.00	4.00	3.00
Hong Kong	2.00	2.00	6.00	2.00	2.00	4.00	5.00	1.00
Korea	4.00	4.00	3.00	1.00	3.00	6.00	1.00	2.00
Japan	1.00	3.00	1.00	4.00	1.00	2.00	3.00	9.00
China	**9.00**	**8.00**	**4.00**	**6.00**	**7.00**	**5.00**	**2.00**	**5.00**
Malaysia	5.00	5.00	7.00	5.00	6.00	3.00	6.00	7.00
Thailand	8.00	6.00	8.00	9.00	8.00	7.00	9.00	7.00
Vietnam	7.00	10.00	9.00	8.00	5.00	9.00	7.00	4.00
India	6.00	7.00	5.00	10.00	9.00	10.00	8.00	6.00
Philippines	10.00	9.00	10.00	7.00	10.00	8.00	10.00	10.00

* The number in the parentheses represents the ranked importance of the sub-scale in terms of its structural loading in the canonical function.

All of these three countries, China; India; and Vietnam, rank relatively low in terms of Inputs and Outputs. Zhu and Xu (2006) have found that the R&D efficiency of Chinese high-tech industries has been growing gradually and steadily. They also found in their study that R&D efficiency is positively related with firm size and market competition. In addition, the study pointed out that foreign investment enterprises had played more important role in enhancing R&D efficiency than state owned enterprises. Based on these findings, the China public administrators should consider a policy to selectively accept foreign investments that will bring in technological capabilities matching Chinese future innovation needs. For a long time, China has emphasized the importance of 'self-reliance' in developing her technological and innovative capability. Foreign investment and importation, however, provides an efficient alternative for hiking up the country's technological know-how, which will help China's development model to become more knowledge-intensive.

The implications of this relative ranking for China in terms of formulating future innovation policy are manifold. First, China should encourage ICT investments to promote the availability and ease of use of ICT, expediting the digitization of more government processes. In terms of promoting citizens' participation in ICT use and processes, speeding up the movement towards e-government is one effective way to boost citizen participation in digitized and streamlined public processes. The lessons we have learned about benefits of e-government include: (a) a government of increased efficiency, which will have a positive impact on increasing the quality of civil services, (b) increased public spending on the ICT related infrastructure, which will contribute to the build-up of innovative capacity, (c) an increased level of human capital quality because of more public participation in public work and information processes, and (d) the increased tendency of the economy to be reshaped into a more information-based one (Jaeger and Thompson 2003, Kumar and Best 2006). All these benefits are promoters of a more innovation-embracing economy and a freer market.

In terms of the second key innovation input factor, R&D, China ranks the fourth after Japan, Singapore and Korea. However, the difference in their measuring indices is much larger than the relative ranking may suggest. As the quality and quantity of the R&D capability and output have a tremendous impact, China should continue to focus on promoting this aspect in her public policy formulation such as in the areas of fiscal and education.

On the KWORKER sub-scale under business sophistication, China's performance was after Singapore, Japan, Malaysia, and Hong Kong ranking fifth. As the accumulation of human capital is an indispensable condition for innovation to take place, businesses foster their productivity, competitiveness, and innovation potential with the employment of highly qualified professionals and technicians. Therefore, the Chinese government should, through the use of encouraging tax legislation, support businesses to invest in staff professional development activities and directly involve in R&D.

The recent global financial crisis has demonstrated how critical it is for a business to attain the ability of credit, investment funds, and access to international markets in order to stay prosperous. China ranks the seventh on the fourth important Inputs factor, the CREDIT subscale. Numerous studies have pointed out that a lot of SMEs in China have difficulties in obtaining the necessary finances for their operations. The role that government can play is to operate more SME financing and micro-financing programs.

CONTRIBUTION AND LIMITATIONS OF CURRENT STUDY

The current study contributes to the existing literature in several ways. First, this study provides an evaluation and a platform for discussions on the readiness, or the lack of such, of China for embracing and enabling innovations in the country as a whole. Second, drawing on INSEAD's GII conceptual framework and a rich set of secondary data, we were able to rank a large set of innovation enabling factors based on the correlations between these factors and the innovation outcome measurements. Third, based on the ranking of the innovation input factors, we come up with recommends for China in regard of the future directions the government may take in formulating public policy that will promote an innovation friendly environment.

Nonetheless, this current study is not without limitations. Two of the more conspicuous limitations are: (a) the limitation in sample size, and (b) the lack of a clear connection between the innovation output measurement and the overall well being and economic prosperity of a country or economic entity. Regarding the first limitation, as the number of data points included in the data set is only 124, while the number of indicators included in the conceptual framework is eighty. The analysis is destined to have to sacrifice the opportunity of analyzing the data at the indicator level (i.e. the most detailed level of measurement) as our study being restricted for the same reason. In the future, revisions must be done to the data collection, such as including longitudinal data, in order to increase the number of data points.

With respect to the second limitation, future studies must include economic measures in the outcome measurement as the focus of the outcome measurement in the current study focuses only on the quantity of the outputs. Such a measurement neglects the impact of specific innovation outcomes may have on an economy's overall well being. Therefore, it does not provide a clear and direct connection to link the two output pillars to economic outcomes or prosperity.

CONCLUSION

Driven by an export-oriented economic development pattern, China has made great progress in terms of innovativeness and technological advancement. Researchers generally recognize that China has gradually migrated from a 'piracy' mode to an incremental innovation mode. This change more or less has reflected on INSEAD's GII ranking: China's ranking in the Global Innovation Index improved from the 43th in 2010 to the 29th in 2011. However, China still has to face with three major challenges: policy formulation and implementation; education system reforms to embrace a more liberal education model to encourage the germination of a creative thinking generation; and transcending from a manufacturing and export based economic development pattern to one that is more knowledge intensive and innovative.

To obtain insights into the interrelationships between the various innovation inputs and the outputs, we performed a canonical correlation analysis at the broader level on the five Innovation Inputs and the two Innovation Outputs. Our objective is to evaluate the strength of the associations among the innovation input scales (the independent variables) and the innovation output scales (the dependent variables). Due to the relatively small data set (only 125 data points), in our preliminary analysis we included only the main scales and left the sub-scales out of the analysis. The data analysis results show that the infrastructure variable (INFRA) contributes most highly in explaining the variances in the differences in the innovation outputs.

In order to develop a further understanding of the specific dimensions in the five innovation input scales have actually contributed to the explanation of the variances in the innovation outputs, we performed another canonical correlation analysis at a more refined level to the subscales of the Inputs and Outputs. Our subscale level analysis indicates that the ICT subscale of infrastructure scale, R&D of the human capital resources, knowledge workers of the business sophistication scale, and the credit subscale of the market sophistication scale contribute most to explain the differences in the innovation outputs.

Based on the findings from the subscale level analysis of the data collected by INSEAD, we make several suggestions to the policy making authorities of China to enhance the Inputs factors. To address the issues presented in the three challenges, first, we recommend public administrators to continue considering a policy to selectively accept foreign investments that will bring in technological capabilities matching China's future innovation needs. Second, China should encourage ICT investments to promote the availability and ease of use of ICT, and speed up the digitization of more government processes. In terms of promoting citizens' participation in ICT use and processes, China should speed up the movement towards e-government for the effective expansion of citizen participation in digitized and streamlined public processes. In addition, China should focus on reforming her education models and contents for the incubation of creative education. Through tax legislation and public policy formulation, Chinese government needs to provide stronger supports for businesses to invest in human resources development and R&D. Finally, as availability of credit to the private sector has been identified to be a key component in market sophistication, the Chinese government needs to be more considerate and flexible in formulating its fiscal policy to operate more SME financing and micro-financing programs.

Authored by Shirley Ye Sheng & Roman Wong, originally published in International Journal of China Marketing Vol. 3(1) 2012, pp. 88-106.

Chapter Two

Cluster Marketing Models and Strategies: The Implications thereof in the Chinese High-Tech Industry

The phenomenon and model of industrial cluster marketing is a cross-linking subject on the industry cluster theory and traditional (geographical) marketing perspectives. Nevertheless, it begs the question, does high-tech industry cluster marketing relate to the traditional industrial cluster phenomenon? This paper focuses on a discussion about whether there is a clear existence of a cluster marketing model to start with. Therefore, the concept of cluster marketing model was defined, thereafter its related areas were determined, and finally a theoretical model for a high-tech cluster marketing model was established. Working with this theoretical framework model, the author proposed the possibility that the cluster marketing model of traditional industries could apply to high-tech industry clusters. The central idea was that the marketing operating mechanisms were the core of the cluster marketing model and that three types of traditional cluster marketing mechanisms (function - interest, regulation, and contract mechanism) can successfully be applied to high-tech industry clusters. As a result, six cluster marketing models for high-tech industries were developed for proposal.

INTRODUCTION

Cluster marketing here is defined as the convergence of distinct activities within an industrial cluster, with the view to achieve, as a whole, organizational objectives by participating more effectively in the competitive market process and the larger macroenvironment, ensuring competitive advantage through better efficiencies and innovation.

Michael Porter claims that industry clusters are "in a particular area under a particular area, with a group of interconnected companies, suppliers, related industries, and specialized institutions and associations." (Porter, 2007) In other words, within industry clusters, not only is the competition very important to a series of related businesses and other entities, but it also often extend downstream to the customer, continuing the river that have relevant skills, technology, public input, complementary products or companies. It extends even so far as when a foreign company continues its investment in the industrial cluster and thereby lends itself to become part of the cluster. Ultimately, these various interrelated aspects of cooperation and competition, ensures that the industrial clusters create a competitive advantage.

Furthermore, significant cluster marketing advantages can be gained through synergies in market research, developments new markets, access to current and new markets, market share, product development, distribution channel development, dissemination of information, sales promotion, etc. through cooperative strategies (Zhu,2003).

China has a total of 53 state-level high-tech development zones, most of these have formed one or more mature high-tech industry clusters with great anticipation for future developments on exclusive high-tech zones. High-tech industrial clusters do not necessarily differ significantly in their cooperate composition or organizational structure compared to traditional clusters such as within the Fujian tea industry, Wenzhou shoes industry, or Shengzhou neckties industry for which cluster marketing was implemented and considered suitable. This is based on the continued successes achieved in recent years through increased competitive advantage in these industries as argued by various scholars (Zhu 2003, 2005; Mu 2007; Feng, 2007)). Furthermore, Guangguan Zheng and Xuemei Chen endeavored to highlight some of the structural elements within the cluster marketing organization. Traditional industrial cluster marketing is divided into three specific models, namely, the "collective marketing" model, "see the customer" model and "share marketing channel" model. They concluded that "cluster marketing adds a significant competitive advantage to small and medium enterprises to develop new markets and an effective means to self-development." (Zheng and Chen, 2006), Therefore, strong clusters contribute to a start-up firm's survival whilst it continues to strive for long-term establishment.

Nevertheless, based on certain variables for example the competitive nature, product obsolesce, and speed of technological change and others, there remain some unanswered questions in terms of high-tech industrial clusters, such as whether the introduction of the traditional marketing model for an industrial cluster is suitable for a highly evolving, complex, and knowledge based high-tech industry? Therefore, one must ask which cluster marketing models are likely to be the best suited for adoption into high-tech clusters and is there a theoretical model to draw from to build these marketing models. In considering these questions and analyzing the industrial cluster theory whilst developing marketing ideas and methods, one could possibly present viable options to improve competitiveness within China's high-tech industry clusters.

This paper consists of five-part bellow: research of the marketing model, designing the organizational structure for cluster marketing, analyzing the operational mechanism of cluster marketing and advantage of cluster marketing and the cluster marketing model for high-tech industry cluster.

RESEARCH: THE MARKETING MODEL

To date, to define the concept of marketing models, marketing theorists do not have a more generally accepted view, may be involved in this concept is too broad, or because many of the concepts we use this point of our view, there is no uniform open-minded. The author looked at domestic and foreign relevant research literature found that even "marketing mode" as its theme or as the article keyword mostly "ignore" on the definition of the concept itself, but more set out directly the form of marketing model. This paper intended to deal with the rigor and the convenience of discussion, the definition of the marketing model is in order to achieve an organization's marketing goals, make a marketing operation mechanism under the guidance of the current marketing idea .The operation mechanism is stable and can be copied. The concept of marketing mode is a high degree of abstraction and generality. It is descriptions and definitions of the composition of the marketing system, the various components of the function, operation and controlling rules. It is knowledge about the marketing system features and operational discipline.

FIGURE 2.1
A THEORETICAL MODEL OF THE HIGH-TECH INDUSTRY CLUSTER MARKETING MODEL

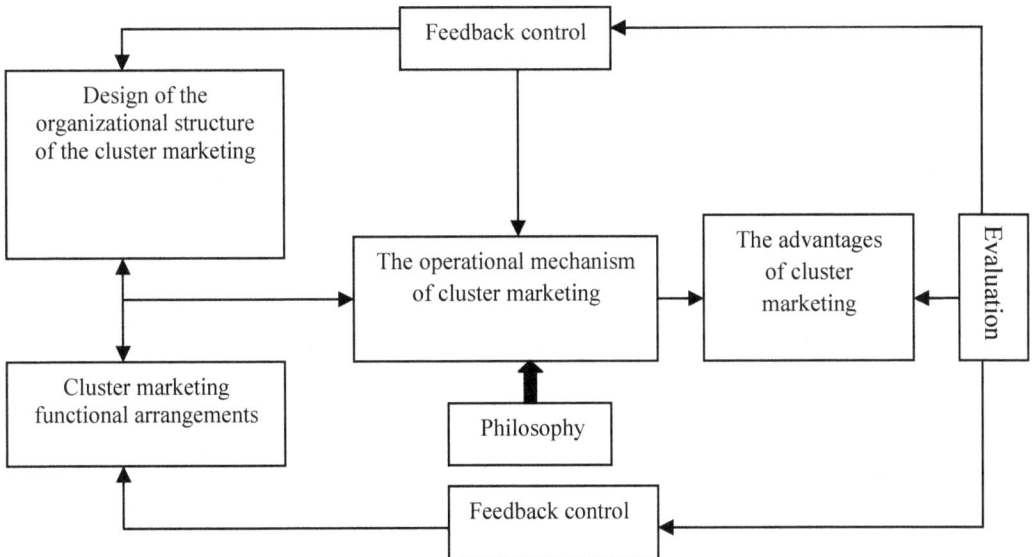

Designing the Organizational Structure for Cluster Marketing

Cluster marketing is the spontaneous cooperation of enterprises within the cluster market behavior, to transform co-marketing awareness into concrete action of the cluster; the primary problem is to think about the micro-organizational structure in terms the cluster marketing. This problem is not solved; it is void and the lack of foundation of cluster marketing. The main participators of the industry cluster marketing include trade associations, chambers of commerce, academic groups, marketing intermediaries and various firms in clusters.

The organizational structure of the cluster marketing has four forms as illustrated below (see figure 2.2).

a) Hierarchical Structure.

Hierarchy is based on the capabilities of the level of cluster marketing to build a marketing organization, as described in the text the cluster brand clusters model and leading enterprise traction model. In terms of the brand cluster model, the top layer relates to a regional brand, the middle layer the corporate brand, and the lower layer the product brand. With regards to the leading enterprise traction model, at the top of the cluster formation is the leading enterprise and its marketing networks which carry out market research and technology development in order to meet the core needs of industry clusters. The middle layer is to provide operational activities such as packaging, logistics, and other services, whilst at the bottom end of the cluster formation are suppliers in support these enterprises.

b) Star-shaped Structure.

The star-shaped structure is characterized by only one center, and is a single layer. Its structure is followed by many common organizations such as an association or technical institute at the center of the cluster marketing. It is more loosely organized, and relies on the industry or technical associations' activities with regular dissemination of ideas, diffusion technology, establishment of rules, and the exchange of information.

c) The Linear Chain Structure.

The linear chain structure is unique, each node represents a marketing function of the virtual organization, each virtual organization can have multiple entities to complete a single or a number of marketing functions, but the virtual organizational structure is linear, that is, except the starting point and end point. Furthermore, each virtual unit occurs only with the other two links.

d) Network Structure.

The network structure is characterized by each node and can be associated with multiple nodes. There is no center, and the network structure is open. Marketing activities within a traditional industry cluster typically use the "see the customer" model and "share marketing channel" model based on this structure, whilst the high-tech industry clusters' "channel network sharing" model can also be considered (discussed below).

Various studies on marketing activities within traditional industry clusters have found that the above-mentioned hierarchical structure, star-shaped structure and network structure are commonly used, but did not use a linear chain structure. The hierarchical structure, star-shaped structure, and network structure can be directly introduced to the marketing of high-tech industrial clusters. Furthermore, because high-tech industrial clusters use information technology at an advanced and sophisticated level, it can accept and adapt to new concepts faster than traditional industries, therefore, a linear chain structure is also suitable.

FIGURE 2.2
THE ORGANIZATIONAL STRUCTURE OF
CLUSTER MARKETING

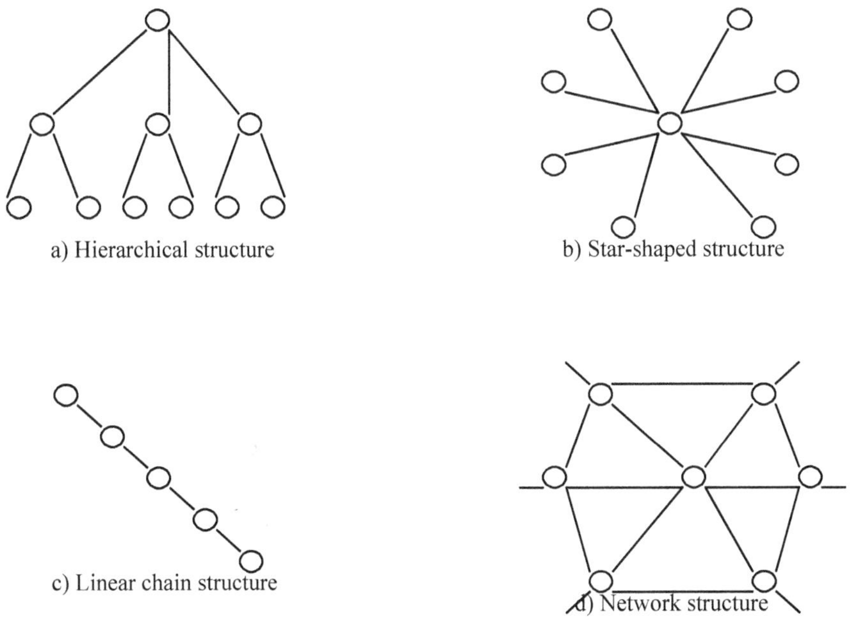

a) Hierarchical structure

b) Star-shaped structure

c) Linear chain structure

d) Network structure

Cluster Marketing Functional Arrangements

The design of a cluster marketing organization must take into account, not only, how to arrange the marketing function in the cluster organization, but also the cluster marketing operation mechanism, and the relationship between them, as shown in Figure 2.1. Cluster marketing functions include, but not limited to, researching markets, developing new markets, access to markets, increasing market share, product development, brand building, channel development, dissemination of information, and sales promotion. Organizations within the cluster should, therefore, endeavor to effectively allocate marketing resources adequately, dominate by a common marketing philosophy, strengthen the cluster marketing operating mechanism through repeated interaction, reach speedy consensus on issues, and ensure the implementation of systems and contracts on sharing cluster marketing functions under this arrangement (marketing operating mechanism).

The Operational Mechanism of Cluster Marketing

The operational mechanism of cluster marketing is under the guidance of the cluster marketing ideas, and upon which the co-participants in the cluster marketing make the rules of cluster marketing operations, specific measures on distribution benefits, incentives and constraints, and the way in which to exert control over the activities of cluster marketing. Function - interest, regulation, and contract are three basic operational mechanisms of cluster marketing.

Function - Interest Mechanism

The function - interest mechanism in the cluster refers to the commitment and benefit from the marketing function which should reflect the rights (interests) and responsibilities for management principles. There is no such thing as a "free dinner" in a manner of speaking, in the clusters marketing co-operation as all actors in the system need exhibit full commitment. The function - interest mechanism is the foundation for a clusters marketing organization to exist and to develop. In this instance it does not matter whether the traditional industry cluster "collective mark" model, "see the customer" model or "share marketing channel" model have followed this principle or not, the commitment remains the same. In the "collective mark" model the embodiment of this principle is in the Chamber of Commerce dues-sharing system. Secondly, in the "share marketing channels" model the embodiment of this principle is in the effectiveness of marketing channels, the power-sharing in the distribution channels, and the resulting benefits. Lastly, in the "see the customer" model the embodiment of this principle is that firm's sales incentive output is according to "see customer worker" performance. The function - interest mechanism also can also effectively be implemented to high-tech industry cluster marketing.

Regulation Mechanism

The regulation mechanism refers to the relationship between industrial cluster marketing organizations and the operating regulation within a certain cluster culture, industry association (technology), the company management system, and the organization's relationship rules. In the "collective mark" model, this mechanism is embodied in the membership system of trade associations, Chamber of Commerce, professional associations (standards), and common rules of behavior. In the "see the customer" model the embodiment of this mechanism is in that of the manufacturers, traders, trading companies, of which "see the customer worker" establish the relationship rules between them. In the "share marketing channels" model the embodiment of this mechanism is the tacit understanding of one another, mutual trust, and full cooperation of the channel members. Compared with the traditional industrial clusters, the existence of a variety of Technology Associations provides more choices of rules for various industrial clusters.

Contract Mechanism

The contract mechanism reflects the market exchange relationships. The marketing cluster organization should not only need to be cooperative, but also ensure effective exchange processes. In essence, the relationship within the cluster marketing organization is a kind of economic system based long-term relationships that will be reflected through a contract. The contract is to coordinate the interests of all stakeholders. The contractual relationship is also the most common relationship of a cluster marketing organization and thus, the contract mechanism is a powerful tool for efficient allocation of marketing resources equitably. In the "collective mark" model, the embodiment of this mechanism is based on the sales of goods that are registered to share maintenance costs of trademarks. In the "see the customer" model, the embodiment of this mechanism is the formation of orders after bargaining between manufacturers, traders, trading companies and "see customer workers". In the "share marketing channels" model, the embodiment of this mechanism is the transactions contract between the members of a channel. Compared to the traditional industrial cluster, a high-tech industry cluster will require more involvement due to complex intellectual property transactions, but cannot change the contract mechanism in its cluster marketing role. Table 2.1 outlines the elements for the traditional industry cluster marketing model and operating mechanisms.

TABLE 2.1
TRADITIONAL INDUSTRIES CLUSTER MARKETING MODEL
TYPES AND OPERATING MECHANISMS

		Traditional Industry Cluster Marketing Model Type		
		"Collective mark" model	"See the customer" model	"Share marketing channel "model
Operating Mechanism	Function - interest	Chamber of Commerce dues-sharing – sharing collective mark	Incentive sales according "see the customer worker" performance	The distribution of channel power and the resulting benefits
	Regulation	Industry, Chamber of commerce, professional associations, and common rules of behavior	Manufacturers, traders, trading companies, and "see the customer worker "established the relationship rules	The tacit understanding, mutual trust, and cooperation of the channel members.
	Contract	Based on sales of goods that are registered to share maintenance costs of trademarks	The formation of orders after bargaining and the commission of "see the customer worker"	Transactions contract between the members of a channel

The analysis above clearly shows that any of the three traditional industry cluster marketing operating mechanisms can be applied to a high-tech industry cluster.

The Advantages and Evaluation of Cluster Marketing
The advantages of cluster marketing are mainly the following:
(1) To enable small and medium enterprises (SMEs) to a certain extent, overcome some of its weaknesses, and to integrated cluster strength to market development.

Industrial clusters of SMEs with human, material and financial resources constraints that embark on independent marketing activities usually result in it carried out ineffectively. A large number of enterprises in industrial cluster and inter-related firms that join forces to carry out marketing activities to help SMEs make up for their deficiencies, using the collective power to achieve their marketing objectives.

(2) Contribute to the establishment of regional brands, which will help the development of enterprises within the cluster.

A regional brand is the inevitable result of the development of industrial clusters. It is a manifestation of the core competitiveness of industrial clusters. It represents the main product and image of the cluster. Regional brands have more than a single corporate brand image, and by using the co-operation of many enterprises to collectively work the enrichment and refinement brands, with more extensive coverage can ensure an ongoing effective branding. Compared to regional brands, in many cases, the individual enterprise's life cycle is relatively short and it takes a vast amount of resources over a long period of time to sustain the individual brand effectively. On the other hand, as long as it is not due to inhibiting internal and external factors such as a change in severe technical or natural conditions, cluster contraction or drastic restructuring, the regional brand can be sustained. A regional brand can achieve better competiveness on a regional industry and enterprise level, enhance regional industry product brands, strengthen corporate brands, bolster cluster brand awareness, and thereby ensure increased brand value on all levels.

(3) The cluster marketing can promote cooperation between enterprises.

Cluster marketing establishes a platform for business cooperation within the group, forming a cooperative mechanism. On the one hand, due to the cluster marketing mechanism by which the market price information is transparent, the corporate generally considers a product differentiation strategy in order to avoid direct price competition. On the other hand, the corporate can more easily access, analyze, and evaluate other firms' product information, to facilitate the coordination of product division among enterprises through the cluster marketing mechanisms, thus contributing to the cluster product diversity, and enhanced cluster attractiveness. Furthermore, firms through the established mechanisms can also promote inter-firm cooperation in other areas, such as product research and development, personnel training, procurement of raw materials, and various other fields of operation.

(4) Help to reduce the cost of operations.

First of all, stronger linkages between industrial enterprises leads to better understand of each other through cluster marketing mechanisms and reduction in transaction costs. Secondly, through cluster marketing, enterprises will be enable to increase their share of trading volume to a certain extent by utilizing the same marketing channels, ensuring decreased unit marketing costs, and creating external economies of scale. Enterprises in the industrial cluster can achieve specialization in the production and trading processes with close cooperation which can lead to better external economies of scale.

In order to assess the advantages of cluster marketing it is necessary to establish a scientific evaluation system based on the four aspects as mentioned above. Once the high-tech industry cluster marketing operation is evaluated after implementation, preemptive action can be taken for future events, problems can be promptly corrected, and adjustments can be made.

THE CLUSTER MARKETING MODEL FOR HIGH-TECH INDUSTRIAL CLUSTERS

According to above theoretical model analysis, we can divide the high-tech industrial cluster marketing model into the following types based on the difference of the marketing mechanism:

The Cluster-Brand Clusters Model

Clusters which incorporate a strategy using cluster brand clusters are structured on a three-tiered layer consisting of cluster brands, corporate brands and product brands. At the top of the cluster-brand clusters is the cluster brand, whereat a collective brand represents one industry cluster. When there is a combination of industry clusters, it becomes a regional brand, of which various trademark registrations is required, which in turn becomes as a collective mark. A registered collective mark is conducive to businesses within the industrial cluster that are more closely related and synergistic to one another.

The value of the cluster brand is enhanced with the strong support of corporate brands within the cluster. On the other hand, strong product brands play an important role in achieving corporate goals. The implementation of the cluster-brand clusters model endeavors to build brand recognition at all levels, focuses on cluster brand development, and the continual pursuit in maintaining a high value market offering. The concept of cluster brand-building is suitable for certain synergistic grouping of firms including local governments, quasi-governmental agencies, industry associations or the economic cooperation organizations, business organizations or industry leaders.

Channel Network Sharing Model

A channel network within an enterprise is mainly responsible for its own products, but in its channel system where spare capacity is available, other enterprises in the cluster with their highly complementary products can utilize the firm's distribution services. Thus, cooperation of this kind result in

50

further benefits between cluster participants as a whole, and can be further enhanced within the channel by assisting one another in disseminating market opportunities, gathering and sharing feedback on market information, sharing potential channel risks, and ensuring greater added value and competitive advantage through increased efficiencies within the channel.

Furthermore, channels within the cluster try to cooperate and build long-term relationships with its suppliers, who in turn provide them with more flexibility and assortment in the merchandise mix and reduction in purchasing costs, thereby enhancing the channel attractiveness to retailers. Lastly, because of the high-tech industry cluster's good grounding in communications infrastructure, the formation of enterprise clusters can be carried out jointly by B2B and B2C.

Leading Enterprise Traction Model

Due to the technology-intensive characteristics of high-tech products, its products have a natural monopolistic tendency in many instances, which gives leading enterprises in an industrial cluster strong bargaining power. SMEs within a cluster can join the brand club or pay for the usage of a certain established or leading firm's brand or trademark. SMEs can also provide the necessary synergistic products and services for the leading enterprise(s), which will enable the SMEs to have enough room for growth with reduced risks associated of entering markets. SMEs working with market leaders can also lead to increased production and further enhance brand influence. For example, Wuhan - China Optical Valley optoelectronics industry cluster applies the leading enterprise traction model which consists of two particularly powerful companies: Fiber Home Technologies Group (FTG) and the Yangtze Optical Fiber and Cable Company Ltd(YOFC). They have a higher brand awareness, strong R&D capabilities and financial strength, provide full access to their core technological research and innovations and perform a guiding role, whilst the large number of small and medium enterprises has formed a successful production network with which to achieve sharing of production capacities, strengthening organizational networking and establishing an integrated market-oriented focus.

Exhibition Promotion Model

The exhibition promotion marketing model is the most familiar and most easy to operate and provide the most effortless results of the marketing model. As stated before, China has 53 state-level high-tech development zones, which are created and government-led, whilst playing a key role, with the view to increase China's development in high-tech industries and to promote a culture of competitiveness among them.

The government has endeavored to promote a good image of industrial clusters as a whole, whether attracting foreign investment or upgrading the influence of region industrial clusters. For example, the government as a stakeholder has successfully promoted the Wuhan East Lake high-tech zone through its yearly "Light Fair" since 2007, attracting investments totaling 11 billion Yuan. Three hundred and twenty internationally funded projects have taken root in Wuhan. The development of this project is not only an extension of the optoelectronics industry chain locally, but it is done with the view to promote China's optoelectronics industry to extend into the international industrial chain. "CRE Council" of China Optical Valley has also successfully held five sessions since its inception 2001 and has attracted foreign investment and even other Chinese nationals from other countries. It is clear, not only is the promotion of the "China Optics Valley" brand in the region successful, but promotional efforts in establishing a solid international brand for the "China Optics Valley" has elevated its external image which brought huge economic benefits for the region locally and the country as whole. Testament of this can be seen by means of the "CRE Council's" efforts in 2006 alone, in initiating 125 contracted projects with the availably 3.07 billion Yuan in capital and the promotion of it in the international sphere.

Cooperative R&D Model

Products of a high-tech industry cluster are regarded as being high value-added, nevertheless, whether it satisfies market demand, needs market testing. A high-tech product life cycle is short, with promotion risks, lead time to product R&D is fraught with further risks, and cooperative research and development of industrial clusters has always been an inherent need. So-called cooperative R&D refers to the corporate seeking "exogenous" resources, competitive advantages, and cooperative innovation. It therefore relies on regional innovation networks, which consist of business and government - financial institutions, research institutions and intermediary organizations, and their technical innovation and product development to effectively enhance SMEs technological innovation and reduce product development risks.

The Marketing Alliance Model

The marketing alliance model refers to a single firm's marketing activities integrated into cluster marketing campaign. By means of brand sharing, product matching, market concentration, channel interdependence, combined regional promotion, and information sharing SMEs can obtain a larger scale of cooperation, reduce marketing costs, market expansion, and share the collective advantages that an industrial cluster offers to better withstand the forces of market competition. Enterprises within industrial clusters usually much more forge stable alliances when sharing resources to conduct joint marketing activities. This approach can often be detected within traditional industries clusters, such as Fujian tea industry clusters and the Zhejiang Wenzhou shoes industry clusters. It can aptly apply to high-tech industrial clusters as well.

CONCLUSION

A theoretical model based on the cluster marketing model was established to compare traditional industry clusters to the high-tech industry clusters. Employing this theoretical model, the author analyzed the possibility that the cluster marketing model of traditional industries can apply to high-tech industry clusters, the following are basic viewpoints:

(1) The concept of any marketing model lends itself to a high degree of abstraction and generality. Nevertheless, it also lends itself to the descriptions, definitions, and composition of the marketing system, of which include various components of the functional, operational and controlling rules. In this paper, it is an understanding about the cluster marketing system features, characteristics, and operational discipline. At its core, is the cluster marketing operation mechanism, and should be stable and can be duplicated.

(2) The operational mechanism of cluster marketing includes three basic components: function - interest, regulation, and contract mechanisms. Function – interest reflects the management principle of the right - responsible; regulation reflects the cultural of the cluster, industry codes of conduct, and cluster stakeholders' requirements in handling mutual relations. The contract component reflects the marketing relationships between the market exchanges within the primary clusters. The contractual relationship is also the most common relationship of cluster marketing organizations and is a powerful tool for efficient allocation of marketing resources. Analysis of the three components (operational mechanism of cluster marketing) has revealed that all of them have been applied to different types of clusters within traditional industries.

(3) By comparative analysis of the operational mechanisms of cluster marketing between traditional and high-tech industrial clusters, it found that all three types of traditional cluster marketing mechanisms can successfully be implemented by high-tech industry clusters. As a result, six cluster marketing models for high-tech industries were proposed.

Authored by Hongbo Tu, originally published in *International Journal of China Marketing*, Vol. 1(2) 2011, pp. 34-44.

Chapter Three

Second Life and E-Marketing in an Online Social Network: The Implementation in China Marketing

Second Life (SL) is leading three-dimensional (3D) virtual worlds working in an electronic environment. The residents have freedom to socialize, explore, meet people and build products and services. The purpose of this paper is to investigate the significance of communication and e-marketing opportunities in the SL virtual world. The theoretical background used in this study was communication theory and social system and media richness theory. Online conversations were performed with SL users to explore their communication behaviors and experiences to conduct marketing activities in Second Life. The findings show that initial capital investment, time engagement and quality of products were equally important in SL as in the real world. Moreover, advertising, customer relations, after sales service and consumer traffic are mandatory for e-marketing promotion. SL was found favorable for technological development, brand promotion, resource management, business strategy and prototyping. The synchronous communication is highly effective for managers and business practitioners in the real world. SL has a significant impact on individual Chinese users and the growth of China's internal market.

INTRODUCTION

Second Life (SL) is one of the fastest growing and leading 3D virtual worlds and latest innovations of information communication technology. The residents have freedom to socialize, create, explore, and meet other residents and build products and services and create an online marketing environment. Communication is vital to perform social and marketing activities. The virtual business has greatly affected the real world economy (Castranova, 2003). SL has the potentiality of business communication, information dissemination and innovation. Due to this, SL is a powerful option for real-world companies. The concept of virtual reality is important in communication research. Virtual reality is the interface between humans and computers in a 3D world interacting directly with virtual objects. It has a number of practical applications with regard to human computer interaction activities. Communication research is the interdisciplinary field of information systems. The synchronicity of communication media in SL has made it a social environment.

Virtual business or v-business refers to a business inside a virtual environment. A business is defined as a process to provide products or services in order to generate revenue as an objective of making profit (Rappa, 2008). The products are virtual, but real revenue can be earned in a virtual world. Most people think of virtual worlds as just a game, but they are evolving toward a society in which social and economic interactions are the main drivers (Zimmer, 2007). Residents can run a global business in real time. Virtual worlds are inspiring both organizations and individuals to make revenue. Real-world companies such as Nissan, IBM and Cisco have been designing and testing new products and services concepts in SL. ABN Amro and Meta Bank have been facilitating opening accounts, making deposits and withdrawing virtual funds. Some universities have been providing online lectures. Residents are running shops, clubs and recreation sites. Some of them are working as a programmer and designer. There is a huge opportunity for education and training, meeting and collaboration, marketing and product testing.

Consumer learning is very important in SL, which bears the concept of word-of-mouth communication. The better the relationship with a consumer, the better the market one can establish. Commutation plays a pivotal role in generating e-marketing opportunities. Advertisement and brand promotion are the key factors of e-marketing in SL (Hemp, 2006). Moreover, modern communication technologies have made distant participants to come closer. They can conduct educational seminars and meetings in a virtual environment. SL is a suitable place for business, academic and non-profit organizations to present their messages to the users. Qualified builders, programmers and artists are found to promote commercial activities. In this connection, SL is known for its recreational and marketing platform. It provides a great deal for real-life businesses to provide an opportunity to engage with customers, suppliers and business partners. SL has strong economic connectivity to the real world.

The purpose of the current study is to learn communication behavior of residents in SL and its scope to create online marketing value. SL is a web-based, computer-simulated virtual environment. So, it has brought a number of opportunities in the e-marketing field. Effective communication is essential for online business. Due to this SL offers numerous trading and learning opportunities through communication. SL is a wide platform for social networking. Besides SL, there are other social networking websites such as Facebook, Myspace, Twitter and YouTube. SL takes high social responsibility and transparency comparing to other social networks. The anonymity of the people is guaranteed that enables residents a much more freedom to perform social and business activities. A further purpose of this study is to learn human communication behavior, interpersonal communication and cognition in a multi-user virtual environment.

The research question of the current study is "What are the opportunities of e-marketing in SL and how important is communication in SL for online marketing?" The importance of the research is that SL is a suitable place for marketing promotion, social interaction, and sharing cultures and ideas among different people residing at different parts of the world and motivating them to enter in this virtual environment. The link between online communication and e-marketing is that communication has interactivity features and has a crucial role in the virtual world to perform social and marketing activities. Educational seminars, conferences and meetings are the outcome of communication. SL facilitates distant participants to come up in one place through this communication medium, thus lowering the cost of learning. It has embraced strong economic and legal connections to the real world. Some of the communication facilities are instant messaging, voice, local chat and blogs. The synchronicity of communication has media richness, which helps to get immediate feedback and facilitate decision making. Richness factors are body language, verbal contents (voice level, volume) and non-verbal contents (appearance, clothing and behavior). SL has broad use of virtual reality which bears the concept of presence and telepresence. Due to the emerging broadband internet access, internet speed is becoming faster. Thus, virtual worlds are rapidly emerging as an alternative means to the real world for communicating, collaborating and organizing marketing activities.

LITERATURE REVIEW

China has the largest online population in the world (David, 2004). The marketers and companies are understanding the importance of having an online presence. China is going to be the second largest advertising market in the world, after the US. Also, the economy is growing 8% to 9% a year (David, 2004). People's disposable incomes are growing quickly. The demographics of the Internet user in China are quite different from other countries (China Online Marketing, 2011). People who are more affluent are the internet users and residing in the larger cities. The Internet, for marketers and advertisers, is a great channel to have access to social networking services by the general public. A majority of Chinese companies have presence in SL for online marketing and brand promotion. The key advantage to working in SL is that it offers much more potential for customers to interact with new products and services.

Chinese online marketing provides a reasonable opportunity for small, medium and large companies in China. Anderson (2009) stated that online platforms decrease distribution costs, including reduced spending on physical stores, rents and shelf space. The number of items sold online can be further extended for a long time. Baidu, the Chinese leading search engine which surpasses Google and controls 76.9% of the Chinese online search market, has moved into the online C2C shopping market in October 2008 and focus at the tempting B2C market (Baidu, 2009). In this prosperous market of high competition and low entry barriers, only the companies that are able to understand and satisfy local customers can utilize the opportunity. Renowned international companies with outstanding technology can easily collapse if consumers are incorrectly approached. The Online and information industry is chosen in China as one of the prioritized industries for governmental assistance (Xinhua, 2009). The Chinese economy is still in a rapid development phase compared to other countries. According to IResearch (2009), high standardized products, like books and CDs, have been some of the most online sold products in China. As online customers gain more experience with online transactions and the convenience of online shopping, online purchases will not be limited to standardized products, but will contain a broader product range for personalized needs.

Virtual Worlds and Second Life

Virtual worlds enable new ways of collaboration and coordination through communication in a 3D environment by Voice Over Internet Protocol (VOIP) (Fetscherin and Lattersmann, 2008). People interact with each other through web 2.0 applications such as voice, instant messaging and video conferencing. SL has become an interactive, collaborative and commercial platform for users, marketers and researchers (Stuart and Brand, 2008). Hence, it offers a huge opportunity to perform e-marketing. The virtual worlds provide flexibility in brand building, advertisement and new product development (Vedrashko, 2006). SL is also a platform to play online games. Enjoyment is one of the important reasons for gaming behavior (Wu, et al., 2008). The games are creating a huge business, and millions of users are motivated to engage in them. People play online games to engage in challenges, make friends, spend time but the basic reason is to enjoy (Davis, *et al.*, 2005; Kim, *et al.*, 2002). Such web-based technologies are useful to create new e-commerce for income generation and consumers' participation (Holsapple, *et al.,* 2005). SL has a scripting tool for monitoring and controlling all communication systems. The podcast is an important communication media to communicate from SL to real life (Lyn, 2008).

SL offers a place for online laboratories to develop and test new products and services (Bainbridge, 2007). It offers scripting and graphic tools for designing, creating and customizing virtual objects and services. Since the virtual market is stable, there is a low amount of investment (Wei and Williams, 2007). Virtual worlds are the hot resource for communication, socialization, collaboration and participation in different activities. A virtual environment is an effective, emotional and simulating environment for users. The customer participation may be active or passive and environmental relationships may be immersive and absorptive. The virtual world is becoming a target place for marketing (Hemp, 2006). SL is a popular and leading online social networking virtual environment. Other social networking web 2.0 applications such as Facebook, Myspace and YouTube are also in operation, but these are limited on their scope for communication, collaboration and coordination (O'Reilly, 2005). The longer the people remain in SL, the more interesting it will be for users. They could learn a number of new activities, make new friends, participate in social activities, conduct business and have interaction with many people around the globe. It helps them to build strong relationships with others, encouraging them to remain in this fantastic world for a long period of time (Castranova, 2001).Voice communication is more important than text as it carries emotional data (Birdwhistell, 1970). Birdwhistell further stated that 65% of information takes place through facial expressions and the remaining 35% through spoken words.

SL has becoming an important place for marketing and brand promotion of real-life products and services. Hemp (2006) stated that virtual worlds have future importance for marketers. They become interactive, collaborative and commercial platforms for all. In this connection there is a huge opportunity for virtual e-commerce. SLs provide flexibility in brand building, new product development, testing and advertisement (Vedrashko, 2006). Virtual presence of organizations may be advertisement or product placement and business-sponsored virtual activities. SL is the computer-mediated shared place for interacting among people (Bray and Konsynski, 2007). SL communication, such as voice, is synchronous. Due to synchronicity immediate response and feedback can be received. This is called "media richness theory." Face- to-face communication in real life has high richness features. Media richness is defined as "the ability of media to overcome different frames of reference or clarify ambiguous issues to change understanding in a timely manner" (Markus 1994, p. 147). The richness characteristic consists of multiple information channels such as voice, gestures, immediate feedback and personal focus. Managers in real life prefer rich media for face-to-face communication, for immediate interaction and decision. Leaner media, such as written media, including e-mail, have low response rates. So managers prefer face-to-face communication for immediate decision making rather than telephone, written memo and email. Interactivity is the key variable in communication research. A majority of people prefer to socialize and participate in social activities. The virtual environment has audio and video contents and different communication media such as instant messaging, text chat and blogs, based on web 2.0 technologies. Communication is preferred for socializing and content sharing (Messinger, *et al.*, 2009).

The inhabitants are responsible for all the contents created in SL (Ondrejka, 2006). Some real life companies such as Toyota, Dell, Adidas and IBM have opened virtual stores in SL for brand awareness. Other companies perform promotional activities of their products and some users are engaged in social activities. Virtual worlds play a vital role to create online social networking and a friendly environment (Hillary, 2007). SL plays a pivotal role in sharing ideas which is essential in information economy (Peter, *et al.*, 2008). Face-to-face meeting in virtual environment is used for knowledge transfer. Facial expressions and body language are shown in graphical form. So, computer-mediated non-verbal communication takes place in SL. People automatically resort to human-to-human interaction but directly to online computer network (Nass and Moon, 2000; Sundar and Nass, 2000). Some people found that virtual life is more attractive than real life (Talamasca, 2006) and avatars could establish networks with other avatars (Bennett and Beith, 2007). Many organizations enter virtual worlds to establish business and generate revenue. The firms design, produce and distribute products. Consumers, on the other hand, purchase goods and services as per their budgetary limitations. Such communication establishes collaboration between producers and consumers. Thus, word-of-mouth communication is highly used in consumer learning. The formation of relationships through interaction in virtual environments is a dynamic process (Ballard and Weigel, 1999). SL bears the concept of presence and telepresence, which is called virtual reality. Presence means being in the environment physically. The avatar represents the virtual presence of a real person whereas telepresence is being in virtual environment by means of communication media (Reeves and Nass, 1996). The virtual reality effect on consumer learning in terms of cognitive, affective and conative dimensions is based on observations made by Li, Daugherty and Biocca (2003). Bandura (1997) stated that individual behavior is the product of the social network through the close social interactions and individuals are able to increase the depth, breath and efficiency of mutual knowledge transformation.

With rich features of social networking and user freedom, users are increasing everyday in large numbers and high numbers of business transactions. Communication has a pivotal role in virtual world to perform social and marketing activities. The development of the internet has raised the use of virtual games. The players develop communities for social interaction and business. Customer relationships and feedback are as important in the virtual world as in the real world. The more we know about the consumer, the more effectively we can communicate and engage in marketing. This is the social aspect of SL. The synchronicity feature of communication in SL is highly effective to perform business activities in a virtual environment. Due to the growing number of users, SL has been facing the problem of system instability that affects online business events. Some other limitations are lack of web interfaces and powerful programming language. SL bears a high social and communication responsibility comparing to other social networking sites such as Facebook, Myspace, Twitter and YouTube.

Communication Theory and Social Systems

Communication is defined as the exchange of information from one place to another. It is an exchange of understanding. SL is an online social network and without communication no activities take place. In this connection, communication research in SL has a broad scope to study human behavior. Communication theory has applications for information systems, psychology, sociology, linguistics and advertising. Many authors and researchers divide communication by 'context' or 'levels' and human users are 'symbol users' or symbol makers. Interpersonal communication tends to focus on dyadic communication, communication involving face-to-face interaction, or communication as a function of developing relationships. The interpersonal communication theory typically focuses on the development, maintenance, and dissolution of relationships. The virtual world has become a strong communication medium allowing distant participants to interact with the real world to enhance collaboration (Leimster, et el., 2004). The development of web 2.0 technology helps policy makers, information system experts and researchers to better understand communication theory (Hsinchun, et al., 2008). Voice communication is more important than text. Birdwhistell (1970) stated that 65% of information takes place through facial expression and the remaining 35% through spoken words. Interactivity is an important characteristic of communication and has great concern to researchers (Norman, 1998). The important factors that contribute to interactivity are speed, range and mapping.

The term "social system" is widely used in sociological systems theory. Social systems are self-referential systems based on meaningful communication. They use communication to constitute and interconnect the events or actions which build up the systems. The environment of social systems includes other social systems, (the environment of a family includes, for example, other families, the political system, the economic system, the medical system, and so on) (Lowry, et al., 2006). Therefore communications between social systems is possible and social systems should have internal and external communication. The basic requirement in a social system is that there should be an interaction between at least two people. Barbara and Gloria (1997) suggested that the collaborative virtual environment can be regarded as a social system. The place is globally shared for communication, interaction and to perform different activities (Messinger, et al., 2009). Communication plays a vital role in SL social systems. The virtual community is globally shared and becoming an online destination of choice for big companies looking to test and sell new products and promote their brands (Messinger, et al., 2009). There are different methods of measuring participation within social systems such as reach, engagement and frequency of participation. All social systems have commonalities. We can assume SL as a place for social networking.

Media Richness Theory

Media richness theory falls under rational theories of media choice (Donabedian, 2006). Media richness theory (Davis, et al., 1989, Kahai and Cooper, 2003) explains the difference between rich and lean media. The richness characteristics include multiple cues, including the use of multiple information channels, such as voice inflection and body gestures incorporated with the verbal message: immediate feedback, which allows for rapid bidirectional communication and quick reinterpretation and clarification of messages; personal focus, which allows for the combination of personal feelings and emotions, as well as the tailoring of messages to the needs and current situation of the receiver; and language variety, which refers to the range of meanings that can be conveyed by the available group of symbols in a language. Previous studies (Carlson, 1993; Ferry, et al., 2001) indicate that the media fall in the same richness order, whether they are arranged by media richness with face to face as the richest medium and electronic media as a lean medium.

RESEARCH METHODOLOGY

Research Design and Development

The research method is mainly categorized into two parts: qualitative and quantitative. Quality defines the character of something whereas quantity determines the amount of something. Qualitative methods help to identify components of a subject whereas quantitative methods determine the number of components. The current study is a qualitative study based on a case study approach that investigates virtual business opportunities in SL. Yin (2003) states that case study is a good choice when the investigator has little control over events or cannot manipulate relevant behaviors. On the other hand, in our research, we had no effect or control on virtual business events during their whole processes. We investigated the phenomenon without disturbing respective individuals or companies. Case study is preferred in examining contemporary events within real life. The strength of case study is its ability to integrate a full variety of evidence, including interviews, documents, and observations (Yin, 2003).

We used interview and observation as methods for data collection. We choose SL as the single case to study as it is one of the most common virtual worlds where the characteristics are most appropriate for e-marketing and the results can be applied to virtual worlds with similar characteristics. The single case design is justifiable when the case represents a critical test of existing theory, a rare or unique circumstance, a representative or typical case, or the case serves a revelatory or longitudinal purpose (Yin, 2003). SL, as our study, is representative as well as typical because of the following reasons:

- Rich communication and business environment: 3D world, community based, creative and potential of e-commerce opportunities.
- Popular among companies. Big brand companies such as IBM, Dell, Toyota and Reuters use it.
- Popular among players. More than 21 million active players.

About a half-million residents regularly visit SL and millions of dollars are spent each month (Second Life, 2010). A majority of people are trying to make money in SL and they are successful. Its popularity among companies and individuals makes SL able to provide plenty of business events with regard to different industries to investigate a wide research scope. In conclusion, the single case study method using SL as the case is suitable to our investigation.

Data Collection: Online Interviews

In the first-step online interview was performed with 30 SL residents in May 2011 for a period of three weeks to study their communication behavior and business experiences. Out of them the best responses of 15 residents with experience of more than two years in SL were taken for analysis. The category of residents included SL players, experienced business practitioners and company representatives. They were selected studying their profile visiting different business places. The profile information was received by clicking the avatar (resident) name. The original interview of users was recorded first and then edited. In the second part of the study, the success history of real world companies was provided based upon the information received from a company representative, SL website, SL online business articles and relevant literature. The qualitative data is received from interview. The qualitative research interview is a construction site of knowledge and leads to specific explanations for the interview results

(Kvale, 1996). It can help to understand the virtual worlds from the subjects point of view and makes use of participants' experiences to analyze virtual business phenomena. As a result, the interview was used as one of the qualitative research methods. The semi-structured interview was used as this provides interviewees' flexibility in asking and answering questions, thus lead to the freedom to explore the phenomena in more details. The objective of the interview is to get a better understanding of how communication is important in SL and its effectiveness in generating revenue. The interview is internet based and not face to face. The interpretation and explanation of the result are based on linking between theories and data to find some pattern matching or common phenomenon. The conversation was performed with SL players, land owners, island owners and business practitioners. Customer benefits in virtual world include scope of product, quality, convenience, ease to access and customer service.

Some observations in SL include watching particular types of events, focus communication related activities and marketing possibilities. Different places were visited to find out how often the products and services exist in SL. Also observed how a resident can find his competitor in SL. Mode of advertising and customer services provided by companies were investigated to learn possible ways of revenue generation. Major coverage of the study in the form of open questionnaires included the following:

- How effective do you find communicating in SL?
- Do you have experience in making real money in SL? How?
- What are the popular products in SL in your opinion?
- How successful are the real-world companies in marketing in SL?
- How effective are virtual events for e-marketing promotion?
- What is the future of SL marketing?
- Do you think communication plays a vital role for marketing promotion in SL?
- What are the problems and challenges for marketing in SL?

Additional information has been collected from the SL website, business articles and relevant literature to make the study more supportive.

Validity and Reliability

Different sources of evidence can be used to the strength of the case study. Yin (2003) formulated the triangulation method to collect multiple resources of the same phenomenon (Oates, 2006; Yin, 2003). There are different types of triangulation method such as strategy triangulation, time triangulation, space triangulation, investigator triangulation, and theoretical triangulation (Oates, 2006). For this study, some kinds of triangulation are adopted such as method triangulation, by using more than one data generation method which are interview and observation to establish the construct validity and reliability of the evidence. Also used was theoretical triangulation by drawing on more than one theoretical perspective from many authors.

About the validity of participants' answers, it was checked whether they really exist in SL and are currently doing business there. Their existence was checked by using the people search function according to their avatar's name. To check whether they are currently doing business in SL, properties of products or lands were checked whether they really owned them. To minimize the errors and biases in the study, not only successful companies but also unsuccessful ones were considered. For website references, for example, SL website and SL wiki were used to describe issues or events that occurred within SL.

RESULTS AND ANALYSIS

Online Conversation with SL Residents

Virtual worlds offer plain text, voice, gestures and emotion for communication. SL has become an interactive, collaborative and commercial platform for users, marketers and researchers (Stuart and Brand, 2008). In this connection, there is a huge opportunity to perform virtual e-marketing. The virtual worlds provide flexibility in brand building, advertising and new product development (Vedrashko, 2006).

Mr. Crank, one of the respondents has been in SL more than two years. According to him, the communication in SL is highly effective to perform marketing activities. People can create products and sell them to make money. But creativity is needed to make products. He says that advertising in SL is useful to promote brands. The negative points are that SL is highly addictive. Thus people do forget their real life. People of all categories gather in SL such as the mentally ill and hackers. In this connection, SL is bigger than real life to perform social and marketing activities. Mr. Creator Byron is an experienced SL user. He finds that SL is useful for global communication. He creates avatars and different body parts. Sometimes he sells them to make money. According to him, the popular business in SL is land sale and body parts such as skin and houses. He says that "Real world companies are successful to promote their products through online events such as meetings and conferences. The problems are slow browsing, copybotters and a new SL viewer (Beta 2) which is not user friendly".

The SL platform has less technical and social problems. Due to this, a large number of people have been joining SL. The communication system is synchronous. Therefore immediate response and feedback can be received. This will be helpful for decision making and engaging in marketing behaviors and increasing social networking. Hence, SL platform follows the theory of communication and social systems.

Mr. Herry Maltz has been working as an active consultant on SL since 2006. According to him "Voice in SL is efficient and easier, and one could not compare SL voice with Skype. Communication in SL cuts the real world cost. Teleconference and email are popular media. Communication is required to conduct business and have interaction. SL is a suitable platform to perform e-marketing and profitable to real-life companies. The problem is competition and fluctuation of land prices. Linden Lab helps to resolve business-related problems". Other challenges in SL as per Mr. Herry are finding qualified persons for public relations and sales, and establishing trust. In his opinion, people are detachable and they frequently change their jobs.

Ms. Precious Ruby has been in SL for two years. She creates things such as flowers and clothes. She argues that real world designers have success in SL. Communication is needed to offer products. According to Ms. Ruby, conference and meetings are highly informative. SL has great potential for designers and business practitioners. The environment is technical, so sometimes it encounters problems.

Mr. Asterion Coen has been in SL for more than three years. He has been working as a solution provider for IBM. He provided information that IBM is exploiting maximum benefit from SL. The company is using SL to test products and services. Moreover, this environment is useful for scripting 3D objects and prototyping. SL reduces real-world costs for meetings and conferences. Thus, SL can be used as a communication tool and real world laboratory. According to Mr. Coen, virtual worlds are the future of the web. The limitation of SL is that the number of avatars gathering in one place is 100. So, he suggests Linden Lab make this more flexible. He further opined that instant messaging (IM) within SL can be used when people are not in the same grid. The IM has secured communication so that no one can know about the conversation. Local chat is open for all and everyone can read the conversations. People prefer voice communication for immediate response. The major social problems in SL are annoyances, harassment and misconduct. The SL virtual world is open to all and has much more freedom.

Mr. Trixie Maddox argues that communication is needed to offer creations and customer relations. He sells avatar body parts such as hair and skin. He has the skill of scripting and 3D designing. He has two islands and provides some space to friends free of cost. Mr. Maddox is satisfied with his revenue. He does advertising to enhance the brands and it is now well established. Moreover, he wants to improve the existing brand as users seek new brands. He has the policy of providing refunds on products customers do not like and sometimes exchanges with other products. Some amount of initial investment is required to open business in SL. The challenging issues are competition, innovation and creativity. He took part in conferences and thinks that a virtual conference saves both time and cost.

The opinions and experiences of Spike Zimerman are that "communication is needed to contact with each other, socialize, run business and conduct online events". He runs a real estate business. Moreover, he is engaged with business consultation, market surveys, advertising and customer-experience projects. He says "we build houses, real estate design, product making, avatar design etc. Other services are exhibitions, video production and customer support. We have an expert team of individuals to perform marketing activities". He buys and sells the land because it is easy to operate. He puts a company's product information on the website so that real world people can visit the site and get information. The challenging issues are time, customer satisfaction and market growth. One must be good in programming, 3D scripting and ought to know the customer's interest. Advertising and communication are vital for brand promotion. He uses word-of-mouth and blogging to secure advertisement of the products. The SL platform is very important to conduct online marketing events. The sustainability of SL cannot be imagined without communication.

Timothy Hoxley expressed his experience as follows: SL is popular and convenient communication software to conduct online events. He sells clothes, accessories, bags and shoes etc. He has focused on women's products because "women want to dress up". This set of products is easy to sell as people want to buy shoes and socks together. Scripting and building skill are required. Mr. Hoxley believes that product quality is as important in SL as in real life. The higher the traffic the higher the sales volume. Customer service is also required in the virtual world as in the real world. He creates advertisements for the products and sometimes provides free products. So he is satisfied with his revenue. Other challenging issues are competition, design, quality and communication skills. Initial investment is required to rent a virtual land and one should pay a land maintenance fee every month.

Mr. Nguway Firelight builds objects in SL. He thinks that communication is required to locate market stuff and advertisement. Moreover, communication is needed to talk with people. Online events are very successful in SL. His girl friend makes money from SL. She is a teacher in real life. He joined SL for recreation and so has no experience of making money.

Deirdre Hyun from Netherlands joined SL in March 9, 2007. In her opinion people make revenue from selling and buying land and from leasing lands and houses and shops. She did modeling in the past in SL and able to generate money. The SL is the best pace for making friends, participating in social activities and having fun and entertainment. She found that the nature of people is same in the real and virtual life. SL has more freedom than real life, so people do not follow the rules and regulations strictly. According to Deirdre, SL is time consuming and she joins SL only during weekends.

Erin Dawodu from USA found that people in SL are helpful and cooperative. He found SL as a place of fun and entertainment and prefers exploring from one grid to another. He prefers to join clubs as it will be more interesting to spend time there and make new friends. The SL is highly social and people participate in numerous social activities. He frequently purchases clothes and body parts.

Liliana Chrome from the USA joined SL in October 12, 2009. The purpose of joining SL is to wander and have fun. She creates clothes and sells them to make money. According to Liliana the SL has an excellent communication system. She frequently uses instant messaging and rarely uses voice. It was learnt that the ultimate goal of people is to achieve entertainment from social activities with effective communication. Communication is useful to conduct online meetings and conferences to offer products and services of companies.

According to Paul Steinberg, an engineer with the Intel software network, E-marketing in SL is a big understanding, exactly mirroring the steps and processes of business in the real world, with manufacturing, distribution, sales etc. Being a successful business in SL might indicate that the person should have experience running a company. Modern web 2.0 communication technologies are highly effective in virtual world.

Table 3.1 shows the summary of findings on communication in SL. SL is an electronic environment and without communication no activities take place. Advertising is a form of communication which is helpful for brand promotion. Online events are highly interactive and informative. Communication is essential for social networking, collaboration and consumer growth. Voice is preferred best as it has a media richness feature. The richness factors include personal focus, immediate feedback and multiple cues. Virtual communication reduces real world cost and time. Furthermore, communication plays pivotal role for customer relationship and locate market. Word of mouth and blogs are means of business communication. SL is the future of the web and has sustainability through communication. Virtual worlds enable new ways of collaboration and coordination through communication in 3D environment by Voice over Internet Protocol (Fetscherin and Lattersmann, 2008). SL is the hot resource for communication, socialization, collaboration and participation in different activities. The virtual environment has audio and video contents and different communication media such as instant messaging, text chat and blogs, based on web 2.0 technologies. Communication is preferred to conduct business, socializing and content sharing (Messinger, *et al.*, 2009).

TABLE 3.1
SUMMARY OF FINDINGS ON COMMUNICATION IN SL

Participant 1: Communication is highly effective to perform marketing activities. Advertising is also a form of communication.
Participant 2: SL is useful for global communication. Online events such as meeting and conferences are reliable source of communication for marketing promotion.
Participant 3: Voice communication is highly effective and cannot be compared with Skype. Communication helps to reduce real world cost and is needed for business interaction. Teleconferencing and email are more popular than other virtual worlds.
Participant 4: Communication is helpful in offering products and services. Conferences and meetings are highly informative.
Participant 5: SL is a Communication tool. Communication reduces real world costs through online meeting and conferences. SL is the future of the web.
Participant 6: Communication is required to maintain customer relationship and offers creations. Virtual conferences save both time and cost.
Participant 7: SL is a popular and convenient communication software and highly reliable to conduct online events. Good communication skills are needed for customer relationships.
Participant 8: Communication is needed to contact people, socialize and run business. Online events are a form of communication and are successful. Advertising and communication are required for brand promotion by using word-of-mouth and blogging. SL has its sustainability through communication.
Participant 9: Communication is required to locate market and for advertisement. Moreover, it is needed for interaction. Online events are highly successful and reduce real world cost.
Participant 10: SL is the place for social networking and communication behavior of people in virtual world is same as in real world.
Participant 11: SL is highly social and a platform for fun and entertainment.
Participant 12: IM is effective to communicate. Communication helps to establish social networking. Online meetings and conferences are useful for products and service offering.
Participant 13: Communication is essential for collaboration and consumer growth.
Participant 14: Web 2.0 communication technologies are highly effective in a virtual world.
Participant 15: Rich media such as voice is crucial for immediate communication.

Table 3.2 presents the summary of findings on e-marketing opportunities in SL. Creativity, quality and communication are vital for customer relations and market promotion. The higher the number of people the higher the sales potential. Popular markets in SL are land, home and body parts. Real world companies are successful in promoting brands through advertising and online events. SL is highly effective for 3D scripting and prototyping. Skilled manpower is needed to conduct business activities. Some challenging issues are competition, innovation and customer support. Real estate businesses are also successful in SL. Some residents have creativity talents. However, some are addicted to the SL environment. Market surveys are very important in SL. The designing cost and time is low so users have creative freedom. SL has become an important place for marketing and brand promotion of real life products and services. Hemp (2006) stated that virtual worlds have future importance for marketers. They become an interactive, collaborative and commercial platform for all. The Virtual world is stable so there is low risk of investment. In this connection, there is a huge opportunity of v-commerce or virtual commerce. Most of the virtual worlds have their own currency. SL provides flexibility in brand building, new product development and advertising (Vedrashko, 2006). Virtual worlds are designed not only for entertainment and business opportunities but for achieving experiences. So a virtual environment is an effective, emotional and simulating environment for users. Virtual presence may be through advertisements or product development and business-sponsored virtual activities. The real identity of a person is hidden so the behavior of the virtual avatars differs from the real world to some extent (Clemons, 2009). Online games in a virtual world are able to generate a good amount of money in real life. Owing to this reason, virtual worlds are an important source of emotional and material benefit (Castronova, 2001). They bear the future scope for the development of e-marketing and internet.

Second Life among Chinese Users

Chinese Second Life called HiPiHi attracted attention in the blogosphere. HiPiHi is already in the beta stage, but it lacks the resources of China's biggest massively multiplayer online role playing company. The graphics look somewhat dated by today's standards, although so do Second Life's (Vili, 2007). The Swedish virtual world Entropia Universe announced that it was teaming up with Beijing municipality, to build a virtual universe that is able to handle 7 million users at any one moment.

TABLE 3.2
SUMMARY OF FINDINGS ON E-MARKETING
OPPORTUNITIES IN SL

Participant 1: Creativity is needed to create products and sell them. Advertising is important to promote brand of the products. SL has the wide potential of marketing opportunities as in real life. The challenges are that SL is highly addictive. Some users are grievers and they break peace of the environment.
Participant 2: He creates avatars and body parts to make revenue. The popular market is land sale, skin and home. Real world companies are promoting their products and services through online events and they are successful. The problems are slow browsing, copybotters and new SL viewer (Beta 2) which is not user friendly.
Participant 3: SL is a suitable platform to perform e-marketing and profitable to real world companies. The problem is competition and fluctuation of land prices. As in real life qualified manpower for sales and public relation is required. Sometimes technical problems prevail in SL.
Participant 4: Working as a solution provider for IBM. IBM is using SL to test products and services. The real world meeting cost of the company has been reduced. SL is useful for scripting 3D objects and prototyping. The environment is useful as a communication tool and real world laboratory. The limitation is that the number of users gathering in one place is restricted to 100 which should be extended.
Participant 5: He creates and sells hair, skin and other body parts. He has two islands. He advertises his products and develops new brands. Customer support and refund policy is important as in real life. Some initial investment is required to initiate business. Virtual conference is useful and it saves both time and cost. The challenges are competition, innovation and creativity.
Participant 6: He does real estate business including market survey, advertising and customer experience projects. Moreover, he builds houses, designs avatars, produce videos and supplies customer support. Buying and selling land is easy to operate. Keeping product information on the website helps people to know about the products. A team of professional people are responsible for marketing opportunities.
Participant 7: He has focused on selling ladies products and prefers to offer a set of products such as socks and shoes. Scripting knowledge is required to create products. Quality and customer service are important as in real life. The higher the traffic the higher the sales volume. Advertisement and offering free products are necessary to attract customers. The business challenges are initial investment, competition, design, quality and

communication skill. He has satisfaction with the revenue generated from SL.
Participant 8: Joined SL for recreation and has no experience in making revenue. However, his girlfriend makes money. Online events are helpful for marketing promotion.
Participant 9: SL is useful for the growth in the real world economy. Professional people are highly benefited as they do not need a full-time job in real life. Some residents have part-time jobs in SL. Creativity and networking are important for offering products.
Participant 10: Modeling experience. Users have creativity freedom but it's time consuming.
Participant 11: Purchases clothes and body parts. He also has creativity skills.
Participant 12: Creation of clothes and sell them. He thinks that marketing in SL is time consuming.
Participant 13: Users should understand the current market. SL is relatively inexpensive but time consuming.
Participant 14: Marketing in SL is similar to that of real world. An experienced person is required to run business.
Participant 15: Designing cost and time is lower and it provides a clear visualization to customers.

David Liu, chief executive of Entropia Universe, claimed that virtual worlds would generate about 10,000 jobs in China (Vic, 2007). He added: "An important aspect for this project is also the positive effects on our environment that we foresee. People will actually be able to work from home inside Entropia Universe as many people do today, even from rural areas, thereby decreasing the amount of pollution generated by travel." He further says "Entropia beat other bidders, including SL, for this venture. Even SL, with a claimed 7 million members, rarely has more than 40,000 on simultaneously, which means that the Chinese venture, if it succeeds, would have a population greater than all but the biggest countries. This raises the prospect that such ventures could become major economies in their own right with no allegiance to any particular administration. These could generate the kind of conditions which lead to massive growth, even, it is sometimes argued, to the emergence of new economic sectors comparable to agriculture or manufacturing - unless China gets there first".

The opinion of one of the Chinese SL users Mr. Gang is that "SL is quite interesting. It contains news, finance, tutorial, tips, map of game, game script, exchange center and so on. SL obviously looks young, but what it does matter here is that the SL has already landed in China. I remember there was a debate when I introduced the new jargon Web3.d to Idea Factory

China (invited only Google group where you can find quite a lot Chinese web 2.0 enthusiasm) and asked for opinion about whether the Chinese can accept the SL model. They said World of Warcraft (WoW) was so popular in China and SL might find a way to make Chinese gamers engaged for a long time. Another fact I have to mention here is –the first SL's millionaire is Chinese".

DISCUSSION

Communication

SL bears the concept of virtual reality in which human computer interaction takes place through communication. Presence and telepresence are inseparable parts of communication. Communication in SL is feasible for games, social networking and e-marketing. Companies use SL for marketing and communication as a tool for engaging with residents. SL has a whole culture and economy within itself. It saves time and money and increases productivity. Computer- based communication is not as effective as face-to-face communication as it misses emotional cues and lacks body language. Voice is equally important in SL as in real life. SL is a place for building community, getting information and buying products and services. Thus SL is becoming a reliable communication channel. Games are helpful to generate real revenue. In this connection, virtual worlds are also called Massively Multiplayer Online Role Playing Games (MMORPG), digital worlds or simulated worlds. The significance of communication in SL is thus categorized into a representative business environment, popular among both real-world companies and players.

Communication plays an important role for establishing collaboration between producers and consumers to generate marketing value and it reduces real-world costs. Communication is required to receive product feedback, build community, engage consumers and raise funds. Moreover, the significance of communication is in brand promotion, organizational information and in providing training and learning skills. Thus SL has been supplementing traditional advertising. Web-based technologies such as SL are useful for creating new e-marketing for income generation and customer interaction and participation. Word-of-mouth communication in this connection is beneficial for consumer learning. The better the relationship with consumers, the better the marketing effort. So virtual communication provides advantages to customers, suppliers, business partners, managers and researchers. Managers prefer rich media such as face-to-face communication for interaction. SL provides synchronous communication for prompt decision making. Communication in virtual world removes geographical constraints and brings people to one place. SL, being a strong communication technology, takes higher social responsibility and transparency than other social networking sites such as Facebook, Myspace, Twitter and YouTube. However, some limitations of SL communication are related to the communication server, speed of the internet, computer systems and viewer software. A computer with standard hardware and software greatly influences the stability of SL and new SL viewer software version 2.0 should be made user friendly.

E-marketing Opportunities

For e-marketing opportunities in SL there are two segments: market segment and the individual segment.

- *Market segments.* Selling of virtual goods, virtual services such as 3D designs, scripting and exhibition, real estate of virtual islands including selling, develop and renting of lands and consulting services on advertising, marketing and other business projects in virtual world.
- *Customer Segments.* This is divided into individual customers and real world companies. Both of them have clear definitions of competitors as they can use powerful search engine to observe and participate.

Individuals and companies have multiple product categories. Some companies focus on single product categories to set up a unique brand name. Quality of product is also important in virtual worlds, similar to real world. Customer attraction strategies are advertising inside and outside SL. Customer traffic is important to increase the business volume. For this some companies provide free products in SL. Sales channels in virtual world as well as on website can be used. Customer service is vital in virtual world to improve and extend market. Skill is required for building, scripting and developing virtual lands. Initial investment is required to open business. Some of the business sources are retail stores, services, real estate, universities, insurance companies and media. Some of the virtual business problems are viewer sessions crashing, low viewer frame rates, limited server capacity, grievers and language.

The biggest business in SL is avatar parts (skins, faces, bodies and hairstyle), avatar accessories (rings, glasses and jewelry) and clothes. Some of the real products are books, music and clothes for which SL provides a website to purchase these products. Thus SL acts as a bridge to real world business. The service provided is 3D designing, building and land development and scripting. Moreover, some real estate marketing involves selling and renting land, houses, apartments and consultation services. SL is limited by virtual experience as there is no sense of smell, taste and touch. SL has no boundary of physical location. Business owners can provide business consultations, market surveys, virtual office design and buildings. Like the real world, SL has competition among products and services. Residents can visit a competitor's location to evaluate quality of the products. The customer benefit focuses on quality, which includes design, beauty and user-friendliness. Many companies provide free products to increase customer traffic. Like traditional business, customer service such as getting feedback, satisfaction guarantees, and refunds for damaged products is important in SL. Advertising is beneficial both inside and outside the virtual world. The outside world includes website and blogs. Important factors regarding market promotion are traffic volume, advertising, demonstration of products and customer surveys after purchase. There are two sales channels in SL: stores in SL and third party purchase. Customers can use both of these channels. The need of multiple contact points, 3D modeling and customer accessibility should be considered. Virtual market effects real world economy. SL communication is thus a powerful option for real world companies, business representatives and players.

The social side in SL is interesting but it's the marketing side that takes a lot of effort and time. Some companies have dropped their projects in SL due to lack of investment and they consider SL as a place for experiment. For some companies and individuals it is a new way of business to reach customers. It has a direct effect on real life and has security and privacy threats.

Theoretical Implication and Managerial Implementation

This study shows that SL is an appropriate place for communication, social networking and e-marketing promotion. The popularity of SL has been increasing every day. A range of trading activities such as buying and selling land, leasing and other services such as scripting, architecture and advertising take place in this virtual environment. There is both a real and virtual economy. Moreover, SL has education as well as training opportunities through effective communication. SL offers several marketing opportunities for real-world products and services. SL marketers are able to generate sustained consumer engagement with a brand. SL is emerging as a test place for new ideas, where real world products can be released at low cost with direct feedback from users. There are many opportunities for innovation and profit making in SL and various business opportunities. A number of residents are generating part or all of their real life income from SL businesses. SL real estate market provides opportunities for residents to establish their own communities and business locations.

This study tests the theory of communication and social system and media richness theory. Communication helps to establish social relations. The outcome of these theories is communication, public distribution and networking. Media richness is linked with communication, which has importance for making prompt decisions in real world practice. Moreover, synchronous communication is needed for organizations, managers and policy makers for decision making. The current study is motivated by a need to understand the roles of effective communication in marketing. The research has key implications for practice. First, the findings suggest that SL bears a higher social and business responsibility than other social networking websites. Hence it helps companies and individuals to make decisions for real life implication of their creation. Secondly, this study shows that communication is a key part that confers eminence and existence of virtual worlds.

The findings and conclusion of our study endeavors contributing to China's expanding internet marketing potential. China has the highest online population in the world. As China's Internet market develops, so does China's Internet marketing. As per the high population of China, the number of Internet users is really growing at a very quick rate, and broadband access is growing rapidly, facilitating interactive marketing growth . Marketers and companies are understanding the importance of having an online presence. China is going to be the second largest advertising market in the world, after the US, overtaking Japan in the next few years. Also, the economy is growing by 8% to 9% a year. People's disposable incomes are growing quickly too, though from a low base. The demographics of the Internet user in China are somewhat different than that of other countries. The people who are better off are in the larger cities (China Online Marketing, 2011). The Internet, for marketers and advertisers, is a great channel to get to these new services by general public.

A majority of Chinese users have presence in SL for e-marketing promotion. SL has been generating more than 10,000 jobs for Chinese users (Nick, 2007). Increasingly, tech-savvy businesses are using virtual worlds to design, create and test product concepts before they launch in the real world. The crucial advantage to working in virtual worlds is that they offer much more potential for customers to interact with new products. In this connection, China having the largest population and number of internet users in the world, has been using Second Life to grow its market both on online and offline environments.

CONCLUSIONS

A number of Chinese users and organizations have been using SL for online marketing promotion. A number of Chinese companies have opened separate places in SL for brand promotion. SL has become a platform for collaboration and e-marketing that removes geographic constraints through effective communication. SL has the responsibility to act as a communication medium to bring real world or distant participants in one place to make collaboration through communication. SL is technologically feasible and highly reliable for e-marketing. Like the real world or the web, many residents play with creation, using the virtual world as a medium for communication and expression. People and organizations building businesses are successful to run their activities. SL communication is synchronous, so it facilitates effective communication among residents. SL is a part of the solution to communication and organizational challenges. With its VOIP capabilities, SL has proven to be an excellent tool in building and maintaining cultures within an organizational team. In this connection, SL has become a regular tool for maintaining trust and connections among residents. The creation of trust and culture at a distance is an advantage over conventional outsourcing and communication technology.

Individual and big companies use virtual worlds as a bridge to their real world business, drawing much attention of both managers and researchers. Their marketing concept and strategies in virtual worlds are worth investigating. This study focuses on professionals and companies rising from web 2.0 communication technologies. Being the largest population of internet users in the world China has been using SL as a social and communication media for e-marketing. A similar study should be performed through empirical data analysis in the form of online surveys from SL residents to investigate the communication behavior and e-marketing opportunities in SL.

Authored by Gajendra Sharma, Li Baoku, and Wang Lijuan, originally published in *International Journal of China Marketing*, Vol. 2(2) 2012, pp. 38-59

Chapter Four
The Real Estate Market in China

This chapter is an exploratory study of real estate in the China market. The study is a correlation analysis which utilizes microeconomic data from the China National Bureau of Statistics. The data consists of (a) GDP, (b) Gross national income and saving, (c) Household consumption expenditure, (d) Social consumption goods, (e) Gross domestic saving, and (f) Housing sales. The findings indicate that the above variables have a strong correlation with each other. The research concludes that the real estate market in China has tended to grow in the recent past and will probably continue to do so in the near future. If China's economy continually grows, housing sales will rise. Housing prices will not fall. Therefore, the oft-predicted real estate bubble in China will not come in the near future.

INTRODUCTION

From the aspect of international business, China's rapid economic growth in the global marketplace has become a dream come true.. Furthermore, China has grown to be a remarkable consumer nation with a powerful effect on the global marketplace. Taking a look at the real property industry in China, one must explore consumers' purchase behavior, specifically the purchase of residential real estate. Some people say there is currently a real estate bubble in terms of some measurement models (Xu, Li, Hui, & Chen, 2010; Feng, Liu, Shi, & Jiang, 2010; Scherbina & Schlusche, 2012). Some people think otherwise, because China has a unique market structure due to its political system, legal system, and culture (Wang & Wang, 2012). Furthermore, specifically, the US financial crisis has happened due to the real estate and subprime mortgage bubbles, factors unique to America and not present in China. At the same time, a large amount of the research utilizes different data and explores various factors which might have had an influence on the real estate market. Considering these issues, the question of how countries might prevent real estate bubbles again becomes an imperative topic for academic research, consumers, and investors. The purpose of this study is to explore the index of microeconomic effects on consumers' residential real estate purchases. The research question is, which index can predict a significant movement in the residential real estate market in China? To estimate or examine whether there will be real estate development or whether, on the contrary, there will be a bubble may not only be based on the Chinese real estate confidence index, price-to-housing income, price-to-rent and price-to-income ratios calculations, but it may also be founded on data analysis from microeconomics. These microeconomic data should illustrate a whole country's economic development circumstances. Therefore, the study adopts an exploratory approach to explore the correlations among such microeconomic variables such as GDP, gross national income and saving, social consumption goods, and housing sales.

Wang and Wang (2012) researched the average price of residential units of ten major cities in China from 1999 to 2010, illustrated at Figure 4.1. These ten major cities cover the southern, northern, central, and western parts of China. It shows that housing prices in China have had dramatic growth during the past two decades. The growth rate in China is from 169% to 431% during the 11-year period. Figure 4.2 displays the GDP of ten selected cities in China from 1999 to 2010. The growth rate of GDP of ten selected cities in China is from 325% to 549% during the 11-year period. Wang and Wang (2012, 275) indicate four reasons which explain why the China real estate market is one of the more important markets among developing countries and summarize these reasons as below:

1. China is the second largest economic body in the world.
2. It has about 19.2% of the world's population.
3. China has a dramatically different political system, legal environment, and culture from the Western world.
4. China has experienced both a dramatic growth in its real estate markets and a huge increase in real estate values during the past decades.

Given that China has one of the most important real estate markets in the world, it is important to know which index can best foresee a real estate bubble? In other words, has any index predicted the circumstances of the real estate market in China? This study adopts microeconomic data from the China National Bureau of Statistics in order to help determine that question.

A decade of recession in Japan was caused by real estate issues present in the Japanese economy since the 1990s. Due to the US real estate mortgage bubble in 2008, there was a widespread global financial crisis that further affected the financial crisis of EU countries which was occurring at the same time. How to prevent or evaluate real estate bubbles became a major topic for academic researchers, consumers, and investors. There are few measurement models to calculate the real estate bubble issue.

FIGURE 4.1
AVERAGE RESIDENTIAL UNIT PRICE OF SELECTED
CITIES IN CHINA

Year	Beijing	Shanghai	Guangzhou	Shenzhen	Tianjin	Wuhan	Chongqing	Nanjing	Hangzhou	Chengdu
1999	4,787	3,102	3,946	5,004	2,157	1,722	1,080	2,808	2,685	1,615
2000	4,557	3,326	3,978	5,275	2,274	1,636	1,077	2,598	2,733	1,608
2001	4,716	3,658	4,047	5,507	2,308	1,745	1,133	2,577	2,624	1,648
2002	4,467	4,007	3,995	5,267	2,414	1,916	1,277	2,780	3,197	1,775
2003	4,456	4,989	3,999	5,793	2,393	2,023	1,324	2,888	3,657	1,908
2004	4,747	5,761	4,356	6,385	2,950	2,463	1,573	3,098	3,884	2,224
2005	6,162	6,698	5,041	6,996	3,987	2,986	1,901	3,850	5,454	2,870
2006	7,375	7,039	6,152	8,848	4,649	3,535	2,081	4,270	5,967	3,499
2007	10,661	8,253	8,439	13,370	5,576	4,516	2,588	5,011	7,432	4,198
2008	11,648	8,115	8,781	12,823	5,598	4,681	2,640	4,808	8,211	4,778
2009	13,224	12,364	8,989	14,389	6,605	5,199	3,266	6,893	10,561	4,875
2010	17,151	14,290	10,615	18,954	7,940	5,550	4,040	9,227	14,259	5,827
Appreciation[a]	258%	361%	169%	279%	268%	222%	274%	229%	431%	261%

Note: The source is the China Real Estate Statistics Yearbook.
[a] Rate of unit price from 1999 to 2010

FIGURE 4.2
GDP OF SELECTED CITIES IN CHINA LITERATURE REVIEW

Year	Beijing	Shanghai	Guangzhou	Shenzhen	Tianjin	Wuhan	Chongqing	Nanjing	Hangzhou	Chengdu
1999	2,174	4,035	2,057	1,437	1,450	1,086	1,480	899	1,225	1,190
2000	2,479	4,551	2,376	1,665	1,639	1,207	1,590	1,021	1,383	1,313
2001	2,846	4,951	2,686	1,954	1,840	1,348	1,750	1,150	1,568	1,492
2002	3,213	5,409	3,001	2,257	2,051	1,493	1,971	1,298	1,782	1,667
2003	3,663	6,251	3,497	2,895	2,448	1,662	2,251	1,576	2,100	1,871
2004	4,283	7,450	4,116	3,423	2,932	1,956	2,665	1,910	2,515	2,186
2005	6,886	9,154	5,154	4,951	3,698	2,238	3,070	2,411	2,943	2,371
2006	7,870	10,366	6,074	5,814	4,359	2,591	3,492	2,774	3,442	2,750
2007	9,353	12,189	7,109	6,802	5,050	3,142	4,123	3,284	4,100	3,324
2008	10,488	13,698	8,216	7,807	6,354	3,960	5,097	3,775	4,781	3,901
2009	12,153	15,046	9,138	8,201	7,522	4,621	6,530	4,230	5,088	4,503
2010	14,114	17,166	10,748	9,582	9,224	5,566	7,926	5,131	5,949	5,551
GDP growth[a]	549%	325%	423%	567%	536%	413%	436%	470%	386%	366%

Note: The source is the China Real Estate Statistics Yearbook.
[a] Rate of growth from 1999 to 2010.

*Source: Wang, H., & Wang, K. (2012). What is unique about Chinese real estate markets? *Journal of Real Estate Research*, 34(3), 278 & 279. Unit: 100 million in RMB.

There is the a market supply and demand equilibrium model calculation can be found in the article of Feng, Liu, Shi, & Jiang (2010). Wang, Chan, and Xu (2012) show the concept of the price elasticity of the housing supply in China. Xu, Li, Hui and Chine (2010) examine the Chinese real estate confidence index (CER index) and describe the changing situations of the Chinese real estate market. Scherbina and Schlusche (2012) use a behavior model to explore real estate bubbles.

Feng, Liu, Shi, & Jiang (2010) describe the direct measurement model for property bubbles as having four constituent models: (a) the Speculative or Bubble Degrees of Real Estate Model, (b) the Ramsey Model, (c) the Market Supply and Demand Equilibrium Model that consists of considering either owned capital or loans, and (d) the Income Capitalization Model. They conclude that (a) major cities like Beijing, Shanghai, Guangzhou, Shenzhen, and Tianjin fit the direct test models the best, and that the predictions of this model for these cities are most consistent with the actual situation than is true for other cities. The authors conclude that the direct measurement model proves that it is a model (of) relative reliability and accuracy" (p.2937). Furthermore, (b) when the direct test model measures these cities in Midwest cities, the results seem more meaningful. Specifically, the real estate prices have continued to rise in the Midwest cities of China since 2008, just as the model predicted

One similar example of research by Xu, Li, Hui and Chine (2010) illustrates the Chinese real estate confidence index (CRE index), which describes the changing situations of the Chinese real estate market by means of the CRE index. Furthermore, the CRE combines three diverse aspects: (a) effective demand and supply, (b) potential demand, and (c) potential supply. The research adopts the case of Shenzhen. The research results indicate that the CRE index is an effective tool to evaluate the real estate market in China.

In overview, from 1990 to 2000, housing prices in China have increased at both the national and city levels. Thus, Wang, Chan, and Xu (2012) examined the price elasticity and supply of housing in China. They adopted data from 35 cities in China from 1998 to 2009. The objective of their research is (a) to estimate a nationwide price elasticity of the housing supply in China and compare it with other countries, and (b) to identify the major elements of variations in housing supply responsiveness through cities in China. Their results indicate that the aggregate price elasticity of supply is between 2.82 and 5.64. When compared with other countries, the estimated price elasticity of China is lower than that of liberal regulatory countries such as the US and Thailand. In contrast with stringent regulatory countries such as the UK, Netherlands, Korea, and Malaysia, the estimated price elasticity of China is higher than that of these countries. According to the empirical results, the research illustrates that geographic, economic, and regulatory factors decide housing supply elasticity across cities in China.

Scherbina and Schlusche (2012) chose to adopt the behavior model to explore the residential real estate market in order to answer why bubbles are ubiquitous in the residential real estate market. The authors subdivided behavioral models of bubbles into four parts: (a) the effect of differences of opinion and short sale constraints, (b) the effect of feedback trading, (c) the effect of biased self-attribution, and (d) the combined effect of the representativeness of heuristic and conservatism biases. The models a and b indicate that the real estate bubble "will deflate when a sufficient supply of the bubble asset is added to the market" (p. 477). However, in models c and d, the real estate bubble "will deflate when positive sentiment is reversed" (p. 477). Consequently, Scherbina and Schlusche (2012, p.487) conclude the following: Real estate bubbles can have more damaging real consequences than equity bubbles because an over-investment in new housing assets is more likely to slow future growth and because the high levels of household and banking sector exposure to real estate can quickly and forcefully transmit the impact of falling prices to the wider economy. As a result, their conclusion indicates that the supply of housing, rising prices, mortgages, and government policy all relate to potential real estate bubbles.

In one example of similar research from Wang, Chan, and Xu (2012), their research indicates that the political environment, legal system, and culture of China are different from that of most mature economies in the western world. Also, Gao (2011) illustrates that influential factors affecting real estate prices in China include (a) economic growth, (b) urbanization and demographic dividend, (c) low cost of real property ownership, (d) the financial system, (e) RMB appreciation, and (f) government supervision. Both research projects illustrate that the environmental structure of China's real estate market is a unique market when compared with the environmental structure of the real estate market in the US or the UK.

The research of Gao points out that some big cities such as Shanghai, Beijing, and Shenzhen have a real estate bubble. However, due to economic growth and a low carrying cost in urbanization, the real estate bubble in China will not burst rapidly, Gao predicts. The above researchers utilize difference measurement models to explore real estate bubbles in the real estate market in China. These above researchers also point out different factors affecting China's real estate market. In similar fashion, this study chooses and utilizes microeconomics data from the China National Bureau of Statistics to explore whether there perhaps might be other factors which can predict the rising or falling of the Chinese real estate market, factors which have not been researched before.

METHODOLOGY AND ANALYSIS

This study adopts microeconomic data from the China National Bureau of Statistics. The data are from 2000 to 2011 and consists of (a) gross national income and saving, (b) household consumption expenditure, (c) social consumption goods, (d) gross domestic saving, and (e) housing sales. These figures are displayed at Table 4.1. There only is one falling figure in 2008, which was housing sales, because of the financial crisis in the American market. On the contrary, the other figures in 2008 did not fall; and, in fact, these figures have increased, such as GDP, household consumption expenditure, and gross domestic saving. These figures have mostly increased from 2000 to 2011. In other words, China's economic growth has been rapid in the past ten years. This phenomenon perhaps can be explained by one reason, that Chinese people tend to purchase housing instead of putting money into savings. The study utilizes the correlation analysis to analyze these variables, in order to explore correlation between them and housing sales.

After correlation analysis, these variables are shown to have a strong correlation in terms of the results shown at Table 4.2. Leedy and Ormrod (2005) illustrate that the strength of the relationship may be divided into three parts: strong, moderate, and weak correlations. The cutting points between 0 to 1 are at 0.4 and 0.6. A weak correlation is indicated by any number below 0.4. A moderate correlation is indicated by the numbers between 0.4 and 0.6. The numbers above 0.6 indicate a strong correlation. Therefore, the findings concluded from these correlations are below:

1) GDP has a strong correlation with gross national income and saving;
2) GDP has a strong correlation with household consumption expenditure;
3) GDP has a strong correlation with social consumption goods;
4) GDP has a strong correlation with gross domestic saving;
5) GDP has a strong correlation with housing sales;
6) Gross national income and saving have a strong correlation with household consumption expenditure;
7) Gross national income and saving have a strong correlation with social consumption goods;
8) Gross national income and saving have a strong correlation with gross domestic saving;
9) Gross national income and saving have a strong correlation with housing sales;
10) Household consumption expenditure has a strong correlation with social consumption goods;

84

11) Household consumption expenditure has a strong correlation with gross domestic saving;
12) Household consumption expenditure has a strong correlation with housing sales;
13) Social consumption has a strong correlation with gross domestic saving;
14) Social consumption has a strong correlation with gross housing sales;
15) Gross domestic saving has a strong correlation with housing sales.

TABLE 4.1
GDP, GROSS NATIONAL INCOME & SAVING, HOUSEHOLD CONSUMPTION EXPENDITURE, SOCIAL CONSUMPTION GOODS, GROSS DOMESTIC SAVING, AND HOUSING SALES FROM 2000 TO 2011

	GDP	Gross national income and saving	Household consumption expenditure	Social consumption goods	Gross domestic saving	Housing sales
	Billion RMB	Billion RMB	Billion RMB	Billion RMB	Billion RMB	Billion RMB
2000	99,214.55	96,358.80	45,854.60	34,152.60	37,698.70	3,572.00
2001	109,655.17	106,703.30	49,435.90	43,055.40	42,721.30	4,625.72
2002	120,332.69	117,381.50	53,056.60	48,135.90	48,516.20	5,721.24
2003	135,822.76	133,648.50	57,649.80	52,516.30	58,137.30	7,670.90
2004	159,878.34	156,721.00	65,218.50	59,501.00	72,325.70	10,375.71
2005	184,937.40	176,908.10	72,652.50	67,176.60	85,886.10	17,576.13
2006	216,314.40	205,586.00	82,103.50	76,410.00	103,682.50	20,825.96
2007	265,810.30	243,176.11	95,609.80	89,210.00	133,577.44	29,889.12
2008	314,045.40	291,747.80	111,670.40	108,487.70	160,622.93	25,068.18
2009	340,902.81	333,738.02	123,584.60	125,342.70	171,628.01	44,355.17
2010	401,512.80	387,718.87	140,758.60	154,553.70	207,397.84	52,721.24
2011	472,881.60	453,567.99	164,945.20	181,225.80	244,320.23	58,588.86

To summarize these results, (a) GDP, (b) gross national income and saving, (c) household consumption expenditure, (d) social consumption goods, and (e) gross domestic saving all have a strong relationship with housing sales. This means that when one of six indexes increases, the amount of the housing sales also rises. The results indicate that the amount of the housing sales in China depends on the national economic development. Or, these indexes describe that when China has a suitable and reasonable economic development, Chinese people should become notable as a population of ever greater purchasing power. Consequently, when the income of consumers is going up, the amount of housing sales also increases. However, due to a multicollinearity issue, this study did not process the regression analysis. Because of that, this study cannot provide any prediction from which indexes to estimate the housing sales in China.

TABLE 4.2

CORRELATION COEFFICIENTS OF GDP, GROSS NATIONAL INCOME & SAVING, HOUSEHOLD CONSUMPTION EXPENDITURE, SOCIAL CONSUMPTION GOODS, GROSS DOMESTIC SAVING, AND HOUSING SALES FROM 2000 TO 2011

		GDP	Gross national income & saving	Household consumption expenditure	Social consumption goods	Gross domestic saving	Housing sales
GDP	Pearson Correlation	1	.999**	1.000**	.995**	1.000*	.981**
Gross national income & saving	Pearson Correlation	.999**	1	1.000**	.997**	.998**	.984**
Household consumption expenditure	Pearson Correlation	1.000**	1.000**	1	.997**	.999**	.982**
Social consumption goods	Pearson Correlation	.995**	.997**	.997**	1	.993**	.982**
Gross domestic saving	Pearson Correlation	1.000**	.998**	.999**	.993**	1	.979**
Housing goods	Pearson Correlation	.981**	.984**	.982**	.982**	.979**	1

**. Correlation is significant at the 0.01 level (2-tailed).

CONCLUSION

As evidenced by Figure 4.1, the average residential unit price in China has increased from 2000 to 2010. If the trend continues, it indicates that the real estate market in China should be growing over the next few years. Specifically, growth can be expected in the areas of Tianjin, Nanjing, and Wuhan. Figure 4.1 displays that without Beijing, Shanghai, Guangzhou, and Shenzhen, the growth rate of these other six cities should be more than

200%. Therefore, on the one hand, looking at the whole of the real estate market in China, the market should tend to grow in the near future. On the other hand, the desire to prevent a future real estate bubble becomes the other important topic for exploration and conversation. Scherbina and Schlusche (2012) indicate that the impact of real estate prices are (a) social, (b) economic, (c) environmental, and (d) governmental. Moreover, in their research they conclude that "circumventing the effect of the latter, the supply of housing frequently increases in response to rising prices" (p.464). It seems the circumstances of real estate are complex. The force of the market (either supply or demand issues), economics, government policy/regulatory issues, population, and locations are all influencing elements that affect the real estate market, its development and its selling prices. Therefore, how to predict or prevent the real estate bubble is a significant topic for academic researchers, consumers, or investors in the real estate market in China.

As a result, the findings indicate one phenomenon to describe China's real estate circumstances. The phenomenon is that if China's economy continually grows, the amount of housing sales will increase and selling prices will not decrease. Also, the real estate environment of China is not same as the U.S. and the U.K. (Geo, 2011; Wang & Wang, 2012). China has a unique market structure (Wang & Wang, 2012). Therefore, the real estate bubble will not burst as Geo (2011) concluded. However, there has been a gap between the incomes of consumers and the selling price of housing, especially with younger generations living in big cities. The selling price of housing is much more worrisome. With such high prices, the real estate purchasing power of the younger generation is limited.

Authored by Wong Ming Wong, originally published in the *International Journal of China Marketing*, Vol. 3(2) pp. 79-86.

Chapter Five

Challenges and Opportunities: The Impacts of Population Aging on Marketing in China and the Chinese Economy

The Chinese population went through the transition from an adult type of population to an aged type of population very quickly at a time when it was not economically affluent. Because of population aging, China might lose the advantage of its labor force and both the Chinese government itself and the pension system sponsored by it would face great financial constraints. China might become a net importer of goods and services due to the lack of a productive labor force in the future. In order to answer the challenge of population aging, China must seek for intensive economic growth, bring the adjustment function of the labor market into full play, implement pension reforms, practice "phased retirement", foster its young generation's saving incentives and control longevity risks by making use of the capital market. The implementation of those measures should create business opportunities for both domestic and international marketers.

INTRODUCTION

As a global phenomenon, the economic consequences and market implications of population aging are under discussions throughout the world. Purcell (2007), after announcing that the continual lengthening of life spans of the American people will result in fewer workers relative to the number of retirees, argued that some means, such as defined contribution pension plans and phased retirement, would encourage people to continue to work when they reach their retirement ages. Maestas et al. (2010) believed that the ultimate impact of population aging in the future depends a great deal on how long people choose to work before they retire from the labor force. Olshansky (2009) revealed why population aging has occurred globally, explained how predictions about the future of human longevity were made, and emphasized the importance of using financial hedging instruments to counterbalance longevity risks. Kune (2009) argued that aging would result in a smaller proportion of the population being employed. Changing demography, fewer workers and more retirees give rise to much concern about the fiscal sustainability of public pension schemes, healthcare systems and other social services.

Population aging refers to the trend and the process of the rising percentage of the aged people in the whole population. As the proportion of the global population over 60 years old continues to grow, the issue of where and how elders are going to live becomes increasingly pressing. Although longer and healthier lives are a boon to individuals and the countries in which they live, these benefits have also been accompanied by significant costs to company pension plans, annuity providers and government age-based entitlement programs whose creators never anticipated that we would or could live this long. The chance that people will live at least twenty years beyond the conventional retirement age is a mixed blessing. For some, the post-retirement years can be a time of warm weather, golfing, and vacations, while for others, it is a period of economic hardship, long-term illness, and isolation. Nevertheless, most of the elderly population, whose lives actually lie somewhere between these two extremes mentioned above, would be unsure what to do with those post-retirement years and whether they will have the economic resources they will need to live on.

Obviously, there are at least four costs associated with population aging. First of all, population aging may cause the GDP per capita of a certain country to fall continuously, since it might decrease the quantity of labor on the one hand while increasing the dependent population on the other hand. Secondly, the social pension system might have a heavier financial burden because of population aging. As population ages, there would be a shrinking labor force to contribute to the retirement income system and an increasing number of retirees. Thus, the cost of the retirement system would rise significantly. Thirdly, as the population ages, more people will need health care for longer periods, while simultaneously the cost of providing health care is rising. Consequently, countries that provide government financial health care for the elderly would find that taxpayer funds are no longer sufficient to cover these rising costs. The fourth cost is that for elders who no longer work and want to remain in their own homes, the need for home care and other community-based services to enable them to live safely and comfortably is increasing. Yet the number of family members who are available to care for elders at home has deceased as most women, the traditional caregivers, are working. Furthermore, the number of professional and paraprofessional workers trained to care for elders at home -- visiting nurses and home aides -- is also declining. So the size of the care-giving workforce, both paid and unpaid, has not kept up with the number of those needs.

The combination of these factors – an economic standstill or even an negative economic growth rate, rising health care costs, a shrinking labor force to contribute to the retirement income system, and a shortage of paid and unpaid caregivers -- means that many elders may be facing a long period of their lives with inadequate income to pay for rising health care and home care costs, and increasing pressure on families who are often needed to provide funds to pay for home care and/or provide that care themselves. (Bookman, 2008)

In 1982, the World Health Organization (WHO) announced " Aging in Place", which is the term for an approach to elder care service delivery that takes place outside of an institutional setting and allows elders to stay in their own homes. Twenty years later, the WHO advanced its version of "Active Aging" at the second United Nations World Assembly on Aging held in Madrid, Spain. Recently, the WHO launched a " Global Age – Friendly Cities Project" in which thirty-three cities from twenty-two countries engaged in a community planning process linking ideas about smart growth with ideas about how to help elders remain active and engaged in their communities with appropriate transportation, housing, health care, and other services.

Castries (2009) warned that long – term care costs of the aged would be a major threat to individual assets and public finances of the developed countries over the next forty years. Existing public schemes covering long – term care exhibit some significant issues, driven by pay–as–you–go designs combined with weak risk definitions. These difficulties would accelerate the need for new financing sources to cover the risk and call for new early preparation by both public and private sectors.

Simonazzi (2009) presented a comparative analysis of various European country models of elderly care to show that all countries were moving towards home care, private provision and cash transfers since rapid population aging had dramatically increased the social and economic cost of elderly care.

Compared with the situations of the developed countries, population aging in China has the following unique characteristics: China has the largest aged population in the world. In addition, China is a typical example of "old before affluent," since the per capita gross domestic product of China was less than $1000 when China became an aged society (Li, 2010, a). The old age insurance sponsored by the Chinese government, which has just transited from an unfunded pay–as–you–go mechanism to a fund-accumulated one, could only offer a comparatively narrow coverage with a minimum income to its elders. Thus, in order to answer the challenges of population aging, China must undertake massive reforms and structural changes from which various business opportunities might emerge.

The second part of this survey describes the peculiarities of population aging in China, and the third section discusses the possible impacts of demographic aging on China's economy. The fourth explores the possible policies that the Chinese government may adopt to deal with the problem of population aging. The fifth part talks about the business

91

opportunities that would emerge from the battle of combating the negative impacts of population aging in China. Finally, some suggestions are made to potential investors in the concluding remarks.

SCENARIOS AND PECULIARITIES OF POPULATION AGING IN CHINA

Population aging is the trend in all of the countries of the world. According to the World Population Organization (WPO) of the United Nations, as long as the population at the age of sixty or above in a certain country or region accounts for at least ten percent of the total population, or the population at the age of sixty-five or above reaches seven percent in the whole population, it can be concluded that the whole population is aging, and this country or region becomes aged (Wang, 2006).

In October, 1999, according to the data published by the National Statistical Bureau of China, the population above the age of sixty reached 126 million, accounting for ten percent of the whole Chinese population (Li, 2010,b).

In addition, the fifth nationwide population census conducted in 2000 showed that China had already had 88.1 million people aged above sixty-five and, this figure, already accounting for 6.96 % of the whole Chinese population, has been growing continuously at an annual rate of 3.39 %. The census revealed that China had already joined the rank of the aged nations, although at an earlier stage than is usual for the typical country.

Research into the Future Trends of Population Aging in China, published by the National Aged Population Office under the State Council of the P. R. of China on Feb. 23, 2010, predicts that， in the period from 2001 to 2100, China's population aging might follow three stages.

The first stage, that is, from 2001 to 2020, is a period of rapid aging. In this period, China will have, with the average annual growth rate of 3.28%， 5.96 million more aged population on the average every year. By 2020, China will have 248 million aged people, accounting for 17.17% of the whole population, among which the very aged population, that is, 80 years old or above， will amount to 30.67 million, occupying a share of 12.37% of the total aged population.

The second stage, from 2021 to 2050, will be a period of accelerating aging. With the people born in "the second baby boom", which lasted from the 1960s to the mid of 1970s in China, reaching their legal retirement age, the Chinese aged population will increase 6.2 million more each year. By 2023, the Chinese aged population will climb to 270 million, equal to the total number of the population aged from zero to fourteen. By 2050, the total of the aged Chinese population will be more than 400 million, accounting for more than thirty percent of the whole population. At the same time, the very aged population at the age of eighty or above would amount to 94.48 million, accounting for 27.78% of the whole aged population.

The third stage, from 2051 to 2100, will be a stable period of severe aging. By 2051, the Chinese aged population will reach its peak of 437 million, about twice the total population aged from zero to fourteen. Simultaneously, the very aged population at the age of eighty or above will occupy a share of 25–30 % of the total Chinese aged population.

The problem of population aging in China has the following peculiarities.

(1) China has the largest aged population in the world. Though already accounting for ten percent of the total Chinese population at present, the people above sixty are increasing at the rate of five percent annually. By the middle of the 21st century, there will have been about 400 million people who have reached the age of sixty, accounting for one-half of the Asian aged population and one-fifth of the aged population of the whole world (Qi, 2005).

(2) From 1980 to 1999, that is, in less than twenty years, the age structure of the Chinese population almost went through the transition from the adult type to the aged type. In contrast, it took Britain eighty years, and Sweden forty years, to go through the similar change.

(3) The increasing age of the population in China is obvious. In recent years, the number of people above eighty, accounting for 9.7% of the whole Chinese population, has been increasing with the speed of 4.7% annually, apparently faster than the annual growth rate of the people aged sixty or above (3.39%). By 2051, people at the advanced age of eighty or above will steadily occupy a share of 20–30% of the whole aged population in China (Li, 2010, c).

(4) When one examines population aging in China, regional differences are obvious. As early as 1979, Shanghai became the first metropolis with the problem of population aging. Later on, provinces and municipalities such as Zhejiang, Beijing, Tianjin, Jiangsu and Liaoning became aged areas one after another. Nevertheless, population aging didn't prevail throughout the western provinces such as Qinghai and Ningxia until 2010, that is, thirty years after 1979 (Duan, 2009).

(5) When the western developed countries became aged societies, their per capita gross domestic product ranged from $5000 to $10,000. As a typical example of "old before affluent", the per capita gross domestic product of China was less than $1000 when China entered into an aged society (Li, 2010, d).

The Impact of Population Aging on the Chinese Economy

Humans are not only an important input and variable factor in economic activities, but also the ultimate beneficiary of those activities. Accordingly, we will argue that population aging will cause the following consequences to the Chinese economy:

(1) China may lose its advantage of a more productive labor force because of population aging. For a long time, a gigantic and cheap labor force with comparatively higher quality has acted as one of the important pillars supporting the continuous economic growth of China. In spite of the fact that China has become an aged country at the beginning of the 21st century, it will have a net increase of 200 million people in the coming 30 years and its working age population, that is, people aged from 15 to 64, will have reached 1.01 billion in 2016, more than the total working age population of all developed countries. Therefore, there will not be a labor shortage in China in a rather long period of time (Ding, 2007, a). However, China will still confront the following structural problems caused by population aging.

Apparently, the first problem is the aging of the labor force structure. It is predicted that from 1990 to 2050, the working population at the age of 15–29 will decrease from 353 million to 257 million, and the share of this age cohort in the total Chinese population will also fall from 48.76 % to 30.2 %. At the same time, the working population at the age of 45–59 will increase from 137 million to 316 million, and their share in the total Chinese population will rise from 18.88 % to 37.6 % (Zhang, 2008).

In 2007, The Development Research Center under the State Council of the P. R. of China made an investigation of 2749 administrative villages all over China, finding that there were no more laborers in their young and robust years to be transferred to the urban areas in almost three-fourths of the villages investigated (Ding, 2007,b).

Secondly, population aging, especially in the economically advanced coastal areas of China, has intensified the problem of insufficient supply of professionals and technicians in China. According to the statistical survey made by the Information Supervising Center of the Chinese Labor Force Market in ninety-four Chinese cities, in the fourth quarter of 2007, the ratios between the demand for and supply of technicians at all levels were greater than one, and the ratios between the demand for and supply of senior technicians, mechanics and engineers were 2.36, 2.36 and 2.2 respectively, which reflected the insufficient supply of technology-based talents in the labor force market (Yang, 2008).

(2) The old-age insurance sponsored by the Chinese government may suffer great financial pressure because of population aging. After entering into the twenty-first century, the Chinese social pension system has

basically completed the transition from an unfunded "pay–as–you-go" mechanism to a fund-accumulated one. However, the governmental pension system, which holds a dominant position in the pension system of China, still has many problems. For example, the financial resources are insufficient, and the insurance coverage is limited and the operation of the insurance funds still needs to be enhanced. Generally speaking, the Chinese pension system will be challenged by population aging in the following three ways:

(a) The period of benefit payment will be prolonged because of population aging and consequently, this will make the pension premium increase and the prime cost of the pension will rise significantly.

(b) Population aging will enormously increase the number of the pension beneficiaries on one hand, while making the cash flow of the pension system increasingly shrink on the other hand.

(c) Population aging will let the people enjoying pension benefits account for a much higher share in the whole population than the working age population does. As a result, the pension insurance institutions will tend to carry out relatively conservative investment strategies, such as reducing the holding of equities, increasing the share of cash and fixed capital in their total assets.

(3) The Chinese government may bear a much heavier financial burden because of population aging. Population aging, together with the well known basic national policy of "one couple, one child", will inevitably require the government to supply the society with public pension insurance, and this will definitely raise governmental social welfare expenditures greatly.

(4) Population aging will cause investment capital to flow from the country whose population is comparatively older to the one whose population is comparatively younger and consequently, whose rewarding rate of capital is probably higher. Under the circumstances of global population aging, national differences of age structure will still lead to a large-scale capital transnational circulation, as well as corresponding structural changes to the international balance of payments of the countries concerned. As a result, those countries whose populations are relatively aging would become the net importers of commodities and labor services because of the capital outflow and the insufficient labor supply.

(5) There will be severe longevity risks in China because of population aging. Longevity risk refers to the actual life spans of retirees extending far past their expected lives. Generally speaking, longevity risks can be defined at two levels -- individual and integrity longevity risks. Individual longevity risk implies that the living expenditure of a person

surpasses his or her accumulated assets in life. This kind of risk could be managed through the participation of the relevant pension plans. The longevity risk of a certain population, also called the concentrative longevity risk, means that the average living span of a certain population is beyond the expected one. Since the concentrative longevity risk is a systematic one which cannot be effectively dispersed by the law of large numbers, all of the longevity risk bearing institutions, such as governmental sponsored pension organizations, insurance companies and pension funds, might be confronted with a great loss and even bankruptcy.

Policy Adjustment and Reform Measurements

China has the largest population in the world, with a total number of thirteen billion. And it is estimated that the Chinese population will reach its peak of 14.65 billion in 2030. Meanwhile, China has the largest aged population in the world. Thus, in the entire twenty-first century, the huge demographic imbalance towards the aged and the heavy financial burden of supporting the aged will continuously interweave and bring severe challenges to the economical and social development of China.

The following policies and reform measures may help to overcome the negative economic impacts of population aging:

(1) Economic growth, especially intensive growth brought out by the increase of productivity, would be conducive for Chinese society to fulfill the duty of supporting its aged population. Different from extensive economic growth, intensive economic growth does not completely depend on the augmentation of inputs, but is gained mainly by the increase of productivity. Therefore, the Chinese government should encourage technical innovation, develop education and offer staff training programs in order to improve productivity.

To a certain extent, the regeneration of a labor force diminished by population aging contributes more or less to the promotion of productivity. Compared with the young generation, aged labors, though somewhat more experienced, have the disadvantages of being less educated, having less enterprise and entrepreneurship ability, being slower to adapt to technical innovations and changes, and demanding higher salaries. Accordingly, it would help to raise productivity by replacing the old with the young.

(2) The possible insufficient supply of labor caused by population aging might be mitigated through bringing the regulating function of the labor market into full play. Nowadays in China, there are some informal employment practices, for example, some enterprises like to hire people by oral bargaining, some entities, including the government organs and the state – owned companies, have the tendency of pasting political requirement on employment, or offering their employees payments much higher than the

market standard. All these practices would impede the normal operation of the labor market. Therefore, If possible, the government should require Chinese enterprises to recruit laborers in the labor market and sign contracts with the employees, which, in the light of the supply - demand relationship of the labor market, have clear terms on the expiration of employment, the job description, the payment term, and the termination or rescission terms of the contract.

(3) Implementing pension reform promptly and conscientiously. The main measures should be:

(a) *Raising the legal retirement age appropriately.* Presently, almost all of the developed countries are now raising their legal retirement age in various degrees. Similar with the western countries, China has millions of "baby boomers" born after the Second World War. It might be a proper choice for China to follow the suit of the western countries to mitigate the great pressures created by the widespread retirement of baby boomers on social pension systems.

(b) *Promoting the development of employer–sponsored pensions and commercial pensions.* At present, China has primarily set up a "three–legged stool"; that is, a pension system composed of pension insurance funded and operated by the government, corporations and the individual respectively. Nevertheless, the government-sponsored pension still holds a dominant position since this "three – legged stool" system is just in its preliminary stage. In this circumstance, encouraging people to participate more in corporate and commercial pension plans, through the incentives of government financial subsidies and favorable tax treatment, would greatly improve the insurance capability of the Chinese pension system.

(c) *Implementing and popularizing "phased retirement".* As mentioned above, there is an insufficient supply of professionals and technicians in China because of population aging. Different from the traditional view of retirement, which holds that a worker moves from full time employment to complete withdrawal from the labor force in a single step, "phased retirement" could be described as "the situation in which an aged individual actively works for an employer for part time jobs or reduces workload as a transition into full retirement. It may also include such conditions in which aging employees receive some or all of their retirement benefits while still employed (Purcell, 2009,a). The concrete methods of "phased retirement" would be: allowing retirement–eligible employees to work fewer days per week or fewer hours per day; permitting employees to reduce their workload through job–sharing; rehiring retired employees on a part–time or temporary basis; and bringing them back through contracts as consultants rather than as regular employees (Purcell, 2009,b).

(4) *Stimulating investment and educating the public, especially young people's awareness of the importance of saving.* This would impede the fall of the savings rate caused by population aging. As is well known, saving is the source of investment, the power behind economic growth, but population aging is likely to make the savings rate fall. In order to stimulate people's enthusiasm for saving, the Chinese financial authorities must manage to raise the return rate of the capital market, and to improve the efficiency of financial intermediary institutions so as to make savings flow into investment fields with a comparatively higher return rate. Furthermore, for the purpose of raising the return rate of investment, the government ought to vigorously encourage fair competition, support and protect technical innovation, develop publicity about and education for the purpose of investment knowledge, speed up the diversification and rationalization of the asset structure through favorable tax treatment and finally, resolutely eliminate the bank practice of offering preferential loan to customers who have special political and economic relations.

(5) China must prevent and control longevity risks by making active use of the capital market. As China is a densely populated country and its social pension system has just in the late 1990s made the transition from the unfunded "pay–as–you–go' mechanism into a partial fund accumulation system, the Chinese government must undoubtedly shoulder a heavy burden of supporting its aged citizens. Besides, China's insurance market, which is now at the underdeveloped stage, can hardly transfer and distribute longevity risks through methods such as re–insurance. Therefore, like the western countries, it would be wise for China to regulate longevity risks through the capital market.

The international experience shows that to scatter longevity risks through the use of the capital market, the first thing that is required is the active participation of influential financial institutions. These institutions need to create a variety of investment alternatives, such as hedging transaction, options, structured notes. They also need to exploit computer software combined with the latest mortality data so that investors can develop their own forecasts.

Considering that longevity norms with public creditability are the basis of issuing longevity financial investment tools, and considering that the Chinese capital market is still at the underdeveloped stage, the Chinese government should, through national demographic investigations, provide reliable information on the life expectancy and survival probability of the Chinese people, so as to enhance public creditability of the longevity risk index created by financial institutions.

BUSINESS OPPORTUNITIES EMERGING FROM POPULATION AGING

Just like one old Chinese proverb says, "good fortune lieth within bad, bad fortune lurketh within good". Population aging, while putting forward challenges to China, also brings about the following business opportunities:

(1) China might employ professionals and technicians, import capital–intensive and high–tech equipment and attract foreign investments innovative in nature from overseas because of population aging. For a long time, a gigantic and cheap labor force with comparatively higher quality has acted as one of the important pillars supporting the continuous economic growth of China. However, by 2020, China will have 248 million aged people, accounting for 17.17% of the whole population, among which the very aged population that is eighty years old or above, would amount to 30.67 million, occupying a share of 12.37% of the total aged population. In order to deal with the aging of the labor force structure, China will have to restructure its economy accordingly, probably through recruiting some technicians and engineers from the advanced countries.

(2) In order to change the Chinese pension system's heavy reliance upon the government sponsored pension program, the Chinese authorities should adopt policies to further develop employer–sponsored pensions and commercial pensions by giving incentives such as government financial subsidies and favorable tax treatment. This, undoubtedly, will advance the development of Chinese private insurance and also the development of foreign insurance companies.

(3) It is imperative for the Chinese government to improve the current health care system to meet the challenges of the long–term health care of the aging population. Long–term health care is needed by those who are unable to perform "Activities of Daily Living (ADL)". In addition to institutional care provided in a nursing home or a hospital when a person has a mental or physical disability, long–term health care includes a variety of services such as shelter, transportation, housekeeping services, therapeutic services, home health nursing care, and nutritional and social support programs. A person who loses his or her autonomy will require more services to perform activities of daily living than others will require. These activities would include bathing, using the toilet, eating, and ambulation. Apart from activities of daily living they may also need assistance with instrumental

activities of daily living. For example, they may need assistance with preparing food, housekeeping, and handling finances. What's more, they may also develop dementia or Alzheimer's disease, which requires around–the–clock supervision and aid with activities of daily living. (Hussain et al. 2009)

Needless to say, long–term care costs are a major threat to individual assets and public finances, but China is far from prepared to answer this major and growing challenge. The reality is that the Chinese government, acting almost alone as the sole provider of long–term care, is financially unable to fulfill this task. In addition, few commercial insurance companies offer long–term care products, which is unfortunate, because many Chinese elders cannot afford expensive long–term care costs, having become old before they became affluent.

It is quite clear that the economic burden that long–term care has on the Chinese economy can greatly impact Chinese people's living standards. Therefore, in order to guarantee that sufficient resources and an effective health system is available fifty years from now when the Chinese elderly population is twice as large as it is today, the following social and public policy measures, whose implementation would undoubtedly create business opportunities for both internal and external private capital, must be adopted right now.

> (a) To cope with China's demographic challenges, and to deal with the financial burdens of the population in case of a severe loss of personal autonomy, the Chinese government should, from now on, be engaged in building a universal coverage of long – term care risks, which would be a cooperative public/private partnership in nature, and on the basis of individual contribution account.
> (b) Now that the existing public schemes with pay–as–you–go designs are not able to cope with funding issues related to aging and a rise in medical and non–medical services costs, the private long–term care insurance markets must play an important role to complement insufficient public benefits. To fulfill this task, insurers will have to develop innovative and robust solutions both in the field of wealth management and regarding protection products.
> (c) Furthermore, some beneficial public/private partnerships must be set up to produce more products and services needed by the aged population, to develop more long–term care institutions such as hospitals and nursing homes, and to promote programs to enhance community involvement, encourage healthy aging, foster social and interpersonal relationship, and so on.

(4) China must prevent and control longevity risks by making use of the capital market actively, since China's insurance market, which is now at the underdeveloped stage, can hardly transfer and distribute longevity risks through methods such as re–insurance. Thus, China must rely on the expertise and financial power of the institutions creating and facilitating investments in the longevity risk market.

CONCLUSION

After thirty years of continuous economic growth, China has become the second largest economic entity in the world. However, despite this wonderful economic performance, China is far from prepared to deal with the challenge of population aging. Being confronted with the largest aged population in the world, China has a pension system that does not have a solid fund foundation and can only offer an essential retirement income to its beneficiaries. At the same time, employer–sponsored pensions and commercial pensions are only at the initial stage. Chinese elders, a generation of " old before affluent" citizens, cannot expect to rely on family care because of the long–time national policy of " one couple, one child'. Therefore, it would be wise for potential marketers to step into the following areas.

(1) Participating in pension or elder care schemes sponsored by Chinese authorities or making exclusive or joint–venture investments in this field.

(2) Making investment in health care infrastructures such as hospitals, nursing homes, and community care giving agencies; or producing health care equipment with relative lower price and higher quality.

(3) Setting up institutions that are engaged in training family caregivers, health care providers, and elder care professionals; or open up continuing education programs to satisfy the needs of some wealthy elders.

(4) Making investment in constructing both the physical and the social environment in which houses, transportation facilities, parks and other public spaces are suitable for elders to have access to personal care services, health care, and physical exercise.

(5) Offering financial services such as re–insurance, hedging transaction, options, organized notes to mitigate the longevity risks caused by population aging.

Authored by Liping Hou, in *International Journal of China Marketing*, Vol. 1(2) 2012, pp. 70-80.

Chapter Six

Marketing Equitable Ethnic Cultural Tourism in China

China is one of the world's great cultural areas and, as such, many people are interested in exploring the country and experiencing its people and heritage. While many tourists focus on well known historic sites such as the Forbidden City, the Great Wall, or Mount Tai, the ethnic minorities of China are gaining increased attention and are spotlighted here. This growing interest in China's cultural diversity is spurring a growing segment of the tourism industry. While marketing efforts are inevitably customer oriented, the impacts of all stakeholders need to be taken into account. Strategies regarding how to do so are discussed with special reference to various indigenous peoples of China.

CONTEMPORARY CHINESE TOURISM AND ITS ORIGINS

The factors leading to the rapid growth of tourism in China are well known. Evolving in relative isolation, China was long distinct from the West and still is. The 19th and 20th centuries, unfortunately, were cruel to China resulting in domination by the expanding colonial powers who viewed the country as a source of markets, merchandise, and raw materials, not the home of a great civilization. Post World War 11 revolutionary activities gave birth to the People's Republic that was established as an alternative to the exploitation, disrespect, and humiliation that had been painfully endured for many years.

Few foreign visitors were able to visit China during the early years of the People's Republic and, as a result, the inbound tourism industry was almost nonexistent. Most citizens of China, furthermore, had little opportunity to travel outside their country and, due to this fact, Chinese demands had almost no impact upon world tourism.

After the vogue of the Cultural Revolution died down, however, Deng Xiaoping gained a significant leadership role in China and is credited with introducing the market system into his country. Among other insights, he understood that the culture and heritage of China was revered worldwide and that by encouraging tourism the cash-starved country could attract foreign currency. In the mid 1970s, Xiaoping gave his blessing to the tourism industry and since that time, its growth has been sustained and remarkable.

Today, advances in the infrastructure of China facilitate continued growth for the tourism industry. Bullet trains make travel quick, comfortable, and convenient. New airports and improvements to existing facilities are making it easier to enter China and quickly travel within it. Fancy

Westernized hotels that cater to foreign visitors are springing up as well as more modest accommodations. Tourism sites are being developed, improved, and promoted.

Approximately 35 years after Deng envisioned tourism as an economic force for China, the industry has emerged as a powerful economic engine that serves many millions of visitors each year while generating generous revenues for the country.

CHINA AS A TOURISM VENUE FOR INTERNATIONAL TRAVELERS

I am lucky to have been able to reside in China for longer than a whirlwind visit. By living in the country and seeing both tourist destinations and the haunts of local people, I have gained insights that are unavailable to the average foreign traveler with only enough time for a brief visit. Although I am far from being an "old China hand", my experiences give me more of an intuitive feeling for the country than many short term visitors are able to develop.

Spending most of my time in Jinan, Shandong Province (in the Northeast portion of China), I have found the local residents to be very friendly and accommodating. I was prepared for people who might be shocked or offended by the appearance of a white person, but I have found just the opposite. Everyone, without exception, has been very friendly and helpful. I feel safe. Although I speak no Chinese, I am able to negotiate with street peddlers who sell fruit and other items, ranging from tennis shoes to screw drivers. An "expatriate quarter" is not required to meet my needs. My only safety net is a piece of paper with my address on it. If I become lost or disoriented, I give it to a taxi driver and he takes me home. Shopping in larger stores is even easier than haggling on the street. Imported products are available at premium prices, but domestic fare of good quality is quite inexpensive compared to American or European prices. Although Western-style facilities, such as hotels, are available, I have not found them necessary and by living in a local neighborhood, I have gained more of a true "Chinese experience" than I would have otherwise enjoyed. When traveling, a variety of modestly priced hostels cater to foreign travelers.

Naturally, a certain amount of care must be taken, especially when dealing with strangers in an alien land. This, of course, is good advice to follow wherever one travels anyplace in the world. I have heard of all sorts of scams and con games such as naïve tourists being lured to a restaurant by "friendly" locals and forced to pay profoundly overcharged prices. By using common sense, however, such problems can be avoided.

My experiences indicate that China is an accessible tourism destination both for foreign travelers who prefer American/European-styled amenities and others, such as the "backpacker crowd" who are more adventurous, on the one hand, and more frugal, on the other.

In recent years, the less populated regions of Western China that are the home of various ethnic minorities have become accessible. Increasingly tourists are becoming interested in these more remote places and transforming them by their presence. As we shall see in a discussion of the Mosuo (below), the issues involved in this process are complex and expand far beyond generating the largest amount of revenue possible in the shortest amount of time.

EXAMPLES OF CULTURAL TOURISM IN CHINA

Although China is largely a culturally homogeneous country, it possesses a number of ethnic and cultural enclaves that are distinct. The situation is parallel to what exists in the North America. Although most of the United States is somewhat similar culturally, in many sparsely populated and out of the way places (such as Appalachia, Alaska, the Dakotas, and the Four Corners region of the Southwest) rural and/or indigenous ethnic enclaves with a distinctive way of life can be found. Many of these groups have emerged as tourist attractions. Chinese ethnic groups have had a similar experience, especially in the Southwest portion of the country. By briefly discussing a number of well known examples of indigenous Chinese peoples who are showcased by tourism, an analysis of relevant issues is presented.

The Bai is an autonomous and recognized ethnic group of almost 2 million located primarily in the Yunnan Province of Southwest China. The language is related to Tibetan. The Bai people are known as creative, being respected for their sculpture, painting, and music. Their appearance is distinctive because of the habit of dressing in white. Bai religious and spiritual life combines Buddhism, local village gods, and the god of Nature.

The Bai people have a number of festivals that have attracted the attention of tourists. The most important is the March Fair that takes place each year at the foot of Mount Cangshan. Originally a purely religious activity, the event has expanded over the years to embrace secular overtones, including performances, traditional athletic competitions, and dancing. A wide variety of local merchandise is available for sale. Another event, the Torch Festival, is basically a harvest celebration; on June 25, the countryside is decorated with banners and at night the people walk their farm fields carrying torches.

In their article "Representing Identities Through Tourism: Encounters of Ethnic Minorities in Dali, Yunnan Province, People's

Republic of China", Doorne, Ateljevic, I. and Bai (2003) look at the role tourism plays both in economics and identity. They argue that culture and history are assuming an increasingly important economic role. Tourism has emerged as a major factor driving the economy; the authors discuss how cultural phenomena are appropriated, manipulated, and constructed in order to attract and cater to visitors.

The Dia people of Yunnan also deserve mention. They are primarily found near the Myanmar and Laotian borders, in the southern part of Yunnan. More than 300,000 Dai live in this region. The Dai are known for their festivals, including the Water Festival held in April. Originally a religious event celebrating the cleansing power of water, the festival has expanded into a good time in which people also playfully splash others with water (including tourists) for the fun of it.

In order for the various peoples of Yunnan Province to showcase their cultural diversity, a Yunnan Nationalities Village has been constructed on the northeastern shore of Dianchi Lake in order portray these diverse cultures and ways of life. This significant cultural endeavor demonstrates that the people of the region are well aware of both the cultural and economic value of their heritage and traditions (Sinohotelguide.com. 2000.) The village exhibits numerous households and other structures representative of specific ethnic groups so tourists can better understand the cultures they visit.

Perhaps the most interesting group is the Mosuo (Moso) of the Lugu Lake region. The Mosuo people are matrilineal (kinship and personal identity go though the mother's line of the family and not the father's.) There is no traditional form of marriage and, as a result, men reside with their mother's family instead of living full time with their mates who, in turn, live with their families. This custom has led many outsiders to imagine that most Mosuo women are promiscuous, which is not true.

Since the 1980s, tourism has become a major backbone of the Mosuo economy and, along with it, a wide number of pressures and changes have arrived including the intrusion of outsiders and the pollution of a hitherto pristine landscape. An account of the rise of tourism among the Mosuo has recently been published by Gang (2011) that chronicles its rise from a cottage industry to a large economic endeavor that is largely planned and managed by the government. In his article, Gang acknowledges that various pressures and problems have occurred simultaneously with economic development involving tourism and outsiders.

To help the people chart their own future, the Mosuo people have established two development associations. One was founded by Cao Jianping, a governmental employee. The other, the Lugu Lake Mosuo Cultural Development Association, appears to have considerable less outside involvement, although John Lombard (an expatriate Canadian) is involved and anthropologists, such as Tami Blumfield, have interacted with the Mosuo over the years.

In my work with indigenous people, I have often seen that different members of a community often hold divergent views regarding the role of outsiders. Mirroring this tendency, Jinping's organization appears to look favorably at outside intervention, such as that provided by the government. The Lugu Lake Mosuo Cultural Development Association, in contrast, appears to be much more wary and centered around the local community. In its statement of purpose, the association emphasizes self determinism by affirming: "All projects and priorities are determined by Mosuo leaders in the Association. Any non-Mosuo who are involved serve in an advisory/supportive position, to help the Mosuo accomplish those goals. Anyone seeking to come in and tell the Mosuo what they should do, or to run their own projects, will not be included in our work." (Lugu Lake Mosuo Cultural Development Association.)

The association is also aware that the Mosuo have an image within the world and wish to be treated with dignity and respect. As an instruction or warning to outsiders who bring their own promotional strategies to the Mosuo, the association insists that:

> No promotion, marketing, or advertising for our programs will *ever* present the Mosuo as a poor, pitiful people. The Mosuo we work with are strong, determined, and proud of their culture. They have already accomplished much on their own, despite meager resources and significant obstacles. We seek to show that determination, strength, and pride to everyone else, and encourage others to work with them as partners" (Ibid.)

Attention is devoted to the fact that the Mosuo should control their own destiny, even in a changing world where outsiders and economic intervention have been thrust within their midst. Thus, the philosophy of the organization says in part:

> ...change is inevitable and unstoppable. It's going to happen -- in fact, it's already happening. The only real question is how that change will affect the Mosuo. In this regard, there are two main possibilities:
> 1) The Mosuo could simply be overwhelmed by the "outside" world, and within 50 years we may see the complete demise of their culture. This is what will almost

certainly happen if the Mosuo do not have the knowledge, skills, and tools to be able to determine their own future.
2) The Mosuo will change, but still retain unique aspects of their own culture; they will integrate aspects of other cultures with their own culture. In this way, although it will change, much of the Mosuo culture will also be preserved. Obviously, it is my belief -- and the belief of all the Mosuo working with me in all of our projects are directed toward that goal.
I can sum it all up in one word – "CHOICE." (Ibid.)

Thus, the Mosuo have two developmental organizations to choose from. This dyad points to a commonly occurring dilemma that indigenous people often face. To what extent can the people control their own destiny and to what extent is the aid of outside specialists necessary and preferable?

THE IMPACTS OF TOURISM

Tourism is routinely lauded as a means of generating business activity in a country or region that needs an economic stimulus. It can often be successful in rustic places as well as providing employment for "unskilled" workers. Pursuing this industry, however, inevitably involves costs (often hidden, unanticipated, and slow to develop) that ought to be acknowledged, weighed, and mitigated as decisions are made and strategies developed. For discussions of the tradeoffs and implications of cultural tourism see (Walle 2010, Rojas and Turner 2011, Mortensen and Nicholas 2010, and Killick (2008.)

Observers of Chinese tourism have long recognized the implications of the industry and its impacts. In 1987, for example, Alan Lew, published "The History, Policies, and Social Impact of International Tourism in the People's Republic of China." As the title indicates, Lew was appropriately concerned with the social context of tourism and the impacts it exerts.

Mirroring Lew's concerns, this paper discusses the varied influences of marketing upon tourism and the hosts who provide tourism services. In specific, cultural tourism often exerts disruptive forces that potentially undercut the local population in hurtful ways. This type of issue has long been analyzed and lamented. Tourism strategies, furthermore, may trigger social changes that have negative implications. As a result, efforts to empower local communities that are becoming involved with tourism often need to be pursued.

In order to explore these issues, models developed in *The Equitable Cultural Tourism Handbook* (Walle 2010) are discussed with reference to China.

MARKETING TO CONSUMERS AND ITS IMPACT

Marketing, of course, involves responding to the needs of a particular target market in strategic ways. Modern marketing is anchored by the "marketing concept" that suggests that the only reason for an organization to exist is to serve its customers.

Ever since it was introduced by E. Jerome McCarthy in the early 1960s, the "4 Ps model of marketing" (that focuses upon 4 controllable variables dubbed "Product", "Place" "Promotion", and "Price") has dominated the field. Some tourism/hospitality marketing texts (such as Robert Morrison's Hospitality and Travel Marketing) expand the number of "Ps" to reflect the uniqueness of the industry; even here, however, the basic approach of the 4 Ps paradigm is preserved: marketing is depicted as (1) developing an understanding of customer demands and (2) manipulating the available controllable variables of marketing to most effectively serve it. In order to demonstrate how this paradigm can be related to cultural tourism, each P will be briefly discussed.

Product

The term "product" refers to what the customer receives (and, typically, what is designed and marketed with the needs, wants, and expectations of the customer in mind. Often, relatively little attention to the impact upon those who provide goods and services.

Tourism strategies, however, need to avoid undercutting the community, cheapening its traditions, or unduly creating stress for the people. Dealing with such details, unfortunately, often falls outside of the range of marketing thought. Under such circumstances, problems can arise if inappropriate demands upon the host culture are made or if impacts are not anticipated and mitigated. In the case of the Mosuo, for example, large hotels and various tourism influences are impacting the culture. While this may be inevitable, the people want a choice. Care needs to be taken so the community is not weakened or undermined in the process of encouraging economic activity.

In short, tourism marketers often feel comfortable adjusting what is offered to respond to customers demands. While doing so is reasonable, efforts should be made to insure that these strategic manipulations are appropriate and respectful to the host community.

Price

Deciding what price to charge can be a difficult issue to negotiate and evaluate. As a result of strategic imbalances, host communities may not be treated in an equitable manner. When a host culture positively contributes to the tourism industry, however, its members deserve to earn an equitable return for their efforts. Not only is such an arrangement ethical, it can help insure the long-term success of the tourism venture. People who do not receive adequate and fair compensation, for example, can easily become demoralized and the quality of the goods and services they provide can decline as a result. Such responses can hurt both the host community and its business partners.

The pricing structure can also be used to control demand. If, for example, a community can comfortably handle only a certain number of guests, the price can be manipulated in order to keep the traffic to a desired level.

Price, of course, often needs to be adjusted in order to mesh with the product itself. When buying a premium excursion to a Chinese tourism destination, of course, patrons expect to be treated accordingly while those taking a cheap whirlwind tour do not demand or anticipate the same level of quality.

Place

The place variable (where cultural tourism activities and experiences actually occur) can have a profound impact on the hosts of cultural tourists. Traditional musicians, storytellers, and other performers who are not accustomed to a large audience may feel uncomfortable being showcased before a big crowd. Efforts need to be taken to minimize the potential for such hurtful experiences and environments. As discussed above, the Bai people have festivals, originally religious in nature, that are becoming important tourism attractions. What are the implications (positive and negative) of this transition? Strategically controlling venues where hosts and tourists interact can be important.

In considering place/distribution issues, decisions should not merely be based upon generating the highest short-term profit. What are the likely side effects of various distribution methods? Should the nature of the merchandise and the speed with which it is produced be considered? These are issues that the mainstream business community might overlook, but they can have a significant impact upon the host community and the ultimate quality of the tourism products and services being marketed.

Promotion

Promotion refers to any way in which an organization communicates with its target market (as well as its partners or facilitators) in order to encourage patronage. On many occasions, promotional strategies that make sense from a customer perspective appear as hurtful when the host community is considered. Above we saw that the Mosuo specifically stated that "No promotion, marketing, or advertising for our programs will ever present the Mosuo as a poor, pitiful people." Nevertheless this kind of inappropriate promotion is obviously a threat; otherwise this possibility would not have been mentioned.

Summarizing this brief overview of marketing, the profession typically views its mission as (1) choosing a target market/markets and (2) catering to its/their demands. Doing so is pursued by manipulating the controllable variables that are available in order to more effectively respond to the market's wishes and expectations. This process is typically called "marketing management."Graphically, this arrangement can be portrayed as Table 6.1.

Marketing, therefore, can be viewed as a strategic science that (1) focuses upon the needs of specific groups of customers and (2) adjusts the organization's controllable variables in order to satisfy the desires and demands of that target market. Currently the most dominant paradigm of the field is the 4 Ps model in which consumer demands are satisfied by manipulating the 4 controllable variables of product, price, place, and promotion.

Certainly, marketing is an ethical and moral activity because helping people achieve their goals and satisfy their needs is a good thing. Nevertheless, mainstream marketing is often so focused on serving customers that the needs of other stakeholders are not adequately perceived and/or adequately addressed.

MACROMARKETING A BROADER VIEW

The type of activity discussed above can be viewed as "micromarketing" (analogous to microeconomics) because it focuses solely upon the benefits that a firm and a target market receive through interacting with one another. Other important considerations that fall outside this universe of discourse tend to be unrecognized or discounted.

TABLE 6.1
MARKETING MANAGEMENT: AN OVERVIEW

Variable	Universe Of Discourse	Impacts	Strategic Implications
Product	The actual good or service being sold to the target market	People seek the tangible and intangible characteristics of the Product. To be successfully marketed, the product must satisfy a need.	The good or service can respond to consumer expectations and/or respond to consumer feelings, such as curiosity.
Price	The price which the organization charges for its goods and services	The price can influence the size of the market and when people will buy the product.	Price is two things (1) a reward for a job well done and (2) a strategic variable.
Place	The distribution network and where the product will be made available	Where the product is and who sells it may influence the level of sales and who buys it.	Appropriately getting the product to where it can be purchased.
Promotion	Communication between the organization, its customers, intermediaries, and other relevant publics that facilitate marketing.	In order to most effectively sell a product, the organization must communicate effectively to appropriate audiences.	Various publics need to be addressed. Communication should reinforce and build upon the other marketing variables.
Marketing Management	Coordinating all of the controllable variables so that the benefits of synergism make the organization and its Products more marketable.	By consciously interlacing the various controllable variables, the organization can more efficiently and effectively market the product.	By overtly combining all the controllable variables in a coherent and synergistic manner, marketing is more effective.

Macromarketing, a sub discipline of the field, however, is concerned with issues that expand beyond the dyad of a firm and its target market. Macromarketing deals with all significant impacts, especially those that are unanticipated and impinge upon stakeholders who are not a part of the patron-client relationship. This kind of analysis can be extremely relevant in situations involving cultural tourism and, as a result, it will be briefly discussed.

Macromarketing focuses upon the full implications of market driven activities. It provides a valuable alternative to micro analysis that might not take the wellbeing of all impacted stakeholders into account. Cultural tourism strategies, for example, can exert a profound impact upon host communities, fragile cultural enclaves, and even entire regions. Macromarketing can help decision makers and their communities to better understand the full implications of their decisions.

Building upon this analytic model, macromarketing is concerned with equitably evaluating the needs of the community while simultaneously enhancing the quality of life that people enjoy. It goes without saying that many host communities that are considering an involvement with cultural tourism can benefit from this kind of analysis.

Charles Slater was a pioneer who affirmed that marketing and its impacts cannot be legitimately viewed in isolation. He, for example observed: "marketing is a part of the whole social process system rather than only a function within each firm or institution" (Slater & Jenkins 1979:374).

From the beginning, macromarketing has employed some form of systems theory analysis; Slater noted, for example, that: "the common thread [of macromarketing papers] was the systems concept of putting marketing in the context of both the firm and society" (Slater 1977:1.)

The systems theory approach in marketing goes back at least to the late 1950s/early 1960s when marketing pioneer Wroe Alderson began modeling the marketing system and its impacts in a holistic manner. Alderson was influenced by the general systems theory model provided by his friend Kenneth Boulding (1956) who envisioned an array of increasingly complex paradigms that can be used to model behavior in terms of interrelationships between the various parts of a system.

These approaches view the elements of culture/society (including marketing relationships) in terms of how they fit into the greater social structure, contribute to it, and, perhaps, function as agents of change. Such a systems analysis is also able to usefully deal with how marketing impacts people who are not involved in a marketing relationship. In many cases, a significant segment of the population receives no benefits, but is hurt by marketing strategies. This reality raises ethical considerations that transcend a customer orientation. Host cultures, their members, traditions, habitats, etc.

might be undercut because of cultural tourism; this possibility needs to be considered, avoided, and where necessary mitigated.

As macromarketing grew, it built upon Alderson's systems theory approach in order to model the full impact of marketing strategies. By 1982, the new field of macromarketing was consciously able to define itself. Thus, in the "Editor's working definition of macromarketing", George Fisk (1982:3) states that macromarketing deals with:

1. Impacts and consequences of society on marketing and actions (marketing externalities),
2. The impact and consequences of society on marketing systems and actions (social sanctions), and
3. The understanding of marketing systems in their aggregate dimensions (macro-systems analysis).

The term "marketing externalities" refers to everything outside of the buyer/seller relationship that is involved with and/or impacted by the organization and its customers. Macromarketing specifically recognizes that external groups are often affected by the processes of marketing and consumption. As a result, the broader implications of these relationships need to be addressed.

Increasingly this view is recognized as important. Thus, Syring (2009) observes in a recent article "In such circumstances...others must absorb the cost of doing business even though they receive no compensation for the price they are unwilling to pay"

If a tourism destination quickly emerges as very popular, for example, it might become overwhelmed, leading to stress and unhappiness. The impact of cultural tourism, furthermore, may undermine the community or prevent people from pursuing other vocations and ways of life. The focus upon tourists might cause artistic traditions to wither. A well developed subsistence way of life might be abandoned. If tourism is abruptly terminated for some reason, these people may have lost their traditional means of earning a livelihood. These concerns are often major issues that host communities need to address.

In such circumstances, the organization, its customers, and a segment of the local population might benefit from cultural tourism while others must absorb the costs of doing business even though they receive no compensation for the price they unwillingly pay. (The classic argument used to rebut such complaints, of course, is that tourism brings jobs and economic activity to the entire community and, therefore, everybody benefits, directly or indirectly, as the fruits of economic activities "trickle down" to the community as a whole). In spite of attempts to argue away this sticky problem, cultural tourism might extract costs that are unfairly paid by those who receive no or few benefits. The sacrifices of these people need to be recognized when cultural tourism strategies are formulated. The systems theory orientation of macromarketing can address such issues in ways that help analyze the true costs of cultural tourism upon the host community as well as determining mitigation strategies.

TABLE 6.2
THE MACRO MODEL: AN OVERVIEW

Issue	Universe of discourse	Ethical Focus	Multiple stakeholders
Externalities	Impacts that extend beyond customers and those who serve them	Ethical behavior needs to consider a wide range of impacts besides benefits to customer and organizations that serve them.	The concept of externalities facilitates an ability to deal with various groups besides customers.
Impacts	Marketing has multiple impacts. Unintentional and unanticipated consequences may impact people who are not part of the patron/client relationship.	The marketing process exerts many impacts. Assessing these impacts and, where necessary mitigating them, is an ethical way to do business.	The impact of micromarketing and marketing management upon external groups is a specific area that needs to be addressed.
Systems Theory	Systems theory, which deals with the relationships between various parts of a larger whole, is a useful perspective of macromarketing.	Macromarketing models are often based upon systems theory. They are particularly useful in developing an appropriate ethical focus involving multiple stakeholders.	Systems theory focuses on interconnectedness. The method is useful when dealing with the needs and vulnerabilities of various external stakeholders.

A relevant issue that host communities often need to consider involves how to structure cultural tourism in ways that lead to responsible marketing and consumption. Doing so involves a far-reaching understanding of the full implications of cultural tourism within a specific community. Especial attention needs to be devoted to envisioning inadvertent and unintended consequences of marketing and consumption that might not be obvious at first glance.

A classic article that deals with these issues is George Fisk's "Criteria for a Theory of Responsible Consumption" (1973). Fisk concentrates upon the fact that technological change encourages certain marketing decisions that, while serving the overt demands of customers, may not be in the best interest of society because of negative long term implications. As a result, Fisk questions the wisdom (and perhaps even the legitimacy) of marketing strategies that fail to recognize and deal with their potential negative legacy. A key issue to remember is that people who are not involved in the buying/selling/consumption process may be unwillingly forced to bear costs associated with these economic activities while receiving no benefits. Cultural tourism potentially creates situations where these potentials may materialize.

In addition, macromarketing has long been interested in the impacts of tourism (Belk and Costa 1999, Jamison 1999, Nguyen 2009.) Since much cultural tourism takes place in rural and developing regions, macromarketing is especially well equipped to serve the industry.

The perspectives of macromarketing usefully transcend the micro-oriented buyer/seller orientation in ways that consider the well-being of all impacted stakeholders. The systems theory model provides a means of addressing the wide range of impacts that marketing and consumption may exert upon the host community. An overview of the macromarketing paradigm is provided in the following table 6.2.

Macromarketers portray their field as a much needed alternative to "4 Ps" marketing management that is based upon the marketing concept and views the patron/client relationship in isolation. These macromarketing perspectives parallel the ideas of tourism theorists such as J. Michael Haywood (1990) who seeks to transcend the marketing concept when assessing tourism strategies. Macromarketing also dovetails with the perspectives of host communities that are concerned about possible negative side effects of cultural tourism and economic development.) Host communities are aware that cultural tourism strategies have often triggered unanticipated and unintended side effects that were not initially obvious. The tools of macromarketing can be used to avoid blindly making decisions without an adequate understanding of their consequences. Graphically portrayed, these differences emerge as shown in Table 6.3.

Both micromarketing and macromarketing are legitimate and needed. Neither orientation should overshadow the other. Unfortunately, in innumerable economic development projects (including many involving cultural tourism) the micromarketing orientation dominates. This discussion urges host communities to temper micro assessments with a macromarketing analysis that deals with the broader implications of a proposed or existing cultural tourism venture.

Looking at the examples of cultural tourism impacting ethnic minorities of China, the value of a macro approach to strategic planning and assessment can be a vital tool. Macromarketers tend to argue that quality of life issues and strategies of empowering local communities need to be given a high priority. By doing so, marketing can best achieve its goal of fostering equity and parity and not merely serving external organizations by pleasing customers.

TABLE 6.3
MICROMARKETING AND MACROMARKETING COMPARED

Issue	Micromarketing	Macromarketing
Focus	The micro patron/client relationship between an organization and its customers.	The broader implications of marketing including, but not limited to the patron/client relationship
Unique perspective	Organizations exist to serve clients. The entire organization should revolve around clients.	Marketing exists within the larger environment and exerts a variety of influences upon it. Marketers should consider these relationships and their implications.
Breadth of field	Choosing a lucrative target market and then strategically manipulating the product to please it.	A broad systems theory analysis, in addition to marketing management needs to be employed.
Significance	Since tourism organizations and host communities need the support of a target market, catering to it in strategic ways is important.	Host communities have specific needs. A macromarketing perspective is best able to factor such variables into strategic planning.
Relevance	Micromarketing/marketing management emphasizes the needs of those who are involved in the buying/selling relationship.	Macromarketing considers the needs of a wide array of stakeholders, not merely customers and businesses that serve them.

DISCUSSION AND CONCLUSION

Starting from humble beginnings in the 1970s, cultural tourism in China has grown to be a powerful force and one that governmental agencies and private organizations use to stimulate economic activity. As a result, in China (as elsewhere) encouraging and planning cultural tourism is an important consideration.

Historically, much of this activity was conducted using what can be called "micromarketing" perspectives. This paradigm focuses primarily (if not exclusively) upon the benefits that accrue to an organization and its customers when they interact with one another. A blind spot in this method, unfortunately, is that the needs, desires, and vulnerabilities of those who provide cultural tourism goods and services can easily be overlooked.

An alternative to such "micro" perspectives is provided by macromarketing, a sub discipline that is dedicated to examining the full impacts of marketing activities and proposing alternatives that are equitable and viable. Increasingly, macromarketing perspectives are employed when marketing strategies are envisioned. Such techniques have a vital role to play when cultural tourism strategies are developed and implemented. By embracing such a method of analysis, local people can be empowered and their quality of life enhanced.

China is home to a wide range of indigenous peoples and many of them have become (or are emerging as) tourist attractions. Some, such as the Mosou, have developed sophisticated cultural development associations that work to insure that tourism policies and strategies are not dictated solely from above, that they are equitable, and that they reflect the desires of the people.

Authored by Alf H. Walle, originally published in *International Journal of China Marketing*, Vol. 1(2) 2011, pp. 57-69.

Chapter Seven

Adjusting to the Local Context: A Japanese Overseas Retailer in Guangzhou, China

This is an anthropological study of a Japanese overseas retail group YOWA in China, with the main purpose to examine its localization process and strategies under the Chinese context. Through the investigations of YOWA's investment in Guangdong province, the business characteristics, as well as transformations it made in China, this paper has three main findings. All of the three findings resulted from the process of YOWA's localization in varying degrees. They reveal its efforts in adjusting to and aligning with the external economic and culture environment of Mainland China.

INTRODUCTION

Against the backdrop of economic globalization, internationalization is an important way for companies to develop. One of the most important questions for multinational enterprises (MNEs) possibly lies in: How can they most efficiently run business in different markets with separate local cultures? 'Localization' seems the key to this question. Localization is the process of adjusting a product or a company to a particular language, culture, and host-country markets. There are several localization strategies, such as production localization, material procurement localization, talent localization, company image localization, management localization, etc. (Wu, 2004)

This paper investigates the localization strategies of a Japanese overseas company under Chinese context, through the case of a famous retail enterprise named YOWA. Although China have opened its door to the outside world since the Open and Reform in 1978, the retail sector was still restricted until several pilot projects of joint-ventures were permitted in the year of 1992. YOWA was one of the early pioneers that embarked on a new adventure in Mainland China. Through fifteen years of management and localization in the Chinese society, YOWA had become a vivid and distinctive example to study.

My interest in the localization strategies of YOWA started from an anti-Japanese demonstration in 2005. I have witnessed that protestors headed to major Chinese cities during those two weeks in April. For Guangzhou, as an estimate, three thousand demonstrators marched to the Japanese Consulate in this city, attacking and damaging Japanese supermarkets and restaurants on the way.

The anti-Japanese demonstration of 2005 indicated that the downturn in Sino-Japanese relations would turn to a bad side of trade relationship as well as fairly negative influence on the overseas Japanese companies in Mainland China, especially the retail groups which connect inseparably with daily life and represent the country's products, life style and cultures. (The anti-Carrefour supermarket demonstration in 2008 was a similar case.) The demonstration convinced me that it is considerably important to study the retail sector which closely related to people's daily life and inspired me to probe into several questions: how do Japanese retailers adjust to the Chinese context? What business strategies will they choose to survive? What are the localization features of their overseas companies in the Chinese context? The present study of tracing localization strategies of an overseas Japanese retail organization YOWA in Mainland China can provide an empirical research anthropologically, and to answer the questions raised above.

LITERATURE REVIEW

In the late 1960s to 1970s, Japanese companies began outperforming their MNEs in the west (Taylor, 1999). Some studies discussed that the motives for internationalism of MNEs can be classified as 'push' and 'pull' factors (McGoldrick & Fryer, 1993). In the case of Japan, high cost of land and labor, increased competition at home and government restrictions on expansion (especially for retailing business) were considered to be the push factors. While the strong Yen and comparative advantages of Japanese companies and management were regarded as the pull factors. (Chen & Brenda, 1995; Horn & Cross, 2009).

When it came to the 1980s, Japanese MNEs experienced a rapid expansion (Horn & Cross, 2009) in East Asia, especially China. China traditionally linked tightly with the Japanese economics for reasons of history, geographic proximity and a common cultural heritage. Thus, a burgeoning number of studies have investigated the activities of Japanese MNEs in China. (Anand & Delios, 1996; Horn & Cross, 2009; Itagaki, 2009; Taylor, 1999; Wong, 1999; Wong & Hendry, 1999) There is a body of literature attributed the reasons of increasing investments in China to its abundance of materials and low cost labor, rather than market expansion. (Anand & Delios, 1996; Ministry of International Trade and Industry, 1997) However, with rapid economic integration and increasing economic linkages between the two countries, there is a growing literature to suggest that China is a prime production location and key market. (Taniguchi, 2005, cited in Horn & Cross, 2009:286). Moreover, Horn and Cross (2009) further concluded that China was influencing the transformation of corporate Japan.

120

The core issue of localization lies in understanding the local culture. To understand the local culture, the consumption market and the human resources pattern are the most important aspects to discuss. Thus within the literature of Japanese MNEs in Mainland China, scholars from the disciplines of business and economics have mainly focused on the issues of business environments, historical process, as well as future trends of this economic relationship, while scholars from the disciplines of management have usually concentrated on the localization of human resource management practices (HRMs) of all aspects.

Within this literature of HRMs, many studies have focused on the issue of expatriates' replacement (Beamish & Inkpen, 1998; Fryxell, et, al., 2004; Heim, 1997), since one of the most important merits management localization brought is the personnel outlay reduction (Beamish & Inkpen, 1998; Fryxell, et, al., 2004; Heim, 1997; Zhang, 2005). Japanese MNEs have long been criticized for lagging behind Western companies in the localization of management practices, as well as its persistence of expatriate-intensive management (Kopp, 1999; Pucik, 1999). This standpoint may have stemmed from the fact that the majority of Japanese MNEs began their foreign activities later than their Western counterparts. (Itagaki, 2009). However, there are increasing studies challenging this standpoint by the fact of the decreasing number of Japanese expatriates and the increasing number of local managers. (Beamish & Inkpen, 1998; Fryxell, et, al., 2004; Heim, 1997; Wong & Hendry, 1999)

The transferability of the HRMs has also received much attention. Kajima believed that Japanese firms (especially those weak firms at home) were more likely to relocate in less developed countries (say China) in order to exploit their comparative advantages. (Kajima, 1978, cited in Chen & Brenda, 1995) On the contrary, Taylor (1999) suggested that cultural proximity was the main reason for the ease of transfer of business and management practices. Zhu and Warner (2000) also pointed out that it was due to the sufficient similarities between Japan's model of employment relations and the industrial and labor system of China. (Cited in Horn & Cross, 2009) Nevertheless, due to the present fluctuate labor systems in both countries and unprecedented mobility in the workforce, especially among the younger generations in Mainland China (Itagaki, 2009), the problems of localizing employment practices in China might be magnified for Japanese companies. (Horn & Cross, 2009) Furthermore, some scholars have indicated that the work style and HRMs developed in their domestic operations were the major competitiveness of Japanese companies (especially for those manufacture companies), thus Japanese MNEs should find solutions of maintaining a competitive edge meanwhile localizing management. (Itagaki, 2009)

Obviously, the above literature has several limitations to understand the issues of management localization of Japanese MNEs in China. The first limitation of these previous researches has been the lack of attention to the context. This limitation would lead to some misunderstanding of the localization process and strategies of Japanese MNEs. Wang's study of effectiveness of Japanese joint-ventures in China (1994) found that among MNEs in different sectors, management styles and HRM patterns would be different from each other. In this sense, it is essential to examine the context of the partners as well as the host countries. Wong and Hendry (1999) also alerted that 'the central issue for international management is not to identify the best IHRM policy per se, but rather to find the best fit between the company's international environment, its overall strategy, its HRM policy and implementation, and keep all these dimensions in direct alignment.' (Wong & Hendry, 1999, p.118)

The second limitation is that these previous studies failed to involve wide-range of sectors into the studies of Japanese MNEs. To date, the majority of these works have been relating to the manufacture enterprises (see Anand & Delios, 1996; Horn & Cross, 2009; Itagaki, 2009; Taylor, 1999; Zhang, 2005). Comparatively, little attention has been given to raising our understanding of other sectors, like retailing, services, consulting, and so on. The third limitation of these studies has been the lack of empirical methods in investigating the Japanese MNEs. Recurrent to these studies was using the documentary research methods, namely, second-hand materials. As noted above, management localization of MNEs is a dynamic process which involves cultural conflicts, manipulation, resistance, as well as power and control. Thus, empirical and qualitative methods would play an important role in it.

The limitations of previous studies imply that the present approaches to management localization are still insufficient. In order to examine the localization features of Japanese MNEs, a more holistic, detailed, and empirical approach should be adopted.

METHODOLOGY

This is an anthropological study of a Japanese overseas supermarket. The methods used in this study contain participant observation, informal interviews, questionnaire, and secondary data.

Participant observation

My six-month fieldwork as an ordinary employee of YOWA was conducted from September 2008 to February 2009, in SEICO Guangdong (SEICO GD), a subsidiary of YOWA, in Guangzhou, Mainland China.

The fieldwork was divided into four steps:

1. one month in the Human Resource department of the headquarters.

2. one month of rotation in four sections of a typical store. (One week for each).

3. three months in a particular section (the Bedding Section) in the store.

4. one month in the Personnel and General Affair Department of the store.

The ice breaking voyage was full of hardships. During the first month in HR department of the headquarters, I tried to develop networks, and familiarized myself with the routine operation, as well as the relationship between the headquarters and stores. I also attended meetings, activities and personal gatherings as much as permitted to, and collected written materials of all kinds, such as the organizational charts, correspondence, in-house publications, etc.

In late October of 2008, I was permitted to work in Sunny Store as a management trainee (abbreviated as MT). I started rotation among different sections in different departments of the store in order to build up an overall concept of the operation on the sales floor. During this one-month rotation, I had worked in four different sections of the store: the Perishable Section, the Grocery Section, the Boys & Girls Section and finally the Bedding Section for one week each. The rotation provided me a chance to draw an overall concept of the operation in the store and also helped me to find a more proper field site for the next step.

After the rotation, things gradually got better and I finally launched my research in all respects. I selected the Bedding Section in the Department of Household as the most suitable field site for another three months finally. I tried to build up networks during the previous one-month rotation and had made a more reliable relationship with the workers (including promoters and regular employees) in the Bedding Section.

I spent most time on informal interviews with the workers in SEICO GD after completed the jobs assigned by the section chiefs. I attended meetings, recruitment seminars, training courses and consultative activities like quality control circles as much as I could, and actively joined in social events on both sides as a photographer (promoters' side and regular workers' side) such as the MT outward bound, picnics, travels, sports day, new year parties, personal gatherings and so on. By participating in these activities, I built social networks gradually, broke down barriers and observed the life and work of the workers in SEICO GD lively in a context.

My final station arrived at the Administration Department in Sunny store where in charge of all the important administrative work including the training, promotion, ranking, attendance checking, and accounting, cashier, security, etc. I collected materials of all kinds, such as the employment statistics of the store over the past eight years, the detailed statistics of turnover rate and so on. Also I got some information about historical background of the establishment of SEICO in Guangzhou via several informal interviews with the store manager.

Informal Interviews

Most of the anthropological studies of organizations and consumers take interviewing as a basic anthropological technique (Jordan, 2003). Also according to Wong (1999), both the participant observation and intensive interviewing would contribute to understanding the context of the phenomena in question. There are several types of interviews, such as informal interview, highly structured interview and in-depth interview. Usually, the informal interview occurs during participant observation when one is asking about the work being observed. (Jordan, 2003) I primarily relied on the results gained from the participant observation through six-month of fieldwork and intensive informal interviews. Informal conversations held in the course of everyday work provided me a more dynamic and extensive view of the whole things happened around and helped figure out the context during the six-month fieldwork.

Questionnaire

Questionnaire, a quantitative method, was also adopted in this research project. A survey was conducted on my return visit in September 2009, which aimed at observing working and living conditions of the promoters. In my study, it was promoters who were responsible for daily merchandise sales in stores. Promoters worked as long-term workers and were completely under regular employees' management. Thus, to some extent, promoters should be viewed as non-regular workers here. The anonymous questionnaire consisted of five parts of contents, including personal information, lifestyles and life goals, employment relationship with suppliers, working conditions in the stores, and interpersonal communications, which were designed into the forms of gap filling, one-choice questions and multiple-choice questions. 300 copies of questionnaires were sent out and 167 copies were collected back within which 55 copies were from the bedding section where I have worked in.

Secondary Data

In this anthropological study, I also resorted to the secondary data. According to Blaxter (2006), secondary data, such as official statistics and governmental data are very valuable to researchers. Therefore I have used data and statistics from company documents and reports, various organizations, official websites and government publications. By comparing the secondary data with the primary information I collected from the fieldwork，some indications like historical changes and the future trends in Mainland China were observed in the research, such as the adjustments in employment patterns. Apart from the secondary data collected from the official organizations, I continue to read authoritative print media everyday such as *Guangzhou Daily* in order to examine the latest events happened in Guangzhou which might affect the operation of YOWA. Other electronic ways like Google Alerts were also used to remind daily updates of relevant topics that might concern. All these instruments and tools helped me analyze the current situation and future trends of Japanese retail groups in Mainland China without delay.

BRIEF INTRODUCTION OF THE COMPANY

YOWA (fictional name), which consists of YOWA Co., Ltd. and more than 150 group companies (as of February 2009), is a famous Japanese retail group based in the Greater Tokyo Area, Japan. With a long history that can be traced its origin back to 18th century, the modern corporation of this company was established based on three local supermarkets in KANSAI(關西) region in 1970. This merger made it the third largest national chain store only smaller than Daiei and Seiyu in the retail sector of Japan then. When entered into the 21st century, the company officially changed its group name into YOWA from 'SEICO' due to continuous business expansions, and the previous SEICO companies had become subsidiaries and affiliates of YOWA Co., Ltd. by then. Several years later, YOWA developed into one of the biggest retail groups in Japan with revenues amounting to over three trillion JPY in 2003(Annual report). In 2010, YOWA was ranked around 130th in the Fortune Global 500 rankings, and ranked the first 20 in the top 250 global retailers measured by retail sales of financial year 2008 (Deloitte Development LLC, 2010).

The YOWA group runs various kinds of business including general merchandise stores (hereafter GMS), supermarkets, convenience stores, drug stores, specialty stores, financial services, shopping centers, internet shopping, merchandise procurement and food processing operations. Among all these business, GMS, multi-supermarket and food supermarket are the three major business of the company.

In the 1980s, taking the saturated domestic consumer market and the increasing tendency of population decline into consideration, YOWA readjusted its business strategies and started to focus on the overseas globalization. YOWA began its overseas expansion in the year of 1985, taking Malaysia and Thailand as original standpoints, and then penetrated

125

into Hong Kong in 1990s. As the business in Hong Kong bloomed, YOWA finally entered into Mainland China in 1995, and established its first store in Guangdong province in 1996. According to the YOWA Annual Report 2009, by the end of February 2009, sixty stores in total had been opened overseas, in Malaysia (18 stores), Thailand (6 stores), China including Hong Kong and Taiwan (36 stores), mostly GMS stores and supermarkets.

Below we can see YOWA's stores in Mainland China. Currently (as of Dec.31th, 2010) there are 25 stores in operation, among which 4 stores in Guangzhou. (Table 7.1)

TABLE 7.1
OVERVIEW OF YOWA'S STORES IN MAINLAND CHINA

Company Name	Location of the Headquarters	Date of Establishment	Number of Stores (as of Dec.30th, 2010)
SEICO Guangdong	Guangzhou, Guangdong	1995.12	10
SEICO Shanghai	Shanghai	1995.12	1(closed)
YOWA Qingdao	Qingdao, Shandong	1996. 3	7
YOWA Shenzhen	Shenzhen, Guangdong	2000. 5	6
YOWA China	Shenzhen, Guangdong	2004. 9	1
YOWA Beijing	Beijing	2007.4	1

INVESTMENTS IN GUANGDONG PROVINCE, MAINLAND CHINA

Japanese companies mainly invest in North China, Yangtze River Delta, and Pearl River Delta region. The Pearl River Delta region in Guangdong province has now become a major manufacturing center and one of the most attractive regions for Japanese companies since the Open and Reform in late 1970s, owning to its open investment environments, integration of different cultures, and geographical advantages. In 1980s, many Japanese electrical and electronic companies invested in this region due to low labor cost, as well as comparatively developed secondary sectors. When it entered into 1990s, these companies gradually transferred to Yangtze River Delta for a larger market share. Instead, Japanese auto industry began to invest from the year of 1999. Since three auto giants Honda, Toyota, Nissan opened factories in Guangzhou, many auto-related companies and service companies had also established their overseas subsidiaries in this region (Guangzhou Daily, 2007). By December 2010, the registered members of the Guangzhou Japanese Chamber of Commerce and Industry have reached more than 600, including 545 companies, 63 individual members and 71 sponsor companies (the Guangzhou Japanese CCI).

YOWA established its first subsidiary and store in the Pearl River Delta region and at the same time devoted a great deal of capitals and human sources here. By the end of 2010 the company had set up three subsidiaries SEICO Guangdong, YOWA Shenzhen and YOWA China in Guangdong Province. The former two are joint-venture companies by YOWA HK and local retailers, and the last one is a wholly-owned company operated by the parent company YOWA Japan. As of Dec.31th, 2010, these three subsidiaries had run 17 SEICO GMS stores and supermarkets in seven cities along the Pearl River Delta. (Figure 7.1)

The open investment environments and good economic situation of Guangdong province is one of the attractions. Firstly, Guangdong province has been a pioneer in the Economic Reform, as well as a gateway to attract foreign investment throughout Mainland. Among the 11 original cities or special economic zones that had been approved for overseas capitals to enter into Chinese market by the central government in 1992, Guangdong occupied four, which made it the most proper site for YOWA's initial deployment in Mainland China. In addition, according to the National Bureau of Statistics of China, in 2008, the GDP of Guangdong province reached ¥3569.646 billion (US $512.69 billion), increased by 10.1% compared to 2007.

As the Figure 7.2 demonstrates, from the year of 1995, the GDP of Guangdong province kept growing at a quite stable speed in spite of various growth rates in different years. The living standards in Guangdong province has been enhancing as well. Furthermore, according to the 2008 Provincial Census, the Pearl River Delta zone had a population of 47.7 million people. By examining the per capita disposable income of the urban households (Table 7.2) in the seven cities where SEICO stores located, we could find that from 2007, this statistic has been growing substantially in recent years and exceeded 20,000 RMB in seven cities except Huizhou, which shows high consumption capabilities of these cities.

FIGURE 7.1
CITIES IN GUANGDONG PROVINCE WHERE
SEICO STORES LOCATE

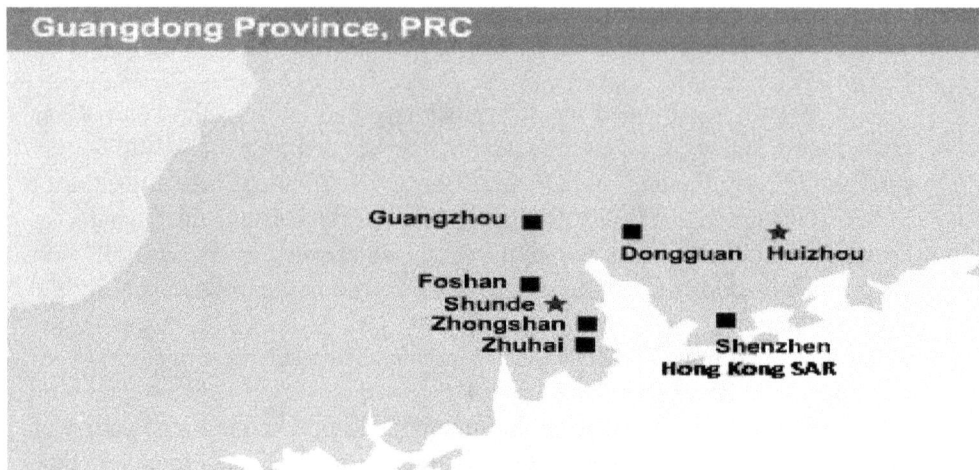

Note: ■stands for GMS or multi-supermarkets ★stands for shopping centers

FIGURE 7.2
LOCAL PRODUCTION AND GROWTH RATE OF GUANGDONG
PROVINCE FROM 1978 TO 2008

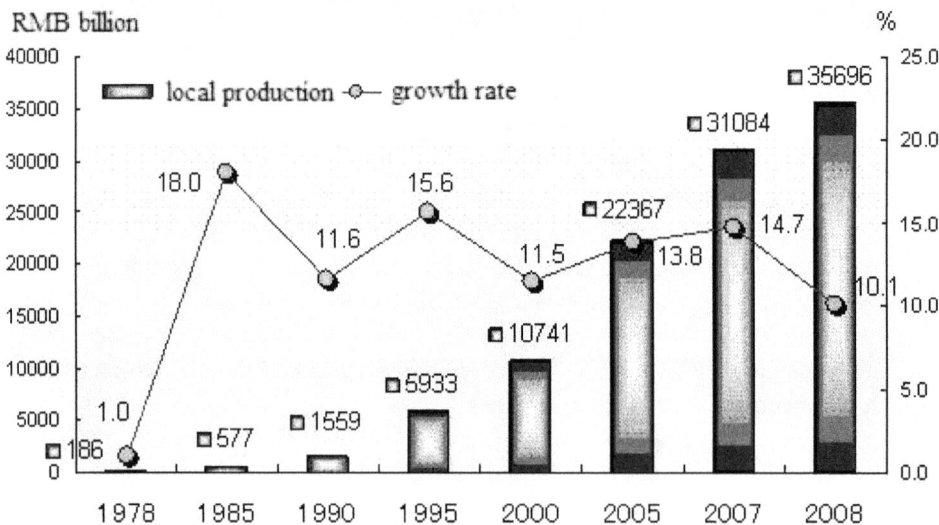

Data Source: National Bureau of Statistics of China

TABLE 7.2
PER CAPITA DISPOSABLE INCOME OF URBAN HOUSEHOLDS
BY CITY (RMB)

City/Year	2000	2005	2007	2008
Shenzhen	21577	28665	33593	26729
Dongguan	14226	22882	28209	30274
Shunde	14394	21015	25301	26433
Guangzhou	13622	18287	22469	25317
Foshan	11977	17680	21112	22494
Zhuhai	15376	18908	20516	20949
Zhongshan	-	17256	20317	21560
Huizhou	10328	15763	18770	19481

Data Source: Guangdong Statistical Yearbook 2009

Another attraction is the geographical advantage of Guangdong province, as a place closely links with Hong Kong, where the parent company YOWA HK locates. The transportation between any cities in Guangdong and Hong Kong is convenient. Take Guangzhou as an example, it is a port city alongside the Pearl River and locates about 120 km (75 miles) northwest of Hong Kong. The fact that it only takes 110 minutes to travel between the two cities makes it convenient to transfer capitals, equipments and resources directly from YOWA HK to Guangzhou.

The final attraction might be the similar cultural influences between Guangdong and Hong Kong. Rooted from the same Cantonese culture, Cantonese people are willing to absorb foreign cultural goods and transform them into local uses as the Hong Kong people. In this way, the successful experience of doing business in Hong Kong enabled YOWA to realize its localization in Guangdong province without much difficulty than in any other cities in Mainland China. YOWA's operation and localization should be understood in this economic and society background.

YOWA'S BUSINESS CHARACTERISTICS IN MAINLAND CHINA

We might make this argument more clearly from a comparative perspective. Here I choose to take YOWA and another Chinese local GMS store Vanguard into comparison. Vanguard GMS store, which belongs to the CR Vanguard retail group, is ranked as No.1 chain store in Mainland China. This retail group is further controlled by the CR Vanguard group, a state-holding enterprise. Although both YOWA and Vanguard are doing business on GMS stores, they still vary greatly from each other.

In terms of the store numbers, the expansions of YOWA has been much slower and geographically limited compared with the local retailer Vanguard. As the statistics of 2010 (collected from the retailer's official website) shows, Vanguard owned 15 GMS stores in Guangzhou, while YOWA had operated 5 stores: one was food supermarket, and the other four were GMS stores. Geographically, the retail group of Vanguard owned 3200 stores (in various retail formats) in more than 100 cities of Mainland China, while YOWA only operated in Guangdong province (in the Southern China), Shandong province (Eastern China), Hong Kong and Beijing (in total 15 cities including Guangzhou, Foshan, Shunde, Shenzhen, Dongguan, zhuhai, Huizhou, zhongshan in Guangdong province; Qingdao, Yantai, Weifang, Weihai, Zibo in Shandong province; Hong Kong and Beijing).

In terms of location selection, all the YOWA stores in Guangzhou were located in major business districts where are directly connected to the subway. On the opposite, all of the 15 Vanguard stores were opened near residential communities. In terms of the overall company image, shopping environments, promotion strategies, quality of merchandises and service, YOWA was distinctive compared to Vanguard. Firstly, YOWA's overall image was impressive with its Japanese identity. There were many special signs and activities help to show its identity, such as the 'Japanese food street', the 'thankful footprint' action, the 'Astro Boy's cleaning action', the sales of lucky bags (fukubukuro, 福袋) as well as some environmental activities. These special activities with unique Japanese style were appealing to customers, especially those who have a certain affinity to Japanese culture.

Secondly, YOWA made great efforts on shopping environments than Vanguard. The YOWA stores were well-decorated with seasonal features and holiday atmosphere, and provide considerate hardware facilities such as clean wash rooms and mothers' lounge. And under the framework of the free-entrance concept, customers could feel free and enjoyable. Also the light music broadcasting in the stores made the shopping environment more relaxed and somewhat upper-class. Thirdly, YOWA's promotion strategies were diverse. It emphasized on good quality rather than low price as Vanguard. It acted quickly to catch the customers by changing the promotion themes and providing shopping suggestions according to holidays and seasons. Fourthly, the service quality of YOWA was relatively high. All the workers were trained to be very polite and helpful. In addition, there were some extra services like free packaging (especially during the gift-giving season) and home delivery which were in favor of customers.

Finally, a difference which can be found from the above discussions is that YOWA and Vanguard targeted different customers. For Vanguard, it mainly tried to attract people living in residential communities nearby, with strong need of everyday necessities, in reasonable or low prices. In contrast,

YOWA was appealing to customers with mid-to-high level incomes who had special demands in symbol consumption, such as quality, service, environments, and standards which lie behind the goods, and provided one-stop shopping experiences of higher level (Yohogi, 2007; Wang, 2009). From the comparison with a local retailer Vanguard, we can see the differences of location selection, overall image, shopping environment, promotion strategies, merchandises and service standards, and targeted customers made YOWA distinctive in Mainland China. It can be inferred that these differences were highly likely rooted in two profound reasons: one is YOWA's competitiveness and distinctiveness as a Japanese retailer and the other is YOWA's adjustments through the localization process in the Chinese context.

YOWA'S TRANSFORMATIONS IN CHINESE CONTEXT

There are two main transformations YOWA made in Mainland China. The first one is YOWA was operated with Chinese-intensive management and changed some of its human resource management strategies. And the other one is YOWA adopted the consignment mode and fully utilized promoters employed by suppliers as non-regular but long-term workers in an attempt to act similarly as its counterparts in Mainland, enhance its dominant position in the retailer-supplier relationship, and most importantly, reduce its labor cost. I will use the statistic of SEICO GD, one of YOWA's subsidiaries in Guangdong Province to demonstrate these two transformations. The company of SEICO GD included the headquarters in Guangzhou, and 10 stores in several cities in Guangdong province.

Human Resource Management Strategy

Japanese MNEs have long been criticized for lagging behind Western companies in the localization of management practices, and its ethnocentric practice, as well as the persistence of expatriate-intensive management (Kopp, 1999; Pucik, 1999). However, my study of YOWA shows a sharp contrast with these studies by the fact of a decrease in the number of Japanese expatriates and a massive increase of local employees. Furthermore, my study also indicates YOWA's changes in human resource management strategies to adjust to Chinese society by the positive use of local female workers, the status change of part-timers, and the new innovation of promoters as main labor force.

Firstly, through a detailed analysis of the employment statistics of SEICO GD in 2009, I found that among the total number of 2039 employees, there were only five Japanese expatriates at the top of the management hierarchy of this subsidiary, and the rest 2034 were local Chinese employees with majority (86.8%) born and educated in Guangdong province. Except for the five Japanese expatriates working in the headquarters, there were no other Japanese or Hong Kong employees working in SEICO GD, and all the rest managerial positions were occupied by Mainland Chinese, including the most essential position in stores: the 'store manager'. It helps to illustrate an orientation that local employees were greatly relied on in SEICO GD.

Secondly, also from the employment statistics, I found regular employees in SEICO GD were predominantly female, especially in stores. Take the Sunny store as an example, of the total 439 regular employees, 319 (72.7%) were women. In terms of gender distribution, the employment in SEICO GD has followed the overall pattern for chain stores in Mainland China that females are regarded as the major labor force rather than short-term commitment workers in Japan. Furthermore, among the 79 employees of the managerial rank in Sunny store, 60 (76%) were women and also, eight out of ten store managers were females. It helps to indicate that the roles female employees played in YOWA were distinctive compared to the parent company in Japan. Women were greatly relied on and placed in high managerial positions with good career prospects. YOWA noticed the differences between Japan and China in the female employment patterns, and adjusted its HRMs to it.

Thirdly, there was an important change in the number of part-time workers in 2008 which can help to understand YOWA's HRMs in Mainland. Part-time workers belong to the category of non-regular workers, those who return to work on a part-time basis or those who were not under the official labor contracts with the company. Part-timers were once the main labor force of YOWA, both in parent company and overseas subsidiaries. However, the new labor contract law which went into effect on January 1st, 2008 suggests: "Non-full-time labor refers to a form of labor for which the remuneration is generally calculated on a hourly basis, the average working hours of a worker each day shall not be more than four hours and the cumulative working hours per week for the same employer shall not be more than 24 hours." Due to legal reasons, the number of part-timers decreased into only one person in SEICO GD suddenly in 2008, and nearly all of them were transformed into regular full-time workers.

Finally, the fully utilization of promoters is also an important issue in discussing the HRMs of YOWA in Mainland China. The promoters in YOWA can also be identified as non-regular workers. They were sent by the supplying company which cooperated with YOWA, and worked in YOWA at the company's complete disposal. The latest statistics of January 2009 shows that there were 1333 promoters working in the Sunny store of SEICO GD. This phenomenon could be easily observed in any supermarkets in China, while hardly existing at all in chain stores in Japan. By adopting others' employees as long-term workers in the stores, YOWA once again made important changes to its HRMs in Mainland.

Consignment Mode and Promoter System

The consignment counter with promoters is a cooperate mode between retailers and suppliers. YOWA adopted this consignment mode and fully utilized promoters as non-regular but long-term workers through the localization process in Mainland China, which is seldom be found in its parent company in Japan.

Under the mode of consignment, YOWA sold merchandises as the dealer of the suppliers for a share of the profits or commissions. For the suppliers, goods on consignment equaled to the articles on a specialty counters inside the consignment store. The suppliers sent several long-term promoters into the stores and in this way had their sales well organized according to both their actual needs and the store's condition, such as sales promotion, tallying, ordering and receiving of the goods. While on the side of YOWA, it only provided space and facilities for the suppliers and arranged promotions occasionally under the name of YOWA. In return, a certain percentage of the total sales were given monthly as commissions by each consignment brand. Besides, an annual rebate of sales, warehouse rentals, utilities, miscellaneous expenses including entrance fees, sponsorships for new-store anniversary celebration, contract renewal fees, new membership fees, etc. had also to be paid to the company of YOWA. To some extent, YOWA here played the role of a lesser, while the suppliers were just like the tenants. The consignment mode in YOWA exactly followed that of the department stores in China.

The phenomenon of promoters happened together with the consignment mode, it can easily be observed in most if not all supermarkets and department stores in Mainland. Promoters refer to people who were employed by the supply companies which cooperate with the retail stores, however work in the latter as sales clerks to improve the sales performance of a certain brand or a company. It is a win-win result of the market liberalization and the fierce competitions between suppliers. It provides more work opportunities in the society, improves the sales performance of the suppliers, reduces the personnel outlay of the retailers, and to some extent, guides the consumers to face massive merchandises. By utilizing promoters, YOWA acted similarly as the other local Chinese retailers, and successfully reduced its personnel outlay.

According to the director of SEICO GD, over 90% of the business of SEICO GD was operated in consignment mode, and virtually all the suppliers had to send promoters as free labor force. An employment statistic showed that in January 2009, there were totally 1333 promoters in one typical store of SEICO GD (93.9% of them were females), while only 279 regular YOWA employees in the same store. The proportion of 1333: 279 was expressive. In other words, there were almost five promoters out of every six workers on average. Therefore, promoters should not be viewed as peripheral or dispensable, but long-term major workforce of YOWA.

From a questionnaire survey of the working and living conditions of promoters, certain characteristics of these promoters turned out to be evident. In the term of age distribution, half of them were between the age of 26 to 35, which was an energetic, mature period of their lives, as well as an age of children rearing and family burden; Concerning their educational background, over half of the promoters graduated from high schools, while the other half were junior school graduates, which indicated a relatively low educational status among this group of workers; Considering the previous working experiences and working motivations, the promoters could be classified into two categories: the laid-off workers"(下崗工人）and floating labor （流動人口）. The lay-off workers here refer to people who became unemployed at the age of 40 or older after the Reform of State-owned Enterprises in the 1990s and the 2000s, while the floating labor refer to people who left hometowns for big cities in order to get better life and opportunities, both of whom were working for supporting their families.

Promoters spread throughout the stores in every section, the basic working units in YOWA, and were under the supervisions of section chiefs and ordinary staff. They were involved into YOWA's organization in everyday operation. Recruited and paid by the suppliers, however worked under the total management of YOWA, promoters were actually subject to dual managerial control of several levels both the suppliers and retailers. Their job contents not only included the sales performance of their own companies, but also extra work assigned by YOWA. They were trained regularly about the service standards and corporate culture of the company, and were checked whether they had mastered through 'mystery shopper', which means a person goes in pretending to be an ordinary shopper and evaluates the customer service received by the store. The management skills towards promoters included both firm controls like fine punishments and conciliatory approaches such as helps on their sales, conveniences given to their personnel arrangements as well as spiritual encouragement and material rewards. By doing so, YOWA fully utilized this group of free labors and reduced its personnel layouts in Chinese markets.

The consignment mode and promoters' phenomenon are resulted in the imbalanced relation in the supply-demand and the transformation from the seller's market to the buyer's market in China at present. In an attempt to compete with its counterparts in Mainland, YOWA adopted the similar strategies which were never taken in its own country. In this way, YOWA enhanced its dominant position in the retailer-supplier relationship, and most importantly, reduced its labor cost.

CONCLUSION

Through the investigations of YOWA's investments in Guangdong province, the business characteristics, as well as transformations it made in China, this paper examined YOWA's localization process and strategies. There are three main findings in this paper. Firstly, from the comparison with a local retailer Vanguard, we can see the differences of location selection, overall image, shopping environment, promotion strategies, merchandise and service standards, and targeted customers made YOWA distinctive in Mainland China. On one hand, these differences were highly likely rooted from its competitiveness and distinctiveness as a Japanese retailer and on the other hand, they were resulted from YOWA's adjustments through the localization process in the Chinese context.

Secondly, YOWA was operated with Chinese-intensive management and changed some of its human resource management strategies. Local Chinese employees sourced the overwhelming majority of the workforce and were placed in important managerial positions. Although the organizational system of YOWA in Mainland was transplanted from its parent company in Hong Kong with minor alterations, we still confirm this feature in the terms of employment pattern, which contained several interesting variations compared to the cases of Nagasakiya (Matsunaga, 2000) and Fumei (Wong, 1999). For example, the positive utilization of local female employees and management trainees, the employment status change of part-timers, the innovation of promoters as main labor force, and so on.

Finally, YOWA adopted the consignment mode and fully utilized promoters employed as non-regular but long-term workers in an attempt to act similarly as its counterparts in Mainland, enhance its dominant position in the retailer-supplier relationship, and most importantly, reduce its labor cost successfully. The employment statistics revealed that, there were five promoters out of every six workers on the sales floor, in a typical YOWA store in China. Promoters sourced vast majority of the workforce in the store and did not cost YOWA any money. All YOWA had to do was supervising and utilizing them.

All of the three findings were resulted from the process of YOWA's localization and in varying degrees, revealed its efforts in adjusting to and aligning with the external economic and culture environment of Mainland China. From the above discussions, we can found that adjusting to the local context is an important issue in localization of MNEs. This paper set out to contribute to the understanding of localization process and strategies of a

Japanese overseas retail group in Guangzhou, Mainland China. Although the paper is based on only one case, the findings concluded may provide insight and relevant information to both academics and practitioners. Further researches based on a deeper analysis should be adopted to explore the interactions between the overseas company with Japanese employees, as well as the relationship among Japanese expatriates and local employees, which constituted the company's institutional culture.

Authored by Huang Wang, originally published in *International Journal of China Marketing*, Vol. 2(2) 2012, pp. 107-122.

Part II: Marketing Mix in China

Chapter Eight

Shanzhai as a Weak Brand in Contemporary China Marketing

Shanzhai as a special brand is widespread in contemporary China. Shanzhai marketing is becoming marketing innovation model for weak brands. The current researches on Shanzhai marketing focus on the Shanzhai marketing phenomenon but are lack of theoretical analysis. This study aims to interpret the theoretical foundations for Shanzhai marketing from various marketing perspectives, and probes the marketing implications for weak brands. It first reviews Shanzhai marketing's origin, background, definition and types, then explores the motivation and possibilities for weak brands to carry out Shanzhai marketing, and finally concludes the marketing implications that weak brands can conduct Shanzhai marketing strategy in its start-up period. It reaches the conclusion that Shanzhai marketing which is given rise to in particular Chinese marketing environment is becoming marketing model for weak brands to develop quickly at low cost, and innovative marketing model which adapts to the dynamic changes in Chinese market and the changes in consumers' behavior.

INTRODUCTION

Since the Reform and Opening-Up, China not only has a large increase in GDP but has gone through profound changes in all the areas. Compared with European and American market, Chinese market has some special features: The mainstream products in the market have monopolistic advantage while small and medium-sized enterprises (SMEs) lack resources either in power or in finance to support and expand the development; Taking advantage of reduced technical doorsill in some industries in recent years, many SMEs even family-run workshops produce different kinds of products to meet people's needs especially people with low-income; Chinese people's average income has risen sharply, and therefore their consuming capacity has been improved greatly, which contributes to a large increase in brand awareness. Although worshipping domestic and international top brands has become a trend in China, most of Chinese consumers don't have enough purchasing power for the big brands; the idea of despising authority and pursuit of personality has become a new and negligible force as the growing up of 1980s and 1990s generation. Influenced by such an idea, the Chinese consumers, especially those who were born in the 1980s and 1990s, stand in an opposition to mainstream products and monopolistic products. Due to the changes in Chinese market and consumers, Shanzhai products are welcomed and accepted as soon as they appear in the market.

Shanzhai phenomenon first originated from the mobile phone industry, then expanded to MP3, game machines, DVD and other different areas before it spreads to the whole digital area. By means of network, Shanzhai has reached to all areas of people's lives. Beginning in 2007, "Shanzhai" is becoming a folk culture in Chinese society. Shanzhai film, Shanzhai star, Shanzhai brands and other Shanzhai appears one after another. K-Touch (天语), an newly-emerged domestic mobile phone brand which integrates many useful and excellent features of mobile phones like Nokia, Samsung and Motorola, and Adivon (阿迪王), a newly-emerged domestic sports outfit brand with Chinese characters meaning of exceeding Addidas, stand as the representatives（Xu, 2009）

OVERVIEW AND BASIC CONCEPT

The Origin and Background of Shanzhai

The rising of Shanzhai phenomenon is related to the Reform and Opening Up. In the beginning, traces of Shanzhai can be found in China's many high-tech companies, private technology enterprises, as well as township enterprises. In fact, as early as 2001, in Zhejiang Cixi, the small appliance manufacturing center, or in IT industry gathering cities, like Guangdong Dongguan, consumers can always see some familiar but confusing ads: "Daneng" washing machine, "BMW" fan, Samsung Okma refrigerator, and NOKLA mobile phone (Xu, 2009). These products are manufactured and sold by means of copying or imitating brand name, but they are welcomed by people with limited consumption capacity for the cheap prices.

Shanzhai originated from the mobile phone industry. Since 2005, Chinese electronics manufacturing industry has lowered its control and technical threshold, so many small companies in Shenzhen, Jiangsu and Zhejiang (most developed provinces in China) started to engage in. Take mobile phone industry for example, a large number of manufacturers, which rely on imitation, innovation and cheap price, have emerged. These manufacturers first imitate mainstream brands' appearance or function, and then make some innovations, finally exceed them either in appearance, function or price. With the policy and technical barriers further reduced, Shanzhai manufacturing is expanding from the mobile phone industry to various fields in the IT industry. Many SMEs are characteristic of small capital investment, low-cost operation, quick response to market, and short product life cycle. So although start from imitation or OEM, many SMEs can survive in the market, even exceed the big brands by developing Shanzhai marketing.

Shanzhai Marketing's Definition and Types

"Shanzhai products" are defined as those products which lack technology, and cheap copies of big brand products. They are provided to satisfy people's desire for some products (cultural products included) they appreciate but can't afford due to limited consumption ability. Those products are quickly provided, can meet people's needs, and sold at low price. They are manufactured in terms of "copy, imitation, learning and improvement" to replace the old and long-existing products which lack innovation and updating. (Tao, 2010)

Shanzhai products are favored by many consumers. Take its source "Shanzhai mobile phone" for example. Its sales growth is impressive because of its low prices. "Shanzhai fighter", "K-Touch" has a bigger sales growth even than mobile phone manufacturing giants Motorola, Samsung, Sony Ericsson, and LG. . CCTV news reports that in 2007 at least 150 million "Shanzhai phone" are produced, almost the same as total sales of mobile phones in domestic market. An online survey shows 66.15% people said they would consider buying Shanzhai phone, 76.2% thought buying Shanzhai phone is reasonable, only 14.5% consider it as infringement and should be cracked down.

Shanzhai Marketing is innovative for the Chinese SMEs to build and develop brands in the start-up period. Shanzhai marketing is an approach which enables SMEs to produce "quickly-provided, to meet civilians' needs, marketable, of multiple functions and low price" products in terms of "copy, imitation, learning, innovation and improvement" in big brands' appearance, functions and even the name; and a approach to realize original accumulation of capital and initial building of its own brand. When SMEs have developed into a certain size and their brands have considerable strength, they develop timely strategies to "de-Shanzhai" to achieve rapid building and development.

SMEs' Shanzhai marketing is a copy and innovation for big brands' marketing. The specific performance of its strategy has the following types:

First, a full copy of digital products is most typical. Shanzhai mobile phone is the source which Shanzhai popularizes. The products are 100% the same as the mainstream brands in style, appearance, technology, function and brand names.

Shanzhai phone are copies of big brands such as Nokia, Samsung, and Sony-Ericsson in function and appearance. Even some brand names are changed to Nokir, Samsing, Suny-Ericcsun to seek similarity. Because of copy, companies can save R&D costs and therefore the price is only one-fifth of the regular products or less. Although the material quality and technologies are lower, its multiple functions and fashionable appearance can make them favored by low-end consumers.

Second, some Shanzhai brands confuse consumers by imitating big brands' brand names, trademarks, packaging and other outside cognitive factors to achieve sales objectives.

Many Shanzhai brands attract consumers' attention by imitating big brands' brand names, trademarks and slogans to achieve sales. Such as the following ambiguous brand names Sqny, Adidos, Fuma, Pama, Hike, Tochifa, which are respectively imitations of Sony, Addidas, Puma, Nike, and Toshiba? Imitation of some familiar brands' cognitive factors can be very confusing for consumers. For example, one consumer purchased a pair of Double Star shoes ("double star" is a famous sport-shoes brand in China). But the shoes are actually branded "Double Star Shoe".

Third, Shanzhai brands imitate big brands' marketing communication strategy and channel operation strategy and therefore are similar in brand advertising planning, creativity and communications, and brand spokesperson, so consumers can be easily confused.

Take Shanzhai spokesman for example. Many domestic TV shows are producing Shanzhai stars, such as Zhou Wings, Zhou Caifeng, Shanzhai version of Jay Chou and Zhou Huajian (both are famous Chinese pop singers). For Many SMEs, on one hand, they want to expand their markets and increase brand awareness and reputation, on the other hand, they have a shortage of capital, so they have to choose Shanzhai stars as their spokesperson, which is consistent with "more, faster, better and cheaper" commercial advertising investment principles. For example, it seems that American President Obama is advertising for "Imperial" clothing because you can see President Obama is smiling on the billboard, but in fact, famous photographer Yilehamu has his signature in the lower corner.

THE MOTIVATION AND POSSIBILITIES FOR SHANZHAI MARKETING

SMEs generally own weak brands. How to build and accumulate brand equity is a problem that troubles the scholars and entrepreneurs. Shanzhai brand strategy is not only one of the shortcuts for companies to build brands in early period of capital accumulation and early period of building brands, but also an innovative marketing pattern for SMEs. Prevalence of Shanzhai marketing is analyzed from brand growth path, marketing strategy and consumers' changing behavior.

Low-cost for Weak Brands' Growth

SMEs generally have weak brands which attributes to scarce financial support. Therefore, weak brands should develop not only innovative and offensive but also defensive and concentrating strategies, rather than dispersing resources to market segments. In the initial stage of brand building, there are two basic routes to take. First, pull by high-cost ads; second, promote by low-cost products. In the second route, SMEs invest limited money in the key factor—products. In brands building, relevant elements of products take an active role through design and planning, advertising withdrawing to a secondary position (Liu, 2007). A dramatic increase in advertising price push high the cost of new product promotion and a strong market competition makes more difficult new products promotion. Under the second route and in the absence of advertising, the average market share is no more than 4 percent. To realize the dream of a strong brand, transformation of the original brand and advertising promotion are compulsive to ensure more than 10% market share.

SMEs Shanzhai brand strategy is an embodiment of the second route. Starting from early imitation, and operating a profitable project based on "short, flat and fast," SMEs quickly finish capital accumulation. In this process, Shanzhai brands take advantage of low cost, big brands' advertising, low prices and "familiar" brand image quickly to open up markets and seize more shares in lower market to achieve sales expansion.

Shanzhai Brand Can Attract Consumers' Attention and Lead to Purchase

About current economic trends, with the development of information, what values is not information but attention. Michael H. Goldhaber (1997) adopts the concept of "Attention Economy" in his 1997 *The Attention Economy and the Net*. It is coupled with the information age, and its biggest feature is the excessive products and scarce attention. The core is to obtain and maintain more consumers' attention. Attention Economy is an economic pattern to maximize future commercial interests by attracting the maximum attention of the user or consumer and therefore developing the potential consumer groups.

In the time when consumers' self-awareness is rising, and access to information is increasingly diversified, rejecting traditional literacy and information-based indoctrination marketing to choose "Eyeball Economy" was particularly important. It is a must and premise for consumers to buy goods. By imitating the appearance of well-known brand products, brand names, product LOGO, and slogans Shanzhai brands lead consumers to discuss in the hope of acquiring consumers' attention, and thus enhancing sales possibilities.

Marketing Environment Changes Lead to Changes in Consumers' Behavior

Consumers' preferences and habits have undergone major changes in the late 1990s. Consumers' lifestyle is a moving target, as is put: society's focus and preferences are constantly changing (Solomon, 2004). One of the current global trends is consumers' need for convenience is increasing; value-oriented consumers want to show their unique personality and they begin to reflect on the past consumption pattern. In showing personality, Shanzhai brands' appearance is beyond comparison for many well-known brands. Their designs show not only current trends, but also international fashion style, and their functions are no worse than all big brands.

The development and change in domestic consumers' behavior cannot be ignored. Chinese consumers' unique behaviors can be divided into Face Consumption, Comparing Consumption, Show-off Consumption and Symbolic Consumption. As digital products popularize in market, consumers have become more rational, value-oriented, emphasizing on the function and role, and more sensitive to price (Lu, 2005).

China's newly emerged consumers are composed of people born in 1980s and 1990s. Many lifestyle changes in consumer behavior are promoted by young consumers. They constantly redefine what is the most popular and what is not. (Solomon, 2004) China's new consumer group is one-child-only generation, or the E generation (referring to the group growing in network and electronic media "Electronic" age). Their consumption behavior and psychology are different from other generations in better tolerance, strong curiosity, a strong self-sense, leading to consumption features like diversity-- a decline in brand loyalty, consumer autonomy -- try before purchase, the effectiveness of their choice -- emphasis on function rather than form. The rise of 1980s and 1990s paves the way for the popularity of Shanzhai products. These people are characterized by contempt for authority, dislike being rule-bound and little care for brands.

Changes in the marketing environment and consumers' psychology and behavior also reflect the current social and cultural environment. On one hand, they fit the current popular culture "anti-authority, anti-monopoly, anti-elite," on the other hand, they have strong characteristics of subverting and destroying the existing social order. Shanzhai brand is part of consumer culture. Shanzhai is a manifestation of pursuing individuality, a mockery of mainstream culture. Therefore, for urban white-collar and the new generation born in the 1980s and 1990s who pursue fashion and personality, Shanzhai brands which are cheap and amusing are welcomed and favored.

CCDVTP 4P Marketing Model Replacing the Traditional Model

Facing a changing marketing, Philip Kotler, "father of modern marketing," modified his "4P" theoretical model and replaced it with the latest marketing model CCDVTP (Kotler, 2003). The so-called CCDVTP means for short: Create, Communicate, Deliver Value, Target and Profit. CCDVTP points out that in order to create a good brand, enterprises must constantly communicate with consumers; deliver brand's unique value while being aware of their target market to take every opportunity to make profits. CCDVTP model is to achieve profitability by means of innovation, communication and value delivery in target market. In Marketing-triumph time, SMEs must adapt to market changes, update their market strategies, find out target market and enhance interactive communication with consumers. Double-way communication, full practice and using CDVTP model are of great significance.

Market has undergone tremendous changes, likewise are consumers' psychology and behavior. On one hand, with the monopoly and control of the market price, big manufacturers make large profits, but ordinary consumers lack sufficient purchasing ability; on the other hand, the popularity of the Internet allows consumers to learn about products' cost. Sales price is far more than those consumers can accept especially in fields as sport outfits, shoes and hats. SMEs Shanzhai brands are copies of big brands in appearance, design, and function but with cheaper price, more functions and appearance that is more original. Shanzhai brands have lower manufacturing costs, advertising costs and marketing costs, so ordinary consumers naturally can accept them, and satisfy the needs for vanity of low and middle income groups (Wang and Shen, 2007).

Although today's market is fragmented, individualized, consumers' demands are different and personalized; Shanzhai brands can fully underpin their adapted segments. Effective segmentation of the market, identification of appropriate target market, SMEs must have effective STP strategies in fierce competition. Shanzhai brand can meet the needs of its target market segments. Low cost, stylish appearance and multiple functions can better grasp consumption trends of segmental market. Generally, Shanzhai brands appear more often in rural markets, urban-rural areas, retail outlets and railway stations in urban areas where migrants' workers concentrate. But consumption groups of Shanzhai brands are not limited to low-income groups. A considerable amount of middle-income consumers are Shanzhai brand loyal customers, who are mainly followers of fashion or practicability and their professions cover IT, university teachers, engineers, and low-income groups also include students who learn up-to-date information (Luo, 2009).

Shanzhai brand is an embodiment of SMEs' market segmentation strategy. In terms of products and market segmentation, products' market coverage model can be divided as follows: a concentrated market, product specialization, market specialization, selective specialization, and full coverage. Shanzhai brand belongs to the third model - the market specialization, that's, SMEs position their products as low price for low-income groups. Companies producing Shanzhai products are small in size and have advantages just as small boat turns easily. It is easy for companies to find entry points in the market, and change producing strategies timely with changes in the market.

Shanzhai brand is the use and presentation of product innovation strategies for SMEs (Ruan, 2009). Take Shanzhai phone for example. Shanzhai is an integration of technology, appearance and process innovation. Producers of Shanzhai phone combines the latest vertical and horizontal technology favored by consumers into a new product to occupy more market share realizing 1 +1> 2, and make greater economic profits. These technologies are mainly presented in Shanzhai phones' design concepts, including individualized appearance, high resolution screen, large volume horn, long standby time, and other kinds of useful features.

Elaboration Likelihood Model and Meaning Transfer Model

In 1980s, R.E.Petty etc. brought forward the Elaboration Likelihood Model (ELM), a type of model for consumer information management, which explains how advertising impacts on consumers' attitudes and emphasizes the influence of consumer involvement on advertising effects (Petty, Cacipoop, & Schuman, 1983). The theory reduces the attitude changes into two basic paths: the central and edge. Central route considers attitude change over the products because of consumers' serious consideration and integrating information. On the contrary, edge route sees the change not as the consequence of considering the features or proves but as the consequence of linking it with many clues. The basic principle for ELM model is different persuasion methods rely on the likelihood of elaborating information. When the elaboration likelihood is high, the central route is particularly effective; and when this possibility is low, the edge route is effective.

Consumers can be confused by Shanzhai brands after borrowing big brands' cognitive elements, and therefore develop impulsive or conforming consumption behavior. Shanzhai brands can be found more often in IT field because homogeneity and popularity are obvious in market. Based on such a model, the elaboration likelihood is low when consumers choose Shanzhai products. Their cognitive process and attitude change belongs to the edge route of elaboration likelihood model. Consumers tend to ignore products' features and functions, and more influenced by the explicit elements attached to Shanzhai brands. In this case, consumers develop some preferences and then promote purchase.

In Meaning transfer model, "meaning" refers to the imitation of the famous brand's image. The process of consumers buying the Shanzhai brand is process of famous brands' transferring. This process includes three phases: first, strong brands have been given a certain symbolic meaning for long-term brand equity accumulation, making them representatives of a certain gender, age, social status, life style and consumption situation. Second, Shanzhai brands are imitations of big brands that can attract consumers who worship big brands but have limited consumption ability. As such, the consumers transfer big brands' image to Shanzhai brands consciously and therefore make Shanzhai brands as the alternatives of big brands, and third, Shanzhai brands' target consumers have access to big brands' symbolic meaning by using or consuming these Shanzhai brands. Figure 8.1 shows these processes:

Shanzhai Marketing = Niche Marketing

In marketing, the long tail market is also named "niche market." The internationally famous marketing professor Philip Kotler argues that a business must differentiate itself in ways that are important to the customer, concentrating on one or two areas in which it can be excellent or stand out, such as speed, reliability, service, design, relationships, features, personality, or technology. According to him, "whereas segments are fairly large and normally attract several competitors, niches are fairly small and normally attract one." His definition of an attractive niche is characterized as "the customers in the niche have a distinct set of needs; they will pay a premium to the firm that best satisfies their needs; the niche is not likely to attract other competitor; the niche gains certain economies through specialization; and the niche has size, profit and growth potential" (Kotler, 2003).

The Long Tail theory which is proposed by Chris Anderson (2004) popularizes as the widely use of Internet. It suggests that a market with a high freedom of choice will create a certain degree of inequality by favoring the upper 20% of the items ("head") against the other 80% ("long tail"). In marketing, enterprises tend to concentrate on the 20% of the market share taken by the mainstream commodities which are purchased by 80% of the customers. They ignored the 80% of the market share taken by only 20% of customers. After China's Reform and Opening-up, Chinese economic model has a transition from Planned Economy to Market Economy. Tens of thousands of SMEs which lack government support seize every opportunity to take the niche market overlooked by the mainstream enterprises by manufacturing various products to satisfy the needs of the 80% of customers.

147

FIGURE 8.1
MEANING TRANSFERRING AND SHANZIZED PROCESS

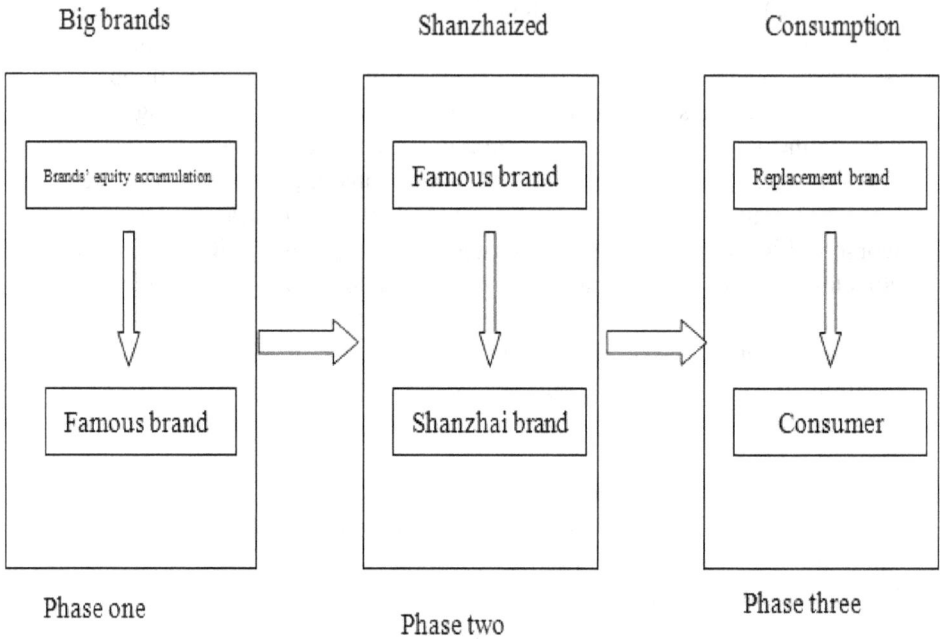

Big brands	Shanzhaized	Consumption
Brands' equity accumulation	Famous brand	Replacement brand
↓	↓	↓
Famous brand	Shanzhai brand	Consumer
Phase one	Phase two	Phase three

So the economy-driven model in China changes from mainstream market to non-mainstream market. The Pareto Principle which was regarded as commercial bible has the potentiality to be changed.

Shanzhai products produced by SMEs make up an essential part of the long tail in Chinese market. CCTV reports that production of Shanzhai mobile phone in 2007 has reached 0.15 billion, which shares between one third and a half of the market share of the year. The production keeps growing in 2008 and has reached 0.2 billion. A considerable number of Shanzhai mobile phone gives multiple choices to customers who have limited consumption capacity or identifies with Shanzhai culture. The Long Tail theory focuses on the market share of the non-mainstream market. It believes "every little makes a nickel" and that the market share can even exceed that of mainstream products. Tao (2010) argues that the number of customers who welcomes Shanzhai products keeps growing, and Shanzhai products are taking more and more market share in the Chinese market.

SHANZHAI BRAND'S MARKETING IMPLICATIONS ON WEAK BRAND

Shanzhai market is a shortcut for SMEs to build their weak brands, and also an innovative marketing approach when Shanzhai culture popularizes. SMEs' Shanzhai brands respond quickly to the market, using strategies of imitation plus innovation and positioning their market accurately. Shanzhai brands choose to avoid strong competitors and target the consumers with lower income to acquire market share. It is because of adapting to market changes and innovative marketing approach that Shanzhai star brands come into being represented by K-Touch and Adivon. Weak brands' Shanzhai marketing strategy brings us many marketing implications.

Shanzhai as the Start-Up Strategy and the Growth Path for Weak Brands

Seeking to develop weak brands through Shanzhai marketing, SMEs must have a deep understanding of Shanzhai brands' different levels. SMEs should persist in innovation based on imitation, discard plagiarism, and never attract consumers' attention by infringement. Low-level Shanzhai is simply plagiarizing while high-level is innovation based on big brands, using SMEs' advantages to carry out innovation which big brands don't work on, such as car phone, music phone, camera-concept mobile phone, and mobile phone equipped with eight overweight bass speakers. Under the pressure of competition in the market, Shanzhai products rise. Many companies realize processing semi-finished products is more convenient than starting from raw materials. Moreover, Shanzhai products have advantages both in price and function through imitations and innovation in appearance and function. Under the precondition of no infringement, no violation of law, imitation is the first step in taking market share, and the first step towards the market.

In the initial stage of brand development there are two basic routes to take; first, pulling through high cost in ads; second, promoting through low-cost products. The second route advocates SMEs to invest limited money in the key point, namely, product itself. In brands' start-up phase, products' related elements take positive role through plan and design while advertising relegates to secondary position. Weak brands' Shanzhai marketing, such as using Shanzhai star as spokesperson and imitating big brands' logo and trademarks, is only a stage and way in the process of building brands, and a speculative choice SMEs have to make in start-up phase. But the starting point and destination of Shanzhai marketing is to make big brands. After acquiring enough original capital, de-Shanzhai strategies must be carried out. Integrated marketing communication strategy can be applied, such as pulling by ads, to raise market share to over 10%, and eventually a strong brand is made.

Weak Brands Need to Innovate on Marketing Communication

SMEs' weak brands have little influence, limited financial support and scarce marketing resources. TV commercials, newspapers, street shows, or new product release cost high for SMEs. Consumers because of its special "Shanzhai" status can reject Shanzhai products. Therefore, SMEs must take marketing innovation into serious consideration, and master accurately key points of Shanzhai marketing communications.

Viral marketing is essentially adding promoting information while providing users with free but valuable services such as free e-books and free email to help users to enjoy network service and entertainment bringing users convenience. If applied correctly, viral marketing can achieve a very significant effect at a very low cost (Leng, 2010). Selecting a unique and valuable topic is particularly important because it can stimulate consumers to purchase through viral marketing's rapid reproduction and dissemination of product information. Adivon is a successful viral marketing model. Creative and humorous network topics edited arbitrarily by netters spread quickly like network viruses. Many Webbers remember "Adivon" after reading posts about "Adivon" online in a delightful manner.

Internet is changing, influencing and dominating people's lives. SMEs must take advantage of network because it attracts a large number of consumers born in 1980s and 1990s who are not offensive over Shanzhai products but very welcome. In terms of network forum, community, blog, online games, QQ group, brands can strengthen interaction with Webbers. Viral marketing not only reduces cost but also has a significant effect on target consumers.

After SMEs have obtained achievements in brand building, their products have gained a certain degree of awareness and reputation, and word of mouth marketing effect begins to take shape, enterprises must develop integrated marketing communication strategy, which means to combine network marketing and traditional TV advertising marketing, to further enhance brand awareness and reputation and increase sales.

Word-of-mouth communication allows people to discuss products and services and makes the dialogue easy and practical. It is an art and a science to start positive and beneficial dialogues between consumers and consumers, between consumers and marketers. Word-of-mouth communication can not only stimulate positive communication, help SMEs to reduce marketing budgets, bring new clients to increase sales, but also play an important role in establishing a good reputation for brands.

Weak Brands Must Specify Appropriate STP Strategy

SMEs must have a clear STP strategy, position accurately the market, and grasp the target market. It is very difficult for SMEs to open the first and second class market with weak brands, so the third and forth class market is appropriate. Most Shanzhai products are highly competitive in that they can always find the lowest-cost supply and the most convenient access channels, so their advantage in cost performance is evident, especially in the third and forth class market. This strategy allows weak brand to evade big brands' competing pressures, discover new market segments, and fill the empty spaces. This is Shanzhai brands' first step towards market.

Weak Brands Can Make Use of Imitation-Plus-Innovation Strategy to Penetrate Into the Market At a Low Cost in the Start-Up Period

SMEs can improve and innovate marketing elements like products, brands, advertising and channel, which are based on imitation. New ideas and concepts are added, different functions are integrated. Similar designs, packaging and brand names attract young consumers' attention. It provides new generation consumes motives for purchase. Compared to high prices of big brands, the low price of Shanzhai brands makes it possible for low-income consumers to satisfy their admiration and vanity for big brands.

Weak Brands Can Make Use of Word-Of-Mouth Marketing, Event Marketing, Story Marketing and Other Emerging Low-Cost Marketing Approaches to Adapt to Changing Trends in Marketing and Consumers' Behavior, Grasp Consumers' Core Needs, and Enhance Brands' Images.

Event marketing is enterprises' involving in public' focus, bringing themselves into the focus, to attract media and public's attention; enterprises can also attract the attention through creative activities planned by themselves. Linking products' core values and elements skillfully with big events, or making news for the need of marketing promotion will undoubtedly enhance brands' awareness and reputation. This is a remarkable way for Shanzhai brands to carry out low-cost marketing. Weak brands relate themselves appropriately to big events, and bring themselves to the center of media and public attention, which will no doubt play an important role in weak brands' promotion and development.

Story Marketing is to put emotions into the brands in the form of story to increase the brands' core culture when products reach a relatively mature phase. It enables the products to move the consumers through releasing their core emotion, assisted by the function and concept needs, and therefore ensure a explosive increase while maintain a stable increase in sales. Weak brands can make use of story marketing to help with word of mouth communication. At present, most products produced by small-sized and medium-sized enterprises are relatively mature and popularized products, having a high degree of market homogeneity. In this case, SMEs should segment the market and position their products accurately. They can design products using story as the starting point, conforming to the target consumers' needs in brand names, products' appearance design and packaging design, create a personalized image, and carry out advertising planning and marketing planning centered on the story to fit the theme of the brand's communication.

SMEs develop Shanzhai marketing, take advantage of new-century consumers' activity and behavior, steer marketing communication, capture "active group" and "opinion leaders", form heated topics, and contribute to interpersonal word-of-mouth communication. With the time of needs for personality coming, enterprise must develop marketing strategies which can apply to consumers' psychological needs, cultivate "opinion leaders" in target consumers, discover and even produce topics appreciated by target consumers. By making use of events, through target consumers' word of mouth communication and viral communication, purchase potentiality can be fully released.

CONCLUSION AND MARKETING IMPLICATIONS

It is necessary to indicate that this study has several limitations. Firstly, it has theoretical analysis of Shanzhai marketing; however, it lacks quantitative research based on a massive investigation into the market. Secondly, it doesn't take into account the differences in different product types, thus it is recommendable that a thorough and specific analysis should be conducted. Last but not least, most of the references quoted in this study are limited to China, so it is suggested that a worldwide research on Shanzhai marketing should be done. The next study is expected to collect more data and materials related to Shanzhai marketing from both home and abroad. Then, it selects a specific product of an industry to carry out a large-scale market investigation into Shanzhai consumers, employees in enterprises manufacturing Shanzhai products as well as the government. By using various statistical models and analyzing the influence of various factors over Shanzhai marketing, it targets to construct the theoretical model of Shanzhai marketing.

Authored by Xionghui Leng and Mingyan Zhang, originally published in *International Journal of China Marketing*, Vol. 1(2) 2011, pp. 81-94.

Chapter Nine

Expecting Marketing Activities and New Product Launch Execution to Be Different in the U.S. and China: An Empirical Study

Most new product studies focus on early steps in the process, trying to speed the process steps to market launch, or trying to control costs via staging and other efficiency actions to increase operations efficiency. Few studies examine the impact of commercialization and launch activities of marketers, the effects of marketing activities on launch execution and timing, and the impact of marketing and launch activities on new product performance. Launch activities are critical in the long term, since they influence the firm's cash flow for the next five years, the average cash flow generating life of a successful innovative product. Our model explores the effects of marketing and launch activity execution, launch timing, and nature of the product on performance, considering also the SBU's level of cross-functional integration and market orientation, and levels of channel cooperation. ** We empirically test the model using new product managers from the U.S. and China, and generate insights into cross cultural differences in marketing conduct, observe the robustness of our model, and provide contextual variations sufficient to reduce frame and sampling biases that haunt the study of innovation success.

INTRODUCTION

There are significant payoffs to successful launch execution. First, launch costs and risks are substantial, indeed launch can easily cost more than R&D, engineering, and development costs combined (Urban and Hauser, 1993; Hultink et al., 1997; Guiltinan, 1999). The launch stage is strategically important as, as that point, the management of the new product effort changes from development to commercialization (Crawford and Di Benedetto, 2008). Finally, proper launch execution increases the reputational value of the firm in the distribution channel, boosts sales force and distribution channel employee morale, may provide a pioneering advantage to the firm, and ultimately positively affects the firm's value (Bowersox et al., 1995, 1999). Interestingly, the academic literature on launch strategy, and specific launch issues such as lean launch strategy or launch timing has been slow in developing (Calantone and Montoya-Weiss, 1994). The majority of the literature on launch strategy has emerged within only the last ten years (e.g., Hultink and Robben, 1995; Hultink et al., 1997, 1998, 1999, 2000; Guiltinan, 1999; Di Benedetto, 1999; Thoelke et al., 2001; DeBruyne et al., 2002; Lee and O'Connor, 2003; Langerak et al., 2004; Calantone et al., 2005; Calantone and Di Benedetto, 2007).

Few, if any, research studies have examined how the launch process differs across national boundaries. One should expect that different cultural or business environments do not do science and technological development all that differently. However, cooperation between supply partners, coordination of distribution channels, prominence and effectiveness of promotion and advertising activities, and many other marketing differences across cultural and business environments could be highly influential at the time of launch. Additionally, levels of environmental hostility may vary markedly from one business environment to another. The economic bets made by innovating firms are extremely high; although the underlying technology may be similar, differences in environmental hostility, effectiveness of marketing activities, and the interactions among these, would impinge on the firm seeking to execute a multi-country launch successfully. All of the abovementioned launch studies were conducted in North America and Western Europe; the antecedents to a successful launch remain understudied in big emerging markets or underdeveloped/developing economies, where the business environment is substantially different from that found in the West. The best empirical testing ground to assess suitable, successful launch practices would be a comparison between a fully developed market and a quite different one such as China, in which cultural and business environment, government policy, stage of economic development, and industrial strategy, are all quite different.

China is, so far, quite understudied in many aspects of new product research. Despite the recent economic reforms and its emergence in the global economy, relatively little research on new products has yet been conducted in China (e.g. Parry and Song, 1994; Song and Parry, 1994; Di Benedetto, Calantone and Zhang, 2003; Di Benedetto and Song, 2003; De Sarbo et al., 2005; Di Benedetto et al., 2008). Furthermore, few of these studies explicitly consider the importance of proper execution of launch activity in China. Greater understanding of the new product development process (including launch) in China is needed, given the relative size of the Chinese economy as measured by the International Monetary Fund, and the reforms underway since the 1980s to stimulate innovation and growth in Chinese business. Indeed, China and the United States are two of the three largest economies in the world as measured by purchasing power parity (the other being the European Union) (www.cia.gov/cia/publications/factbook, 2001). China represents close to one-fourth of the world's population, and its trade surplus with the U.S. (well over $100 billion) surpasses that of Japan

154

(*biz.thestar.com*, Jan. 20, 2006). China is generally considered one of the most important Big Emerging Markets that will dominate the global economy in the coming decades.

Our research objective is to carry out a macro-level comparison between a developed and a rapidly developing business market (respectively, U.S. and China). In this study, we propose a new product performance model, in which the execution and timing of launch activities, as well as the execution of marketing activities, directly impact new product performance. Our theoretical model makes a contribution to the literature, because we explicitly model the role of launch execution and launch timing, which are important components of a successful launch but whose specific effects on performance have remained understudied in the literature. We also include internal and external antecedents of launch execution and timing, such as cross-functional integration, market orientation, level of channel cooperation, and other key marketing activities. While the literature suggests that all of these are related to a successful launch, the specific ways in which these affect launch timing and execution of launch activities is not understood. We derive a set of hypotheses from our theoretical model and empirically validate our model by testing our hypotheses in both countries. Based on differences between the U.S. and Chinese cultural and business environments, we derive additional hypotheses concerning the relative importance of the antecedents of new product performance across the two countries. Our model is based on broad theory comparing developed to developing economies, which helps us to generalize our findings and draw theoretical contributions and managerial insights appropriate to other business environments.

To accomplish our research objective, we gather data from 183 new product products developed by U.S. firms, and an additional 261 new product projects developed in China. In general, we find strong support in both the U.S. and China for the research hypotheses derived from our hypotheses. Specifically, we find that the business unit's level of resources and skills, the amount of cross-functional integration, and the level of market orientation positively affect the execution of marketing and launch activities and the extent of channel cooperation (directly or indirectly); and new product performance is positively affected by the execution of the marketing and launch activities, business unit resources, and launch timing. We also find and discuss several significant cross-national differences, as well as similarities, in importance of antecedents to new product performance. Our findings have managerial importance as well as theoretical significance, and we discuss the managerial implications in the concluding section.

CONCEPTUAL DEVELOPMENT

In our theoretical model, we hypothesize that the timing and quality of execution of launch both directly impact the performance of the new product, as does the product's level of innovativeness. We also hypothesize direct relationships between the quality of execution of marketing activities, and the extent of channel cooperation, on new product performance. We are also interested in exploring the factors that impact quality of launch execution and launch timing. These antecedent factors include the level of cross-functional integration, the firm's resources and market orientation, and the extent of channel cooperation. Figure 9.1 illustrates the hypothesized relationships among all of these variables. The following paragraphs explain and develop each of these relationships more fully.

Cross-Functional Integration

Cross-functional integration can be defined as unity of effort across the functional areas involved in NPD (marketing, R&D, manufacturing, and so on) (Song and Parry, 1997b). Cross-functional team implementation in NPD increases knowledge sharing among functional areas and avoids "functional silo" product development (Gupta, Raj and Wilemon, 1986; Gupta, 1988; Griffin, 1992; Towner, 1994; Olson, Walker, and Ruekert, 1995; Dyer, 1996; Sherman, Souder and Jenssen, 2000, Atuahene-Gima and Evangelista, 2000; Troy et al., 2008). Effective cross-functional teaming is critical to meeting new product performance metrics such as shorter time to market, higher quality, and greater financial success (Griffin and Hauser, 1992, 1993; Norton, Parry, and Song, 1994; Song and Parry, 1996; Ruekert and Walker, 1987a,b; Ayers, Dahlstrom and Skinner, 1997; Swink, 2002).

The benefits of integration are derived from improved information gathering and transmission, and ultimately improved proficiency of both marketing activities and launch activities (Ruekert and Walker, 1987a,b; Song and Parry, 1997a,b). With respect to launch, Integrating distribution and logistics in the new product process leads to synergies across functional areas, increases flexibility in the supply chain, ultimately leading to improvements in launch effectiveness and efficiency, and boosting the firm's ability to meet customer requirements (Bowersox et al., 1995, 1999; Calantone et al., 2005; Calantone and Di Benedetto, 2011). We hypothesize:

> H1a: A higher level of cross-functional integration positively affects the quality of the launch execution.
>
> H1b: A higher level of cross-functional integration positively affects the quality of execution of marketing activities.

156

Business Unit Resources

Many studies of new product performance view the business unit's level of marketing and technical resources as an antecedent of product success (Cooper, 1979a,b, 1983; Cooper and Kleinschmidt, 1987, 1993; Calantone and Di Benedetto, 1988; Parry and Song, 1994; Montoya-Weiss and Calantone, 1994; Calantone, Schmidt and Song, 1996; Song and Parry, 1996, 1997a). The relationship between resources and ultimate success has often been modeled indirectly. Having a higher level of resources allows a business unit to carry out specific activities pertaining to the marketing and the launch of the product more proficiently; proficiency in carrying out these tasks is positively related to product success (Calantone and Di Benedetto, 1988; Song and Parry, 1997a,b; Gatignon and Xuereb, 1997; Moorman and Slotegraaf, 1999). We hypothesize the following direct effects:

H2a: A higher level of business unit resources positively affects the quality of the launch execution.

H2b: A higher level of business unit resources positively affects the quality of execution of marketing activities.

Much research supports the hypothesis that the levels of skills and resources positively affect product performance. A meta-analysis of the NPD literature found that product marketing and technology capabilities are very important factors underlying new product success (Montoya-Weiss and Calantone, 1994), a finding supported by later research (e.g., Song, 1997a,b; Gatignon and Xuereb, 1997; Moorman and Slotegraaf, 1999; Guiltinan, 1999). The strategic factor market literature (e.g., Barney, 1986) notes that a business unit can strategically make investments in skills and resources (such as through acquisition) that provide sustainable competitive advantage since they can be difficult for competitors to acquire or imitate. These skills and resources ultimately generate above-average economic performance, further suggesting a direct link between the possession of skills and resources and ultimate performance levels. We propose:

H2c: A higher level of business unit resources positively affects the performance of the launched product.

Some channel research has explored the effect of resource dependency on channel member behavior and channel efficiency (Gassenheimer and Calantone, 1994; Gassenheimer et al., 1995).

FIGURE 9.1
RESOURCE-BASED DRIVERS OF SUCCESSFUL PRODUCT LAUNCH

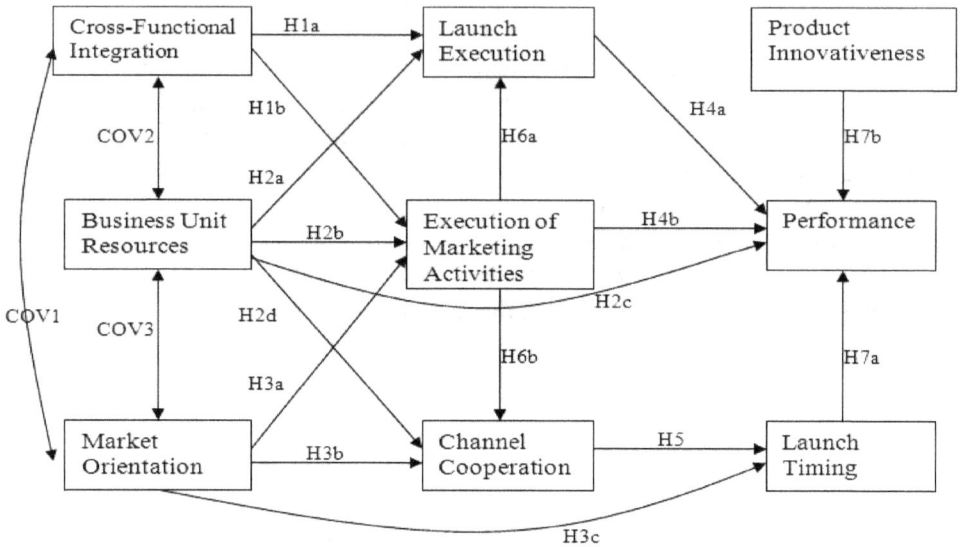

Cross-National Hypotheses:
H8a: The effect in H3c is *lower* in China.
H8b: The effect in H5 is *higher* in China.
H8c: The effect in H3a is *lower* in China.
H8d: The effects in H1b and H2b are *higher* in China.
H8e: The effects in H2c, H4a, H4b, H7a are *lower* in China.
H8f: The effects in H7a and H7b are *higher* in China.

The embeddedness literature suggests that strong ties between a manufacturer and its distributors will lead to an open exchange of information, more innovative new products, and ultimately, improved performance (Morgan and Hunt, 1994; Rowley, Behrens and Karckhardt, 2000; Bonner and Walker, 2004). A mutually beneficial relationship exists between manufacturer and distributor. The manufacturer can gain several advantages by cooperating with distributors, since the latter knows customer needs best (Kalwani and Narayandas, 1995); similarly, the distributor is dependent on the manufacturer's ability to continuously improve product offerings and better satisfy the customer (Rowley, Behrens and Karckhardt, 2000; Bonner and Walker, 2004). Certainly, manufacturers will be able to gain competitive advantage through their ability to provide economic support to their distributors (Gassenheimer and Calantone, 1994). The more resources the manufacturer has, the greater the economic dependence of the distributors on the manufacturer, and the more compliant the distributors'

158

behavior will be. We hypothesize that the level of channel cooperation achieved will be related to the business unit's resource level:

H2d: A higher level of business unit resources positively affects the level of channel cooperation.

Market Orientation

Market orientation is defined as the organization wide generation and dissemination of market information and intelligence regarding customer needs and wants, and organizational responsiveness to such information (Jaworski and Kohli, 1993; Kohli and Jaworski, 1990; Narver and Slater, 1990; Narver, Slater and MacLachlan, 2004). In terms of product development and launch, a market orientation can be manifested in many ways: frequent meetings with customers, interdepartmental meetings to discuss competitive strategies or market trends, periodic checking of product development to keep it in line with customer needs, taking corrective action when customers are unhappy with service quality, and so on. A higher market orientation is related to greater knowledge about the marketplace and about competition, which allows firms to execute their marketing activities better and thus have better success at launch (Deshpande et al., 1993). Further, as market orientation increases, a greater level of cooperation with external channel partners is stimulated, which increases the channel members' willingness to cooperate at launch. Finally, a firm with greater knowledge about the competitive environment and the marketplace is likely to have a better sense of the "right time" for market launch, so we expect a relationship between market orientation and launch timing. In sum, we hypothesize:

H3a: A higher level of market orientation positively affects the quality of execution of marketing activities.

H3b: A higher level of market orientation positively affects the level of channel cooperation.

H3c: A higher level of market orientation positively affects the timing of the launch.

Execution of Marketing and Launch Activities

An early empirical study, Project SAPPHO, found that the most critical determinants of product success included understanding users' needs and the magnitude of the marketing efforts (Rothwell, 1972). The execution of marketing activities (such as selecting customers for product use testing, conducting test marketing, training the sales force, and developing and testing the advertising) increases a product's competitive advantage as viewed by the customer, ultimately increasing the level of success attained by the product (Cooper, 1979a, 1983; Calantone and Di Benedetto, 1988; Cooper and Kleinschmidt, 1987; Song and Parry, 1994, 1996, 1997a,b).

In addition, product launch activities (such as providing service and technical support to the customer, having appropriate pricing, advertising, and distribution at launch, having adequate product availability) also determine of the product's performance level (Cooper, 1979a, 1983; Maidique and Zirger, 1984; Cooper and Kleinschmidt, 1987, 1990; Calantone and Di Benedetto 1988; Song and Parry, 1994, 1997b).

There is a small but growing literature on the importance of the launch stage (for a review, see Calantone and Di Benedetto, 2007). The launch stage is often the most expensive stage in product development by far (Urban and Hauser, 1993; Guiltinan, 1999; Langerak, Hultink and Robben, 2004); and effective launch activity execution is a significant precursor of market performance (Calantone and Di Benedetto, 2007; Cooper, 1979; Cooper and Kleinschmidt, 1990; Parry and Song, 1994). Poor execution of product launch can result in marketplace failure, even if other stages in the product development process are carried out well (Montoya-Weiss and Calantone, 1994). Many firms emphasize executing a "lean" launch, characterized by small commitments of resources, slow manufacturing ramp-up, and low commitment of inventory (Calantone et al., 2005). Lean launch activities can lead to significant cost efficiencies and time-to-market improvements, resulting in improved product performance (Bowersox et al., 1995, 1999).

Carrying out marketing activities well provides the firm with a better understanding of the marketing efforts required at the time of launch as well as target customers' responses to price levels, resulting in better tactical launch decisions such as improved timing (Calantone and Di Benedetto, 1988, 2007; Hultink and Robben, 1999; Langerak, Hultink and Robben, 2004). The product development literature shows that effective execution of launch activities is related to superior market performance (Calantone and Cooper, 1979; Cooper and Kleinschmidt, 1990; Parry and Song, 1994; Guiltinan, 1999; Calantone and Di Benedetto, 2007, 2011).
We hypothesize:

> H4a: A higher quality of launch execution positively affects the performance of the launched product.
>
> H4b: A higher quality of marketing activity execution positively affects the performance of the launched product.

Channel Cooperation

Tight cooperation among channel members permits more efficient sharing of information. Cooperation results in a state of "mindfulness," meaning that there is a shared understanding of goals and constraints among all participants (Bowersox, Stank and Daugherty, 1999; Petersen, Handfield and Ragatz, 2003). Cooperation also increases synergy: the result of NPD is more satisfactory than what would have been accomplished by any one of the participants individually (Jassawalla and Sashittal, 1998; Song, Montoya-Weiss and Schmidt, 1997). These factors, taken together, allow for better, more responsive product development. That is, tighter ties among channel members help them respond more rapidly to customer needs and bring products to market more quickly. The ability to execute a flexible, lean launch, and to extract the benefits mentioned above (cost efficiencies, and accelerated time to market), will be dependent on the firm's ability to coordinate and cooperate with its supplier partners (Bowersox et al., 1995, 1999).

There is limited academic research specifically on launch timing (for an exception, see Calantone and Di Benedetto, 2011), but the product pioneering literature suggests that delaying a launch is detrimental to long-term market share (Robinson and Fornell, 1985; Robinson, 1988; Lambkin, 1988; Karakaya and Stahl, 1989; Kerin, Varadarajan, and Peterson, 1992; Song, Di Benedetto, and Zhao, 1999; Robinson and Chiang, 2002). It is also possible that a launch can be too early, at a point when marketplace information is still missing or it is still unclear which technology will be most appropriate for the market (Calantone and Di Benedetto, 2011). This is conceptually similar to the management concept of the strategic window (Abell, 1978), which suggests that there is an optimal time to capitalize on a marketplace opportunity. We therefore hypothesize:

> H5: A higher level of channel cooperation positively affects the timing of the launch.

Marketing Competitiveness

If the firm proficiently assesses market potential, carries out good test marketing, and performs other marketing activities well, it will have a better idea of the intensity of promotion and distribution that will be required at launch, and will ultimately conduct its launch activities better. It will also have a better idea of its target customers' likely responses to differing price levels, and can set prices accordingly (Calantone and Di Benedetto, 1988). In short, better marketing information will allow the firm to make better tactical launch decisions (Hultink et al., 1997; Hultink and Robben, 1999). Furthermore, excellence at executing marketing activities increases the level of cooperation of channel members, since the assistance they receive from the manufacturer (in the form of marketing support) helps them to achieve lean-launch efficiency targets and also attain levels of distribution desired by the manufacturing firm.

Thus, we propose two hypotheses:

161

H6a: A higher quality of marketing activity execution positively affects the quality of the launch execution.

H6b: A higher quality of marketing activity execution positively affects the level of channel cooperation.

Performance

Launch timing is a critical variable determining ultimate product success, and there appears to be a close relationship between product performance, launch timing, value delivered to customer, and likelihood of success (Cooper and Kleinschmidt, 1990; Zirger and Maidique, 1990; Lilien and Yoon, 1990; Parry and Song, 1994; Guiltinan, 1999). In the NewProd empirical study, 13 percent of the product failures occurred because a similar and better product was launched by a competitor at the same time; if the product had been launched earlier it may have had a chance to become established and ultimately succeed (Calantone and Cooper, 1979).

As mentioned earlier, it is possible for the launch timing to be too late or too early, both with potentially detrimental effects on performance. There are many anecdotal examples of firms that delayed too long in launching a product, only to be beaten to the market by competitors (Crawford and Di Benedetto 2008, p. 445).

At the same time, firms are often under pressure to accelerate time to market (Millson, Raj and Wilemon, 1992) and may ultimately launch too early without fully understanding the risks involved (Crawford, 1992). In a recent launch study, evidence was found that an "optimal" launch time exists, and it is influenced by the objectives of several stakeholders: top management, customers and consumers, and distribution channel members (Calantone and Di Benedetto, 2011).

We hypothesize:

H7a: Better launch timing positively affects the performance of the launched product.

The empirical literature has not yielded consistent results regarding the relationship between the product's degree of innovativeness and its performance. The Project NewProd studies have produced equivocal results (see, e.g., Cooper, 1979a; Kleinschmidt and Cooper, 1991): highly innovative products outperform incremental products on some measures of success, while the reverse was true for other measures of success. These authors noted that there are two ways to view the relationship between innovativeness and performance: (1) highly innovative products have higher performance because they create greater opportunity for competitive advantage; (2) less innovative products have higher performance because they carry less risks and uncertainties. They speculated that there might be a

U-shaped relationship between innovativeness and performance (i.e., moderately innovative products will be outperformed by both highly innovative and incremental products. Some later empirical evidence suggests, however, that highly innovative products outperform all others on one specific performance variable: whether the product meets the firm's profit objectives (Song and Montoya-Weiss, 1998). Therefore, consistent with this later work, we hypothesize:

H7b: A higher level of product innovativeness positively affects the performance of the launched product.

Cross-Cultural Hypotheses

While we expect this model of new product performance to be generalizable across various countries, we expect differences in the relative importance of the various factors leading to new product performance, due to differences in the cultural and business environments. By gathering data from both the U.S. and China, we are able to develop and test hypotheses concerning the differences between a large, fully-developed, free-market economy and a large, rapidly-developing, centrally-planned economy.

China is an important and unique business environment and a rapidly-emerging global market economy. It is traditionally a centrally-planned economy, and in an attempt to boost global competitiveness, central planning has been focusing on stimulating new product development, particularly in high-tech industries (Gadiesh, Leung and Vestring, 2007; Li and Zhang, 2007; Luo, 2003; Mu, Peng and MacLachlan, 2009). Chinese as well as foreign firms view China's enormous market potential and have sought to increase efficiency and effectiveness of new product launch there (Atuahene-Gima, Slater and Olson, 2005). Nevertheless, despite great advances in its global presence, China is still characterized by a volatile business environment, and a lack of market institutions that support product innovation. During times of great economic transformation, this lack of market institutions can hamper innovative activities (Luo, 2003). In addition, many Chinese firms are still state-owned, and there is significant government involvement in investment and hiring (Henley and Nyaw, 1986), and governmental reforms have focused on technology and innovation stimulation (Schermerhorn and Nyaw, 1992; Jefferson, Rawski and Zheng, 1992). In a centrally-planned economy, other things being equal, we would expect that marketing and launch activities designed to increase a new product's competitiveness in free market competition would be relatively less critical to its performance. Factors such as greater cooperation through the distribution channel or greater cross-functional integration would be relatively more important to marketing and launch execution and, ultimately, to new product performance. We hypothesize:

H8a: The effect of market orientation on launch timing will be lower in China than in the U.S.

H8b: The effect of channel cooperation on launch timing will be higher in China than in the U.S.

H8c: The effect of market orientation on execution of marketing activities will be lower in China than in the U.S.

H8d: The effect of (i) cross-functional integration and (ii) business unit resources on execution of marketing activities will be higher in China than in the U.S.

H8e: The effect of (i) business unit resources, (ii) launch execution, (iii) execution of marketing activities, and (iv) launch timing on new product performance will be lower in China than in the U.S.

H8f: The effect of product innovativeness and launch timing on performance will be higher in China than in the U.S.

METHODOLOGY AND DATA COLLECTION

A retrospective methodology was employed in this study, as had been successfully done in several previous studies of NPD and product launch (Cooper, 1979a,b, 1983; Cooper and Kleinschmidt, 1987; Calantone and Di Benedetto, 1988; Calantone et al., 1996). A mail survey instrument was developed for data collection, based on the NPD literature. Respondents were requested to select one of their company's most recent new product launches (i.e., launched no more than five years ago) which was "characteristic" of their firm at the time of launch and for which they would be able to provide detailed information. Except for the performance measures, each of these was measured on 0 to 10 Likert-type scales.

The model was tested in the U.S. with a sample of product managers derived from the Product Development & Management Association member database. The model was also tested using a second sample derived from a study in China, using mailing lists obtained from four Chinese industry ministries. Gathering data in both business environments allows us to carry out the macro-level comparison between developed and developing business markets, which is a stated research objective, and also permits us to assess the robustness and generalizability of the theoretical model outside the North American environment.

The following sections detail the instrument development process and the data collection in the U.S. and China.

Instrument Development and Validation Process

To ensure that we had a survey instrument that provided valid, reliable measures of the constructs under study (Churchill, 1979), we used a two-step process to develop the instrument. This was particularly important since scales previously validated in other studies were not available for some of the constructs (for example, timing of launch).

In the first step, we identified relevant scales from the marketing and related literature wherever possible to build an initial pool of scale items. We grouped scale items derived in this way into constructs. To the initial pool, we added new items wherever it was felt that the domain of the construct had not been sufficiently covered by the identified items (Mintu, Calantone & Gassenheimer, 1994). For example, few items pertaining to launch timing or channel cooperation were available, so new items were added (the Appendix indicates which scales were developed for the specific purposes of this study).

In the second step, we assessed the construct validity of the scales being developed, and corrected ambiguous or confusing scale items, by pretesting the questionnaire. The pretest sample included 50 individuals, who were all practicing managers participating either in a university executive training program or in an evening MBA program. Participants were asked to fill out the questionnaire, and then in the debriefing they were asked if they felt all the questions were clear and that the scale items represented the desired constructs adequately and captured the appropriate "shades of meaning." Only minor corrections and adjustments needed to be made to the questionnaire based on the feedback from the pretest. The appendix provides a list of the final measure measurement items and the response format employed in the questionnaire.

Construct Measures

Market orientation was measured using a 14-item scale developed by Narver and Slater (1990) and also used by Song and Parry (1997a). This scale includes a set of questions regarding the extent of formal and informal meetings regarding customer needs, competitive strategies, and the dissemination of customer satisfaction information.

The level of cross-functional integration was measured using a six-item work group structure scale that explored the involvement of cross-functional teams in strategic decisions and the presence of liaison personnel and/or task forces to facilitate interdepartmental collaboration (Bowersox et al., 1995).

The next three constructs (business unit resources and skills, execution of marketing activities, and execution of launch activities) were measured using scales derived from the Project Newprod studies of Cooper (Cooper, 1979a; Cooper and Kleinschmidt, 1987). A seven-item scale measured the marketing, R&D, and manufacturing skills and resources present in the business unit. The marketing activities scale contained fifteen items measuring the quality of execution of tasks such as customer selection, in-use testing, test marketing, planning the product launch, studying customer feedback, and planning the sales force, advertising, and distribution activities. Finally, the seven-item launch activities scale assessed the quality of execution of the selling effort, advertising, product availability and distribution, pricing, and technical support at the time of launch.

The nature of the product (new-to-the-world product, new product or line to the company, addition to an existing line, or modification of existing product) was measured using a single-item scale used by Cooper and Kleinschmidt (1987).

We developed new scale items to measure launch timing and channel cooperation. These were pretested on a sample of about two dozen students in executive MBA programs for clarity. The seven-item launch timing scale required the respondent to assess the timing of the launch relative to business unit goals, competition, and customers, as well as the overall launch timing. The channel cooperation scale contained five items, and assessed the level of cooperation and coordination attained in the channel, the speed of deployment of the product into the channel, the timeliness of channel promotion, and the timeliness of the launch.

Ten measures of perceived new product performance were gathered. Recent literature has suggested that a unidimensional performance scale is an oversimplification (Griffin and Page, 1993; Hultink and Robbin, 1995). Measuring only profitability, for example, may be a misleading indicator of the product's success, relative to the objectives specified by the firm. Therefore, the following measures of success were used: perceived overall profitability, and perceived profitability, sales and market share relative to the business unit's other new product launches, to competing products on the market, and to the business unit's objectives for the product launch. Each of these was measured on a Likert-type scale of -5 to $+5$ (scale items appear in Appendix).

U.S. Data Collection

The U.S. survey was mailed to a list of corporate managers whose principal responsibility was new product commercialization. This sampling frame was chosen because these individuals were felt to be representative of the most knowledgeable managers active in new product management and commercialization. A follow-up call and second mailing were used to boost response rates. A key informant method was used for data collection: this method has been frequently used in new product research (Song and Parry, 1997a,b; Cooper and Kleinschmidt, 1987; Calantone, Schmidt and Song, 1996). All respondents were experienced practicing managers in new product management, and were the most knowledgeable source of information on the product's launch and commercialization (Phillips, 1981). The sample

166

included practitioners from firms producing consumer goods as well as business-to-business goods and services. A total of 1005 questionnaires were sent, of which 183 usable questionnaires were returned; this represents a response rate of 18.2%.

Most respondents held either Manager, Assistant Manager, or Director positions. About 6% of the respondents held Planning, Corporate Planning, or Strategic Planning positions within their firms; the remainder of the sample was roughly evenly split across Technology, Marketing, New Product Development, and Other Management. These demographics (by functional area and job title/level) are very representative of the overall sampling frame characteristics. Additionally, for evidence of reliability, the sample was split into two halves (early and late respondents), and, with only one exception, no significant differences were found between halves of the sample obtained on any of the scale items. The two halves were not different in terms of any of the performance measures used. We therefore conclude that the earlier and later respondents are not significantly different from each other in any way that would bias our results. This finding can also be used to infer a non-threatening level of non-response.

China Data Collection

We explicitly sought to avoid applying an American bias or shade to the research. It is important to ascertain the "comparability" of data collected in different cultural contexts (Douglas and Craig, 1983), thus the research was designed with the intent of establishing equivalent measures for the study of the Chinese NPD process.

To make sure the translation was accurate and that the question meanings were not altered, we used a two parallel-translation/double-translation method to translate the questionnaire into Chinese (Douglas and Craig, 1983, Sekaran, 1983). Four Chinese professional translators assisted in preparing the Chinese questionnaire. Two people prepared independent Chinese translations of the English-language questionnaire and the other two independently translated the Chinese translations back into English. A comparison of the resulting questionnaires revealed considerable consistency across translators. When disagreements could not be resolved, phrasing favored by a majority of the translators was selected. The appropriateness of the selected translation was further confirmed by consulting with 6 Chinese managers.

The final stage of measurement development consisted of two pretests of the resulting questionnaire. The first pretest was conducted by interviewing 9 Chinese graduates from a well-regarded U.S. business school and 11 Chinese executives who had been involved in more than 20 NPD projects in two Chinese firms. All were fluent in both English and Chinese.

These respondents were asked to complete the questionnaire and raise questions as problems or ambiguities arose. After these interviews, the instrument was corrected and professionally drafted. The second pretest was conducted using all the team members of a recently introduced product in a Chinese firm. These respondents were asked to complete the questionnaire for a recently developed project. The final version of the questionnaire reflected a very few modifications, as suggested by participants in the pretests. The underlying purpose of these exhaustive steps is to insure equivalence to the greatest degree possible.

The sample frame consisted of mailing lists obtained from four Chinese ministries: Aerospace, Electric Machinery, Chemicals, and Electronics. After deleting enterprises with less than 11 employees, the list was reduced to 966 companies. In administering the survey, we followed the total design method for survey research (Dillman, 1993). The first mailing packet included a business card, a personalized letter to the contact of the company in Chinese, a questionnaire in Chinese, and a pre-addressed postage-paid return envelope. The package was sent to all 966 firms in China. Respondents were guaranteed confidentiality and offered an executive summary of the results. Following the procedure given by Dillman (1993), a followed up letter, a second wave of mailing with questionnaire, and a final follow-up letter were sent to non-respondents. In addition, a personal phone call was made to the non-responding firms two weeks after the fourth reminder letter.

Of the 966 questionnaires initially mailed, 42 were returned as undeliverable, yielding an adjusted sample size of 924. We obtained 261 usable responses, for an effective adjusted response rate of 28%. Of the 261 enterprises in our sample, 194 were state-owned enterprises, and 23 were joint ventures involving a state enterprise and a foreign partner.

To examine concerns about the validity and reliability of the information provided by respondents, two Chinese researchers conducted 27 randomly selected follow-up telephone interviews (30 were originally selected, but 3 managers declined to participate). We concluded that the information was reliable and valid because: (1) each questionnaire was completed by a project manager identified as a knowledgeable source regarding all aspects of the project's development (Phillips, 1981) and 25 of the 27 project leaders consulted with other managers or team members before completing the questionnaire.

RESULTS

We combined the U.S. and China data samples and conducted an exploratory factor analysis, in which we set the number of factors equal to the number of constructs. After promax rotation, almost all scale items mapped onto factors which were a priori consistent with the constructs (the few that did not map clearly onto a factor were eliminated). This was then repeated with the samples not pooled, and a clean set of items on factors obtained. The fact that all constructs fit cleanly in both countries provides elementary, basic evidence of universal construct validity across the two countries. This was followed by more formal tests of construct and item equivalence.

TABLE 9.1
CONSTRUCTS AND COEFFICIENT ALPHAS*

Construct	Mean (Standard Deviation)	Coefficient α
Marketing Orientation (14 items)	6.48 (1.30)	0.861
Cross-Functional Integration (6 items)	5.75 (1.67)	0.817
Business Unit Resources and Skills (7 items)	5.61 (1.45)	0.841
Execution of Marketing Activities (15 items)	5.70 (1.41)	0.894
Channel Cooperation (5 items)	5.50 (1.81)	0.891
Launch Timing (7 items)	5.26 (2.02)	0.921
Launch Execution (7 items)	6.01 (1.49)	0.793
Performance of Launched Product (10 items)	1.22 (2.11)	0.957

* All constructs measured by multiple Likert-type items measured on 0-10 scales, except Performance measured on a +5 to -5 scale.

The means and standard deviations for all factors for the combined sample, and all coefficient alpha statistics, are presented in Table 1. The path model of Figure 9.1 was run as a two-group model with the U.S. and China samples as the two groups. The overall model fit is excellent both for the exact fit test and alternate test criteria ($\chi^2 = 62.29$, $p < 0.055$; CFI = 0.990; RMSEA = 0.027). All coefficient alphas are higher than the accepted cutoff value of 0.70, presenting an alternate indicator of convergent validity and internal consistency. All standardized parameters for both the U.S. and China samples are presented in Table 9.2, together with the overall model fit statistics. A two group CFA was then performed to assess the presence of multiple forms of construct invariance across the two settings (Myers, Calantone, Page and Taylor, 2000). Excepting two items, all items loaded on correct factors and were invariant (equivalent lambdas and constructs) between countries; the two offending items were removed from further analyses. Furthermore, instrument invariance obtained, tested using the measurement error covariances (theta delta) in each country. Since invariance obtained at the item, construct and error levels, we proceeded to test next for common method bias.

Common Method Bias

We used several procedures to empirically examine if common method bias obtained and threatened interpretation of our results. These were the Harmon one-factor test, questionnaire ordering, a confirmatory factor-analytic approach to Harman's one-factor test (McFarlin and Sweeney, 1992; Sanchez and Brock, 1996), a variant of the Myers et al. (1999) test for instrumentation bias, testing common covariance between unhypothesized pairs of constructs, correlation between endogenous and exogenous errors, a full mediation test, and a moderation test.

The rationale for the initial tests is that if common method bias poses a serious threat to the analysis and interpretation of the data, a single latent factor would account for all manifest variables (Podsakoff and Organ, 1986). A worse fit for the one-factor model would suggest that common method variance does not pose a serious threat (Sanchez et al., 1995). The one-factor model two group CFA yielded a $\chi^2 = 4105.56$ with 416 degrees of freedom (compared with the $\chi^2 = 1344.77$ and df=398 for the measurement model). The fit is considerably worse for the unidimensional model than for the measurement model, suggesting that common method bias is not a serious threat in the study. Similarly, the one factor model derived using principal components analysis did not obtain (this latter 'test' is considered to be weaker, as suggested by Podsakoff et al. (2003)). Next, the Podsakoff et al. suggestion of testing a single common factor against the error structure of the CFA was applied, and a common factor did not obtain a passable fit; the CAIC difference was greater than 2600, which again suggested a multi-construct CFA.

The next two tests compared the fit of the overall CFA when the errors of the endogenous variable items were allowed to co vary with those of the exogenous variable items. This test would obtain no significant difference from the original CFA χ^2 result, or a better fit (smaller χ^2) if a "commonness" of instrumentation result obtained from employing single source data. Such a result did not obtain, thus the Myers et al. (1999) demonstration of absence of any instrument bias is in evidence. This result is also consistent with the Podsakoff et al. suggestion of the instrumentation component of a common instrument being not detectable.

Finally, the presence of both strong and significant mediations (launch execution, channel cooperation and marketing activities) as well as significant moderation (country fixed effects) suggest logically that common method bias did not obtain since the presence of either effect argues that the single informants per firm reliably captured significant effects of the phenomena without bias. If bias obtained due to common method or instrument, it would persist through contingencies (moderation) and partial direct paths (mediation), neither which is observed in this study (Blalock, 1964, 1971). Next, we proceeded to test the structural hypotheses employing the PHI matrix from the invariant CFA results.

Results from U.S. Sample

We consider first the results from the U.S. sample. As shown in Table 9.2, strong support is found for almost all the hypotheses. Increased cross-functional integration is related to better execution of launch and marketing activities (path coefficients for H1a and 1b2 = 0.118 and 0.224, both significant at the 0.05 level). Greater business unit resources are related to improved execution of launch and marketing activities and also increased performance and channel cooperation (coeffs. for H2a and H3b = 0.410 and 0.252 respectively; coeffs. for H2c and H2d = 0.287 and 0.263 respectively; all significant at the 0.05 level). A greater market orientation is related to improved execution of marketing activities, increased channel cooperation, and better launch timing (coeffs. for H3a, H3b, and H3c = 0.408, 0.097, and 0.014 respectively, all significant at the 0.05 level). Better execution of marketing activities is related to improved performance, better execution of launch activities, and improved channel cooperation (coeffs. for H4b, H6a, and H6b = 0.242, 0.333, and 0.341 respectively, all significant at the 0.05 level). Better channel cooperation is related to improved launch timing (coeff. for H5 = 0.520, significant at the 0.05 level), and improved launch timing is related to improved performance (coeff. for H7a = 0.266, significant at the 0.05 level). Furthermore, there is a significant effect between increased product innovativeness and performance, though weaker (coeff. for H7b = 0.064, significant at the 0.10 level). No support was found for the hypothesized direct relationship between launch execution and performance (coeff. for H4a = 0.058, not significant).

TABLE 9.2
SUMMARY OF PARAMETERS AND TESTS
ON TWO GROUP MODEL

Hypothesis	Path	U.S.	China	χ^2
H1a	Cross-Functional Integration – Launch Execution	0.118**	0.116**	--
H1b	Cross-Functional Integration – Marketing Execution	0.224**	0.226**	--
H2a	Business Unit Resources - Launch Execution	0.410**	0.404**	--
H2b	Business Unit Resources - Marketing Execution	0.252**	0.401**	DIFF
H2c	Business Unit Resources –Perform.	0.287**	0.090	DIFF
H2d	Business Unit Resources - Channel Cooperation	0.263**	0.261**	--
H3a	Market Orientation - Marketing Execution	0.408**	0.216**	DIFF
H3b	Market Orientation - Channel Cooperation	0.097**	0.097**	--
H3c	Market Orientation - Launch Timing	0.114**	0.113**	--
H4a	Launch Execution – Perform.	0.058	0.060	--
H4b	Marketing Execution – Perform.	0.242**	0.241**	--
H5	Channel Cooperation - Launch Timing	0.520**	0.748**	DIFF
H6a	Marketing Execution - Launch Execution	0.333**	0.326**	--
H6b	Marketing Execution - Channel Cooperation	0.341**	0.336**	--
--	COV (Cross-Functional Integration - Mkt Orientation)	0.485**	0.362**	--
--	COV (Business Unit Resources - Market Orientation)	0.333**	0.402**	--
--	COV (Business Unit Resources - Cross-Functional Integration)	0.291**	0.523**	--
H7a	Launch Timing – Performance	0.266**	0.270**	--
H7b	Product Innovativeness – Perform.	0.064*	0.064*	--

Overall Statistics: $\chi^2 = 62.29$; df = 45; $p < 0.055$; CFI = 0.990; RMSEA = 0.027; C.I. (RMSEA) 90% = (0.000, 0.043)

Note: All parameters are reported from a completely standardized solution.

**: Significantly different from zero at $p < 0.05$ (tested on raw parameters)

*: Significantly different from zero at $p < 0.10$ (tested on raw parameters)

"DIFF" indicates cases that equality constraint release between groups obtained a significant statistical improvement in the model fit as indicated by LM-test.

Results from China Sample

Table 9.2 also includes the results obtained from the China sample. As indicated in Table 9.2, the model appears to be very generalizable to the Chinese setting. Since the results are very similar, we will focus our presentation here on the main differences between the two country samples. All the hypotheses supported in the U.S. sample are supported in the China sample as well, with only one exception: H2c was not supported. That is, no significant direct relationship was found between business unit resources and performance (path coeff. for H2c for the China sample = 0.090, not significant). In addition, cross-national differences were also estimated, by allowing the equality constraint between groups (nations) to be released and determining whether the model was significantly improved. These results are also shown in Table 9.2. As indicated, there are only four hypotheses for which a significant cross-national difference in parameter magnitude was found. One of these was H2c, as noted above (a significant relationship between business unit resources and performance was found only in the U.S.). The other three differences were found for H2b, H3a, and H5. The relationships between business unit resources and execution of marketing strategy, and between channel cooperation and launch timing, were stronger in China than in the U.S. (coeffs. for H2b and H5 for the China sample = 0.401 and 0.748 respectively; both significantly larger than the equivalent coefficient for the U.S. sample at the 0.05 level). Also, the relationship between market orientation and execution of marketing strategy was stronger in the U.S. than in China (coeff. for H3a for the China sample = 0.216, significantly smaller than the U.S. coefficient at the 0.05 level).

Cross-National Results

Table 9.2 indicates that there are many similarities between the Chinese and U.S. empirical results. The standardized coefficients are only significantly different for a few hypotheses as shown in Table 9.2. Several specific cross-national differences were hypothesized, and support was found for only some of these. Specifically, the effect of market orientation on launch timing was lower in China (H8a supported), the effect of channel cooperation on launch timing was higher in China (H8b supported), and the effect of market orientation on execution of marketing activities was lower in China (H8c supported). The effect of business unit resources on execution of marketing activities was found to be significantly higher in China, though a hypothesized difference in the effect of cross-functional integration on execution of marketing activities was not found (H8d partially supported). Surprisingly, of the several hypothesized cross-national differences in effects on performance, only one was found to be significant: the effect of business unit resources on performance was lower in China than in the U.S. (H8e partially supported; H8f not supported). Indeed, this was the only case where a significant relationship in the U.S. model was not found to be significant at all in China. In sum, while there are some cross-national differences which are consistent with hypotheses, we find evidence that many of the relationships found in the U.S. model are generalizable, even to a very different business and cultural environment such as China. We expand on these surprising similarities and differences in the discussion section.

THEORETICAL AND MANAGERIAL IMPLICATIONS, AND CONCLUSIONS

Many firms have begun to appreciate that product innovation is an important driver to sustained financial performance and competitive advantage. In an environment where cash-to-cash (time from initial investment to revenue generation) is an important performance metric, the firm must manage its NPD activities so that the launch is successful and not delayed. In the development of new consumer or business products, the launch phase is often the most expensive (sometimes by a substantial amount), and strategic and tactical decisions made at the time of launch are of critical importance. Despite a large literature on the relative merits of being first to market, relatively little research attention has been aimed at understanding the constellation of decisions made at the time of launch, including launch timing, launch execution tactics, and resource allocation. Importantly, the effects of marketing activities, distribution channel support, market orientation, or cross-functional integration on launch have also not been fully taken into account. This lack represents an important gap in the literature, since marketing and related activities have direct impacts not only on innovation success rates, but also on the firm's revenue realization.

A further hindrance to our understanding of the launch phase in NPD is that most research studies have been conducted in a single geographic region, usually either North America or Europe, so there is little evidence of the empirical generalizability of the findings.

In this article, we have presented a model that integrates several key constructs leading to new product success. We specifically account for launch timing, launch execution, and marketing activities carried out at the time of launch, as well as other constructs shown in previous studies to have impact on success (cross-functional integration, market orientation, and channel cooperation). We attempt to find some evidence of empirical generalizability by testing the model using samples drawn from two very different business environments, the United States and China. Overall, we find substantial support for the integrative model: in both country samples, all the hypotheses are strongly supported (with only one exception in the U.S.

and two exceptions in China). Our results add to the recently emerging literature on new product launch (e.g., Hultink et al., 1997, 2000; Di Benedetto, 1999; Calantone et al., 2005; Calantone and Di Benedetto, 2007), and suggest that further study of the importance of launch timing, and how to get the timing right for optimal new product performance, is warranted.

Despite the strong empirical support for the model, the fact that one of the hypothesized relationships (strong launch execution improves performance) was *not* significant merits further discussion. Recall that in this study, launch execution was defined in terms of the selling, advertising, promotional, and service technical support for the product at the time of launch, product availability and distribution, and price level at launch. As shown in Figure 9.1, four other direct effects on performance were found to be significant. Consistent with many previous studies (e.g., Cooper and Kleinschmidt,1987; Calantone and Di Benedetto, 1988; Song and Parry, 1997), type of new product, business unit resources, and execution of marketing activities are strongly linked to performance. While launch execution is not found to be significant in this study, launch timing is strongly significant. The findings presented here are of importance to practicing managers, as they suggest that the timing of the launch (in terms of business goals, and with respect to different shareholders including the competition, the customers, and top management) may be even more important to product success than the execution of the launch activities listed earlier. That is, management may execute the marketing programs at the time of launch well -- yet if the launch is mistimed with respect to one or more of the stakeholders, the ultimate performance of the product is thrown into question. The fact that launch timing, a previously under researched component of the launch phase, proves so critical to performance (in both country samples) is intriguing, and suggests that timing is of great importance to managers and potentially a rich area for future research.

As noted above, the model appears to be generalizable to at least one different business and cultural environment, China. Again, however, minor differences in the U.S. and China results merit further discussion.

Only one cross-national hypothesis regarding antecedents to performance was supported: the effect of business unit resources on new product performance was lower in China (actually not significant in China) than in the U.S. This perhaps is not surprising, given the vast differences between the two business environments. A great number of Chinese firms are state-owned, and over the part thirty years or so, managerial reforms designed to stimulate technology, innovation, and competitiveness have been implemented in China (Schermerhorn and Nyaw, 1991; Jefferson, Rawski, and Zheng, 1992). Despite some decentralization in recent years, the Chinese government is still very involved in investment, hiring, and performance-

175

target setting (Henley and Nyaw, 1986, Parry and Song, 1994). Thus, management of a small Chinese state-owned enterprise may be lacking in resources, but still be able to launch innovative new products successfully due to government support and investment. Although the direct relationship between resources and performance was not significant, the Chinese enterprise's resources were nevertheless found to affect marketing activity execution and channel cooperation, both of which indirectly affect performance (H2a, H2b and H2d all significant). The interrelationship between the Chinese state-owned enterprise, centralized government decision-making, and ultimate performance is therefore a complex one, provides valuable information to support managerial decision-making, and is worthy of further investigation especially during this transitional time in the Chinese business environment.

There were three other differences found between the two country samples, as shown in Table 9.2. The relationship between business unit resources and execution of marketing strategy was higher for the Chinese sample (H8d partially supported). Perhaps in a business environment in transition such as China, enterprises with fewer resources have more difficulty executing marketing strategy due to relative inexperience (i.e., marketing strategy decision-making may have only been decentralized to the enterprise level comparatively recently). The relationship between channel cooperation and launch timing was also stronger in China than in the U.S. (H8b supported). This may be evidence of relative inexperience or a structural competitive difference at the macro level. Chinese managers with little experience in making launch timing decisions on their own may be dependent on the expertise of their channel partners to help them time the launch. Finally, the relationship between market orientation and marketing strategy execution was stronger for the U.S (H8c supported). Having a market orientation was presumably less important in a centralized economy, and many Chinese enterprises may be only increasing their market orientation levels very recently. Hence, the positive effect of market orientation on strategy execution, while significant, may not be yet fully manifested in China. While some of these explanations may be conjectural, the differences between the fully developed U.S. business environment and the transitional, yet very fast developing Chinese business environment, and their effects on decision-making and investment in new products, nonetheless remain topics worthy of greater understanding and future research.

We recognize the limitations of our study. Response rates are less than ideal, yet there is no evidence that they are not representative of the populations of interest. The U.S. sample may be biased in favor of firms that prioritize product development as an important strategic component since the

176

frame is members of a professional NPD organization. Another possible limitation is our reliance on a retrospective methodology and our use of single informant data. Although these methods are commonly used in NPD research studies, the retrospective methodology may result in some halo effect bias since the true outcome of each project (success or failure) is known by the respondent. The single informant method may introduce bias if that individual is not the most knowledgeable person within the organization to complete the questionnaire (Phillips, 1981). We tried to minimize this bias by carefully selecting the respondents and also requesting the recipients to pass on the questionnaire if there was another person more qualified to respond. Further, several recent studies have found that the key informant method provides reliable and valid data on strategic decisions and performance at the senior management level (Kumar, Stern and Anderson, 1993; Zahra and Covin, 1993; Menon, Bharadwaj and Howell, 1996). The model gives every indication of being robust across the two very different business environments of the U.S. and China, yet caution suggests further studies may be required to ascertain the empirical generalizability of the model in other geographical locations.

APPENDIX

SCALE ITEMS USED IN THIS STUDY

Note: Except where otherwise noted, the scale used was 0 = strongly disagree; 10 = strongly agree.

Type of New Product (Source: Cooper, 1979a; Cooper and Kleinschmidt, 1987)

Into which category did the product fit? (Check only one from the following list.)

___ An innovation: a totally new product to the world that opened up a brand new market (e.g., nylon)

___ A totally new product to the world, but one where there was an existing market, i.e., replaced other products, functional substitute (e.g., laser printer)

___ A totally new product to our company that offers new features to the market (existing market).

___ A new product line to our company (existing market and existing products sold by others).

___ A new item in an existing line.

___ A significant modification of an existing product.

___ A minor modification of an existing product.

Execution of Launch Activities (Source: Cooper, 1979a; Cooper and Kleinschmidt, 1987)

How would you rate the quality of each of the following elements *in the launch of this product?* (Scale: 0 = very poor; 10 = excellent.)

Selling effort, e.g. the right people, properly trained, etc.
Advertising.
Promotion (e.g., discounts, trade shows, events).
Service and technical support for the customer, e.g., right people, qualified, responsive.
Product availability: sufficient inventory available.
Product distribution: on-time delivery, quick response.

Pricing: appropriateness of pricing level(s).

Business Unit Resources and Skills (Source: Cooper, 1979a; Cooper and Kleinschmidt, 1987)

To what extent does each statement listed below correctly describe this selected market launch?

For the selected product launch,
...our marketing research skills and resources were more than adequate.

...our sales force skills and resources were more than adequate.

...our distribution skills and resources were more than adequate.

...our advertising and promotion skills and resources were more than adequate.

...our R&D skills and resources were more than adequate.
...our engineering skills and resources were more than adequate.

...our manufacturing skills and resources were more than adequate.

Cross-Functional Integration (Source: Bowersox et al., 1995)

In assuring the compatibility among decisions made in one area (e.g., logistics) with those in other areas (e.g., marketing/sales), certain integrative mechanisms may or may not be used. Please indicate the extent to which the following are used in your selected product launch.

For the selected product launch,
...interdepartmental committees were set up to allow departments to engage in joint decision-making.
...task forces or temporary groups were set up to facilitate interdepartmental collaboration.
...liaison personnel existed whose specific job it was to coordinate the efforts of several departments.
...cross-functional teams made decisions concerning *manufacturing strategy*.

...cross-functional teams made decisions concerning *distribution or logistics strategy*.
...cross-functional teams made decisions concerning *marketing or sales strategy*.

Execution of Marketing Activities (Source: Cooper, 1979a; Cooper and Kleinschmidt, 1987)
Please indicate how well your business unit undertook each of these activities, *relative to how well you think it should have been done*. (Scale used: 0 = done very poorly or omitted; 10 = done excellently.)

Selecting customers for testing market acceptance.
Submitting products to customers for in-use testing.
Executing test marketing programs.
Interpreting the findings of the market testing.
Finalizing plans for manufacturing.
Finalizing plans for marketing.
Establishing overall direction of this product launch.
Delegating or contracting specialized research work to outside contractors.
Launching the product into the marketplace.
Studying feedback from customers regarding this product during launch.
Studying feedback from customers regarding this product after launch.
Training the sales force.
Planning and testing the advertising for this product.
Executing the advertising strategy for this product (e.g., good copy placement, adequate number of insertions).
Managing distribution channel activities for this product.

Market Orientation (Source: Narver and Slater, 1990)

Market orientation is defined as the organization wide generation of market and competitive intelligence pertaining to current and future customer needs, dissemination of the intelligence across departments, and organization wide responsiveness to it. The following statements describe some characteristics of market orientation that may or may not apply to your business unit.

When developing this new product,
...our marketing people met with customers frequently to find out what products or services they needed.
...individuals from our manufacturing department interacted directly with customers to learn how to serve them better.
...several of our departments generated competitive intelligence independently.
...we periodically reviewed the likely effect of changes in our business environment (e.g., regulation) on customers.
...a lot of informal "hall talk" in our business unit concerned our competitors' tactics or strategies.
...we had frequent interdepartmental meetings to discuss market trends and developments.
...marketing personnel in our business unit spent time discussing customers' future needs with *other* functional departments.
...data on customer satisfaction were disseminated at all levels in this business unit frequently.
...we tended to ignore changes in our customer's product or service needs for one reason or another. (Reversed)
...we periodically reviewed our product development efforts to ensure that they were in line with what customers want.
...if a major competitor had launched an intensive campaign targeted at our customers, we would have implemented a response immediately.
...we were quick to respond to significant changes in our competitors' pricing structures.
...if we found that customers were unhappy with the quality of our service, we would have taken corrective action immediately.
...if we found that customers would like us to modify a product or service, the departments involved would have made concerted efforts to do so.

Performance (Source: Cooper and Kleinschmidt, 1987; plus additional new items added)
New product performance can be measured in a number of ways. Please indicate, from what you know today, how successful this market entry was or has been, using the following criteria.

(Scale used on first item: -5 = a great financial failure; +5 = a great financial success.)

How successful was this market entry from an *overall profitability* standpoint? (Scale used on remaining nine items: -5 = far less; +5 = far exceeded.)

Relative to your business unit's other new product launches,
…how successful was this market entry in terms of *profits*?
…how successful was this market entry in terms of *sales*?
…how successful was this market entry in terms of *market share*?

Relative to competing product launches,
...how successful was this market entry in terms of *profits*?
...how successful was this market entry in terms of *sales*?
...how successful was this market entry in terms of *market share*?
Relative to your business unit's objectives for this product launch,
…how successful was this market entry in terms of *profits*?
…how successful was this market entry in terms of *sales*?
…how successful was this market entry in terms of *market share*?

<u>Launch Timing</u> (Scale developed and pretested in this study)
Please comment on the relative timing of the product's launch.

Relative to **our business unit's goals**, the timing of our launch was on target.

Relative to **our direct competition**, the timing of our launch was perfect.

From the point of view of our **major customers**, the timing of our launch was excellent.
The timing of our launch helped us achieve a competitive advantage.
The product went from development to launch with no delays.
The product was launched at the appropriate time.

Top management believed the timing of our market entry was excellent.

<u>Channel Cooperation</u> (Scale developed and pretested in this study)
Please state your level of agreement with each of the following.

From the distribution channel's point of view, the product was launched at the right time.
Channel <u>cooperation</u> was well developed ahead of time.

Channel <u>coordination</u> was accomplished as planned.

We achieved rapid deployment of our product into the distribution channel. Channel/trade promotion was executed on time.

Authored by Roger J. Calantone, C. Anthony Di Benedetto, & Michael Song, originally published in *International Journal of China Marketing* Vol. 2(1) 2011, pp. 14-44

Chapter Ten

The Art of Price War: a Perspective from China

This paper proposes a framework to understand the prevalence of price wars in China and it also uses the framework to articulate the art of planning and executing a price war.

INTRODUCTION

A price war is something to be avoided in the West. However, Chinese companies have earned a reputation for starting price wars. Many US companies know too well that the first sight of a Chinese company in a US market means a price war is coming: it always offers a price that is 30-50% lower than its closest competition (Engardio and Roberts 2004). By now, many US companies have a taste of that terrifying "China Price." Many practitioners and experts question the rationality for Chinese companies to start price wars. "Why can't they just lower the price by 10% or even 20%," many wonder aloud. "That way, they can still keep their damned price advantage and do much better for themselves, too?"

In the West, academic researchers and practitioners alike know that the outbreak of a price war means disastrous consequences for firms involved and hence they all view price wars in an industry as the failure of managerial rationality. A *Fortune* magazine article captures this prevailing view accurately. "What are price wars good for?" the article asks (Henderson, 1997). In the same breath, the author answers the question definitively: "Absolutely nothing." If price wars are good for "absolutely nothing," of course, no firm should ever initiate them. If a firm does, it must be driven by insanity. In that case, "[t]he best way to escape a damaging price war is *not* to jump into the fray at all" (Rao, Bergen, and Davis, 2000).

Chinese companies obviously do not share the same code of business conduct. They are not just "war mongers" in the US markets. They also take their gloves off in their own domestic markets and have no hesitation to start a price war if it is deemed necessary to achieve their sales and profit objectives. In the past ten years, firms in China have fought large-scale price wars in a wide range of industries, including consumer electronics, home appliances, personal computers, mobile phones, telecommunications, cables, and, most recently, automobiles. It is in their domestic markets where they hone their skills in waging price wars. Indeed, price wars are widely considered as a legitimate, effective marketing strategy by executives and business thought leaders in China. It is not uncommon for today's executives to talk about the "business arena" as the "battleground," and they do not just talk about it metaphorically, either. In fact, strategy in Chinese, "战略," literally means "battle plans" or "combat strategies."

The rub is that while Western companies seem to suffer whenever they start, or they are caught in, a price war, Chinese companies seem to thrive on price wars they start and many emerge from them stronger, bigger, and more profitable. Like any other war, victories in price wars also produce many legendary "generals" in China. Some of them become idols for aspiring managers and some even become national heroes thanks to the extensive media coverage of price wars in China.

In 1995, for example, IBM, Compaq, and HP were the three best selling PC brands in China, but three years later, the top 5 PC brands in China were all locals who had fought their way up through price wars. In 1999, China's mobile phone market was dominated by Motorola, Nokia and other foreign brands with all the local brands together having less than 5% of the market. However, only four years later and after a series of intense price wars, the local brands took more than 50% of the market. Most recently in 2005, Chery, a local automobile company with only 10 years of history, launched several rounds of price wars and beat many global players to take the fourth place in terms of market share, and is now preparing for an aggressive assault on the US market in the coming years.

The sharp contrast in the attitudes toward price wars in China and in the West raises an intriguing question: are those Chinese companies simply lucky survivors in chaotic price wars, or do they know something about how to wage price wars that their Western counterparts do not? We will offer an answer to this question by taking a detailed look at two price wars that took place in China in the color TV industry and in the microwave oven industry during the mid-1990s. Our study has convinced us that luck has nothing to do with being a victor in a price war. Good planning and execution are the keys to winning. In other words, Chinese companies do seem to know something about price wars that the executives in the West do not or have forgotten.

No one should be surprised by the fact that firms in a country where executives routinely draw strategic inspirations from Sun Tzu's *The Art of War* may have a distinct perspective on price wars. What is somewhat surprising is the fact that we know very little of that Chinese perspective in the West. How do Chinese companies assess their business environment to identify the opportunity for a price war? Apparently, they do not just randomly start a price war or start it everywhere. Then, the question is how do they decide whether and when to start a price war? Like in any other war, the forces unleashed in a price war can be very destructive and unpredictable and hence careful planning and execution are a necessity to stay in control of those forces. How do Chinese companies prepare for and execute such a war?

The answers to all these questions are critically important for the Western companies who do business in China or who compete with Chinese companies in the West. With many foreign companies counting on China' growth to drive sales and profitability, and with more and more Chinese firms entering global markets, frequent price wars in China and elsewhere seem inevitable. One must understand how Chinese companies use price wars as a strategic weapon to be able to see their coming, to fight price wars effectively, or even to avoid them altogether.

We offer answers to all those questions. We will first analyze two well-known price wars in some detail to see how Chinese executives make their decisions about starting a price war and how they plan for it. From these analyses, it is clear that Chinese executives *do* treat price wars as an opportunity, and that there are rational reasons for them. Indeed, putting all these reasons together, one begins to see a rational framework for initiating and planning for price wars and hence to appreciate "The Art of Price War." This framework helps us to address the question of whether a price war should be initiated, by which firm, in what industry, and under what structural conditions in the marketplace. This framework can be applied to Chinese markets to shed some light on why they are rife with price wars, and to markets in the West to explain why Chinese companies are so aggressive with their prices and why Western companies are reluctant to start, or get involved in, price wars.

ANATOMY OF TWO PRICE WARS

The Color TV Industry

In early 1996, China's color TV industry was highly fragmented, with more than 130 manufacturers. Each manufacturer had, on average, less than 120,000 units of sales. Only 12 had annual sales of over half a million units, and only 4 had annual sales of more than 1 million units. As a result, few manufacturers could take advantage of economies of scale and most of them operated inefficiently. However, they all slogged along because a vast majority of these companies were owned by local governments and they were protected in their local markets. Thus, there was very little room for any ambitious Chinese company to expand their sales and to achieve scale economies through market entry or mergers and acquisitions (M&A).

The upward mobility was also very limited for a Chinese company at the time. China's color TV market was a two-tier market. Foreign brands served the high-end market and enjoyed a 20 percent price premium over local brands. With that price premium, foreign brands, Japanese brands in particular, still held a dominant position in China, especially in the Chinese urban markets. Although the quality of domestic products was comparable to that of foreign brands, local brands were in general competing with each other in the low-end market, and import buyers would seldom consider local brands.

Thus, in this market environment, a Chinese TV manufacturer had little horizontal or vertical mobility to increase its sales. In fact, the breathing room for Chinese companies was quickly shrinking in late 1995. At the time, there was a good deal of smuggling of color TVs, which was a significant drag on the stability of TV prices. In addition, Chinese companies were under increasing downward pricing pressure from a number of sources. First, import tariffs were slated to go down in 1996 for small-screen color TV's from 60% to 50% and from 65% to 50% for large-screen color TV's. Second, lured by the sheer size of the China market, foreign investments in the Chinese TV industry were red-hot. All 10 of the largest TV manufacturers in the world at the time were rapidly expanding their production in China. It was estimated that in two years' time, if all the announced expansion plans were fully executed, they would add an additional 10 million units of annual capacity in the Chinese market. The sales of foreign brands were expected to cascade down at the expense of Chinese companies. In fact, one business plan prepared by a large global color TV manufacturer boldly suggested that in three years' time, by investing some $3 billion in China, the company would destroy Changhong, the largest local competitor.

With 17 production lines concentrated in one place, Changhong ran the largest and most efficient color TV production in China. Its capacity at that time at least doubled that of the second largest Chinese manufacturer. Changhong was also the largest manufacturer for many key TV components, such as plastic injections, electronic components, remote controls, etc. As a highly vertically integrated company located in Sichuan, one of the less developed regions in China at the time, Changhong enjoyed cost advantages and earned the highest profit margin among all domestic color TV manufacturers. The net profit margins for Changhong were around 20%, far ahead of most of its domestic rivals.

Despite being the strongest domestic TV manufacturer, Changhong had to worry about its long-term survival, and it had to find ways to increase its market share quickly to shore up its future. Changhong's CEO, Mr. Ni Runfeng, spent several months in late 1995 and early 1996 weighing alternative strategies to increase the company's market share. The top executives at the company, including the CEO, talked with a number of pricing experts, carried out a number of marketing surveys in various regions, and extensively analyzed the survey data. Through these interviews, surveys, and analyses, they collectively came to the conclusion that would startle any

186

Western executive: a price war was the weapon of choice for Changhong to achieve a leadership position in the marketplace. They had their reasons.

On the one hand, a price war would put small, inefficient domestic TV manufacturers between a rock and a hard place: they could either cut their prices and suffer significant losses through margins, or maintain their high prices and suffer significant losses through volumes. In either case, they would have to struggle mightily to survive without any help from the local government. Such help was not forthcoming in early 1996 as readily as in earlier years, as the central government had tightened its fiscal policy, cascading down all the way to the local governments. Such help would become even less forthcoming if quick, costly, and significant damage could be inflicted to those local manufacturers. A decisive price war would do all that.

On the other hand, a significant price cut by a large local color TV manufacturer would also put foreign competitors, especially the Japanese TV manufacturers, in a predicament. If they were to stay out of the fray, Changhong would gain at their expense. If they were to join the fray, they would leave a lot of more money on the table for their high-end customers without much increase in sales and hence significantly reduce their profitability. Moreover, low prices and mud wrestling with a Chinese manufacturer could, certainly in the minds of foreign manufacturers, only erode their brand equity and undermine their brand image. On top of all this, for any drastic pricing changes, they needed to get the approval from their foreign parent firms, which could be a lengthy process. For those reasons, Changhong did not expect any significant price cut by foreign manufacturers, at least not initially.

Thus, what Changhong counted on, by initiating a premeditated, determined price war, was a huge increase in sales volume, taking customers away from weaker domestic rivals and possibly from foreign rivals, too. Changhong's confidence in its ability to increase its sales was further enhanced by the fact that in early 1996, China's color TV industry was at a fast growth stage. With a significant drop in the prices for color TVs, the industry demand could expand significantly and Changhong could corner a significant chunk of that demand. Changhong was the first color TV manufacturer to be listed in China's stock market and it enjoyed a high level of brand awareness and a high-quality image among domestic brands.

Aside from its low cost position relative to other domestic manufacturers and its brand awareness and image, Changhong recognized a number of other advantages going for it once a price war broke out. In early 1996, Changhong had an inventory of around 1 million units with a total estimated value exceeding 2 billion RMB. Changhong's efficiency suffered because of the huge inventory. However, this ready supply of a large quantity of color TV's provided the ammunition that Changhong would need in a price war to boost sales volumes. Changhong was also better prepared than any other domestic competitor to ramp up its production in case of surging demand. As the largest local color TV manufacturer, Changhong had built, over the years, a very close relationship with key component suppliers in the color TV industry. Once a price war got under way, Changhong could count on the reliable supplies of key components for its production. What also played to the advantage of Changhong as the initiator of a price war was the fact that smuggled color TV kinescopes, a key component for color TVs, were flooding the market in China and local component manufacturers had a large number of unsold color TV kinescopes in their inventory. According to one estimate, there were as many as 1.25 million units of inventory in 8 local kinescope manufacturers in early 1996. Changhong could tap a significant number of them to fight a price war.

With an uncertain future but ample ammunitions, Changhong thus found it an opportune time to stir up the industry with an unprecedented price war. After careful analyses, executives at Changhong decided that its price cut did not need to be a huge one for the price war to be effective. A 10% cut would enlarge its price differential with foreign brands to about 30% (before the price war, the price gap between local and foreign brands was around 20%) and put many domestic rivals in the red. The price cut was also affordable for Changhong given its 20% profit margin at that time. On March 26, 1996, Changhong fired the first shot, announcing a price reduction of 8% - 18% for all its 17"–29" color TVs, leading to price reductions ranging from RMB100 to RMB850.

The price war evolved mostly as Changhong had expected. All domestic TV manufacturers, especially the small ones, were shocked and angered by Changhong's price reduction decision. However, they reacted with hesitation. Initially, most local players decided to stay out of the fray. The four biggest domestic players (Konka, Panda, SVA, and Peony) did not follow suit until June 6 when Konka announced a price cut of up to 20%. The main reasons for them to wait were threefold. First, they were caught by surprise and were not prepared for the price cut and were not sure how to respond. Second, many underestimated the possible impact of a price war because of the fragmented nature of Chinese TV market, with many different brands dominating in different regions. Third, some state-owned enterprises (SOEs), such as Panda and SVA, had high costs per unit and a thin profit margin to start with. An 8%-18% price cut was not affordable for them. Also, it did not help that Panda was getting ready for its IPO in Hong Kong in May 1996. Panda and Peony pinned their hope on government intervention to stop Changhong's "reckless" pricing behavior. The thought of government intervention could only dull their fighting spirit.

Some domestic manufacturers did react quickly to Changhong's price cut. TCL, a medium-sized TV manufacturer at that time, was the first to react. On April 1, it announced a price cut of 120 – 300 RMB. Xiahua, another medium-sized player, announced a price cut of 10%. Due to the capacity constraint and the shortage of key components, however, Changhong's rivals could cut prices for small-sized TVs only.

Foreign brands did not follow Changhong's price reduction, just as Changhong had expected. Sony and Panasonic, for instance, all decided to take the high road: they would focus on quality and functionality, not on price.

Changhong's decision to initiate an unprecedented price war generated a barrage of publicity throughout the country and had a very positive impact on its sales as expected. A few months after the price war, Changhong's overall market share increased from 16.68% to 31.64%, with its share in the 25" market jumping from 20.76% to 45.25% and in the 29" market from 14.37% to 17.15% (in 1997, the overall share was further increased to 35%). Some medium-sized local players, TCL and Xiahua in particular, who followed suit quickly, had also benefited from the price war. They both increased their market share by more than 2%. In the meantime, small domestic players (sales less than 200k) in the market suffered mightily. During January – March 1996, there were a total of 59 local brands that had sales in the one hundred largest department stores in China. By April, this number dropped to 42. In the process, the market share for these small players dropped by 15.19%. Those big domestic manufacturers who did not follow suit saw their market shares dwindling, too. Panda's market share dropped from 7.6% to 5.8% and SVA from 5.5% to 2.6%.

Foreign brands also suffered. Before the price war, imports and joint venture products accounted for 64% of the market and local manufacturers for only 36%. After the price war, the market share of domestic products significantly increased with a total of around 60% by the end of 1996. The once all-powerful Japanese brands were all humbled and ended up with a much reduced market share. In 1997, 8 out of the top 10 best selling brands in China were Chinese and three local players, Changhong, Konka, and TCL became the best selling color TV brands in China, with their market shares at 35%, 15%, and 10% respectively. Only two foreign brands, Panasonic and Philips, made it to the top ten, each with about 5% of the market. Thus, the first ever large-scale price war in China drastically changed the landscape in the industry in favor of Chinese companies and the CEO of Changhong, Ni Runfeng, became a hero for Chinese national industries.

The Microwave Oven Industry

While Changhong might still be considered as a lucky survivor of a risky price war where the chips happened to fall its way, Galanz, a microwave oven manufacturer, has to be considered as a recidivist "warmonger" who has thrived with a deliberate price war strategy. From August 1996 till October 2000, Galanz initiated five major price wars and, through them, became the world's largest microwave oven manufacturer, with about 30% of the worldwide market and 76% of the Chinese market (see Table 10.1).

In 1995, China's microwave oven industry was at its infancy and less than 2% Chinese urban households owned microwave ovens. To a Chinese household, a microwave oven was a luxury item and the total unit sales in that year were about 1 million. The profit margins were very high for manufacturers at the time (30%-40%). The high profit potential attracted many entrants in the industry and there were already 28 small domestic manufacturers throughout China. By 1996, that number was to become 116.

TABLE 10.1
GALANZ'S SALES INFORMATION FOR YEAR 1995 – 2003

Year	Sales volume (in '000)	Local market share	Int'l market share
1995	200	25.1%	
1996	650	34.5%	
1997	2000	47.6%	
1998	4000	61.4%	15%
1999	6000	67.1%	20%
2000	10000	76.0%	30%
2001	12000	70.0%	35%
2002	13000	70.0%	40%
2003	16000	68.0%	44%

Galanz entered the microwave oven business in 1992 and by 1994 it produced 100,000 units of microwave ovens with a market share of about 10%. Soon afterwards in 1995, it achieved a market share of 25% and became a formidable competitor. It has done so by attracting talent from all over China, by purchasing an advanced production line from Japan, by devising effective marketing strategies (e.g., successfully entered the Shanghai market, the most important microwave oven market in China), and by responding to market changes very quickly.

Galanz's major competitor at the time was the Whirlpool-Xianhua (W-X), a joint venture formed in May 1995 between Whirlpool and the sizable Chinese manufacturer Xianhua, with Whirlpool owning the majority interest. In early 1996, Galanz and W-X each had about 25% of the market share in the microwave oven market, and they were far larger than the other competitors in China. However, relative to W-X, Galanz had a clear advantage: it was a more focused company with a streamlined, short decision-making process. At the time, Whirlpool was new to the Chinese market (it entered in late 1994) and was still learning the ropes of how to operate in China. It had four joint ventures in four different cities with four different Chinese partners in four different product categories (microwave ovens, air conditioners, refrigerators, and washing machines). Understandably, it encountered many problems in its China operations and could not pay sufficient attention to W-X. In addition, all key decisions in W-X had to be approved by Whirlpool's China head office, then its Asia Pacific office, and then by its U.S. headquarters. The whole process often took three months. Galanz, of course, took a note of that.

Galanz's decision to initiate the first price war in August 1996 was not an easy one. Senior executives at Galanz had long and heated debates on the risks and benefits of a price war and contemplated all scenarios. The majority of senior managers at the time opposed the price war strategy and preferred a safer strategy of maintaining the current high profit margins. In the end, the CEO made the call, siding with the minority, to get ready for war.

There were a number of reasons behind Galanz's decision, although the company was on a healthy growth trajectory. First, a significant portion of Chinese households were ready to modernize their kitchen with the purchase of a microwave oven, along with other appliances. A focus on high-end households and on high margins precluded riding that wave. Galanz estimated that significant price reductions would increase sales by about 100%.

Second, as one of the largest manufacturer in China, Galanz took upon itself the task to reorganize the industry for a sustainable future of growth. In an interview with one of the authors for this paper, Yu Yaochang, the VP of Galanz, recalled that one of the purposes of the first price war was to consolidate the industry by marginalizing small, inefficient players before they had a chance to grow and discourage new entrants. A high profit margin in the industry would both encourage excessive entry and hide inefficiencies going forward.

Third, perhaps, most importantly, a well-planned and executed price war could significantly benefit Galanz in terms of establishing its cost advantages in the marketplace. Galanz recognized that a significant price cut could substantially increase its sales through expanding the market as well as take customers away from weak competitors. Then, a substantial increase in the company's sales could substantially reduce its unit cost through scale economies in production, distribution, and components sourcing, which in turn would make the price cut profitable in the first place. The trick here was to make sure that the cost decrease would outpace the price decrease so as to increase the company's profitability. Galanz believed that it had a chance to do this, as long as it was deliberate and meticulous in planning and executing the price war.

Two months before launching the price war, Galanz began to run its production lines on a 3-shift, 24-hours a day schedule, so that it had an ample supply to meet the expected surge in demand. In August 1996, Galanz launched its first price war with a price reduction of 40% on some of its key products and with an average price reduction of 20.1%. The size of the price cuts surely put customers as well as rivals on notice. In a number of cases, Galanz's price reduction levels on some products were higher than their current gross profit margins. Galanz picked August to start the price war, as it was the off-peak selling season when manufacturers would generally downscale their production and distribution.

The news of Galanz initiating a price war was reported widely in all major Chinese media. Retailers embraced the price war with open arms, as it could help them build store traffic and sell more of their other products. In many cases, they were even willing to take lower profit margins, 8% instead of the usual 20%, on Galanz products during the price war period. Competitors were caught unprepared and dazed. Most of the small manufacturers did not respond quickly, as they believed that Galanz was simply dumping its excess inventory in a low selling season. Galanz's main rival W-X was, as expected, particularly slow in responding to the price reduction.

The outcome of the first price war could not have been more positive for Galanz. By the end of 1996, Galanz's market share had increased from 25% to 34.5%. Before the price war, the gross profit margins for Galanz were close to 40%. After the price war, sales had increased by about 200% and the average unit cost was reduced by around 50%. Galanz's net profits also increased significantly. Even from the products where the magnitude of price cuts was bigger than that of profit margins, Galanz made profits because of cost reductions.

The huge success of the first price war had convinced the executives at Galanz that a deliberate price war strategy was a viable strategy, not only in the short term, but also in the long-run. From October 1997 to October 2000, Galanz initiated four more price wars and executed them with increasing sophistication. In each round of price wars, Galanz cut its prices substantially with double digit percentage point drops (up to 40% in some cases). The sales increases were also substantial, all around 100% - 200%. As a result, the company became more and more dominant as indicated in Table 1 by its ever rising market share. In each round of price wars, Galanz achieved an average unit cost reduction of about 30% - 40%. Because of those victories, in the Chinese media, Galanz became the ever-victorious army and its executives the ever-victorious generals.

The secrets behind the ever-victorious army were, of course, its cost advantages. To achieve the cost advantages, Galanz needed to drive up its volumes relentlessly. Pricing helped the firm to achieve high volumes. Ever since the first price war, Galanz adopted a simple and systematic way in setting its price to drive volumes. It set its price at the break-even level for its nearest competitor. For example, if the second player's annual sales were 2 million units, then Galanz would set its price at the break-even level for the 2-million units. During price wars, Galanz's price would even go significantly lower than this breakeven point. Using this strategy, Galanz always made rivals reluctant to cut prices and thus it always stayed ahead of competition in capturing more volumes. As the process unfolded, Galanz encountered fewer and fewer competitors. In 1996, there were about 120 microwave oven manufacturers. By 2003, the three largest microwave oven manufacturers took over 90% of the market.

THE ART OF PRICE WAR

The two examples of firms initiating and executing price wars successfully, of course, do not make price wars a smart marketing strategy. Indeed, there are incidents, even in China, where firms initiate price wars on impulse and bring ruin to themselves as well as to everyone else in their industry. What they do demonstrate, however, is the fact that price wars can be a potent, effective marketing strategy when they are deployed with forethought and skills and in the right circumstances. What constitutes right circumstances? How should a firm plan and execute a price war?

From the two examples discussed previously, we see that the Chinese executives did not start the price wars on impulse and they planned and executed the price wars with great care. Consciously or unconsciously, they were making rational calculations to make sure that they benefit from a price war and control its outcome. These calculations that they were making, it turns out, neatly fit into a simple framework with which the executives in the West are all too familiar but have not made the connection. Implicit in this framework is (almost) everything that an executive ever needs to know in order to plan, execute, and fight a price war. The Chinese executives in the two cases discussed previously merely applied the framework, consciously or unconsciously. This framework is the so-called Incremental Breakeven

Analysis (IBEA). With it, one can have a comprehensive, systemic understanding of the incentives facing firms in initiating and fighting a price war.

Incremental Breakeven Analysis (IBEA)

A price war always starts with a firm initiating a deep price cut in an industry, *e.g.* Changhong in the color TV industry and Galanz in the microwave oven industry. When the firm initiates such a price cut, by and large, it expects to benefit from it either right away or at some point in the future. Putting aside any long-term benefits or costs for now, the firm can only benefit in the short term if its sales go up sufficiently. To determine the threshold sales increase that is needed for a firm to benefit from a price cut, one can conduct the so-called incremental breakeven analysis. What this analysis does is to identify the sales change that will make a firm's profits after the price change to stay the same as before, or the breakeven sales change. In Figure 10.1, we display the formula for this threshold sales increase for a given price cut when a sales increase could lead to a change in a firm's marginal costs.

To use the formula, let's go back to the Galanz case. As we have discussed before, while planning for the first price war, Galanz reduced its product price by as much as 40%. So, let us take Δp=40%. To evaluate whether doing so could increase its contributions, Galanz could calculate the threshold sales increase it must generate with the 40% price cut to stay at breakeven. At the time, Galanz's average contribution margin---the contribution per unit sales before the price change (price minus marginal cost) as the percentage of the pre-change price, was about 40%, or cm = 40%. The company expected that the price cut would generate enough volume to reduce its unit cost by 30-40%, or on average Δc 35%. By plugging all these numbers in the formula, we have Δq = 0.905 or 90.5%. This suggests that if the demand for Galanz's products would increase by more than 90.5% as a result of the 40% price cut, Glanz would make more profit by implementing the price cut. Then, Galanz could focus on the question of whether it was possible to generate that much sales increase given the market environment it found itself. At the time, Galanz expected its sales to increase by 100%, fully anticipating competitors' reactions (the actual sales increase was about 200%). Therefore, initiating the price war was the rational thing to do.

FIGURE 10.1
INCREMENTAL BREAK-EVEN ANALYSIS FORMULA

$$\Delta q = \frac{\Delta p - (1-cm)\Delta c}{cm - \Delta p + (1-cm)\Delta c}$$

Definitions:

Δq---the breakeven sales increase in percentage;

Δp---the magnitude of a price cut;

cm---the contribution margin in percentage (before the price cut);

The Art of Price War

The value of IBEA goes far beyond that simple calculation, of course. Some rigorous analyses of that formula will help us to understand the incentives facing a firm in initiating a price war. By analyzing those incentives, we can begin to understand how the Chinese executives in the previously discussed two cases planned and executed price wars.

From the IBEA, we can see that it is more tempting for a firm to initiate a price war if it faces a small Δq, all else being equal. In other words, if it does not take much sales increase for a firm to benefit from a deep price cut, the firm should have more an incentive to use price as a weapon and to initiate a price war. This means that we can analyze the formula in Figure 10.1 to see when Δq is small to know where a price war is more likely to break out and what kind of firms may have the most incentive to initiate it.

To start, we note in the formula that if cm is larger, Δq is smaller. This means that if the current profit margin is high, it does not take much in increased sales for a firm to benefit from a price cut, and thus there should be more of a temptation for such a firm to engage in price competition. This analysis suggests two insights. First, across different industries, the ones that have (unusually) high margins tend to be the ones where price wars break out, all else being equal. Indeed, in China, price wars do not break out randomly across different industries. When the first price war broke out in the color TV industry in China, it was a high profit margin industry that had supported a large number of manufacturers, however inefficient they were. When the first price war broke out in the microwave oven industry, that industry was also characterized by high profit margins and excessive entry. Indeed, all subsequent price wars in China happened in high margin industries such as consumer electronics, home appliances, personal computers, mobile phones, telecommunications, cable TV, and, automobiles. Second, within the same industry, the firm that has the best margin, typically due to a lower cost, has more of an incentive to initiate a price war. Changhong was such a firm, Galanz was such a firm, and so were many other price war initiators in China.

Based on these two insights, we can also understand why Chinese companies tend to start price wars when they enter the markets in the West. Chinese companies have cost advantages and a favorable exchange rate, and they encounter a small number of competing firms in every market they enter. To them, every business in the West is a high margin business!

We also note that as Δc in the formula increases, Δq is always smaller. This means that in industries where significant scale economies were involved, price wars are more likely to break out. In those industries, firms face significant incentives to ramp up their sales and to stay ahead of competition in going down the cost curve. All those industries in China that have been plagued by price wars are the ones where significant scale economies exist. Indeed, even in the West, price wars periodically flare up in industries with significant scale economies such as for PCs, electronics, and airlines. Furthermore, the fact that Δc decreases Δq also suggests that within an industry, the firm that is most skillful in taking advantage of scale economies is more likely to be the one that initiates a price war and benefits from it, all else being equal. Both Changhong and Galanz were such firms that consciously and skillfully exploited scale economies to their own benefit.

Interestingly, when a firm enters a new market starting with a clean slate, it typically does have lots of scale economies to exploit. This is because studying the market, setting up distribution channels, and advertising all take significant fixed costs. In this sense, the aggressive pricing behavior on the part of Chinese companies to carve a slice of market share when they enter into the markets in the West is rather expected.

Finally, in the formula, a larger Δp will lead to a larger Δq. On the surface, this relationship merely suggests that a large price cut needs to generate a larger volume increase to breakeven. However, upon reflection, this relationship also tells us something about how price wars are related to product differentiation. In a highly differentiated industry, it would take a huge price cut to persuade customers to switch from one firm to another. This, in turn, means that a huge increase in sales has to be expected in order to justify the price cut in the first place. Therefore, in a differentiated industry, price wars are less likely to break out. It is almost unnecessary to repeat the cliché here, except the fact that it conforms with the Chinese experience with price wars very well. Price wars almost always break out in an industry in China when products in the industry become standardized, with little room for further technology innovations and quality improvements. In addition, the fact that the foreign brands charged a 20% premium and it only took about 10% price cut to draw customers away from foreign brands had certainly helped Changhong to make up its mind to start the price war.

The preceding analyses answer the questions of what kinds of firms in what kinds of industries would have the most incentive to start a price war and benefit from it. However, they do not answer the question of how to plan and execute a price war. For that answer, we need to look deeper into Δq. To benefit from a deep price cut, a firm must generate enough sales increase to cross the threshold of Δq. Where does this sales increase come from?

From a firm's perspective, its sales q comes from the demand in the industry Q and its market share s, i.e. $q = sQ$. Thus, its sales change will come from either its market share change, or the industry demand change, or both. In fact, some algebra will show $\Delta q = \Delta s + \Delta Q + \Delta s \Delta Q$, where Δs is the change in the firm's market share in percentages and ΔQ is the change in the industry demand in percentages. What this means is that a firm can cross the threshold sales increase either through a significant market share increase or through a significant increase in the industry demand (or both of course). We now take up each source of sales increase in turn to see how a firm could maximally tap each source.

To benefit from a price war, a firm can try to increase its market share Δs so that it can generate enough sales increase to cross the threshold Δq. For instance, if $\Delta q = 20\%$, a firm can cross the threshold if its market share increases by more than 20%, or $\Delta s > 20\%$, even if the industry demand does not change, or $\Delta Q = 0$. Therefore, while planning and executing a price war, a firm should give itself the maximal chance to increase its market share. There are a number of things that a firm can consider here.

First, to the extent that it is easier for a firm with a small initial market share to increase it, a small market share firm is better positioned to use price as a weapon and to initiate a price war, and a big market share firm may want to think twice about it. For that reason, we rarely see firms with a dominant market share starting a price war. Second, the timing of starting a price war is very critical. A firm has a better chance to increase its market share if competition is unable or unwilling to react swiftly. A clumsy, half-hearted response from competition would give the war-initiating firm the time and space to stuff distribution channels and to occupy new sales territories. Both Changhong and Galanz, as discussed before, have thought hard about competitive reactions and about an opportune time to fire the first shot.

Third, even if competition reacts swiftly by bringing down their own prices, an astute firm can still increase its market share if it has prepared for a price war adequately. As competing firms lower their prices, the firms that will gain in market share will be the ones that have products on hand to sell. A firm that has prepared for a price war, through building up its inventories, ramping up its productions, and boosting up its production capabilities, will be best positioned to increase its market share. From the discussion before, we see that both Changhong and Galanz had made elaborate preparations in those activities before they fired their first shot, while competition was caught napping. Of course, competitor could have seen that ramp-up and acted accordingly.

Fourth, a firm can gain a larger market share when less cost-effective firms in an industry are weeded out. A price war will put strains on all firms in an industry. However, less efficient firms will buckle first and surviving firms will fatten their market shares. Clearly, in both cases that we have discussed in this paper, the Chinese companies made explicit calculations to consolidate their respective industry and achieved that objective. In fact, looking more broadly, this motivation has surfaced again and again in many other Chinese industries where price wars break out. Indeed, an industry with a large number of firms and a wide distribution of sizes and operating efficiencies is a fertile ground for price wars. As China has many of those industries, while in the West there are few, it is not surprising that there are more price wars in China than in the West and Chinese executives may seem to be feistier.

Through many price wars, Chinese executives have also learned that to weed out cost-inefficient firms in a market, they do not necessarily need to fight a prolonged, bloody fight. A "shock and awe" strategy can quickly convince an inefficient rival to get out of the way, as any resistance is either futile or fatal. Both Changhong and Galanz thought of this in planning and executing their price wars. From this perspective, it is perhaps understandable that Chinese companies are gung-ho about charging a price 30%-50% lower than competition, rather than a gentlemanly 10% or 20% lower, when they invade a market in the West.

Of course, not all bets are off if a firm cannot increase its market share by starting a price war. Another important factor in a firm's price war calculus is ΔQ, the change in the industry demand. When a price war breaks out, even if all competing firms in the market are equally efficient and they all follow suit cutting their prices so that no firm can gain any additional market share, firms can still benefit from price wars if they expand the industry demand sufficiently. In the West, people tend to forget the times when the markets for mundane products such as microwave ovens, color TV's, refrigerators, etc., were growing at a fast pace and the total demand for them was price elastic. However, in China, they are all high growth industries with high price elasticity and hence substantially lower prices can open the floodgate for consumer purchases. This is also one of the key reasons why there are so many price wars in China but not in the West. Changhong was betting on this surge in the industry demand and so was Galanz. What this also means is that as the growth of an industry levels off, one should begin to observe fewer price wars and more focus on non-price competition.

CONCLUSIONS

We hope that our discussions so far, based on the experience of Chinese companies have achieved two objectives. First, they demystify rampant price wars in China and combative pricing behavior on the part of Chinese companies. There is nothing intrinsically Chinese, as far as we can detect, about the calculus that the Chinese executives use in planning and executing price wars. What is intrinsically Chinese, however, is the fact that a whole generation of Chinese executives have grown up in a business environment characterized by growing markets, heterogeneous firms with a wide distribution of cost-efficiencies, and new technologies with significant scale economies. This business environment provides many profitable opportunities for them to engage in price wars and to hone their skills, whereas in Western markets, oligopolistic competition among (mostly) equals in mature markets encourages more finesse in devising marketing strategies. In both cases, firms are weighing the same factors, albeit making different strategic choices in the end.

Second, price wars are not *per se* a nonstarter as a marketing strategy, and the stigma associated with them in the West is not helpful for executives who have to fight in the trenches. As with any other business strategy, the usefulness of price wars depends on the circumstances. A company can take a quite rational approach to plan and execute a price war when opportunities arise. Chinese companies seem to have a knack in identifying those opportunities and seizing upon them. However, one need not look far to discover the art of price war, and the familiar incremental breakeven analysis or IBEA provides one with a guide for planning and executing a price war.

Up to this point, we have purposefully left two issues untouched. First, price wars have long-term consequences beyond what the short-term payoffs capture. How could IBEA be adjusted to incorporate these long-term effects? Second, the art of a price war is all about how to plan and execute a price war and it seemingly says little about a firm at the receiving end. If a

Chinese company comes to a US market, how could a US company prevent it from starting a price war? If it cannot discourage the Chinese company from charging a price 30-50% lower, what should it do?

The first question is easier to answer. If you can assess specific long-term benefits or losses from a price war in terms of its impact on the future cash flows, you can always adjust Δq downward or upward accordingly. Thus, for instance, if Philip Morris expected that a 20% price cut on the Marlboro Friday (April 2, 1993) would have had the long-term effect of disciplining generic brands and thus stabilizing price competition in the future, it should have been willing to accept a much lower immediate sales lift, sacrificing short-term profits for the long-term gains.

The questions related to defensive strategies are harder to answer. Depending on the situation in which a firm finds itself, the answers can be quite different. We are currently developing detailed answers to those two questions, based on specific case studies. However, one already gets all the clues to those answers from IBEA if one thinks like a contrarian. IBEA suggests two broad principles for fighting a price war.

First, as Sun-Tzu put it best in his <u>Art of War</u>, "the highest realization of warfare is to attack the enemy's plans" so that one can subjugate "the enemy's army without fighting." Specific to fighting a price war, what this means is that you want to do things that can prevent any company from starting and benefiting from a price war. In the parlance of incremental breakeven analysis, you want to increase Δq facing your rivals, so much so that they never have a chance to increase their sales significantly to cross that threshold.

Second, when a price war has to be fought, you cannot fight it by merely taking a defensive posture. Once again, Sun-Tzu put it best, "One who cannot be victorious assumes a defensive posture; one who can be victorious attacks." In the parlance of IBEA, you want to do things that can put your own company in the position to capitalize on a rising industry demand (ΔQ) and on the possible redistribution of market shares (Δs) in the industry.

Authored by Z. John Zhang and Dongshen Zhou Originally published in *International Journal of China Marketing*, Vol. 1(1) 2010, pp. 17-30.

Chapter Eleven

Demand Attributes and Market Segmentation: An Evaluation of Refrigerator Purchase Behavior in Rural China

Conjoint analysis is the most widely used method of analysis of consumer's demand preference in marketing research. In this paper, we use conjoint analysis model to study peasant' cognitive attributes to refrigerator product, through a detailed analysis of 5872 effective questionnaires collected from 14 provinces. The questionnaire and the analysis model are constructed from the peasant consumption psychology point of view. The result demonstrates that the Chinese peasant' demands of refrigerators vary along with the differences in price, brand, quality, and region. There is a "threshold value" of income for peasant. Based on consumer demands attributes evaluation, we argue that there are three market characteristic Segments in Chinese rural market, "the type of comprehensive benefits", "the type of the brand-oriented", "the type of the price advantage".

INTRODUCTION

Durable goods usually consist of several attributes. The different combinations of attributes form different specific products. Consumers make decision by integrated value of different product attributes. Conjoint analysis is the best method to research the product attributes. The basic idea of conjoint analysis is to value the relative importance and utility of each attribute by measuring the consumers 'whole preference to products of multiple attributes. Conjoint analysis can help us to understand the intrinsic value system of the consumer psychology, and to know why consumers choose a certain product rather than other products.

Conjoint analysis is the most widely used method of consumers 'preferences research in the field of western marketing. Luce and Turkey firstly introduced this method in 1964; Green used it to do marketing research in 1971. Since then, the technology of conjoint analysis model has been developed rapidly, and has been more and more widely applied in academic research, as well as in business research（Carroll, Green，1995；Green，Krieger, Wind，2001；Wittink，Vriens, and Burhenne，1994）. From the mid 1990s, some scholars in China began to use conjoint analysis in the fields such as marketing (e.g. Huixin Ke et al., 1994; Xiaoqun He etc.,

2000; Kaocong Tian et al., 2003;Zhe Xu etc., 2004). Some consulting companies also began to use this technology at that time.

Although, many scholars and experts use conjoint analysis to research product attributes, there is a lack of systematic first hand research on Chinese peasants' cognition of the attributes to durable appliances. The peasant consumer behaviors are significantly different in dissimilar cognition of product attributes. For peasants, the products can be observed; the differences in cognition of the product attributes come from the differences of consumer psychology. In the process of the rural market development, enterprises should have a better understanding of the product attributes as well as the combination of consumer behavior and psychologies. The examination of peasant cognition of the attributes for popular refrigerators in rural electronic appliance markets is accomplished by using the random coefficient model of conjoint analysis. The perspective of peasants consumption psychology is used to construct the research models. The hope is that the outcome of the research will be useful for the enterprises to develop new products and market segmentation in rural markets.

RESEARCH MODEL

Conjoint analysis is a statistic method to study the importance of product attributes to consumers, as well as the consumer utility from the same attribute levels. A product is usually composed of several attributes. The different combinations and specific levels of each attribute makes products different. For different consumers, the importance of product attribute s and the utility values on different levels of the same attribute are not the same; this is the core difference of consumer demand. The evaluation of the product attributes and the utility values of the specific attribute level are appropriate standards in market segment.

There are various methods of collecting data in conjoint analysis. In addition, the methods of the model estimation are different. For example: (1) whole outline method (WOM); (2) mixed method, MM (Conjoint analysis and individual mixed Conjoint Analysis); (3) self-interpretation method (SIM); and (4) discrete-selection method (DSM). However, the degrees of difficulties for different methods to collect data are not the same. There is no conclusion on which method is the best fitting to consumer inside value system. Nonetheless, the WOM is a traditional conjoint analysis method, which is still widely used nowadays, especially, in China.

Usually, the WOM includes the following steps: (1) to determine the important product attributes and the specific levels of each attribute; (2) to determine the product mix using orthogonal designing method; (3) to score each product mix by the possibility or the preference of purchase; and (4) to estimate the utility coefficients of the model by using the least squares method (OLS) linear regression (Marhotala, 2002).

In a conjoint analysis, we often need to estimate two levels of utility coefficients, the individual level and the whole level. In WOM, the individual level utility coefficient is estimated by regression of individual all data points There are usually two ways to get the whole level utility coefficient: the first is the arithmetic mean values of the individual levels utility coefficients; the second is OLS linear regression of all respondents' data. The main problems of the above approach are (1) when we estimate the individual level utility coefficient using alone regression, the number of data is limited and the number of independent variables is too large (there are more coefficients need be estimated), and therefore, the model freedom of motion is very low. The consequence is that the model will fit into the data excessively, and the estimation of the individual level utility coefficient is not stable; (2) the whole level utility coefficient is not stable by using arithmetic mean value of individual level utility coefficient; (3) if we get the whole level coefficients by the regression of all the data points, we could ignore the differences of the coefficients between different individual levels,.

The random coefficients model can be used to solve the problems above with advantages as follows: (1) it can be used to estimate the coefficients of the individual level and the whole level at the same time through same model.; (2) it can be used to do statistic test of the differences of the individual levels coefficients; and (3) it can be used to make the shrinkage estimation for each individual level coefficient, it makes the individual level shrinks towards statistical population, which reduces the possibility of extreme values in individual coefficients, it makes the individual coefficient more reliable.

Basic Conjoint Analysis Models

The whole outline method (WOM) can be expressed by the following utility function.

$$U(X) = \sum_{i=1}^{m} \sum_{j=1}^{k_i} a_{ij} X_{ij} \qquad (1)$$

Formula (1): there are $i = 1...m$ product attributes. Attribute i has $j = 1...k_i$ levels. $U(x)$ is the total utility of a product mix. a_{ij} is the partial utility value of attribute i of level j. X_{ij} is a dummy variable ($X_{ij} = 1$ when X (attribute i and level j) is exists, otherwise $X_{ij} = 0$).This is a common basic utility model which only has main effects, no cross effects.

The importance I_i of attribute i can be expressed as the utility range which is the biggest difference in the partial values.

$I_i = \{\max(a_{ij}) - \min(a_{ij})\}$ (for all the levels of attribute i) (2)

The relative importance W_i of attribute i is got from the standardized calculation of. I_i

$$W_i = I_i / \sum_{i=1}^{m} I_i \qquad (3)$$

The purpose of conjoint analysis is estimating the utility coefficient of each attribute's level through score of each attribute's level of each specific product from the respondents .The utility coefficients of the WOM are usually estimated by the way of the dummy variables regression (Marhotala, 2002).

The Regression Model of Individual Level

Before random coefficient model, we need to define the model of individual level. For the conjoint analysis which includes m attributes and attribute i has levels, we need to estimate $\sum_{i-1}^{m} k_i - m$ coefficients in addition to distance. For the k_i level of each attribute i , we need to define one reference level. The reference level coefficient is 0, and then we could estimate the other k_{i-1} coefficients. The attribute's level coefficient estimated represents the difference from the reference's level. If the coefficient >0, it is meaning the utility of this attribute's level is higher than the reference's level. If the coefficient <0, it is meaning the utility of the attribute's level is lower than the reference's level. For convenience, we assume $t = \sum_{i-1}^{m} k_i - m$, this is based on some experimental design methods, such as orthogonal design. Every respondent need to score at least s product mixes, so everyone has s data points. For respondent h and product s, $S = 1 \ldots s$, the linear regression equation can be expressed as:

$$Y_{0hs} = \beta_{0h} + \beta_{1h} X_{1hs} + \beta_{2h} X_{2hs} + \ldots + \beta_{th} X_{ths} + e_{hc} \qquad (4)$$

Formula (4): Y_{hs} is the score of product s by consumer h . $X_{ihs}^{t_{i=1}}$ is dummy variable of different attribute's levels of product s. β_{ih} are model coefficients of the respondent h . β_{0h} is the model distance, $\beta_{ih}^{t_{i=1}}$ is utility

204

coefficient of different attribute's levels of the consumer h. e_{hs} is the model residual error of product s for consumer h. We assume $e_{hs} \sim N(0,\sigma^2)$.. We assume that the model residual error of products s and respondents h obey this distribution.

Random Coefficient Model

From the Formula (4), we know that each consumer has his own model coefficient. For the model coefficients of consumer h, the coefficients can been expressed as equations. Every equation is about the average model coefficient of all the consumers and the random residual error of consumer h. It is as follows:

$$\beta_{0h} = \gamma_0 + \mu_{0h}$$
$$\beta_{1h} = \gamma_1 + \mu_{1h}$$
$$\beta_{2h} = \gamma_2 + \mu_{2h}$$
$$\dots$$
$$\beta_{th} = \gamma_t + \mu_{th} \tag{5}$$

Formula (5): γ_0 is distance, $\gamma_i \overset{t}{\underset{i=1}{}}$ is the population mean of the model coefficients of each attribute's level. $\mu_{ih} \overset{t}{\underset{i=0}{}}$ is the coefficient random residual error for consumer h. We assume that residual error obeys the law of normal distribution, average is 0, and variance is $\tau i \overset{t}{\underset{i=0}{}}$ .It is as formula (6).

μh~ N(0，τ0)
μh~ N(0，τ1)
μh~ N(0，τ2)
...
μh~ N(0，τt) (6)

If we put formula (5) into formula (4), we will get the random coefficient model by whole outline method (WOM):

$$Y_{hs} = \gamma_0 + \gamma_1 X_{1hs} + \gamma_2 X_{2hs} + \dots + \gamma_t X_{ths} + \mu_{0h} + \mu_{1h} X_{1hs} + \mu_{2h} X_{2hs} + \dots + \mu_{th} X_{ths} + e_{hs} \tag{7}$$

Through this model, we can estimate the population means coefficients, $\gamma_0, \gamma_1, \gamma_2, \dots \gamma_t$, and the random coefficients of consumer h ,$\mu_{0h}, \mu_{1h}, \mu_{2h}, \dots \mu_{th}$. In statistics, the population mean coefficient is also called the Fixed Effect, and the individual's random residual error is also called the Random Effect. The fixed effect is the value of Best Linear Unbiased estimation (BLUE); the random effect is the value of Best Unbiased prediction (BLUP). The model coefficient of each respondent h is the sum of the fixed effect and the random effect. The random effects can be obtained by shrinkage estimation. This method not only considers the internal differences in each person, but also considers the differences between different people. The biggest advantage of this method is that the coefficient of the individual level draws close to overall average coefficient, it reduce the possibility of the extreme value on the individual level (Littell etc, 1996). In addition, we can test the random effect variance $\tau_i^t{}_{i=0}$, if $\tau_i^t{}_{i=0} \neq 0$, it assumes the difference in this coefficient for the different consumers is significantly. Otherwise, the coefficients of the different consumers are more convergent (Bryk etc, 1992; Littell etc, 1996; Greene, 2000).

Some scholars recently proposed other methods to estimate the utility coefficients of individual level and whole level. The two main methods are hierarchical Bayes (HB) and finite mixture (FM). The HB is carried out through fitting the Monte Carlo Markov Chain (MCMC); the FM is carried out through the maximum likelihood method or Expectation-Maximization (EM) method. The HB is better than FM fitting the random coefficient model logic (We can also take random coefficient method as a kind of empirical Bayes), because we make hypothesis to be coefficient distribution of individual level. However, there are no significant difference between the coefficients of individual estimated with the method of the Bayes and the FM. (Allenby etc, 1995; Lenk etc, 1996; Andrews etc, 2002).

RESEARCH DESIGN AND DATA COLLECTION

This research subject is refrigerators, which is a popular electrical appliance for peasants in China. The refrigerator is the key product subsidized by the government in accord with the national significant policy "home electric appliances to the countryside policy". It is also the key product that peasant like it more and more. This research has practical significance and value to research no matter for the nation or for the home electric appliance enterprises. The research samples are peasant consumers from 14 provinces, the method of multi income steps (high, medium, low) cluster was adopted. The first step, we randomly choose 14 provinces in order of different income level proportion .The second step, we randomly choose cities and towns in every province in order of some distribution. The third step, we randomly choose peasants in the cities or towns. Finally, we received 5872 valid questionnaires. The sample regional distribution and sample sizes can be seen as in table 11.1 below.

TABLE 11.1
THE DISTRIBUTION AND CAPACITY OF SAMPLE

Province	Number of cities or towns	Sample Capacity
Anhui	29	503
Fujian	57	392
Hebei	45	449
Heilongjiang	29	400
Hunan	61	463
Jiangsu	76	499
Jiangxi	33	252
Neimeng	12	478
Shandong	46	501
Shanxi	65	450
Shanxi	35	496
Yunnan	56	297
Zhejiang	33	194
Sichuan	79	498
Total	656	5872

We designed the conjoint analysis through the following three steps. The first step is the determination of product attributes. Through fieldwork, we understand the product attributes which sales clerks and appliance buyers considered. We identify the related attributes of refrigerators through qualitative research. Then, we get 300 questionnaires about score of these attributes from qualitative research, the questionnaires come from the Heilongjiang and the Shanxi provinces randomly, According to the score sorting, we select 7 important attributes of the refrigerator to research, as the table 11.2. The second step is the determination of the levels of the every attribute. After fieldwork in Guomei super market, we determine the levels of each attribute. According to the prophase-survey, we find the peasant think many factors are important for brand (is it domestic famous or just-so-so), and there are many different brands. So, according to peasant'opinion, we merge the brands to four brand categories (the Euramerican brands, the Japan or Korea brands, the domestic 1 brands and the domestic 2 brands). The domestic 1 brands include Haier, New-fly and Rhombohedrons. The Domestic 2 brands include Little-swan, Hisense, Principle, Kelon, Rongsheng, TCL, Oakes curled, Konka and AoKeMa. The Euramerican brands include Electrolux and Siemens. The Japan and Korea brands include

207

Samsung, Toshiba, Panasonic and LG. The ridge has 22 attribute levels in total (table 11.2).

The third step is the determination of product mixes. According to the refrigerator's attributes and the number of their levels, the refrigerator has 4 x 4 x 3 x 2 x 3 by 3 x 3 = 2592 possible product mixes. They are too many obviously. So we determine 32 kinds of product mixes for the refrigerator using orthogonal design method.

Finally, we design questionnaire about these 32 product mixes and we let the peasants score these product mixes between 0~100 according to the purchase possibility.

TABLE 11.2
THE ATTRIBUTES AND LEVELS OF REFRIGERATORS

Brand	Price (RMB-Yuan)	Color	Structure	Power Consumption (KW/hr)	Volume	Cooling Capacity
Euramerica Japan-Korea	⟨1500 1500-1800	white grey	wide door short vertical door	⟨0.6 0.6-0.8	⟨170L 170-200L	⟨3kilos 3-5kilos
Domestic 1	1800-2000	others		⟩ 0.8	⟩ 200L	⟩ 5kilos
Domestic 2	⟩ 2000					

Data Analysis and Results

The refrigerator has 7 attributes, every attribute has 22 levels. We need to estimate some model coefficients including the distance using dummy variable regression method. And we estimate the fixed effects and random effects of the refrigerator coefficients using of Proc Mixed (SAS), limits maximum likelihood method (REML) and between–within degrees of freedom (DOF) calculation method. Because the random coefficients are too many, we assume that the random coefficients inside covariance=0, and we just need estimate their variances $\tau_0, \tau_1, \tau_2, ... \tau_t,$. This assumption is as follows:

$$Var \begin{vmatrix} \mu_0 \\ \mu_1 \\ \mu_2 \\ \vdots \\ \mu_t \end{vmatrix} = \begin{vmatrix} \tau_0 & 0 & 0 & \cdots & 0 \\ 0 & \tau_1 & 0 & \cdots & 0 \\ 0 & 0 & \tau_3 & \cdots & 0 \\ \cdots & \cdots & \cdots & \cdots & \cdots \\ 0 & 0 & 0 & \cdots & \tau_t \end{vmatrix} \qquad (8)$$

The Utility Coefficient Analysis of Whole Level

From whole average model coefficients table (table 11.3)，we know the attribute levels significantly ($p<0.01$) influence the possibility (utility function) for peasant to buy refrigerators besides some attributes (volume, domestic 1 brand, wide door structure, color and power consumption of 0.6-0.8 kilowatt hour). Based on the model coefficients table 11.3, we will analyze the relative importance of the refrigerator attributes and the partial utility values of each attribute level.

According to the formula (2) and (3), we separately calculate the biggest utility range and relative importance of the refrigerator 7 attributes (table 11.4). The brand is the most important product attribute in all attributes, importance score is 30.4%. The second is price (importance score =23.9%) and cooling capacity (importance score =23.2%). The power consumption importance score= 15.8%. Volume importance score =4.0%. The structure importance score=1.8% and color importance score= 0.9 %. so for Chinese peasants, They pay more attention to not only the brand but also the price because their income is still low, this result can be explained on one hand the peasants have showing off consumption psychology (the importance of brand > performance), on the other hand they also have the practical consumption psychology (the price is the second important attribute).

In conjoint analysis, the relative distance of the partial utility values (the different levels of the same attribute) is the most important, which reflects the relative size of the utility of different attribute levels. Even if we make the partial utility values of different levels of the same attribute plus or subtract a constant, their relative contribution have no change.

For brand, the domestic brands have absolute superiority, and their partial utility values are higher than the foreign brands. There are no significant difference between the domestic famous brands and the domestic general brand; this could be caused by the chaos of refrigerator market and lack of super homebred brand. To the homebred brands, the competitiveness of foreign brands (Euramerican or Japan-Korea refrigerator) is still much inferior.

209

TABLE 11.3
**THE COEFFICIENTS OF THE WHOLE AVERAGE MODEL OF
THE CONJOINT ANALYSIS OF REFRIGERATORS（N=5752）**

Variable	Coefficient	Standard Deviation	Degree of Freedom	T	p
Distance	53.484	0.335	5751	159.790	<.0001
Brand[a]					
Japan-Korea	-6.376	0.224	180000	-28.490	<.0001
Euramerica	-5.610	0.207	180000	-27.120	<.0001
Domestic 1	-0.084	0.155	180000	-0.540	0.588
Price[b] 1500-					
1800yuan	-1.417	0.148	180000	-9.570	<.0001
1800-					
2000yun	-2.693	0.155	180000	-17.430	<.0001
〉2000yuan	-5.018	0.193	180000	-26.050	<.0001
Color[c]					
White	0.188	0.123	180000	1.530	0.127
Grey	0.058	0.142	180000	0.410	0.684
Strucure[d]					
Wide Door	-0.382	0.100	180000	-3.810	0.000
Power Consumption Kilowatt hour					
0.6-0.8	-0.882	0.123	180000	-7.190	<.0001
〉0.8	-3.313	0.143	180000	-23.180	<.0001
Volume[f]					
170L-200L	0.829	0.129	180000	6.440	<.0001
〉200L	0.285	0.127	180000	2.240	0.025
Cooling Capacity[g]					
3-5kg	2.333	0.135	180000	17.280	<.0001
〉5kg	4.854	0.170	180000	28.500	<.0001

Note：a: The reference group of brand is domestic 2; b: The reference group of price is below 1500 Yuan RMB; c: The reference group of color is other colors; d: The reference group of structure is short vertical door; e: The reference group of power consumption <0.6 kilowatt hour; f: The reference group of volume <170L;g: The reference group of cooling capacity <3 kg. These coefficients =0.

TABLE 11.4
THE RANGE AND RELATIVE IMPORTANCE OF THE
ATTRIBUTES OF REFRIGERATORS

Attribute	Utility Range	Relative Importance
Brand	6.376	0.304
Price	5.018	0.239
Color	0.188	0.009
Structure	0.382	0.018
Power Consumption	3.313	0.158
Volume	0.829	0.040
Cooling Capacity	4.854	0.232
Total	20.960	1.000

For the attribute of price, as we know, the higher the price is, the lower the partial utility value is. The difference of the utilities is smaller between 1500 Yuan and 1500-1800 Yuan than other price range, which shows that the peasants have lower sensitivity of price in these price ranges. Even if manufacturers increase the price to close 1800 Yuan, it wills not significant difference for the purchaser's total utility value. However, if the price is too high, for example, it is more than 2,000 Yuan; the total utility value will dramatically decline. This shows that the peasant's high price capability is relatively lower.

For the attribute of color, peasants do not do not pay more attention to color. Merely peasant prefer traditional white color than other colors, the strategy that manufacturer try to attract peasant consumers by changing the color of the refrigerator maybe not work. For the door structure attribute of the refrigerator, there is not so much difference on whether with the door handle or not. .

As for the attribute of power consumption, the less the power consumption is, the higher the partial utility value is. We can see that the peasants care much about the attribute of power consumption, and they satisfy to the refrigerators with the power consumption below 0.8 kilowatt hour. It will be more attractive to energy-saving refrigerators in the rural market.

The attribute of volume is very interesting. The all-level partial utility values are almost same, i.e. peasants do not do not care so much about the refrigerator's size. After further research, we find many peasants pay more attention to who buy refrigerator or not, they do not do not care how big the refrigerator is. They do not do not understand the concept "liter" very well. In addition, peasants self-sufficient lifestyle and habit result in the use frequency of refrigerators is low and some family even use the refrigerator as furniture decoration. They do not think the refrigerator is necessity in life so much; they buy it just because other people buy it. So when manufacturers develop product in rural market, they should communicate to peasants about the knowledge of refrigerator and life quality as same time.

The attribute of cooling capacity is also interesting factor. The bigger cooling capacity, the more peasants like it. Influenced by the traditional consumption idea, peasants think capacity is signal of quality, they forget the bigger cooling capacity, and the more power consumption is. Peasant decision-makings by cooling capacity and power consumption are so contradictory, which explains the peasant is not rational when they evaluate durable goods and making decision.

The Difference Analysis of the Utility Coefficient on Individual Level

The model's random effect coefficients and residual error variances are given in table 11.5. Through test the variances of random effects, we know the partial utility values of some attribute levels are significantly different, and others are not. Because we cannot test reference groups attribute levels directly, we make them equal to 0. The 0 doesn't mean that reference groups attribute levels' partial utility values are same for all the consumers. If there are significant differences between the other levels of the same attribute, the partial utility values of the reference groups attribute levels should have differences too. This is because it is simple linear relationship with partial utility values of other attributes (the reference group model coefficients are equal to the values when all other attribute levels of the same attribute are equal to 0).

After the difference test of the every level of each attribute specifically, we get the results as following: (1) the random effect coefficient variances of Euramerican and Japan-Korean brands are significantly different, it is meaning the attractions between Euramerican and Japan-Korean are different for different peasants. For the same reason, there are different between domestic 1 and 2 brands for peasants. (2) The partial utility values in the whole price ranges are significantly different, it is meaning that peasants have significantly different price sensitivity, and the sensitivity to high or low price is much more different. (3) White color always is the main color in refrigerator market. The attractions or identities of white color have significant difference, grey color does not. (4) The appearances of the refrigerator are basically same. The peasants do not care the refrigerator has door handles or not. (5) Peasants have same agreement on low-power-consuming refrigerator, but they have significant difference for the power consumption more than 0.8 kilowatt hour. (6) There are significantly difference for peasant's evaluation in volume. (7) There are significantly difference for peasant's evaluation in cooling capacity.

To sum up, the refrigerator structure, 0.6-08 kilowatt-hour power consumption and gray color have no difference for the peasants. Brand, price, volume and cooling capacity are four attributes whose differences for peasants are bigger. For attribute combination, there are two difference combinations, high prices combination and high capacities combination. This is meaning for the some classes refrigerators, especially the high-grade class, there are very big difference in peasant's value judgment. Therefore, manufacturer should develop different products according to the difference of peasant value judgment.

Utility Coefficient Analysis on the Individual Level

The utility coefficient of the individual level is the sum of the whole utility coefficients (fixed effects) and the individual random errors (random effects). From Figure 11.1, we give the distributions of individual level's utility coefficients whose attribute are significantly different. Some differences of partial utility values of some attribute levels for peasants are very big.

DISTRIBUTION OF INDIVIDUAL PARTIAL UTILITY VALUES

For example, average utility values of the Japan and Korean brands are higher than domestic 1 brands', but there are some extreme utility values in Japan and Korean brand are very low(-63) it is far less than the lowest utility value of domestic 1 brands (-12.6), it is meaning for these peasants, Japan-Korean brands are completely unnecessary. So it will make their preference low if providing them the Japan and Korean brands refrigerators. In figure 11.1, we know the partial utility values of the some attribute levels (such as the attributes of "0.8 power consumption", "5 kg cooling capacity or above" and "2000 Yuan or above") have big differences for peasants. The differences of utility values on the individual level indicate the refrigerators-market in rural is multi- market. Different peasant consumers prefer different refrigerator mix.

TABLE 11.5.
THE RANDOM EFFECT COEFFICIENT VARIANCE AND MODEL RESIDUAL VARIANCES OF REFRIGERATOR

Variable	Estimated Value	Standard Deviation	Z	p
Intercept	442.450	8.946	49.460	<.0001
Brand[a]				
Japan- Korea	172.670	4.809	35.900	<.0001
Euramerica	130.620	4.042	32.320	<.0001
Domestic 1	21.889	2.155	10.160	<.0001
Price[b]				
1500-1800yuan	10.832	1.800	6.020	<.0001
1800-2000yuan	21.924	1.980	11.070	<.0001
〉2000yuan	97.961	3.320	29.510	<.0001
Color[c]				
White	0.864	1.085	0.800	0.213
Grey	0.000	—	—	—
Structure[d]				
Wide Door	0.000	—	—	—
Power Consumption[e]				
0.6-0.8 kilowatt hour	0.000	—	—	—
〉0.8 kilowatt hour	30.929	2.022	15.300	<.0001
Volume[f]				
170L-200L	8.636	1.624	5.320	<.0001
〉200L	6.076	1.581	3.840	<.0001
Cooling Capacity[g]				
3-5kg	18.333	1.869	9.810	<.0001
〉5kg	80.312	2.964	27.090	<.0001
Residual	461.620	1.919	240.520	<.0001

Note: a: The reference group of brand is domestic 2; b: The reference group of price is below 1500 Yuan RMB; c: The reference group of color is other colors; d: The reference group of structure is short vertical door; e: The reference group of power consumption <0.6 kilowatt hour; f: The reference group of volume <170L; g: The reference group of cooling capacity <3 kg. These coefficients =0.

FIGURE 11.1
DISTRIBUTION OF INDIVIDUAL PARTIAL UTILITY VALUES

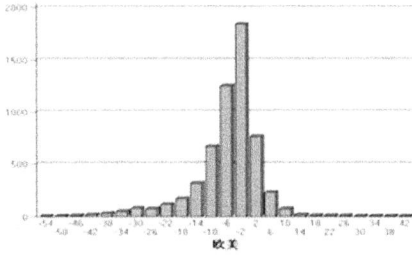

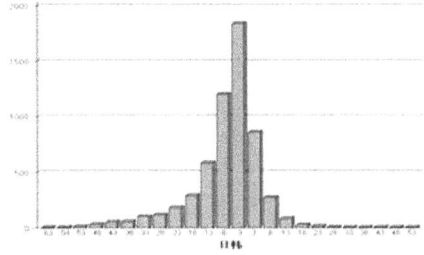

Euramerican Brand

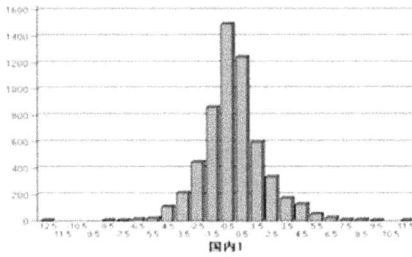

Japan-Korean Brand

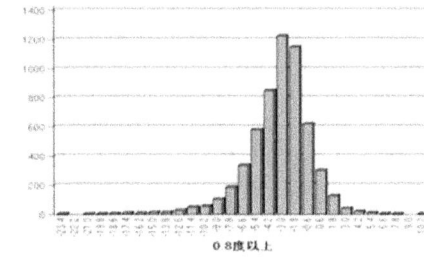

Domestic 1 Brand

Consumption Above 0.8 degree

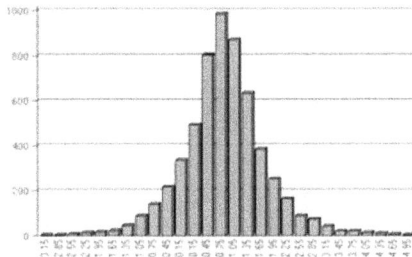

Volume of 170-200L.

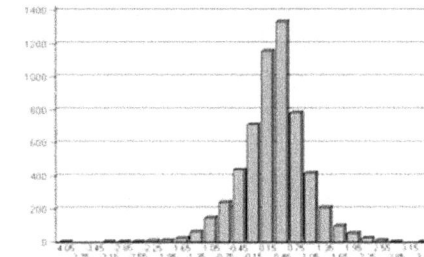

Volume above 200L

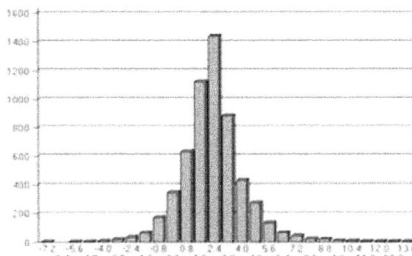

Cooling Capacity of 3-5Kilos.

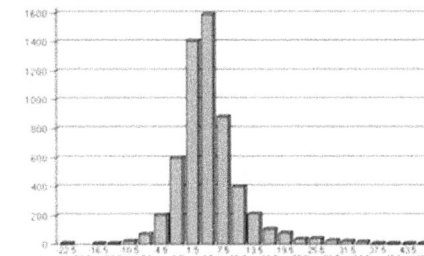

Cooling Capacity of above 5 Kilos.

215

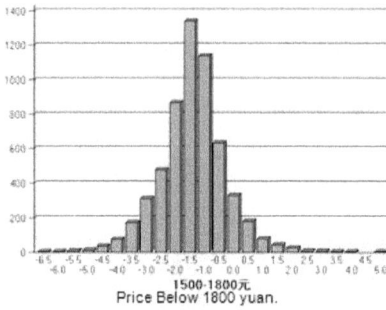

1500-1800元.
Price Below 1800 yuan.

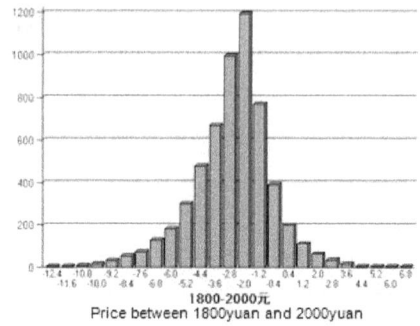

1800-2000元.
Price between 1800yuan and 2000yuan

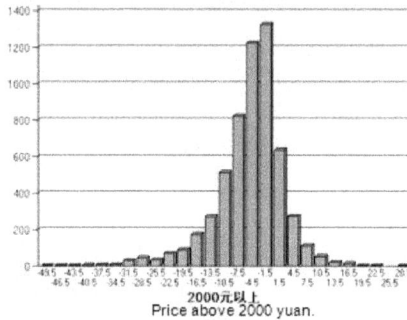

2000元以上.
Price above 2000 yuan.

Enterprise should analyze peasant consumers' difference value system. Market segmentation should been carried according to the peasant preference. They should provide attractive products in view of different segments of the market, even one-to-one marketing.

After SAS software running, we get cluster analysis result of the partial utility values on the individual level. The cluster process is shown in figure 11.2.

Based on figure 11.2, that is appropriate to choose three segments of the refrigerator market in rural. We can calculate the importance of each attribute of segment market and all market (table 11.7), through value the partial utility of each segment market' s attribute levels (table 11.6).

216

FIGURE 11.2
**THE CLUSTER ANALYSIS OF PARTIAL UTILITY VALUES ON
INDIVIDUAL ATTRIBUTE LEVEL**

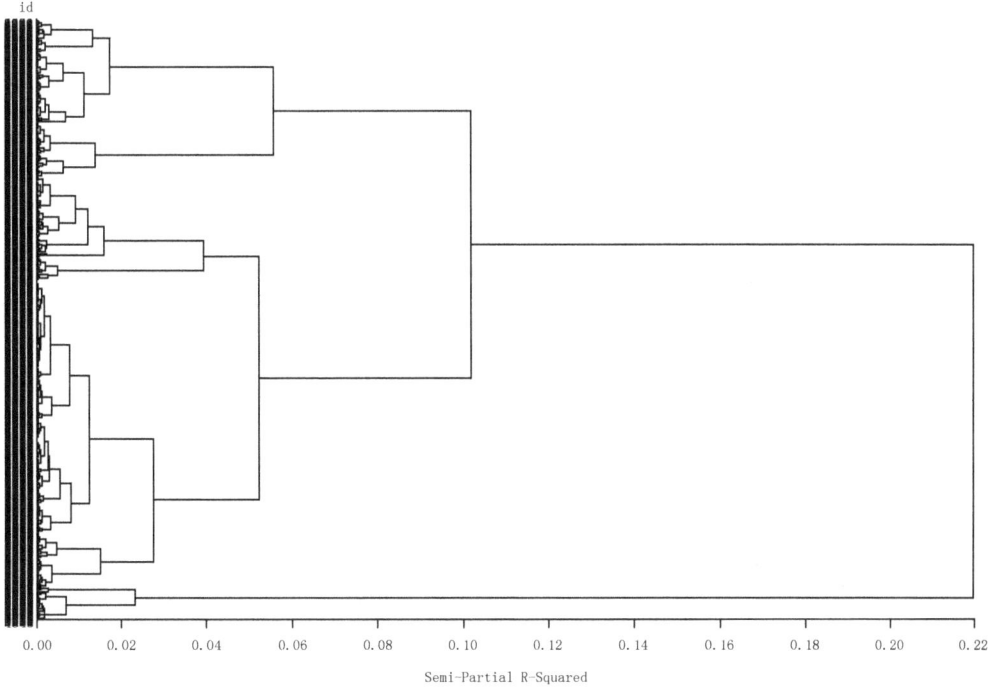

Semi—Partial R-Squared

From the results of table 11.6 and table 11.7, the refrigerator attribute preferences are significantly different for research sample. It is unable to reflect this difference only using the whole market model, if enterprises do not subdivide the attribute preference differences, their products' attraction will decline. There are the peasant consumers' characteristics in segment market in table 11.6 and table 11.7.

We can get three types of segment market.

"The type of comprehensive benefits" segment market: Namely segment market 1, it is 68.57% in the whole market. They are the biggest consumption group of the market, and these consumers pay the most

TABLE 11.6
THE CLUSTER ANALYSIS OF PARTIAL UTILITY VALUES ON INDIVIDUAL ATTRIBUTE LEVEL

Attribute	Level	Market Segment			Whole Market
		1	2	3	
	Market Scope	3944	308	1500	5788
	Market Share	68.57%	5.35%	26.08%	100.0%
Brand	Japan-Korea	-1.289	-21.395	-5.097	-3.359
	Euramerica	-1.003	-12.353	-4.768	-2.592
	Domestic 1	0.898	18.720	5.045	2.934
	Domestic 2	1.394	15.028	4.821	3.017
Price	〉 1500yuan	1.710	2.079	3.828	2.282
	1500-1800yuan	0.217	0.710	2.601	0.865
	1800-2000yuan	-0.954	-0.081	0.947	-0.411
	〉 2000yuan	-0.973	-2.708	-7.375	-2.736
	White	0.110	0.104	0.098	0.106
Color	Grey	-0.026	-0.023	-0.020	-0.024
	Other Colors	-0.084	-0.081	-0.078	-0.082
Structure	Wide Door	-0.191	-0.191	-0.191	-0.191
	Short Vertical Door	0.191	0.191	0.191	0.191
Power Consumption	<0.6degree	1.340	1.381	1.555	1.398
	0.6-0.8degree	0.458	0.499	0.673	0.516
	〉 0.8degree	-1.799	-1.880	-2.227	-1.915
Volume	<170L	-0.365	-0.396	-0.383	-0.371
	170L-200L	0.418	0.479	0.557	0.458
	〉 200L	-0.053	-0.084	-0.175	-0.087
Cooling Capacity	<3 kilos	-2.369	-2.006	-2.545	-2.396
	3-5 kilos	0.040	0.142	-0.375	-0.063
	〉 5 kilos	2.329	1.864	2.920	2.458

attention to the cooling capacity whose importance is 32.3% for them, the second important attribute is power consumption whose importance is 21.6%. The brand and price attributes importance are same 18.4%, these attributes attraction for peasant are relative same.

They like the refrigerators, which have "5 kg refrigeration ability" and "power consumption of 0.6 kilowatt hour or below", they do not care international high brand, and the domestic brand is ok. They like low price of fewer than 1500 Yuan. So the refrigerator with low price, domestic brand, electricity-saving and big power is most attractive for the 1/3 market consumers.

"The type of brand-oriented" segment market: namely market segment 2, it is 5.35% the whole market. These consumers pay most attention to brand whose importance is 76.9%. And they like domestic brands more than foreign brands. For some consumers, the difference of domestic brands is the most attractive decision –making factor.

"The type of price-brand" market segment: namely segment market 3, it is 26.08% in the whole market. They relatively pay attention to price and brand. The price importance is 34.9% for them; the brand importance is 31.6% for them. The degrees of importance for the two attributes are not significantly different. Meanwhile, the price attribute importance of segment market 3 is higher than segment 1 and 2 markets'. The difference of peasant partial utility values of the two levels of price "below 1500 Yuan" and "price between 1500 Yuan and 1800 Yuan" is relatively small （from 3.8 to 2.6）. The utility value will become negative if the price pass 2000 Yuan, and consumers more possible refuse this kind of high price refrigerators.

STATISTICAL VARIABLES' INFLUENCE ON THE SEGMENT MARKET

To research the relationship of the peasants consume behavior characteristic and segment market, we discusses the family income and family population in this part.

The Analysis of the Influence of Family Income on Segment Market
From table 11.8, the consumers mainly belong to "the type of comprehensive benefits" market consumers.

TABLE 11.7
THE IMPORTANCE OF ATTRIBUTES ON INDIVIDUAL LEVELS
OF REFRIGERATOR MARKET SEGMENTS

Attribute	Market Segments			Whole Market
	1	2	3	
Market Share	68.57%	5.35%	26.08%	100%
Brand	0.184	0.769	0.316	0.563
Price	0.184	0.092	0.349	0.131
Color	0.013	0.004	0.01	0.007
Structure	0.026	0.007	0.01	0.014
Power Consumption	0.216	0.063	0.12	0.114
Volume	0.054	0.017	0.03	0.029
Cooling Capacity	0.323	0.049	0.170	0.142

The income type is important factor, for example, the consumer groups with high sideline income or other incomes; they value brand's importance more high. Most of families buy refrigerator with 4-5 members. The family income amount has not significant relationship with segment market (table 11.8).

The Analysis of Variance of Market Segment and Income Amount
From table 11.9 to table 11.14, the every $p > 0.05$, so there is no significant difference between income amount and segment market of refrigerator; it is meaning peasant income amount is not a valid constraint in refrigerator consumption. There are two possible reasons. The first reason is that refrigerator is so popular in peasant family. If without refrigerator in home, householder could care about neighborhoods look down him. The psychology of vanity and showing off make peasant give up considering income amount constraints, when they making decision. The second reason is "income threshold".

TABLE 11.8
THE TABLE OF FAMILY INCOME AND MARKET SEGMENTS

Variable	Segment Markets			The Whole Market
	Comprehensive benefits type	Brand-oriented Type	Price-brand Type	
Market Share	68.57%	5.35%	26.08%	100.00%
Agricultural Income (Yuan)	9570.70	8918.23	8539.70	9267.30
Part-time Income (Yuan)	14228.35	10799.17	13420.42	13843.17
Sideline Income (Yuan)	6730.87	7101.02	6145.35	6599.30
Other Income (Yuan)	4159.16	5624.23	4081.74	4212.26
Overall Income (Yuan)	28856.27	25416.99	26295.07	28004.20
population (person)	4.12	4.02	4.15	4.12
Average Individual Income (Yuan)	7565.66	6985.06	6805.76	7335.12

TABLE 11.9
THE DIFFERENCE BETWEEN AGRICULTURAL INCOMES IN REFRIGERATOR MARKET SEGMENTS

Variable Resource	Quadratic Sum	Degree of Freedom	Mean Square Deviation	F	p
Between the Group	1.10E+09	2	5.50E+08	1.43	0.24
in the Group	2.04E+12	5291	3.85E+08		
Total	2.04E+12	5293			

TABLE 11.10
THE DIFFERENCE BETWEEN WORK INCOMES IN REFRIGERATOR MARKET SEGMENTS

Variable Resource	Quadratic Sum	Degree of Freedom	Mean Square Deviation	F	p
Between the Group	3.22E+09	2	1.61E+09	0.61	0.54
in the Group	1.35E+13	5113	2.64E+09		
Total	1.35E+13	5115			

TABLE 11.11
THE DIFFERENCE BETWEEN SIDELINE INCOMES IN REFRIGERATOR MARKET SEGMENTS

Variable Resource	Quadratic Sum	Degree of Freedom	Mean Square Deviation	F	p
Between the Group	3.35E+08	2	1.67E+08	0.65	0.52
in the Group	1.10E+12	4261	2.59E+08		
Total	1.10E+12	4263			

TABLE 11.12
THE DIFFERENCES BETWEEN THE OTHER INCOMES IN REFRIGERATOR MARKET SEGMENTS

Variable Resource	Quadratic Sum	Degree of Freedom	Mean Square Deviation	F	p
Between the Group	3.29E+08	2	1.64E+08	0.39	0.67
in the Group	1.29E+12	3097	4.18E+08		
Total	1.29E+12	3099			

Some previous macroscopic studies showed the family income amount have significantly important relationship with consumers' consumption of durables. But our research result is contrary. Because if there is an "income threshold" for peasant, i.e. before real income < "income threshold", it is difficult to activate their purchase intention and behavior, income amount constraint works. But real income> "income threshold", the consumer behavior is affected by psychological variables and marketing variables more than income, so income amount constraint could doesn't work.

TABLE 11.13
THE DIFFERENCE OVERALL INCOME OF EACH SEGMENT OF REFRIGERATOR MARKET

Variable Resource	Quadratic Sum	Degree of Freedom	Mean Square Deviation	F	p
Between the Group	9.31E+09	2	4.65E+09	1.22	0.29
in the Group	2.19E+13	5749	3.81E+09		
Total	2.19E+13	5751			

TABLE 11.14
THE DIFFERENCE AVERAGE INDIVIDUAL INCOME OF EACH SEGMENT OF REFRIGERATOR MARKET

Variable Resource	Quadratic Sum	Degree of Freedom	Mean Square Deviation	F	p
Between the Group	6.52E+08	2	3.26E+08	1.05	0.35
in the Group	1.73E+12	5593	3.10E+08		
Total	1.74E+12	5595			

TABLE 11.15
THE GEOGRAPHICAL DISTRIBUTION OF THE MARKET SEGMENTS OF REFRIGERATORS

Province	comprehensive benefits type %	Brand-oriented Type%	Price-brand Type%
Anhui	72.84	2.21	24.95
Fujian	66.67	3.31	30.02
Hebei	63.92	4.90	31.18
Heilongjian	51.24	23.02	25.74
Hunan	76.99	5.53	17.48
Jiangsu	72.82	3.57	23.61
Jiangxi	76.96	0.87	22.17
Neimeng	53.28	5.29	41.43
Shandong	68.10	3.91	27.99
Shanxi	71.13	8.69	20.18
Shanxi	78.99	2.33	18.68
Sichuan	63.73	4.40	31.87
Yunnan	77.74	1.71	20.55
Zhejiang	70.00	3.68	26.32

These parts classify the sample area according to the characteristics of the market segmentation (table 11.15). The characteristic of the peasant consumers in Heilongjiang is relatively outstanding. The Brand-oriented consumers are the first place, and the proportion is more than the other provinces. Although the southeast coast provinces' economy is advanced, in their provinces, the consumer's Brand-oriented consuming habit is not formed yet. Shanxi and Yunnan provinces' economy is developing, and consumer pay most attention to the comprehensive benefits. What it means for them is that the traditional cost performance psychology is dominant factor. They have limited brand awareness, which is just in cognitive stage, without brand-oriented motivation, behavior or emotion.

To analyze the different characteristics of peasant consumer behavior in the regional area, we reclassify the market share according to the three consumer behavior patterns and three consumption types (table 11.16). Totally, peasants underline cost-performance, they pay more attention to the capacity and the using cost. Those are the cooling capacity and power consumption attributes. The consumer demand on durable goods is various, in the regional market segment, the characteristics of product attributes are various too.

TABLE 11.16
THE DISTRIBUTION OF CONSUMPTION BEHAVIOR PATTERN
OF EACH SEGMENT

	comprehensive benefits type %	Brand-oriented Type%	Price-brand Type%
ENM	70.10	3.50	26.40
CNM	68.09	6.85	25.06
FNM	68.38	4.58	27.04

Note: ENM, Extensive Needs Mode; FNM, Functional Needs Mode; CNM, Core Needs Mode.

CONCLUSION

According to our research on refrigerators, we can have the following conclusions: (1) there are different on cognition of product attributes for peasant consumers in the different consumer behavior patterns and different segment markets. (2) Peasants are especially practical, and the comprehensive benefits type products have the biggest share in the market. The peasants more like the function and performance of refrigerators. (3) Sometimes, peasants have the same cognition to different product attributes.

This is meaning that the purposes of peasants' intrinsic psychology are different. (4) Peasant' decision of electrical appliances is not rational yet. They like products of lower prices, but they like the big one same time, the decision-making process has contradiction. (5) Through variance analysis that income amount and the income type are different influence for peasant consumption of the refrigerator. In the research review, we mentioned that some scholars did not consider wealth constraint when they research American consumption of durable goods, the reasons are: 1) the aim of the consumer behavior research is the general principle whatever individuals or groups decision-making process; 2) the theoretical foundation of the consumer behavior research is less considers the family finance; 3), the consumer behavior research borrowed more from the psychology and the sociology etc not finance. These explain the empirical result is reasonable that the income amount is not significant importance for peasant decision-making.

In general, the most important is that the peasant consumer evaluations of product attributes in different regions and markets are not the same different. Therefore, in the keen competition market the market segmentation is very important for enterprises. When they make the policy, they must make it based on their understanding on the peasant evaluations of product attributes as well as the demand characteristics in different segment markets.

Authored by Baoku Li, Lijuan Wang, and Bingru Li, originally published in *International Journal of China Marketing*, Vo. 1(2) 2011, pp. 13-33.

Chapter Twelve

China Compared with the US: Cultural Differences and the Impacts on Advertising Appeals

An important first step to successful global marketing is to understand the similarities and dissimilarities of values between cultures. This task is particularly daunting for companies trying to do business with China because of the scarcity of research-based information. This study uses updated values of Hofstede's (1980) cultural model to compare the effectiveness of Pollay's advertising appeals between the U.S. and China. Nine of the twenty hypotheses predicting effective appeals based on cultural dimensions were supported. An additional hypothesis was significant, but in the opposite direction as predicted. These findings suggest that it would be unwise to use Hofstede's cultural dimensions as a sole predictor for effective advertising appeals. The Hofstede dimensions may lack the currency and fine grain necessary to effectively predict the success of the various advertising appeals. Further, the effectiveness of advertising appeals may to moderated by other factors, such as age, societal trends, political-legal environment and product usage.

INTRODUCTION

Previous research indicates that the effectiveness of advertising is highly dependent on cultural variations (Cheng and Schweitzer, 1996; Culter and Rajshekhar, 1992; Monga and John, 2007; Shavitt and Zhang, 2004). Scholars have studied whether advertisements with appeals adapted to the audience's important cultural values (e.g., individualism for North Americans and collectivism for Chinese) tend to be more persuasive and better liked than appeals unadapted to such values (Zhang, 2004). More recently, Hornikx and O'Keefe (2009) conducted a meta-analytic review of the research and found that adapted ads are somewhat slightly more persuasive and better liked than unadapted ads.

Generally, researchers have paired countries to test for differences in several values portrayed in advertising to determine the most effective methods. Albers-Miller and Gelb (1996) conducted the largest and most widely recognized study of this nature using Hofstede's (1980) four cultural dimensions and Pollay's (1983) list of common advertising appeals. Unfortunately, they did not compare the value systems and perceptions of effective advertising of the Mainland Chinese with those of the United States.

As such, smaller marketing firms are forced to develop advertising programs based on data extrapolated from research on Korean and Taiwanese value systems (Emery and Tian 2003).

China's gross domestic product is reported to be $1.335 trillion by the middle of 2010, surpassing Japan's GDP of $1.286 trillion, making China the second largest economy in the world (Gustin 2010). Accordingly, the Chinese consumer market is the second largest in the world in terms of Purchasing Power Parity (PPP) and is growing at a double-digit pace since 1990s (Sun 2007, Fraser and Raynor 1996). As early as in 2001 it was predicted that the Peoples Republic of China would be the second largest Internet user and that the Chinese language will be the most used language on the Internet by 2005 (Rodrigues, 2001). This prediction was witnessed to be true in the end. As of June 2010, the population of China's Internet users climbed to 420 million, 36 million more than at the end of 2009 (Gao, 2010). The fast growth of the economy, coupled with Chin's enormous population of over 1.4 billion people, has made China attractive for global marketers. It was reported that multinational agencies mostly headquartered in the United States have been seeking markets in China and bringing their offices to China. At the same time along with their increased incomes, the Chinese people have started to demand a wider choice of products and services. Chinese consumers have become more used to employing advertising as their information source to make purchasing decisions, and in addition, more and more companies use advertising as the means to promote their products and services (Chang and Chang, 2005; Gustin, 2010).

Advertising has become one of China's fastest-growing industries. According to Nielsen Media Research, the United States ranked first in advertising in 2005, and China ranked third, after only the United States and Japan (China Advertising Yearbook, 2006). At the current annual advertising spending growth rate, China is expected to become one of the world's top five advertising markets within a few years (China Association of Advertising, 2009). All this equates to tremendous opportunities for international advertising firms to help their present clients expand into China or to assist the Chinese with marketing their products abroad.

This task, however, is particularly daunting for companies trying to do business with China because of the scarcity of empirical research. **Cultural differences serve as the hardest barrier to overcome as they have been deeply ingrained in the Chinese citizens over thousands of years. In fact, as some American firms have learned advertising that are effective in other markets may not work at all in the China market; more interestingly, that some advertisements which are effective in certain areas of China may not work in other areas in the same country (Kurlantzick, 2002, Tian, 2000). Meanwhile the cross-cultural pragmatic failure in English advertisements translated from Chinese has been identified as a significant issue for Chinese marketers to consider when launching advertising campaigns in the Western country markets (Sun, 2007).

A review of cross-cultural advertising studies published in 18 major periodicals between 1980s and earlier 1990s found that only one study pertained to China and none compared China with the United States (Samiee and Jeong, 1994). Emery and Tian (2002a, 2002b) updated this study between 1992 and 2001 and found three studies pertaining to China and only one that compared China with the United States. Since then although no systematic study has been done on this subject scholars have started to pay attention to it. For instance in her recent new book *Brand New China*, Wang (2008) offers us a unique perspective on the advertising and marketing culture of China, demonstrates the influence of U. S. branding theories and models on advertising in China. The purpose of this study is to partially address this movement by comparing effective advertising appeals between China and the United States.

THEORETICAL BACKGROUND

Cultural Values

The first step to successful cross-cultural marketing is to understand cultural differences (Briley and Aaker, 2006; Lillis and Tian, 2010). The reasoning is that consumers grow up in a particular culture and become accustomed to that culture's value systems, beliefs, and perception processes. Consequently, they respond to advertising messages that are congruent with their culture, rewarding advertisers who understand that culture and tailor ads to reflect its values (Cheng and Schweitzer, 1996; Culter and Javalgi,1992, Desmarais, 2007). Albers-Miller's (1996) study of 55 country pairs indicates that similar cultures have similar advertising content and dissimilar societies have dissimilar advertising content. Hofstede's (1980) seminal study regarding the relationship between national culture and work-related values is the most frequently cited benchmark for cross-cultural understanding (Tian, 2000). Hofstede considered that a country's value system could be depicted along four dimensions: individualism (IDV), power distance (PDI), uncertainty avoidance (UAI), and masculinity (MAS).

Hofstede explained that the dimension of individualism was the degree to which individual decision-making and actions are encouraged by society. This dimension reflects the way people live together. In a collectivistic society, at the lower end of the individualism-collectivism continuum, individualistic behavior may be seen as selfish.

The power distance dimension indicates the degree to which power differences are accepted and sanctioned by society. In other words, it indicates how different societies have addressed basic human inequalities in social status and prestige, wealth, and sources of power. The societal norm in a country with a high score on the PD dimension is for powerful people to look as powerful as possible. People with power are considered to be right and good. Powerful people are expected to have privileges. In countries with large power distance, the exercise of power gives satisfaction and powerful people try to maintain and increase power differences (Hofstede 1980).

The uncertainty avoidance dimension represents the degree to which society is unwilling to accept and cope with uncertainty. People use law, religion, and technology to address uncertainty. This dimension is related to anxiety, need for security, dependence on experts, and the application of information (Hofstede, 1980).

The masculinity dimension indicates the degree to which traditional male values (*assertiveness, performance, ambition, achievement*, and *materialism*) are important to a society. The opposite end of this continuum has been labeled femininity. The societal norm in a country with a high score on the MAS dimension is to try to be the best while valuing achievement, productivity and "machismo". In these countries, big and fast are considered beautiful (Hofstede 1980).

Hofstede's research has been instrumental in furthering an understanding of cross-cultural consumerism and is often used as the basis for selecting between customized and global approaches to marketing (Tian, 2000). Unfortunately, Hofstede was not able to map the Mainland Chinese culture at the time of his 1980 study. Later Hofstede explained that his 1980 study used the cultural values of IBM employees in offices around the world. At that time China did not have IBM offices and access to comparable employees was denied (Hofstede, 1993). Fernandez, et al. (1997), however, updated the original Hofstede study and for the first time included dimensional values for Mainland China. It is important to note, however, that Fernandez, et al. used undergraduate and graduate students in their study. The relationship between China and the U.S. in that study is presented as a standardized score in Table 12.1.

Advertising Appeals
The second step to successful cross-cultural marketing is to understand a society's sensitivity to advertising appeals. Advertising appeals are the specific approaches advertisers use to communicate how their products will satisfy customer needs by embedding a culture's values, norms, and characteristics (Arens and Bovee, 1994; Hornikx and O'Keefe ,2009).

TABLE 12.1
COMPARISON OF HOFSTEDE DIMENSIONS (Standard Scores)

Dimension	China	U.S.
MAS	2.20	-.58
UAI	.31	.59
IDV	-.96	1.52
PDI	1.05	-.01

Note: 1990 data excepted from Fernandez, Carlson, Stepina, & Nicholson (1997)

The appeals are typically carried in the illustration and headlines of the ad and are supported and reinforced by the ad copy. Researchers have argued that cultural values are the core of advertising messages and typical advertisements endorse, glamorize, and inevitably reinforce cultural values (Desmarais, 2007; Pollay and Gallagher, 1990).

Advertising has been long viewed as a mirror to reflect the values of certain cultures and previous studies have reported that advertising content differs across cultures (Cheng and Schweitzer, 1996; Nelson and Paek, 2005). Evidence indicates that different cultures seem to emphasize different advertising appeals. For example, Japanese ads have been found to contain more emotional and fewer comparative appeals than American ads (Hong, Muderrisoglu and Zinkhan, 1987). Advertising in China has been found to contain more utilitarian appeals that focus on state of being and promise a better life (Chan and Cheng, 2002).

Combining Cultural Values and Advertising Appeals

Although sparse, research on cross-cultural advertising appeals is generally conducted by pairing countries to test for differences in several values portrayed in advertising to determine the most effective methods (Zinkhan, 1994). Albers-Miller and Gelb (1996) conducted, perhaps, the largest and most referenced test of cross-cultural advertising appeals using Hofstede's (1980) four cultural dimensions and Pollay's (1983) list of common advertising appeals in eleven countries. Pollay developed a list of 42 common appeals by drawing on previous advertising literature and values research in other disciplines. Albers-Miller and Gelb, however, did not examine China because of the lack of Hofstede dimensional measures.

TABLE 12.2
RELATIONSHIPS OF APPEALS TO HOFSTEDE'S DIMENSIONS
AND HYPOTHESES

Appeals	MAS	UAI	IDV	PDI	Hp
Effective	+				C>US
Convenient	+				C>US
Natural	-				C<US
Innocence	-				C<US
Tamed		+			C=US
Adventure		-			C=US
Untamed		-			C=US
Magic		-			C=US
Youth		-			C=US
Independence			+		C<US
Distinctive			+		C<US
Family			+		C<US
Popular			-		C>US
Succorance			-		C>US
Ornamental				+	C=US
Vain				+	C=US
Dear				+	C=US
Status				+	C=US
Cheap				-	C=US
Humility				-	C=US

Note: Plus and minus symbols indicate convergence or divergence between Pollay's appeals and Hofstede's dimensions.

Albers-Miller and Gelb (1996) used six coders from various countries (i.e., Taiwan, India, France, Mexico, and two from the United States) to relate Pollay's appeals to Hofstede's dimensions. The coders were instructed to relate each appeal to one end of a single cultural dimension or to indicate that the appeal related to none of the dimensions. Appeals retained for their research were ones for which at least four of the six coders indicated the same hypothesized relationship. Twelve of the 42 appeals were eliminated because of the lack of agreement about a hypothesized relationship or because the appeal did not relate to any of the dimensions. Additionally, 10 of the remaining 30 appeals failed to support the hypothesized dimensional values at $p<.10$. The relationships between the dimensions and the 20 significant appeals are summarized in Table 12.2.

Advertising Appeals in the Chinese Context

Advertising as a means of marketing has been widely accepted by Chinese society after Deng Xiaoping launched his reform and open-door policy. Advertising in China has riveted the attention of scholars not only within China but also scholars from the West. In the earlier stage of the market economy oriented reforms, Chinese consumers were suspicious of advertised products, because they perceived that only bad products needed to be advertised. This phenomenon is perhaps a reaction to the fact that early Chinese advertisements often used exaggerated claims, destroying all credibility for their so-called miracle products (Liang and Jacobs, 1994; Zhang, 2004; Sun, 2007). It has been discovered, however, that Chinese consumers generally indicate foreign advertisements are attractive and trustworthy. This makes Western advertisers have an advantage over their local counterparts, since Chinese consumers have a high regard for products imported from the West (Ha, 1996; Zhang and Shavitt, 2003; Yan, 1994; Wang, 2008).

Zhang and Neelankavil (1997) conducted an empirical study by investigating the effects of different advertising appeals used across cultures; their findings indicated that cultural differences along the individualism-collectivism dimension affect people's reactions to certain advertising appeals. It was suggested that appeals that emphasize individualistic benefits are more effective in the USA than in China. When appeals emphasizing collectivistic benefits are employed, they are generally more effective in China. However, such effects can be moderated by product characteristics. Different product types may serve to influence the effectiveness of culturally congruent advertising appeals (cf. Zhang and Shavitt, 2003). In the study done by Zhao and Shen (1995) the findings clearly demonstrate that most of the respondents use mass advertising as their chief source of information about products.

In recent years there has been a growing interest in the Chinese market, in particular the use of social networks in China for business purposes. This type of social network or personal connection has been termed as *Guanxi* in Chinese. It is suggested that *Guanxi* can be classified into three categories, namely 1) expressive ties for family members, 2) instrumental ties for strangers, and 3) mixed ties for familiar people. Lee and Dawes limit their study to *guanxi* of the mixed-tie type because most business situations fit this type (Lee and Dawes, 2006).

Because of its relational nature, some have identified Guanxi with a traditional form of relationship marketing. Understanding and managing Guanxi is not only useful in the development of partnerships under the current economic situation in China, but also is necessary for access to the Chinese market in terms of advertising and promotion (Tomás and Arias,

1998). Guanxi is the foundation of Chinese business negotiations; the meaning of Guanxi and using it can also be applied in advertising to differentiate between the characteristics of Chinese and Western negotiations in the marketing context. Guanxi is a characteristic of Chinese culture and provides a starting point for understanding Chinese consumer behaviors. Western cultures have inherently different characteristics. As culture is so important in the marketing process, it is necessary to apply the five dimensions of culture as outlined by Hofstede (1991) and to place these in the Chinese context (Buttery and Leung, 1998).

METHOD

The Design of the Study

This study uses the 20 advertising appeals employed in the Albers-Miller and Gelb study (1996) that were found to be the most highly correlated with the Hofstede dimensions (coder inter-rater reliabilities >.77 and correlation values above .40 at p<.10). Using Pollay's list (1983) of appeals and synonyms, the Chinese and American researchers selected several descriptive words from each of the 20 appeal categories that were most likely to have the same meaning within each culture. For example, the terms beautiful and detailed are often used cross-culturally to represent ornamental appeal. In turn, these descriptors were refined by a focus group of five English-speaking Chinese students and five U.S. students until there was an agreement on which descriptor would be used to represent a particular appeal. Each descriptor was translated into the Chinese language and dialect of the participating university students and placed on questionnaires administered by the U.S. and Chinese researchers

All items were measured on a 7-point Likert-type scale ranging from (1) "extremely important" to (4) "important" to (7) "not important". The scale descriptions were translated into Chinese and then back-translated into English by different bilingual translators. Again, scale variances were subsequently resolved by the focus group of students to ensure equivalency between versions. The country scores were calculated by summing the responses for each appeal across the individuals within a given country and then calculating the means of those individuals' scores. The significance of differences between the means of the appeals was determined by a t-test. The probability, however, of finding a significant difference by chance alone increases rapidly with the number of tests. One solution to this multiple testing problem is to make a Bonferroni correction to the probability associated with each test by multiplying it by the number of tests executed (SPSS Applications Guide 2001). We considered only those values less than p=.002 to be supportive.

The study used undergraduate college students in an attempt to capture the perceptions of new consumers as they begin to integrate their view of appeals with their value system. Although this group did not have years of purchasing experience, it was hoped that their perceptions might be predictive of future trends. Further, students and young adults have an inordinate influence on purchasing in China because of the deference families give to their only children. Lastly, we believed it was important to use of young adults in this study in order to parallel the Fernandez, et al. (1996) reference study.

Data from a randomized (gender, age, socio-economic class, martial and minority status) sample consisting of 300 undergraduate college students at three state universities in metropolitan cities in northeastern and northwestern China and 300 undergraduate students at two state universities and one private college in the southeastern United States was collected. While neither China nor the United States is a culturally homogeneous society, we believe that our sample groups adequately represent the young, college age population. Lastly, using a selection of ads the students were given 15 minutes of training on advertising appeals. They were also trained on the questionnaire's scale. Ninety-Eight percent of all the questionnaires received had useable data.

Hypotheses

Directional hypotheses were created for each of the 30 appeals based on the notion that a country's value system (Hofstede dimensions) would be reflected by the importance their citizens placed on the appeals (Table 9.2). For example, the Mainland Chinese culture is considered very masculine (Fernandez et al., 1997). As such, one would expect the Chinese to rate the masculine appeal of effectiveness as very important. Conversely, one would expect that they would rate feminine appeals as not very important.

For the purpose of developing comparative hypotheses, the value systems were considered significantly different, if the cultural dimensions between countries differed by more than 1.64 standard deviations ($p < .05$). For example, the difference between China and the U.S. on the MAS dimension is 2.78 standard deviations or a significance of $p<.01$. As such, we hypothesize that Chinese consumers would consider appeals associated with masculinity (e.g., effectiveness, convenience, success) to be significantly more important than U.S. consumers (i.e., C>US). Additionally, because the Chinese and U.S. differed by 2.48 standard deviations, we posited that U.S. consumers would consider appeals associated with individualism (e.g., independence, distinctiveness, self-respect) to be significantly more important than Chinese consumers (i.e., C<US). Lastly, because the differences between the Chinese and U.S. consumers on the importance of appeals associated with

uncertainty avoidance and power distance dimensions were less than 1.64 standard deviations, we hypothesized that the differences between the two cultures would be indistinguishable or non-significant (i.e., C=US).

RESULTS

The results of the hypothesis testing are summarized in Table 12.3. A Levene's test indicated that equal variances could be assumed for each of the appeal items. Overall, the findings appear to suggest that the Hofstede dimensions offer only moderate value in predicting the importance of various advertising appeals in China. The results failed to support each of the four hypotheses developed from the masculinity dimension; in fact, one was supported in the opposite direction. Specifically, the appeal of "natural" which was thought to be more important to U.S. consumers was, in fact, more important to Chinese consumers. This non-support of the appeals is particularly noteworthy, since the Chinese culture was the most masculine of all 15 countries in the Fernandez et al. (1997) study by more than one standard deviation and significantly ($p<.001$) more masculine than the U.S. Interestingly, both the U.S. and Chinese consumers rated "effectiveness" as the most important of the 30 appeals. Surprisingly, however, the Chinese consumers gave high rating to the appeals of "innocence" and "natural", which are generally considered more feminine.

Support was relatively strong for the hypotheses suggesting that there would be significant differences in appeals associated with individualism. Four of the five hypotheses were significantly supported at $p<.001$. Appeals, such as distinctiveness, family and popular were predictably important to U.S. consumers. Similarly, *succorance* (e.g., expressions of gratitude and pats on the back) which is normally associated with a collective society was predictably high for Chinese consumers ($p<.002$). Although the appeal of *independence* was indicated as much more important by U.S. consumers, it was only significant at $p<.014$. Additionally, it is interesting to note that the appeal of "family" was significantly supported as an individual appeal and not as a collective appeal. This was the same result as the Albers-Miller and Gelb (1996) study in examination of collective and individualistic societies. The fact that 80 percent of the hypotheses in this dimension were supported is particularly noteworthy, since the U.S. has been considered in past studies (e.g., Fernandez et al., 1996; Hofstede, 1980) as the most individualistic country in the world.

TABLE 12.3
DESCRIPTIVE DATA AND HYPOTHESIS TESTING

Dimension	Appeal	Mean		SD		P-	Hp
		China	USA	China	USA	Val.	
Masculinity	Effective	2.02	2.26	1.41	1.46	.221	NS
	Convenient	3.31	2.89	1.40	1.30	.029	NS
	Natural	2.64	3.17	1.21	1.30	.002	S-O
	Innocence	3.35	3.87	1.43	1.61	.013	NS
Uncertainty	Tamed	2.45	3.31	1.52	1.40	.001	NS
Avoidance	Adventure	4.73	2.73	1.63	1.91	.001	NS
	Untamed	4.54	4.45	1.96	2.06	.729	S
	Magic	4.44	5.05	1.93	2.04	.030	S
	Youth	3.98	4.24	1.78	1.70	.288	S
Individualism	Independence	3.74	3.21	1.66	1.41	.014	NS
	Distinctive	4.83	3.91	1.76	1.77	.001	S
	Popular	4.31	3.63	1.61	1.82	.002	S
	Family	4.56	3.65	1.92	1.62	.001	S
	Succorance	2.96	4.12	1.54	1.65	.001	S
Power Distance	Ornamental	3.92	3.52	1.71	1.62	.087	S
	Vain	3.93	3.98	1.87	1.76	.823	S
	Dear	4.66	3.67	1.77	1.61	.001	NS
	Status	4.82	3.57	1.81	1.47	.001	NS
	Cheap	3.27	3.19	1.58	1.62	.714	S
	Humility	4.73	3.76	1.61	1.74	.001	NS

Note: S=support, NS=nonsupport, and S-O=support in the opposite direction

Support was moderate for the proposition that the U.S. and Chinese consumers would react similarly to appeals associated with uncertainty avoidance. Three of the five hypotheses were supported as the two non-supported hypotheses were significantly different at $p<.001$. Interestingly, the two non-supported appeals indicated that China might be slightly higher in uncertainty avoidance than the United States. The fact that the Chinese students considered the "tame" appeal particularly important and the "adventure" appeal as particular unimportant is a key indicator of a society high in uncertainty avoidance. This seems to be in keeping with most studies of Asian cultures, but is different from the findings presented by Fernandez et al. (1996)

Support was mixed for the notion that the U.S. and Chinese consumer would view the appeals associated with power distance in a similar manner. Three of the six hypotheses supported this proposition. While the three non-supported appeals are significant at the $p<.001$ level, they seem to send a mixed message. For example, the U.S. consumer considers the appeals of dear (e.g., expensive), status and humility to be significantly more important than the Chinese. The first two of these would normally be associated with a high power distance country and the third would be associated with a low power distance country. Further, the Chinese consumers indicated that the appeals of dear and status were less than important (i.e., mean score more than 4). This is particularly surprising for a country with a non-representative style government and a small middle class. Lastly, an examination of demographical differences (i.e., age, marital status, gender and minority status) within the groups of the Chinese and U.S. indicated that there was no significant difference in their ratings.

DISCUSSION

Anthropologist Hall categorizes cultures into high context cultures and low context cultures. According to him the cultural context has certain impacts on the effectiveness of advertising. In "high context" cultures, such as the collectivist Asian cultures of Japan and China, the context in which information is embedded is as important as what is said. In low context cultures, such as the individualistic oriented North American cultures of USA and Canada, the information is contained in the verbal messages; in these cultures, it is important to provide adequate information relating to the product or service in order to satisfy their need for content. Conversely, people in high context cultures are often more effectively reached by image or mood appeals, and rely on personal networks for information and content (Hall, 1976; Lillis and Tian, 2010; Tian, 2002).

It has been widely accepted that Hofstede's cultural dimensions could be accurately used as predictors of appeal effectiveness; the study by Albers-Miller and Gelb (1996) has reinforced this acceptance by providing an enlarged content and scope. However, the results of this study tend not to fully support the above notion when applying the Hofstede's instrument as well as the improved format of the instrument by Albers-Miller and Gelb from a cross-cultural perspective, particularly within the cultural content of modern Chinese society. There could be several explanations for difference in predictability beyond the validity and translation of the instrument.

First, the eleven countries (e.g., Japan, Taiwan, India, South Africa, Israel, France, Finland, Brazil, Chile, Mexico, U.S.) used in the previous study by Albers-Miller and Gelb (1996) have significantly different market economies, political-legal and advertising systems than that in modern China. As such, the significance of individual appeals might vary considerably due to these differences. Second, Hofstede's dimensions although with updated values (1990) might be somewhat too old to be used in predicting the effectiveness of appeals as the business environment in terms of social-economical-cultural-technological structure has experienced tremendous changes all over the world. Third, the appeals may have significantly different values from one age group to the others given changes stated above, and moreover, given the fact that the Albers-Miller and Gelb (1996) study was conducted by using an adult population. Fourth, the product usage visualized by the respondents may have moderated the effect on the importance of appeals. Fifth, cultural dimensions may not be fine grained enough to predict the effectiveness of appeals. In other words, changes in the perceived importance of advertising appeals may take place much more quickly than changes in cultural values; in fact, changes in the importance of advertising appeals may mimic current societal trends and may be precursors to cultural changes.

China as the largest developing country in the world has many special characteristics that differ from the United States, the largest developed country in the world, in terms of social system, economic development level, and cultural values. For example, the higher than predicted values of uncertainty avoidance for the Chinese consumers might be based on the lack of a well established legal system to protect consumers as well as the large amount of poor quality and counterfeit products. Therefore, American marketers should try to use appeals of caution, security and stability and seek endorsements from recognizable and trusted figures. A possible explanation for the appearance of a consumer power distance index lower than the U.S. might be that appeals such as ornamental, dear, status, and lack of humility are avoided because they are symbols of luxury which are widely viewed by normal consumers as appeals to the fubai fenzi (corrupt officials) only.

Although the economy of China has enjoyed a great progress in the last two decades, compared with Americans the great majority of Chinese people still have low incomes. The Chinese official statistics in 2008 indicated that China's annual per capita income was less than 16,000 Yuan rmb (about $2400 USD). Households with the highest incomes accounted for 10 percent of the total population, with these annual disposable incomes averaging less than 44,000 Yuan rmb (about $6500 USD). American advertisers should stress appeals such as economical, inexpensive, simplicity and humility to draw the Mainland Chinese consumers' attention. Awareness of these differences in terms of business communication is essential to ensure effective advertising. According to Zhao and Shen (1995), the foreign advertisements that are the biggest hit with Chinese consumers are those for popular products that they can afford to buy, that they use often or plan to buy. The same study shows that there are ways of generating a positive attitude towards an advertisement and a brand image. One is to come up with a creative and entertaining advertisement by using innovative images;

another one is to make the advertisement captivating and lively by using dynamic scenes with lots of action. It is interesting that Chinese consumers are very skeptical with regard to advertisement endorsed by celebrities; they believe the testimonials are false as actors are paid to say good sides about the products.

Here again, pitfalls could arise due to differences in color association or perception. For instance, in many tropical countries, green is associated with danger and has negative connotations. Red, on the other hand, is associated with weddings and happiness in China. Moreover, appeals to humor or sex also need to be treated with considerable care as their expression and effectiveness might be simply opposite from what the American advertisers perceive in the Chinese context. The dry American sense of humor does not always translate effectively into Chinese language.

The fact that China scored lower than the United States on uncertainty avoidance represents a cultural reversal and is a particular indicator that China has experience a remarkable transformation from a socialism system (i.e., a low risk taking philosophy) to a market oriented socialist-capitalism system (i.e., a mixed opportunist risk taking philosophy). This major change in ideology, however, might have been a catalyst of social value changes. The Chinese might be more curious of different ideas and more willing to take risks as their society moves more toward a market economy. On the other hand, the possibility exists that the relative change between the two countries is the result of the U.S. becoming more resistant to uncertainty. The shift made by the United States from being a weak uncertainty avoidance country in Hofstede's study to one of strong uncertainty avoidance seems reasonable in light of the political, economic, and social changes the United States over the past two decades. In particular, the increased uncertainty about the economic power of the United States may be a factor in the change.

Gender should be an important indicator for cultural difference, it is widely accepted that gender identity may have various functions cross-culturally in ways of social activities, including consumption behaviors. However, the result from this study indicates that in terms of masculinity appeal in advertising there seems to be no difference between American respondents and Chinese respondents, a rational possible explanation for the lack of a difference in masculinity between the two groups could be simply because of their age. There is a strong and universal relationship between masculinity and age; as the hormones associated with sexual productivity decrease, there is a corresponding increase in feminine values (Hofstede 1991). As such, both groups indicated a relatively high importance to those appeals associated with masculinity. Therefore, American marketers may be successful in using the same masculine appeals in the Chinese youth market as they do in the U.S. market. Similarly, age may have had a powerful affect on the differentiation between the U.S. and Chinese students on the dimension of individualism/collectivism. Youth are at a stage in their life cycle where they are trying to be more independent and as such, may reflect more independent appeals. Additionally, the transition of China to a market economy coupled with increasing wealth and purchasing power may suggest more interest in appeals of independence and less on community.

CONCLUSIONS

The significance of cross-cultural differences in advertising has become even clearer as we continue to move toward a globalized marketplace. As such, it is important that marketing personnel not let old stereotypes drive their advertising strategies; this is particularly important in the Asian market, as China and Taiwan become formal members of the WTO. Our findings indicate that heuristics such as Hofstede's cultural dimensions may be too broad to capture the detailed differences required in launching an effective advertising campaign. A possible explanation is that cultural values change much more slowly than consumer values and therefore cannot be used to effectively predict consumer behavior. While the continued development of advertising heuristics is important, marketing personnel must continue to use the tried and true method of the focus group. This prevents the mistake of assuming that you know what the consumer thinks is important. In fact, the results of this might be considered as coming from a mini-focus group.

While the findings do not provide unequivocal recommendations for developing advertising, they do provide some general information for marketing practitioners seeking to do business in China. For example, one should consider the seven appeals (i.e., effectiveness, safety, tamed, durable, natural, nurturance and succorance, in descending order of importance) whose means were less than 3 to be very important to selling a product. Conversely, those ten appeals (i.e., casual, distinctiveness, community, status, adventure, dear, family, untamed, magic and popular, in descending order of least important) whose means were more than 4 should be avoided. In any case, the findings strongly suggest the need to consider market segmentation and to consult with an expert in Chinese consumer behavior before developing ads for their market. Lastly, the results suggest the need for future research on factors that may moderate an appeal within a culture (e.g., age, socioeconomic status, significant event).

Finally, it is necessary to indicate that this study has several limitations. While our study intentionally used college students to get a "heads-up" on future consumer behavior, their perceptions may be significantly different from national perceptions. This is true particularly in the case of Chinese college students who are often the only child in the family and therefore might have limited purchasing experience. In addition the small sample size (numerical and geographic) prevents generalization and the differences in their college environments and socio-economic status may be significantly moderating perceptions. It is recommended that future studies should focus on a large scope in terms of geographic coverage and wrap a more complicated cultural content with a particular attention to the tremendous transformation in business world to a cross-cultural perspective.

Authored by Charles Emery and Kelly R. Tian, originally published in *International Journal of China Marketing*, Vol. 1(1) 2010, pp. 45-59.

Chapter Thirteen

Information Handling Styles, Advertising and Brand Attitude: A Chinese Brand Case Study

The purpose of this paper is to examine the effect of mixed advertising on brand attitude for a Chinese brand in the telecommunication services industry. Previous studies indicate that emotional advertising contributes to increasing positive customer brand attitude. An individual's recognition needs and information processing styles both have an influence on the advertising perception. However, few empirical studies so far have monitored the effect of mixed advertising on brand attitude. The "Qingqin 1+" advertisement is taken as the example analyzing both the effect of ad perception on brand attitude and the interactive effects of an individual's information processing style on advertising perception and brand attitude. The findings will help to reveal the effect of advertising perception on brand attitude, namely that emotional advertisements are more efficient than rational ones in the case that is studied. Brand developers should keep in mind the effect of mixed advertising when designing their communication campaign. Few studies have been published on the effect of Chinese brand advertising on consumers, hence this has a significant value for Chinese brand managers.

INTRODUCTION

Emotional advertising gives a brand some of its specific characteristics (Aaker, 1995), which impact the brand differentiation and the customers' decision-making process. One of the differences between rational advertising and emotional advertising lies in the advertising appeals (Gierl & Praxmarer, 2007; Albers-Miller, & Stafford, 2007; Dens & De Pelsmacker, 2010). Rational advertising aims at persuading customers by using reason, logic and objective information, which include product/service functions and how to match customer needs. On the other hand, emotional advertising focuses on the specific psychological experience: it sends information about self-satisfaction, social identity and sensual stimulation and relates to self-improvement and emotional appraisal (Puto & Wells, 1984; Ratchford, 1987; Heath & Feldwick, 2007).

The process of customer brand attitude is a process of perception and acceptance. Advertising can affect the brand attitude (Andrew, 1986; Fisher, 1998; Keller, 1998), therefore the customer perception of an advertising appeal is an important component of brand attitude (Ruiz, 2004). The perception of advertising appeal can be divided into two perceptions: the perception of emotional information and the perception of rational information, which can both influence the customer's brand attitude through different channels (Petty *et al.,* 1983). However, in real life, a large part of advertising messages belong to the mixed advertising category. But so far, little serious study has been made to understand how mixed advertising affects brand attitude (Ruiz, 2004).

A customer's perception of advertising is influenced by his/her individual profile (Edson & Stern, 2003; Page, Aaron *et al.*, 2005). Research on this topic has found that the features of individual profiles include a person's information handling characteristics and need for cognition (which refers to the tendency of an individual to invest effort in thinking about and handling information) (Sojka & Giese, 1997). Experimental studies found that when the individual's information handling style matches the advertising style, advertising can contribute to a greater degree to brand attitude (Ruiz, 2004). Compared with the need for cognition and preference for affect, the individual's information handling style is also an important variable that may affect the relationship between the advertisement and brand attitude, and possibly a more stable variable. Until now, few studies have empirically studied this modulation effect.

The sample advertisement used for this paper is a printed media advertising of a telecommunication service product, known as "Qingqin 1+" in Chinese. Conveyed by three printed pictures, the advertisement is translated into English as "the whole family cares about each other" and belongs to the mixed advertising group category. This paper empirically studies the modulation effect of individual information perception styles on the perception of advertising appeal and brand attitude. In the case of "Qingqin 1+," the results reveal that customer's perception of emotional information of telecommunication service product advertising significantly and positively affect brand attitude, while the perception of rational information has no such significant effect. In addition, the individual's information handling style influences the relationship between the perception of information and brand attitude. The results of this paper will help us amplify the understanding of advertising and brand attitude.

LITERATURE REVIEW

Rational Advertising and Emotional Advertising

Based on previous studies, we have used information content analysis to distinguish rational advertising from emotional advertising by using three sets of criteria. As suggested by Resnik & Stern (1977), if the advertisement contains one of the following information cues, then it can be regarded as rational advertising. The coding categories of the information content include some of the following information cues (first set of criteria): product/service price, quality, function, material, purchasing time and place, sales promotion information, information on taste, product nutrition, packaging, promise to customer, product safety, independent research results and new product concept as researched by the company. If the advertising contains none of the above information content, then it can be considered as emotional advertising.

The second set of criteria was introduced by Geuens & Pelsmacker (1997): it is based on advertising appeal: humor, enthusiasm, nostalgia, sex, anger, fear and other emotions. It holds that if the advertisement relates to one of the types of appeal listed above it can be regarded as emotional advertising. If not, it comprises rational advertising. If it is difficult to decide between the two categories, it belongs to the mixed advertising category.

The third set of criteria was suggested by Flint-Goor & Liebermann (1996) and includes two kinds of information content. Among them, the types of information related to rational content are price, product characteristics or make-up, function, purchase time and place, sale information, product packaging, promise of product quality, market share, research results, convenience, health and nutrition and product safety. The types of information related to emotional content are sex, position and prestige, youth, sports, beauty, gender, enthusiasm and living style. Based on this, the authors divided advertising into five categories: high rational advertising, mixed-rational advertising, mixed advertising, mixed-emotional advertising, and high emotional advertising. As this kind of criteria is suitable for analyzing mixed advertising, we selected this method for our research.

Emery and Tian (2003 and 2010) have described the significance of a fourth set of criteria coming from the cross-cultural differences of advertising perception that may influence the communication strategy of enterprises operating in many countries. The studies demonstrated that groups of Chinese and US students reacted differently to advertising appeal in relationship to the Hofstede work-related values (1980). The customer's perception of advertising appeal and its impact of brand attitude have practical usage for the customer (Keller, 1998). Katz (1960) describes different aspects of brand attitude such as utility function, value expression function, self-protection function and cognitive function. Aaker (1995) points out that brand attitude can help convey customer needs satisfaction, express customer attributes and simplify the decision-making process. The process of brand attitude is a process of perception. Brand popularity is the primary source of customer brand attitude (Aaker, 1997). Advertising is an important promotion method, beyond its promotion function of the product and service. After receiving the stimulus from the advertisement, the individual will feel attraction or repulsion for a specific brand. Research by Mackenzie & Lutz (1982) corroborated that the stimulation of advertising influences brand attitude.

The Elaboration Likelihood Model (ELM), as proposed by Petty et al. (1983), supports the relationship between an advertisement and change in customer attitude. The ELM distinguishes two routes through which an advertisement may influence the customer: a central route and a peripheral route. The model explains that the effects of advertising on customer attitude are related to the degree of elaboration of the message through either a high-involvement central processing route or a low-involvement peripheral processing route. If customers are highly involved in an advertised product when exposed to the ad, they are very likely to ignite the central processing route, where customers will consume a great deal of effort in processing the message, and elaborate on ideas in the message. However, when customers are not involved in the product, then the advertisement is processed through the peripheral route. According to the Elaboration Likelihood Model theory (ELM) through the effortful reasoning process, customers integrate the information provided into their own belief structures, which may cause attitude change. On the other hand, the peripheral route involves a less effortful reasoning process that does not rely on scrutinizing the content and merits of the message.

Although the ELM posits that attitude change created through the more effortful central route will be longer lasting, more resistant, and more predictive, behavior can also change through the peripheral route. The perception of both cognitive information and emotional information advertising information will affect the customer's brand attitude. The central approach much more likely contributes to brand attitude through rational information, and the peripheral approach contributes to brand attitude through emotional information (Percy & Rossiter, 2006).

Based on this, we can formulate the following hypotheses:

H1: In mixed advertising, customer perception of the emotional appeal will positively affect brand attitude in a significant manner.

H2: In mixed advertising, customer perception of the rational appeal will positively affect brand attitude in a significant manner.

Customer Type and the Response to the Advertising Appeal

Customer behavior studies have shown that the individual's style of information handling generates different responses when submitted to advertising stimuli (Moore *et al.*, 1995). The individual's cognitive needs and affective needs influence the handling of advertising information (Petty

& Cacioppo, 1982; Mantel & Kardes, 1999; Peltier & Schibrowsky, 1994; Brett *et al.*, 2003). The empirical study found that when the information style of advertising appeal matches the advertisement audience's style of handling information, the advertising message can be more persuasive (La Barbera *et al.,* 1998). Ruiz and alumni did the experimental study of three photo product print advertisements, in a 2*2*3 multi-variable experiment design; the results showed that the match between individual information handling style and the advertisement's emotional or rational style will lead to higher advertising persuasiveness, brand satisfaction and purchasing tendency. This implies that if the individual has high cognitive needs, rational advertising is better than emotional advertising. If the individual has high affective needs, emotional advertising is preferable to rational advertising (Ruiz, 2004).

The individual's needs might influence his/her behavior, but not definitively. Up until now, few studies have analyzed the influence of individual's information handling style on preference of advertising appeal. In personality theory, personal information handling style can be divided into two kinds: sensing style and intuitive style (Kozhevnikov, 2007).

Sensing and intuition are information-gathering (or perceiving) functions. They describe how new information is understood and interpreted. Individuals who prefer sensing are more likely to trust information that is in the present, tangible and concrete. That is, information that can be understood by the five senses. They prefer to look for details and facts. For them, the meaning is in the data. On the other hand, those who prefer intuition tend to trust information that is more abstract or theoretical, that can be associated with other information (either remembered or discovered by seeking a wider context or pattern). They may be more interested in future possibilities. They tend to trust those flashes of insight that seem to bubble up from the unconscious mind. A sensing style individual can catch the rational information of the advertising appeal more easily.

Intuitive style refers to an individual's perception of the whole picture, relationship and the possibility of receiving more insight into the specific context and handling the abstract concept of meaning and its relationship. Compared with a sensing style person, an intuitive style person will pay more attention to the complicated synthesis beyond a huge amount of information, rather than simply sensing the information.

FIGURE 13.1
THE RESEARCH FRAMEWORK

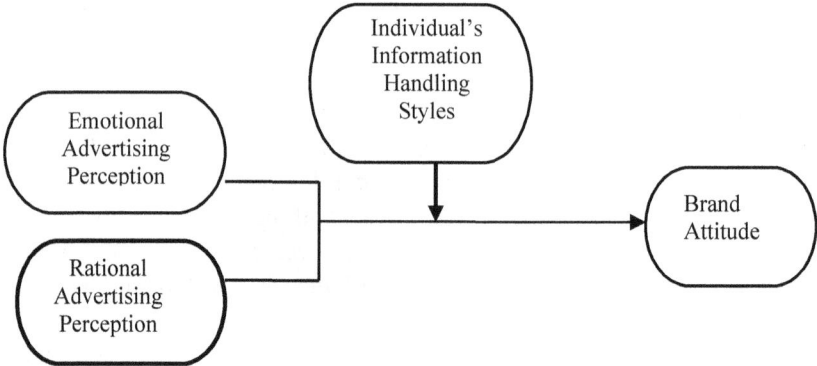

According to a recent study, the sensing-intuitive style of MBTI (Myers Briggs Type Indicator) is similar to the concrete-abstract style of Gregorc's & Kolb's perception part of personality theory (Kozhevnikov, 2007). The emotional information content related to youth, enthusiasm and living style are much more context-based and abstract, whereas rational information content is much more specific and concrete. Hence the intuitive style individual is more sensitive to the emotional information content than the sensing style individual. Therefore, we can hypothesize the following:

H3: In a mixed advertisement, the customer perception of the style of advertising appeal is influenced by the customer's information handling style.

H3.1: If the customer's information handling is sensing style, the perception of rational information will positively influence the brand attitude to a great degree.

H3.2 If the customer's information handling is intuitive style, the perception of emotional information will positively influence the brand attitude to a great degree.

The research framework of this study is presented in figure 13.1, which means the perception of advertising appeal style will influence the brand attitude, and the customer's information handling style will modulate them.

METHODOLOGY

The Background Information About "Qingqin 1+" Brand.

"Qingqin 1+" is an integrated telecommunication service brand. It was created by Chinese Telecom, one of the main telecommunication service suppliers in China. Given the background of the changes to the Chinese telecommunication industry in the recent past, competition in the services market became more aggressive, and Chinese Telecom found that telephone customer turnover was increasing. In 1996, in order to deal with this serious competition, the Chinese Telecom company innovated an integrated service production system combining fixed telephone service, internet access service, mobile phone service and other value-added services. These entirely new product packages were conceived under a single brand name, known as "Qingqin 1+". The target customer of this brand was the family customer, and the brand launched its own print media advertising campaign (see figure 13.2). During 2007 and 2008, the advertising expenses of this brand in Beijing comprised more than 15 million RMB Yuan.

Before beginning this empirical study of "Qingqin 1+", we completed a pre-stage survey to determine the advertising style of "Qingqin 1+". The survey was carried out in more than thirty samples, according the criteria suggested by Flint-Goor & Liebermann (1996). As it turned out, the style of advertising belonged to the mixed advertising category. This was later confirmed by questionnaires of 307 additional samples.

Samples

From November to December 2009, we selected 32 typical telecommunication product stores from all the eight districts in Beijing and ran a random sample survey.

FIGURE 13.2
CHINESE UNICOM BRAND ADVERTISING "FAMILY 1+"

All the elements of the sample were asked the following questions: "Where did you learn about "Qinqin 1+?" and "Have you use Qinqin 1+ product before?" If the former answer is "No" and latter answer is "Yes", the element was rejected from the sample. The total size of the samples was 404, and 307 questionnaires were accepted, with an effective response rate of 76.75%. Among them 53.1% were male, 46.9% were female, with the average age equal to 35.7 years.

Measurement

We used the brand attitude measurement suggested by Chan (1995) for the following questions: "What is your general attitude to "Qingqin 1+"?" and "To what degree do you like "Qingqin 1+"?" etc. (Chan, 1995). The Cronbach's Alpha index came out to 0.776.

The popularity of the Brand is measured by asking the following question: "To what degree have you been informed about the "Qingqin 1+"". The Cronbach's Alpha index result was 0.753.

These variables were measured by using the Likert 7 scale, with the "1" standing for "strongly disagree" and "7" standing for "strongly agree".

When measuring the emotional and rational perceptions of advertising appeal with the method suggested by Flint-Goor and Liebermann, the Cronbach's Alpha index came out to 0.805 and 0.792. The information handling style of the individual responder was measured by the 7 MBTI items suggested by Salter (Salter *et al.*, 1997) and included the feeling style and intuitive style. These two variables were calculated by comparing the categories score. The result is the category with the bigger number. All the data were processed using SPSS16.0 software.

DATA ANALYSIS

Effect of Individual's Information Handling Style on the Relationship Between the Advertising Perception and Brand Attitude

Firstly, we used Cronbach's Alpha index to test the measure of validity. By using the SPSS16.0 software, the Cronbach's Alpha index of the entire questionnaire was 0.823; all the sub-measurements Alpha indexes were above 0.70, which means that the validity was reasonable.

In order to test hypotheses 1 and 2, the popularity of the brand was used as a controlled variable. We then conducted the regression of brand advertising appeal on brand attitude. It turned out that the brand popularity positively influenced the brand attitude in a significant way ($r=0.505$, $p<0.001$), and the perception of rational advertising appeal had no significant effect on brand attitude.

Hence hypothesis 1 was rejected. However, the perception of

emotional advertising appeal positively influenced brand attitude to a significant degree (r=0.165, p<0.001), hence the hypothesis 2 was accepted (see table 13.1).

We then tested hypothesis 3 (the moderator role of individual information handling style). First, the rational perceptions of the advertising and individual information handling style were mean-centered in order to reduce the multicollinearity between the main effect and the interaction variables (Aiken, 1991).

Then we used hierarchical linear regression in order to test the interaction hypotheses. Brand popularity was entered in step 1. In step 2, rational perception of the advertising and the individual's information handling style were entered at mean time.

TABLE 13.1
INFLUENCE OF ADVERTISING STYLE PERCEPTION
ON BRAND ATTITUDE

Dependent	Brand Attitude	
	Step 1	Step 2
Positive brand awareness	.505***	.459***
Perception of the rational advertising style		.034
Perception of the emotional advertising style		.165***
R^2	.255	.286
Adjusted R^2		.021***
F	104.228***	40.412***

Notes: *p<0.05 ** p<0.01 ***p<0.001

In step 3, the interactive variable was entered. The result showed that the interaction effect was positively significant (β=0.173, p<.01). Table 13.2 summarizes the regression results and figure 13.3 demonstrates the pattern of the two-way interaction.

TABLE 13.2

MODERATE EFFECT OF INDIVIDUAL'S INFORMATION HANDLING STYLE BETWEEN RATIONAL ADVERTISING STYLE AND BRAND ATTITUDE

Dependent	Brand attitude		
	Step 1	Step 2	Step 3
Brand popularity	.505***	.470***	.455***
Rational perception of the		.137**	.022
advertising(X1)		.089	.237**
Individual's information handling			.256**
style(X2)	.255	.262	.274
Interaction(X1*X2)		.15*	.014*
R^2	104.228***	37.290***	29.891***
Adjusted R^2			
F			

Notes: *$p<0.05$ ** $p<0.01$ ***$p<0.001$

FIGURE 13.3

THE RATIONAL PERCEPTION OF ADVERTISING

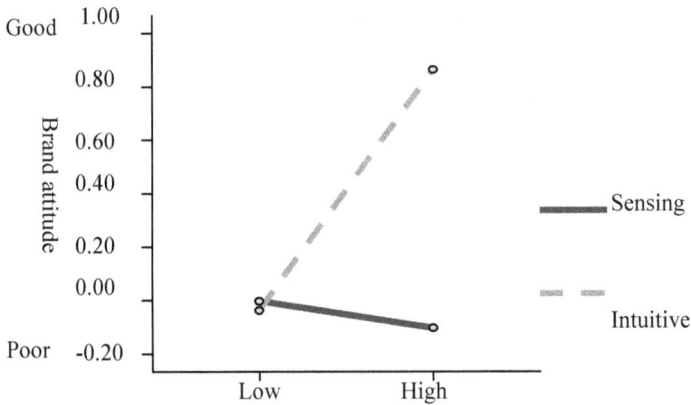

TABLE 13.3
MODERATE EFFECT OF INDIVIDUAL'S INFORMATION HANDLING STYLE ON THE EMOTIONAL PERCEPTION OF BRAND ADVERTISING AND BRAND ATTITUDE

Independent	Brand attitude		
	Step 1	Step 1	Step 1
Positive brand awareness	.505***	.456***	.432***
Rational perception of the advertising(X1)		-.076	-.142**
Individual information handling style(X2)		.217***	.092
Interaction(X1*X2)			.217**
R^2	.255	.289	.306
Adjusted R^2		.034***	.017***
F	104.228***	41.081***	33.335***

Notes: *p<0.05 ** p<0.01 ***p<0.001

The hypothesis 3.1 supports the fact that individual information handling style modulates the rational perception of advertising and the brand attitude.

Following the same method, it turns out that individual information handling style influences the emotional perception of advertising and brand attitude (β=0.205, p<.01). The regression result is summarized in table 13.3, and Figure 13.4 illustrates the pattern of the two-way interaction. The hypothesis 3.2 supports the fact that the individual's information handling style influences the emotional perception of advertising and the brand attitude.

CONCLUSION AND MANAGERIAL SUGGESTIONS

Emotional advertising is better than rational advertising in promoting the telecommunication service brand. This result obtained in this study of a Chinese service brand corresponds to those coming from the previous studies on service advertising strategy. This study is one of the few existing for Chinese service bands. The individual's information handling style can influence the relationship between the perception of advertising style and the attitude toward the brand. Intuitive style customers are more sensitive to the emotional content of advertising, and if they receive this kind of information, their attitude towards the brand will improve. On the other hand, sensing style customers prefer rational advertising content, and this type of content will help to lead to better brand attitude.

FIGURE 13.4
THE EMOTIONAL PERCEPTION OF ADVERTISING

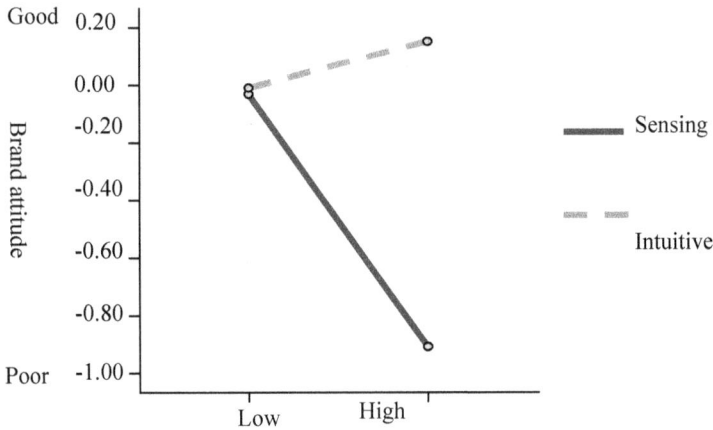

We suggest that even in the case of mixed advertising, individual information style is a key element in the process through which customers select some specific type of information. Brand attitude will be influenced by the specific information they receive. Therefore, advertising information style should be an important decision-making element for marketing managers. We find that the two kinds of information that co-exist have not hindered the way advertising contributes to the potential change in the customer's brand attitude. The mixed advertising style may be a good compromise in order to attract more populations, with individuals having different types of information handling, and it may be less risky strategy to attract both types at the same time.

One of the limitations of this study lies in the fact that we only analyzed one Chinese brand, coming from the telecommunication industry. In addition, all data are based on a self-reporting questionnaire. In the future, different types of data collecting methods should be considered to avoid common method bias (Padsakoff & Organ, 1986).

Authored by Tang Chaoying, Sun Jian, and Francis R. Ille, originally published in. *International Journal of China Marketing*, Vol. 1(2) 2011, pp, 45-56.

Part III: Consumer Behavior in China

Chapter Fourteen

From Motivation to Store Choice: Exploring Northwest Chinese Consumers' Shopping Behavior

Although China has become the largest consumer market in the world, there is limited research on Chinese consumers' shopping behavior, particularly shoppers in the inland China. This study explores the shopping experiences of consumers from Northwest China. In-depth interviews reveal that the participants are much more than functional shoppers as they also shop to satisfy personal and social needs. In addition, they use merchandise, store and service criteria to choose among retail stores. The study contributes to the literature on Chinese consumers' store patronage behavior and provides valuable insights for retailers aiming to explore the Northwest Chinese market.

INTRODUCTION

China has experienced rapid economic growth since the 1980s when the country started its economic reform. With annual average economic growth rates of about 10% since the year 1990, consumer spending power has increased dramatically. The annual per capital disposable income of urban residents increased about 250% from 2000 to 2008 (China Statistical Yearbook, 2009). The improvement of consumer living standards and a growing wealthy middle class have attracted many international retailers to Chinese markets. An increasing number of international retailers also entered the Chinese market after China joined the WTO in 2001 (Liu, 2007). With the entrance of international retailers and development of the domestic retail industry, China's retail market has thus become very competitive (Chaney and Gamble, 2008). Chinese consumers' characteristics, however, are different from those of their western counterparts because of the country's unique social, economic, political, and cultural environments. Chinese consumers' unique shopping behaviors and attitudes constrain the success of some foreign investors (Mai and Zhao, 2004). Many western companies have failed in China despite its huge market size and fast economic development (Wang and Zhang, 2005). To realize the full potential of China's consumer markets, international retailers cannot simply apply western marketing and merchandising strategies to Chinese markets.

China is composed of a number of regional markets (Tsang *et al.,* 2003) and consumers from different regional markets have very distinct shopping and purchasing behaviors (Tse *et al.*, 1989; Cui, 1997; Cui and Liu, 2000). The differences are caused by many factors, including unbalanced economic development between costal and inner regions and changes in personal values as part of a changing social environment (Zhang *et al.*, 2008). At the forefront of Chinese economic reform, the eastern and southern regions of China have become wealthier and more advanced than the western and interior regions. As a result, the majority of research on Chinese consumers has been done in the cities of eastern and southern China such as Shanghai, Hong Kong, and Guangzhou (e.g. Fan and Xiao, 1998; Tang *et al.*, 2001; Wang *et al.*, 2004; Tai, 2005). After the West China Development project was initiated in early 2000, however, the relatively understudied area of western China has drawn more attention because of its rich resources and market scope. With the rapid growth of both domestic and international retailers, more retailers would expand aggressively to inland regions (Liu, 2007). However, there is yet very little information available to help international marketers and retailers understand consumers' consumption and shopping behaviors in this part of the country.

The purpose of this study is therefore to explore the shopping behavior of Chinese consumers in northwest China. Lanzhou is one of the most important cities in northwest China with a population of 3.3 million. Though Eastern Chinese cities have attracted foreign retailers because of greater sales potential, Lanzhou is attractive for its lower relative costs and government efforts to curb pollution and attract commerce (US-China Business Council, 2002). With the opening of the first supermarket — Lanzhou Hua Lian in the year 2000, a greater variety of stores became available in the marketplace. The changing retail landscape of Lanzhou and its importance in the western region makes it an ideal place to explore consumer shopping behavior. Hence, this study provides the insight that domestic and international marketers and retailers need to better cater to northwest Chinese consumers' needs and wants. This information will be useful to retailers competing in the modern Chinese retail environment. Additionally, this study contributes to the literature on Chinese consumer behavior by addressing a gap in knowledge about the relatively unexplored consumer behaviors in northwest China.

BACKGROUND

Chinese Retailing Industry and Its Consumer Markets

The retail industry in China went through three phases (Wang *et al.*, 2008). The first phase was from 1981 to 1990, during which the state-owned stores were still in control. The major stores in China were either department stores or grocery stores. There was a shortage of supply, and consumers could not purchase all they wanted or needed (Wang *et al.*, 2008). During this phase Chinese consumers did not worry much about product quality, services, and shopping environment because of limited choices (Li and Wang, 2006). During the second phase, from 1991 to 2000, the retail industry experienced tremendous changes. With new government regulations, the Chinese market opened its doors to foreign retailers. Meanwhile, different stores, including "super markets, warehouse club, large scale specialized stores, convenience stores, modern department stores, and shopping malls" all came into being (Wang *et al.*, 2008, p.156). The coexistence of different stores and foreign retailers significantly changed China's modern retail landscape (Powers, 2000). China became a buyer's market. Consumers gained freedom of choice with abundant consumer goods and retail stores. They started to pay attention to other market elements such as service quality and shopping environment (Wang *et al.*, 2008). Phase three, which began in 2001 sees a further transition of the Chinese retail industry with the retail market became totally open to foreign retailers by the end of 2004 (Liu, 2007). China has become a major battleground with both international and domestic retailers competing to increase their market share and attract wealthy middle class Chinese consumers (Chaney and Gamble, 2008). Some consumer goods are oversupplied, and consumers have become the dominant force in the marketplace (Wang *et al.*, 2008). Economic value of the merchandise, store image, shopping conditions inside the store and service quality all affect Chinese consumers' satisfaction (Wang *et al.*, 2006).

To be successful in this increasingly competitive retail market, it is critical to understand factors that affect Chinese consumers' consumption and shopping behavior. Many factors affect modern Chinese consumers' shopping and consumption behavior, including demographic changes, as well as the social and cultural backgrounds of consumers. The profound role of family, importance of the group and the role of consensus in shaping attitudes, willingness to take risks, and regional diversity are some key social and cultural influences on consumption in China (Garner, 2005).

China has very diverse regional markets. Based on economic development and consumer purchasing behavior, China can be divided into seven regional markets that include South, East, North, Central, Southwest, Northwest, and Northeast (Cui and Liu, 2000). While south and east regions represent China's most developed regional markets, the northeast and northwest are still untapped markets. Chinese consumers in different regional market have unique tastes and consumption behavior (Tsang *et al.*, 2003; Garner, 2005). The differences among the regional markets are created not only by geographic size, linguistic differences, and historical legacy (Garner, 2005), but also economic disparities between coastal and hinterland regions created by government policy. Compared to consumers from the less developed northwest and northeast regions, consumers from the affluent east and south regions are more individually oriented and have a more active lifestyle (Cui and Liu, 2000). Individualism has become a more important personal value for Chinese consumers from coastal regions (Zhang *et al.*, 2008). Podoshen *et al.* (2011) suggest that materialism and conspicuous consumption is rising among young adults in urban Chinese areas. However, although western individualism has become more evident, there still exist intense personal relationships in China, called "guanxi." Guanxi affects such areas of consumption as gift-giving and conspicuous consumption (Garner, 2005).

The important role that Chinese consumers play in global markets has led to a rise in consumer research in the nation. Researchers have tried to understand Chinese consumers' consumption behaviors and the factors that affect consumer characteristics. Important topics include consumer decision making style (Fan and Xiao, 1998; Wang *et al.*, 2004), brand choice and preference (Lin and Chang, 2003; Yang *et al.*, 2005; Zhou and Wong, 2008), consumer values (Schaefer, *et al.*, 2004; Tai, 2005; Wong and Dean, 2009; Xiao and Kim, 2009), and store patronage behavior (Wong and Yu, 2002; Uncles and Kwok, 2009). However, limited studies have focused on Chinese consumers' shopping and patronage behavior, especially those of consumers in less developed inland China such as northwest China.

Shopping Motivations

For decades, consumer behavior researchers favored the traditional cognition, affect, and behavior (CAB) model to understand consumption behavior. Based on the CAB model, consumers go shopping when they need to purchase certain products or services. However, in 1972 Tauber argued that shopping behavior is motivated by a range of psychosocial needs that go beyond the acquiring of products and services. Following Tauber's seminal article, a number of researchers have focused on understanding consumers' shopping motivations (e.g. Westbrook and Black, 1985; Arnold and Reynolds, 2003). Further studies have shown that shopping motivation can be more product oriented (acquiring products or services) or experience oriented (not related to acquiring product or services) (Dawson *et al.*, 1990). The experience orientation is also referred to as a hedonic shopping orientation, which focuses on fun, sensory excitement (Babin *et al.*, 1994; Arnold and Reynolds, 2003), and the fulfillment of such needs as gaining ideas, improving personal well being, and socializing with others (Tauber, 1972; Buttle and Coates, 1984).

Existing studies present Chinese consumers as largely functional shoppers, meaning that they are more likely to shop for acquiring products or services and less likely for having fun and being entertained. Tsang *et al.*

(2003) compared the mall shopping behavior of consumers from Xi'an and Hong Kong, and concluded that primary shopping motivations for these consumers were making a specific purchase and browsing. In a similar study, Li et al. (2004) compared the mall shopping behavior of Chinese and American consumers and concluded that Chinese consumers' mall visits were mainly motivated by a purchase purpose while American consumers tended to have multiple motivations. Fan and Xiao (1998) investigated young Chinese consumers' decision making style and found out that consumers from their sample were not interested in recreational shopping. With the growth in the Chinese economy and improvement in personal well-being, however, Chinese consumers may have become more similar to western consumers. That is, the Chinese consumer may go shopping for a number of reasons, some of which may be more experience oriented.

Store Choices

Many factors affect consumers' store choice decisions. The perception of product price and quality, service quality, time/effort cost, and psychic cost (mental stress or emotional factors) are all important store choice criteria (Baker *et al.,* 2002). Furthermore, store atmosphere, consumer characteristics and store reputation all affect consumers' choices of retail stores (e.g. Dawar and Parker, 1994; Ou *et al.,* 2006). The emergence of new retail channels and outlets in China has prompted researchers to explore how Chinese shoppers are different from or similar to their Western counterparts with respect to store choices. Li *et al.* (2004) found that for Chinese consumers, mall selection criteria, in order of importance, are shopping atmosphere, merchandise assortment and variety, and location. Tai (2005) showed that working women in both Shanghai and Hong Kong did not display loyalty to particular stores. Chinese consumers' choice of retail outlets and stores is affected by many factors such as social, economic, and geographic differences. Wong and Yu (2002) found that higher income consumers in China tend to be more concerned with the location, layout and store design, style of merchandise, and service quality when choosing a shopping center. Chaney and Gamble (2008) conclude that both geographic and demographic factors play a role in perceptions of local vs. foreign stores. They found that consumers in Shanghai preferred foreign stores, whereas those in Chengdu (a second-tier city), lower socio-economic groups, and older consumers preferred local stores. Overall, a comprehensive body of research about Chinese consumers' patronage behavior does not yet exist. With the likelihood of even more competition in China's retail industry as market development continues, more information in this area will help retailers to compete effectively and gain market share.

METHODOLOGY

In order to explore Western Chinese consumers' shopping motivations and store choice criteria, a qualitative study was conducted in Lanzhou city, Gansu Province. A qualitative research methodology was necessary to gain insight into consumers' behavior from their own perspectives (Denzin and Lincoln, 1994). Additionally, because of the lack of relevant research in the field and the exploratory nature of the study, the in-depth interview method was selected, which proved to be very effective. Given the exploratory character of the research, the interviews were lightly structured, that is, the interviews used focused yet open-ended and non-directive questions in which discussion followed the participants' responses and issues (Mariampolski, 2001). The interviews first asked participants to describe their most recent shopping trip in detail and then asked about their general shopping motives, store choice criteria, and factors affecting their shopping experiences.

Eighteen adult Chinese consumers from different age groups, education levels, occupations, and income levels participated in the study, ensuring a variety of views and opinions. The participants were recruited through posters and word of mouth (WOM) in several local communities and neighborhoods. The diversity among the participants can be clearly shown through their employment status, which included office personnel, researchers, homemakers, small-store owners, retired factory workers and doctors. Ten of the participants were in their 20s and 30s, six in their 40s and 50s, and two were 60 or older. The majority of the participants were females (14), and four participants were males. This sampling approach helped to ensure that the results would be in accordance with the subject of investigation (Ruyter and Scholl, 1998). The interviews were conducted in Chinese and lasted between 30 and 60 minutes each. The interviews were audio-recorded with the participant's consent and transcribed for further analysis. The transcripts were then translated into English and then back-translated into Chinese to ensure accuracy of the English translation (Malhotra, 1996). Table 1 presents the age and gender distribution of the interview participants.

Several cycles of part-to-whole interpretive procedures were conducted to organize the raw data and to generate conceptual schemes based on the data. First, using an intra-text strategy, the interview data from each participant were read and coded to gain a holistic view of each text.

TABLE 14.1
DEMOGRAPHIC CHARACTERISTICS OF INTERVIEWEES

Gender	Young adult (20s – 30s)	Middle aged (40s – 50s)	Senior adult (60 +)	Totals
Male	3	0	1	4
Female	7	6	1	14
Totals	10	6	2	18

Then, through an inter-text strategy, data were analyzed across all the interviews for the emergence of similarities and differences (Spiggle, 1994). The third step consisted of interaction between intra-text and inter-text, a cycle of moving back and forth between them, which allowed for evaluation across all interviews. Finally, an overall holistic interpretation was generated through the combination of the researchers' frames of reference and the data (Thompson, 1997). Two major categories are used to structure the interpretation of responses: shopping motivations and store choice criteria. Themes that emerged within both categories are discussed.

INTERPRETATION

Shopping Motivations
The data suggests that besides purchasing products, northwest Chinese consumers go shopping to satisfy multiple needs that include product needs, social needs and personal needs. Participants strongly suggested six major shopping motivations in addition to product needs that include market exploration, social obligations, socialization, self-gratification, diversion from routine, and visual appreciation.

Market Exploration
Market exploration was very common among participants. Consistent with the existing literature, participants explored the marketplace for similar reasons as their western consumers. Some participants explored the market to learn the newest fashion trends and popular styles, while others tended to check out new products and study the ones that they are interested in.

> Well, I notice, sometimes even if I don't need to buy anything, I would go to see if there is any changes in the market. Is there any new product or any new trend in pricing? That is, to gain some information. There is lots of information in the market, such as products and prices. (#1, Female, 50s)

Some liked to observe market trends such as price changes, and to seek out deals and bargains. Others noted that they explored the market for more than one reason.

> Sometimes I just look around to see what is good or if there is a good deal. If so, I would buy some. I think you need to shop the market more often, otherwise how can you find all the good deals. If you shop often, you can find things you want that are on sale. If you miss that opportunity, you cannot get that deal. (#10, Male, 70s)
> If I have some money, I would like to shop for electronics. Like in the Electronic Market, I would buy a couple CD, or some software, or a USB if it is a good price. In fact, I like to shop at Electronic Market most, especially recently because I plan to buy a better laptop. So, I would shop there to see what is new, and fantasize a little bit too. (#14, Male, 20s)

Overall, the majority of the participants were very excited about exploring the marketplace and what they could learn and find from it. It is an important medium for them to learn about markets and products.

Social Obligations and Socialization

Shopping is not all about purchasing products (Tauber, 1972); for many consumers, shopping is a social occasion (Pooler, 2003). Similar motivations emerged within the participant responses, with two specific social shopping motivations surfacing most frequently: shopping as a social obligation and the opportunity for socializing that shopping affords. Some participants go shopping because of obligation, whether going with their colleagues, girlfriends, or relatives. This is especially true for shoppers who claimed they do not like to go shopping with others, but do so because of an invitation.

> I like going shopping by myself. You have more freedom when you shop by yourself, and you can take your time. But it does not happen a lot. Usually colleagues will ask one another, and then we all go together. (#1, Female, 50s)

Other participants go shopping to socialize with friends and families.

> Shopping is usually about hanging out with friends, spending time together, or finding an environment to talk with each other. Like

264

asking a friend you have not seen for a long time for a shopping trip, you talk and gossip. (#7, Female, 30s)

In this case, shopping is about getting a chance to spend some time with a friend that one has not seen in a while, or to interact with the family to do something fun when they are bored. Overall, participants strongly emphasized social shopping motivations, pointing to a focus on the hedonic, rather than utilitarian, side of shopping.

Self-gratification

Participants revealed that they also go shopping for *self-gratification*; that is they go shopping to release stress, to relax, to improve negative moods, or to treat themselves (Arnold and Reynolds, 2003). Some participants go shopping to lift their mood. When they are down and upset, the marketplace is an ideal place to help them to forget their problems and make them happier.

> I like to go shopping, especially when I feel troubled in my mind. I go and look around, which helps me to improve my mood. It is helpful because there are lots of people and things in the market. Sometimes you can see interesting things happening or find very nice products which can help to divert my mind (from what troubled me). (#4, Female, 40s)

Others go shopping to relax after the hard work of the day.

> Sometimes you feel quite tired after work and want to relax a little bit. Then you may shop at Chaoshi. You may just buy one item, like a cold drink, which makes you feel pretty good. You feel quite relaxed. You don't need to spend a lot, but you treat yourself. (#8, Female, 20s)

Diversion from Routine

Participants also go shopping because they get bored at home and there is nothing else to do. In this case, shopping is treated as a leisure activity. This motivation may be enhanced by the existence of a wide range of retail stores and shopping centers as well as the lack of nearby outdoor activities and facilities in many Chinese cities. It may require much more effort to go to a park than to a nearby shopping center. Shopping is therefore an easy way to seek stimulation or entertainment. This is especially common among older participants. At the same time, shopping can help to pass the time, as some participants mentioned shopping during lunch hours or while waiting for someone.

In fact we did not really want to buy something. We started around 3:30pm. We were bored and had nothing to do so we went shopping. We only shopped about 30 minutes. And then we went to KFC to eat fried chicken.... And sometimes I will go shop and look around a little bit during lunch hours. (#15, Female, 20s)

Visual Appreciation

Some participants saw shopping as a way of appreciating beautiful products such as arts, crafts, and jewelry, or the visual appeal of retail stores.

Sometimes you shop, but not to purchase anything. It is kind of appreciating (pretty things). Brand-name merchandise such as "Feng Mang" is always folded neatly. The merchandise is displayed in large plates with knife and fork beside it. It feels very good and looks very nice. Visually it feels different. May be same clothing, but displayed differently, with some ornaments, feels very good. (#8, Female, 20s)

Retailers in China, especially high-end department stores, have begun to focus on visual merchandising. Some participants go shopping just to appreciate beautiful merchandise and attractive visual displays because doing so makes them happy.

Well, sometimes I like window shopping. Sometimes my daughter doesn't like going to certain stores [selling arts or crafts] and says that we cannot afford shopping there. I don't agree with her. We can go window shopping without buying anything. I like to look at crafts. They are so expensive, but I still like appreciate them in the store and feel good about it. So, I like to look. (#4, Female, 50s)

For this participant, shopping is about appreciating beautiful things, which provides a means of having fun.

Store Choice Criteria

Since the opening of the first supermarket in the year 2000, the retail market of Lanzhou has changed tremendously. Local retail system reform has brought forth a number of new retail formats and an abundance of novelty products. Major retail formats in the local markets include: (a) the free (street) market, (b) specialty stores, (c) convenience stores (also called "small Chaoshi"), (d) department stores, and (e) supermarkets (called "Chaoshi"). Besides different retail stores, there are a number of wholesale markets selling a variety of consumer goods from electronics, apparel and accessories to medicines. Vendors in all the wholesale markets also cater to individual consumers shopping for large quantities. Local consumers have become more educated about store and product choices. The shoppers interviewed for this study revealed that store choice has become an important element in their decision making process. Seven major store choice criteria surfaced within and across the interviews, indicating various factors that participants take into consideration when they decide to shop. Some criteria are focused on the merchandise (product quality/trust, price, style, assortment), while others are focused on retail stores and services (store location, shopping environment, and customer service).

Product Quality/Trust
    Participants revealed that they choose to shop at stores providing good quality merchandise. For the majority of participants buying authentic merchandise, that is, getting what the merchandise is claimed to be, is a big concern. Because counterfeit merchandise is quite common in China and a consumer protection system is still underdeveloped – especially in inland China – participants desire to shop at trustworthy stores, regardless of whether they are purchasing food, cosmetics or apparel.

> I buy food there [at Chaoshi], like sugar, salt, rice. Usually we don't buy fresh fruit there. The fruit there usually are not fresh. Those are pre-packaged, and have preservatives. We bought fruit there before, it was not good. The produce from fresh food market is pretty good and I feel safe buying it too. (#4, Female, 50s)

Dawar and Parker (1994) argue that perceived retailer reputation is one of the important product quality indicators for consumers. The interview data reveal that some participants prefer to shop at supermarkets and/or high-end department stores for certain merchandise because they assume that larger stores have better managerial and quality control abilities. This is especially important when it comes to food and expensive goods such as jewelry. When considering different retail outlets, one of the top two reasons cited by western consumers for shopping at big box stores is low prices (Brennan and Lundsten, 2000). However, the interview data reveal that for participants the appeal of big box stores is not necessarily low prices, but the availability of authentic or quality merchandise.

> I think the shopping environment is good [at Chaoshi] and there are less counterfeit products too, especially food. It is trustworthy. Like apparel, if it is labeled as 100% cotton, it must be. In fact the prices

in Chaoshi are not necessarily lower than those at small shops. But you are not sure if what you bought at those shops is exactly what it is claimed to be. The garments bought in small stores are more likely to shrink a lot. (#18, Female, 20s)

Price

Participants feel that price is another important criterion of store choice. This finding is consistent with the literature that reveals that Chinese consumers are very price-conscious (e.g. Fan and Xiao, 1998). The traditional wisdom is to shop around and get the best price. Under the planned economy, consumer goods were scarce so consumers could not put emphasis on prices. With a more competitive retail environment, shopping around became normal for many Chinese consumers. For certain goods, such as socks and underwear, some participants like to shop where prices are lower or more reasonable. As in western countries, retailers use discounts and seasonal promotions to attract consumers.

I am more attracted to prices. If I see a promotion such as the sign of sales (at some store) I will shop there. I would go inside and have a look, not necessarily to buy anything. (#9, Female, 30s)

Style

Participants also revealed that when it comes to fashion goods, the *style* greatly affects their store choices. They like to shop at stores carrying merchandise that matches their lifestyle or fashion taste. This indicates that some Chinese consumers, including young women, are not necessarily interested in following the latest fashion trends, but instead are concerned with their own personal style and taste.

There are just some stores that are not right for me to shop at. I don't go to those kinds of stores, like those very fashion-forward ones. It is not because I don't like those stores. They are just not right for me to shop there. (#15, Female, 20s)
I don't go to stores selling very fashion forward apparel. Some of those styles look so weird to me. It makes me feel that those products are not for normal people. (#16, Female, 20s)

This information is especially valuable for western retailers looking to explore China's fashion market. Although Chinese consumers are becoming more accepting of western culture and fashion, some consumers in this region, however, clearly have different fashion tastes from that of western consumers.

Assortment

The participants also use product assortment/variety as an important store choice criterion. They revealed a preference for stores carrying a large variety of merchandise. Participants appreciate broad merchandise categories and deep assortment within each category. So an abundance of choice is highly valued.

> They [supermarkets] have quite a lot of merchandise, so my shopping goals can be fulfilled over there. You don't need to go to different stores and you can buy all you want in one store. (#6, Female, 20s)

As in western countries, a large variety of merchandise provides consumers one-stop-shopping convenience. That is why many participants chose to shop at supermarkets for their daily needs. As a newer retail format in China, supermarkets also provide consumers a good opportunity to find new and novel products. Some participants shop there to explore new merchandise. Novelty is exciting and it turns shopping into a fun activity. Meanwhile, they become more educated consumers through exploring different brands and merchandise.

> And there are large varieties of product [at Chaoshi]. And for each product there are several brands. So you have lots of choices. In fact, compared with other stores, I like shopping at Chaoshi. There are very useful products for everyday life that you never saw before. So, you can get these kinds of information in Chaoshi, but not in other stores. So, there are large of variety products which can be very advanced and unique and not available anywhere else. (#15, Female, 20s)

Store Location

Location or the distance of shopping from the home is important for participants. The data reveal that participants like to shop at stores near where they live or work. Although personal cars are becoming popular in China, many still depend on public transportation. It is inconvenient to shop at stores that are far away, especially if direct bus lines are unavailable. The literature reveals that the distance to stores is often a critical determinant of store patronage decision for Shanghai Consumers (Wong and Yu, 2003; Uncles and Kwok, 2009). So, the distance to stores may be a common issue for Chinese consumers.

But compared with Jiashijie [a major supermarket], I like Haulian [the first supermarket opened in Lanzhou] better because it is close to my home and it is very convenient shopping there. I can go whenever I want to go or need to go; it can be on a daily basis. (#10, Male, 70s)

Shopping Environment

Shopping environment is another important factor affecting participants' store choices, and most of them preferred a clean shopping environment. Free markets and outdoor wholesale markets are full of dust and dirt, which keeps some from shopping there. This may suggest an important trend, because Chinese consumers are traditionally known for shopping at free markets for produce and groceries. Prices are usually lower in those marketplaces and one can bargain too. But with the improvements in living standards and availability of modern shopping outlets, it is possible that consumers are now choosing modern stores over traditional markets.

Chaoshi has cleaner shopping environment than other small vendors and shops. Although there are so many people and the air is not necessarily fresh [in Chaoshi], at least you don't have dust and dirt flying everywhere. The merchandise looks clean too. (#6, Female, 60s)

Participants also revealed that they like large stores that are spacious, have smaller crowds and less noise.

I dislike Eastern Wholesale Market most. There are so many people and vehicles. Sometime it is even dangerous because of the traffic. Too much noise too. Uh, there are so many thieves there too. They steal people's money. But this is not the case when you shop at Hualian or Jiashijie. (#10, Male, 70s)

They also like stores that are well-organized, and mentioned that disorganized merchandise often keeps them from shopping at a store. Elements such as lighting and scent all affect participants' store choices.

I like Beisheng [an upscale department store] and Xidan [another upscale department store] because of the better shopping environment and quite upscale merchandise. As an environment, you talk about good layout, light … (pause) which is kind of neat, unlike some smaller shops which are so disorganized. (#3, Female, 50s)

270

Customer Service

Customer service has been a weak component in many Chinese retail stores. For example, it is very difficult to exchange or return merchandise after the purchase, especially in small private shops. With the increasing competition, some retailers have started to focus more on customer services. To avoid conflict and unpleasant shopping experiences, some participants try to avoid stores that have poor customer service.

> I remember [there was] a convenience store beside my University. The service was very bad and the prices were pretty high. It would ruin your good mood if you shop there. Sometimes I was hungry late at night and cannot get anything elsewhere to eat except that store. I would rather be hungry than going to that store. That was bad. Like you would argue with them whenever you shop there, that gets old. (#14, Male, 20s)

CONCLUSIONS AND IMPLICATIONS

With a large population and strong economic growth, China has become one of the fastest growing consumer markets. This study investigated the shopping behavior of northwest Chinese consumers and its findings contribute to our understanding of consumers' shopping motivations and store choice criteria in this region. Several important findings surfaced from the interview data. Although the existing literature suggests that Chinese consumers are more likely to be motivated to go shopping for utilitarian reasons (Tsang *et al.,* 2003; Li *et al.,* 2004), the findings of this study tell a different story. **With the advances in the Chinese economy and increased access to retail outlets and consumer goods, the shopping behavior of northwest Chinese consumers now resembles that of western consumers. That is, participants shop for a variety of reasons including, utilitarian, hedonic, and social reasons.

Among the variety of shopping motivations that surfaced, social motivations appear to be especially important for local consumers. The modern Chinese retail environment provides a good setting for consumers to socialize. The participants of this study frequently go shopping to socialize with friends or family. Furthermore, some participants shop with others simply for fun and companionship. In fact, the majority of participants claimed that they like to shop with others even if they do not like to shop. Similar to shopping behavior in western countries, these shopping companions, also called "shopping pals," serve both functional and social roles (Kiecker and Hartman, 1993). Some participants shop with others for product advice and some for help with decision making and bargaining.

Given the important role of bargaining in Chinese shopping behavior, having a good shopping pal is apparently crucial for many consumers. In contrast to studies on western consumers, however, participants of this study did not shop to obtain social status or authority (Tauber, 1972; Cox et al., 2005) or to meet people (Haytko and Baker, 2004). This implies that northwest Chinese consumers have different social needs and shopping motivations. As a modern society with a collective culture, pleasing others in a social group is still important for many Chinese consumers. The literature indicates that although western individualism has become more apparent in China, consumers in less developed northwest China are the least individual-oriented (Cui and Liu, 2000). This might explain why some participants go shopping because of an invitation from friends or colleagues even if they have no personal shopping needs or generally prefer to shop alone.

It is also important to note that for the participants shopping does not equate to purchasing or buying. For the majority of participants shopping is about satisfying personal needs such as relaxation, appreciation, and recreation. For those participants shopping sometimes is about having fun, fantasy and entertainment. Participants enjoy the pleasure provided by modern retail outlets, which not only offers modern commodities but also a fantasyland to explore. Shopping not only provides immediate material satisfaction but also becomes a form of leisure pastime whether or not a purchase is made. Although Chinese consumers from less developed cities tend to have lower expectations for shopping experiences, the findings of this study imply that the shopping experience has become more important for northwest Chinese consumers, and many of them actively seek hedonic shopping value.

Participants also revealed that they use a variety of criteria to decide where to shop. Factors such as variety, quality, price and style, as well as in-store shopping environment, customer service, and store location are all important store choice criteria. Given the fact that socialization and other hedonic shopping motivations become important for participants, it is not surprising to see that in-store shopping environment and customer service are cited as key criteria. In order to have pleasant shopping experiences, some participants even try to avoid the traditional marketplaces. Furthermore, although prices are important for participants, some of them do choose to pay higher prices for better service. For most participants, product quality is associated with authenticity. Chinese consumers are becoming less adventurous in the marketplace because of the dramatic consequences of choosing inferior quality products, especially with food purchases (St-Maurice et al., 2008). Finally, northwest Chinese consumers may not purchase fashions that do not match their lifestyles or tastes. Providing merchandise that better satisfies local consumer lifestyles and needs may

272

become a key success element. Based on all the criteria that surfaced from the study, the majority of participants prefer to shop at supermarkets. Modern retailers should not only focus on providing quality merchandise, but also address other factors that affect the overall shopping experience.

This study contributes to the literature on Chinese consumer behavior, shedding light on the behavior of northwest Chinese consumers. Because of the exploratory nature of this study and because the interviews were conducted in only one region, the findings cannot be generalized to the larger Chinese population. Findings reveal that there are some differences between Chinese and western consumers with respect to shopping motivations and store choice criteria but also that the similarities are increasing. It is therefore important to conduct more research to develop a deeper understanding of these consumers. Additionally, with more and more consumers seeking extra in-store experiences, it is important to study Chinese consumers' shopping experiences and the factors that affect those experiences. These future research objectives can provide valuable information for both Chinese and international retailers to better serve Chinese consumers and compete in an increasingly challenging retail market.

Authored by Lizhu Davis, Joseph Peyrefitte, and Nancy Hodges, originally published in *International Journal of China Marketing*,.Vol. 3(1) 2012, pp. 71-87.

Chapter Fifteen

Cross-Cultural Customer Satisfaction at a Chinese Restaurant: The Implications to China Foodservice Marketing

Increasingly, Americans are consuming the cuisine of other cultures. Is this an indication that globalization is having an effect on our eating habits? Are Americans embracing and savoring multiculturalism? This study examines the factors (e.g., reliability, assurance, empathy, cultural awareness, cultural atmosphere, responsiveness, control, etc.) contributing to customer satisfaction in an ethnic restaurant. The results reaffirm the notions that reliability and value are the primary indicators of customer satisfaction. Moreover the findings from this study do not confirm some previous studies that cultural awareness of ethnic food has positive effects on customer satisfaction, an issue that needs more explorations. The findings are used to make suggestions to the China food marketers as how to effectively satisfy foreign travelers for their food consumption when they are in China.

INTRODUCTION

Since the very beginning of human history, food has assembled peoples in the way that not any other things have been able to do. No matter it was the ancient agora or today's modern day supermarket or restaurant, the market of food has always played a central role in human's lives, communities, communication, and culture (Huddleston et al., 2009; DeJesus and Tian, 2004).. Culture is often defined as a system of values as well as a determinant of consumer behavior. Members of a particular culture transform their experiences with their physical and social environments to an abstract level of belief about what is desirable and what is not (Lillis and Tian 2010). Such encoded beliefs, called values, act as a general guide for everyday behaviors, including those pertaining to buying and consumption. Cultural values differ among nations along Hofstede's four dimensions of national character (Emery and Tian, 2003; Hofstede, 1984; Tian, 2002). The growing amount of international business has increased the need to understand consumer behavior from a cross-cultural perspective (Mooij, 2004; Senguder, 2001; Sunderland and Denny, 2007; Tian 2002 a). A number of satisfaction models have been accepted by researchers and practitioners, but these models explain the phenomenon at the individual level, independent of the cultural environment of the consumers (Oliver, 1997; Senguder, 2007).

The objective of all marketing efforts is to maximize customer satisfaction (Rust et al., 2004). If for the marketers to satisfy the customers with the same cultural background is not that easy, then to satisfy the customers with different cultural background, which we termed as cross-cultural customer satisfaction, will be even more difficult. According to existing research, valued benefits have impact on satisfaction responses following consumption. Therefore, satisfaction is the function of the congruency between perceived performance and valued benefits derived from consumer personal values, and the formation of consumer values is influenced by central cultural values (Senguder, 2007; Westbrook and Reilly, 1983).

Consumer satisfaction is important to the marketer because it is a determinant of repeat sales and consumer loyalty. Satisfaction is also important to the individual consumer because it reflects a positive outcome from the fulfillment of unmet needs. Customer satisfaction is an important determinant of post-purchase attitude and product choice. The growing amount of international business has increased the need to understand customer satisfaction from a global or cross-cultural perspective (Choi and Mattila, 2006; Katherine et al., 2001; Senguder, 2007; Spreng et al., 1996). Generally, when Americans think about the influence of globalization on consumer behavior, they think it in terms of the United States' influence on the consumerism of other cultures. The reverse, however, may also be true (Tian, 2002 a, b).

Interestingly, over the last two decades, the popularity of ethnic restaurants has grown faster than any other category in the U.S. (Panitz, 2000; Pillsbury, 1998, Silverstein, 2009). Furthermore, this increase seems to directly parallel the increase in overseas trade. On the other hand, the fast growth of China economy as well as China becomes more open to the world, the number of foreign visitors to China is increased to a new high record of almost 55 million tourist visit it annually, which apparently stimulates the foodservice market in China. The purpose of this paper is to examine the factors (cultural and otherwise) contributing to the customer satisfaction of new and repeat customers at ethnic restaurants. It probes the factors that are influencing customer satisfaction any different for an ethnic restaurant than for an American restaurant. Thus to answer the question: does cultural authenticity or cultural familiarity influence customer satisfaction? In so doing the authors aimed at providing some useful suggestions to China foodservice marketers in general and to the Chinese restaurant industry in particular as how to satisfy foreign travelers' food consumption when they are traveling in China.

THEORETICAL ISSUES AND HYPOTHESES

Customer satisfaction is commonly defined as the organization's ability to meet or exceed customer expectations. Research conducted by Parasuraman et al. (1988) suggests that customer service expectations can be categorized into five overall dimensions: reliability, tangibles, responsiveness, assurance, and empathy. Specifically, reliability is the ability to perform the promised service dependably and accurately. Tangibles are the appearance of physical facilities, equipment, personnel and communications material. Responsiveness is the willingness to help customers and provide prompt service. Assurance is the knowledge and courtesy of employees and their ability to convey trust and confidence. Lastly, empathy is the caring, individualized attention provided to the customer.

Additionally, it is important to note that the reliability of service outcomes is the most important dimensions in meeting customer expectations. This is particularly true in the restaurant business. The quality (e.g., aesthetic appearance, aroma, temperature, and taste) of the food is the primary reason for visiting the restaurant (Schiffman and Kanuk, 2009). The process dimensions (assurance, responsiveness, and empathy), however, are the most important in exceeding expectations (Ziethaml et al., 1990). Note, the lack of influence that tangibles have as satisfiers or delighters on customer satisfaction. This is particularly surprising since customers experience the service within the environment of the service facility. Therefore, we believe that:

H_1: Of the various service and cultural dimensions, service reliability will have the largest effect on customer satisfaction.

H_2: The atmosphere of the restaurant (e.g., décor and music) will not have a significant effect on customer satisfaction.

Bateson (1985) suggests that the dynamics or control of the service encounter play a significant role in customer satisfaction. Every service encounter involves an interaction between a customer and a service provider; each has a role to play in an environment staged by the service organization. Furthermore, management has an interest in delivering service as efficiently as possible to protect their margins and remain competitive. These rules and procedures tend to limit the extent of service provided for the customer and the resulting lack of customization that might result in an unsatisfied customer. Additionally, the interaction between contact personnel and the customer has the element of perceived control by both parties. The contact people want to control the behavior of the customer to make their own work more manageable and less stressful; at the same time, the customer is attempting to gain control of the service encounter to derive the most benefit from it. In short, the more control that a customer has over the service; the more the customer is likely to be satisfied. This might be particularly true in situations when a customer is in a foreign environment. Consequently, we expect that:

H_3: The customer's desire for control will have a significant effect on customer satisfaction.

Why do customers choose one service over another - restaurant A over restaurant B? Cost, one may answer. Ambiance or any of several other good reasons are also viable answers. The bottom line, however, may be culture, because the underlying culture helps to determine the value that customers place on the service (Schwartz and Davis, 1981). In other words, when an American customer repeatedly chooses an ethnic restaurant, he or she may have a more positive perception of the restaurant associated with its culture, which may contribute to the value of the service. As such, we anticipate that:

H_4: The customer's perception of the restaurant's culture will have a significant and positive correlation with customer satisfaction.

Additionally, the work of Hofstede (1984) on cultural dimensions may have some effect on whether an individual is willing to take part in a cross-cultural experience. Specifically, Hofstede suggests that countries (e.g., the United States) with a relatively low sense of uncertainty avoidance are more apt to seek out new experiences and to be more tolerant of differences. Further, Bennis et al. (1973) suggest that the more one becomes aware of a foreign culture; the more one is likely to enjoy the culture. Therefore, we imagine that:

H_5: The customer's level of understanding of the ethnic food culture will have a significant and positive correlation with customer satisfaction.

THE STUDY AND METHOD

In order to get a sense of whether other ethnic food cultures influence the U.S. food culture, the authors wanted to select an ethnic culture that was the most dissimilar to that of the U.S. As such, the authors used the Hofstede (1984) dimensions as a guide, and also used a list of the available ethnic restaurants in the city to select one that is most suitable for our study. The area is relatively more diversified in terms of ethnicity and the population is more concentrated than in many other small cities in the U. S. Among many different ethnic restaurants we determined that this particular Chinese restaurant would be the most suitable for our study because it is located in the center of the city and can be easily accessed from all directions. Moreover, we ourselves are regular visitors of this restaurant and have established "guangxi" (social network) with the owners and the service staff. Additionally, we wanted to select a restaurant that had high volume for lunch and evening meals in order to capture statistics on both types of clientele. Further, we wanted to select a geographic area that was rapidly increasing its dependence on world trade.

The site selected was a Chinese buffet style restaurant in a city of approximately 100,000 residents along one of the major interstate highway corridor. The corridor, in general, and this area specifically, is consider by many authorities as one of the country's most rapidly increasing areas in terms of generating foreign revenue. The restaurant is located next to a major shopping mall, in a commercial complex on a heavily traveled four-lane street. There is a commercial plaza across the street with several American style restaurants and fast food services. Additionally, there are two other Chinese restaurants within two miles. A third Chinese restaurant one-half mile away recently went out of business.

The parking lot can accommodate 85 cars and the restaurant is designed to have a serving capacity of 180 customers at a time. There are five seating areas, among which, one is designated as a smoking area with 40 seats. The restaurant is nicely decorated with a beautiful waterfall screen between the waiting area and the eating areas and two large pictures of Hong Kong and the Great Wall in the two main dining rooms. The four buffet bars are next to the kitchen and between the two dining rooms. There is an excellent variety of foods consisting of 4 variations of rice, 15 steamed or fried dishes, 16 fried entrees, 18 vegetable entrees, and 18 deserts and soups. All entrees on each bar are even numbered according to the Chinese cultural value of *hao shi cheng shuang* (good things are in pairs).

Based on authors' observation, the consumers and their consumption behaviors at this restaurant vary from lunches to dinners, from weekdays to weekends. Generally, the consumers for weekday lunches are mainly working adults and drivers; the consumer for weekday dinners are families, mainly husbands and wives; the consumers for weekend dinners and lunches are mainly families, most with children. It is observed that the consumers for Sunday lunch are mainly extended families with grandparents, parents, and children after their church activities (See Table 1 for detailed information about consumers' structure).

There is a manager and a hostess to control the cash register and the waiting area and seven waiters/waitresses and one busboy to handle the dining areas. Except for the manager, hostess and a few servers, the majority of the employees are unable to freely communicate with the customers in English. The service persons are all from Mainland China. They do not get paid from the owners but are tipped by the customers. They work six days a week and long hours per day. The owners provide them with accommodations, including food and shelter. On the other hand, the owners clearly understand the importance of the cook in a Chinese restaurant; the owners pay the cook very well compared with what they pay the other employees and with what other Chinese restaurants pay their cooks. Overall, the manager says the restaurant serves approximately 3,500 customers a week and makes a nice profit despite their relatively low prices.

TABLE 14.1
OBSERVED CONSUMER STRUCTURES IN VARIOUS
TIMES OF A WEEK

Items	WK day Lunch	WK day Dinner	WK end Lunch	WK end Dinner
Dates of observation (days)	May 25 (Thu.)	May 23 (Tue.)	May 28 (Sun.)	May 26 (Fri.)
Times of observation*	12:30 p.m.	6:15 p.m.	1:15 p.m.	6:00 p.m.
Consumers (smoking)	33	6	8	17
Males	23	3	4	8
Females	8	3	4	7
Children	2	0	0	2
Consumers (non-smoking)	97	47	113	63
Males	62	23	45	30
Females	31	21	51	24
Children	4	3	17	9

* Times when the observer arrived at the restaurant.

Three instruments were developed for the purpose of this study. The first instrument was a 20-item, five-point Likert scale questionnaire developed by operationalizing each of the proposed factors affecting customer satisfaction. This questionnaire was given to a random sample of 72 lunch and 88 evening patrons. The second instrument was a seven-question open-ended interview sheet that focused on the issues of cultural awareness, the atmosphere, and reasons for choosing this restaurant. These interviews were given to a random sample of 25 daytime and 32 evening customers. Lastly, a five-item, five-point Likert scale cultural awareness survey was developed and distributed to 100 customers and 100 community members. In all, the data collection process covered a five-week period and was conducted by the authors and eight undergraduate student workers.

FINDINGS AND DISCUSSION

The first, second and third hypotheses were tested using a stepwise regression analysis of the following variables: reliability, assurance, responsiveness, empathy, tangibles, cultural familiarity, cultural atmosphere, and customer control. Separate analyses were performed on the lunch and dinner customers. Both results supported the first hypothesis, which suggested that reliability would be the most dominant variable influencing customer satisfaction (lunch adjusted $R^2 = 0.324$; p < .01; dinner $R^2 = 0.356$, p< .01). Other factors with adjusted R-squares above 0.05 were responsiveness (lunch adj. $R^2=0.181$, p < .01; dinner $R^2 = 0.153$, p < .01) and customer control (lunch adj. $R^2 = 0.233$ p< .01; dinner $R^2 =1.211$, p < .01). None of the other variables had levels of significance less than .05. On this basis, one can see that both the second and third hypotheses were also supported. The atmosphere did not have a significant effect on customer satisfaction (p < .05) and customer control did have a significant and meaningful effect on customer satisfaction.

The fourth and fifth hypotheses were tested using a correlation analyses. The fourth hypothesis, which suggested that customer satisfaction would be correlated with a customer's perception of the organization's culture, was generally supported (r = .63, p < .01). The fifth hypothesis, which posited that customer satisfaction would be correlated with a customer's understanding of the ethnic food culture, was not supported (r = .18, p > .05). This finding conflicts with findings in previous studies (DeJesus and Tian, 2004, Pillsbury 1998, Tian 2001), and therefore more careful studies are necessary. On the other hand, although not hypothesized, there was a strong and significant correlation (r = 63, p < .01) between a community member's knowledge of China/Chinese culture and their frequency of eating in Chinese restaurants.

Ninety percent of the lunch hour customers and 78% during the dinner hour customers were repeat patrons; mean values of repeat visits were 12.3 and 7.2 for the noon and evening meal respectively. Incidentally, there was a strong correlation between the number of repeat visits and the customer's belief that they were recognized by the manager and/or hostess (r = 73, p <. 01). Of the first time customers, 70% of the daytime and 67% of the nighttime customers said that they would be back. Only 11% of the customers perceived the food to be authentic Chinese. However, of the customers who perceived that the food wasn't authentic Chinese, only 5% cared. The other 95% did not seem to mind. Also, the four top reasons that customers indicated as reasons for their intent to return were: (1) taste, (2) variety, (3) quantity, and (4) price. The two most common reasons for customers indicating that they "would not return again" or "probably would not return again" were: (1) they didn't find the food to their tastes (65%), and (2) they didn't like the buffet style of service delivery (23%). Further, it is interesting to note that although a relatively high percentage (45%) of customers believed that there could be miscommunication with the servers, most (82% bottom two blocks) didn't see this as a problem or as a source of dissatisfaction.

Additionally, a comparison of the results of the community survey to the customers offered some interesting insights. First, fifty-nine percent of the community members believed that an ethnic restaurant should have an authentic décor and delivery system. In contrast, less than 15% of the satisfied buffet patrons believed that the décor was authentic and none of the satisfied patrons believed the delivery system was authentic. Second, the average community member perceived that Chinese have significantly stronger work ethics (58% to 20% top two blocks) and significantly higher morals (62% to 32% top two blocks) than Americans, but they are less attentive to cleanliness (19% to 32% top two blocks). Lastly, the demographic findings indicated that the patrons were relatively evenly distributed by age, occupation (professional vs. nonprofessional), gender, and education level. It did seem, however, that there were not as many families with young children (ages 5-12) as might be expected in a comparable American style restaurant.

Support for the first three hypotheses gives a strong indication that the factors influencing customer satisfaction at the Chinese buffet do not differ much from those influencing customer satisfactions in a typical American restaurant. It is interesting that the atmosphere, in general, and Chinese décor, in specific, did not influence customer satisfaction. This should be noteworthy to most of the proprietors of Chinese restaurants, since they spend a good deal of money on decorations. Perhaps atmosphere in a Chinese restaurant would be classified by Hill (1989) are a "qualifier" or by Kano (1984) as a "basic need".

On the other hand, since atmosphere would be considered by Parasuraman et al. (1991) as a process delivery dimension, it could be used an opportunity to exceed customer expectations. Additionally, it may be that as people become more familiar with China, they may appreciate efforts to improve authenticity or to receive information about China during the meal. We believe, however, that a buffet style restaurant is not a good candidate to test this proposition since most people indicated they were there for other reasons (e.g., control, speed, quantity, sampling opportunities).

TABLE 14.2
SUMMARY OF TESTED HYPOTHESES

Concept/Issue	Hypothesis	Finding and Interpretation
The relationship between reliability of service and customer satisfaction.	H_1: Of the various service and cultural dimensions, service reliability will have the largest effect on customer satisfaction.	Supported, which means that reliability would be the most dominant variable influencing customer satisfaction.
The influence of environmental factors on customer satisfaction.	H_2: The atmosphere of the restaurant (e.g., décor and music) will not have a significant effect on customer satisfaction.	Supported, which means that the atmosphere did not have a significant effect on customer satisfaction.
Customer's control over the service and their satisfaction.	H_3: The customer's desire for control will have a significant effect on customer satisfaction.	Supported, which means that customer control over the service has a significant and meaningful effect on their satisfaction.
The underlying culture helps to determine the value that customers place on the service.	H_4: The customer's perception of the restaurant's culture will have a significant and positive correlation with customer satisfaction.	Supported, which means that a customer satisfaction would be correlated with his or her perception of the service organizational culture.
Cultural awareness of ethnic food helps to increase customer satisfaction.	H_5: The customer's level of understanding of the ethnic food culture will have a significant and positive correlation with customer satisfaction.	Not supported, which means that a customer's satisfaction might not be correlated with his or her understanding of the ethnic food culture

Also, it is not surprising that this restaurant was doing very well financially. A buffet style restaurant is an excellent mix of Porter's (1980) cost leadership and differentiation strategies. The buffet standardizes service delivery by imposing strict operating procedures and, thus severely limits the discretion of the contact personnel. Although personalized service is not available, customers are presented with a vast array of items to choose from. This is a particularly good strategic fit since the customers are interested in controlling time, cost and variety and the restaurant doesn't have to worry very much about the English skills of its service staff

Further, it is important to note that the customers' sense of the restaurant's organizational culture was correlated with their level of satisfaction. This is probably an extension of Bitner's (1990) theory on the effect of attribution on satisfaction. In other word, since the customers perceived the Chinese as having a strong work ethic, they would not attribute any dissatisfying experiences as the fault of the restaurant. Also, it was surprising to note that customer satisfaction was not correlated with a customer's knowledge of the ethnic food culture (i.e., H_5). Especially since our survey of community members indicated a positive correlation between their knowledge of the Chinese culture and their frequency of eating Chinese meals.

We suspect this disparity is because there are a large number of people who like Chinese food, yet know nothing about China or the Chinese food culture. As such, we believe the effect (direct or moderating) of ethnic knowledge on customer satisfaction deserves further study. Additionally, it might be worthwhile to investigate the correlation between a person's level of uncertainty avoidance (Hofstede 1984) and their penchant for cross-cultural cuisine. Such a correlation would suggest an interesting opportunity for micromarketing. In short, however, the study simply affirms America's love for Chinese food and the buffet style of service delivery (self-service and variety). Apparently, the customers studied in this case did not expect to get a one-hour trip to China and they did not expect authentic Chinese food and that was just fine with them. The question remains, however, what are Americans or other foreign travelers in China expecting for their food consumption? How the Chinese food marketers effectively market their food and service to those foreigners who are traveling in China? In the next section we will make some of our suggestions based on this particular study.

THE IMPLICATIONS TO CHINA FOODSERVICE MARKETERS

China is a quite unique and diverse country market in various aspects including business practices, distribution and product development as well as legal systems, which differ from those of any other countries. The China food market is huge and unique as well with a great growth opportunity in the next few decades as the process of China urbanization goes and more foreign tourists travel in China (Trend Hunter World 2010). China's restaurant and catering industry is one of the most growing sectors in China since its reform and opening in the end of 1970s. The Chinese foodservice industry was valued at nearly Y 500 billion RMB (about $70.2 billion USD) in 2006, the leading profit foodservice area was the restaurants channel. It is expected to achieve yearly average growth of 18 percent with a goal of Y 3.3 trillion RMB (about $478 billion USD) in sales by 2013. The industry employed nearly 20 million people in 2009, with another 2 million would be added each year (Xinhua News Agency 2009). It is observed that in recent years, the Chinese domestic restaurant market has greatly changed. Not only the changing of consumer behavior but also the customer structure, such as more and more foreigners become the customers, requires that the operators of restaurant industry to engage more accurate brand positioning and better service.

There is no doubt that the fast increase in tourism has benefited the foodservice market in China, this is particular true during 2008 Olympic Games time in the summer of 2008. China has become a major tourist destination following its reform and opening to the world in the late 1970s instigated by Deng Xiaoping. In 1978, China received about 230,000 international foreign tourists, mostly because of the severe limitations that the government placed on who was allowed to visit the country and who was not. In 2006 China received 49.6 million international visitors, making it the fourth most-visited country in the world. In 2007 international tourist arrivals to China increased to 54.7 million, and the foreign exchange income was about $42 billion USD. According to the WTO in 2020, China will become the largest tourist country and the fourth largest for overseas travel (China National Tourist Office homepage).

Although the main purpose of foreign tourist visit China is not for enjoying the Chinese food culture, it is true that to provide a variety of good food choices and services will be definitely helpful to increase the satisfaction of foreign tourists when they travelling in China and thus will be helpful to attract more foreign tourist travelers in the future. The foreign tourist visitors differ from the origins (see Table 3) and thus they must have different food cultures from that of Chinese food culture. It is important and necessary for the food marketers to understand and familiarize themselves with some major foreign food cultures and to customize their food and service to their foreign customers from different countries. It is also important that the food service managers to allow their foreign customers certain degree of self control as what type of food to be served, the buffet foodservice format might be a better choice for most foreign foodservice consumers.

TABLE 14.3
FOREIGN VISITOR ARRIVALS IN 2009

Nationality		Age					Sex	
	TOTAL (10,000 Person)	Under 14	Age 15-24	Age 25-44	Age 45-64	Over 65	Male	Female
ASIA	1,377.93	49.76	102.91	653.58	488.77	82.90	923.59	454.34
AMERICA	249.12	19.00	17.68	85.05	106.02	21.37	158.99	90.13
EUROPE	459.12	17.33	44.86	213.46	163.93	19.54	275.87	183.25
OCEANIA	67.24	5.26	4.32	25.74	27.30	4.63	41.50	25.74
AFRICA	40.12	0.70	2.12	26.35	10.45	0.50	30.07	10.04
OTHERS	0.22	0.01	0.01	0.11	0.09	0.01	0.13	0.09
TOTAL	2,193.75	92.05	171.90	1,004.28	796.56	128.95	1,430.15	763.60

Source: China National Tourist Office Homepage
http://www.cnto.org/chinastats_2009ArrivalsByPurpose.asp

It is also suggested that the foodservice marketers in China should learn to effectively educate their foreign customers by providing them the basic information about the Chinese food cultures, demonstrating the proper way that the Chinese food being served, so that their foreign customers will be able to format their positive perceptions about Chinese food they are served. Finally but not lastly, it is very important that the foodservice marketers in China to train their service staff to effectively communicate and serve their foreign customers. The previous studies conducted by the scholars (such as Tian 2001) demonstrate that effective communications between customers and service staff at any restaurant will play an important role to get customers satisfied and to retain the customers' loyalty, therefore it is suggested that the Chinese foodservice leadership should realize the importance of foreign language training to the foodservice employees.

CONCLUSION AND SUGGESTION FOR THE FUTURE STUDY

Cultural factors play an important role in consumer food consumption and satisfaction. Satisfaction is vital to individual consumers because it reflects a positive outcome from the fulfillment of unmet needs such as eat food when feel hungry. To marketers, especially to the service marketers, such as restaurant operators, customer satisfaction is a very significant because it is a determinant of customer loyalty. Various factors influence customer satisfaction in foodservice sector, such as the reliability of the service, customer control over the service, customer cultural awareness of the service organizational culture, and ethnic food culture (a factor that previous studies have confirmed). It is important that ethnic restaurant operators to educate their customers have a better understanding about their service organizational cultures and their ethnic food culture as well.

Most consumers are aware of the differences between the Chinese food cultures and the American food cultures but need to know more about how and why they differ from one another. The study treats the consumers as the cultural participants but it needs more probes as to how the consumers behave themselves at various situations. The relationship between consumers and employees is not analyzed because of the limitations of the data, although it is suggested that the employees have much influence on consumer behaviors.

The growing amount of international visitors to China in recent years has increased the need to understand customer satisfaction from a cross-cultural perspective by the foodservice marketers in China. In order to create competitive advantages, cross-cultural customer satisfaction should be systematically studied by the Chinese foodservice marketers. It is highly recommended that the foodservice marketers in China should have a better understanding of the determinants of satisfaction responses of their foreign customers.

Future research will investigate the consumer behavior of food and service consumption in more detail and will include a survey of the foodservice employees. Particular areas of interest are how consumers define food cultures; the extent to which consumers are knowledgeable of Chinese food culture and what element consumers identify as the most important factors that cause them to behave differently in such an ethnic restaurant, if there is any difference. The authors are also interested in finding out how the foodservice providers, in this case the Chinese foodservice marketers, understand the differences between their own food cultures and other people's food cultures from an inside-out perspective. Moreover, it is important to find out the cross-cultural factors and their affects on consumers' food consumption and satisfaction.

Authored by Robert Guang Tian and Camilla Hong Wang, originally published in *International Journal of China Marketing*, Vol. 1(1) 2010, pp. 60-72.

Chapter Sixteen

The Choice Behavior in Fresh Food Retail Market: A Case Study of Consumers in China

The supermarket and the wet market are two major fresh food retail models in China. While the supermarket is competitive in food safety and quality, a wet market has the advantage of providing fresher food in a cheaper and more convenient way. There are already some studies on the factors which influence Chinese consumers' decisions between supermarkets and wet markets. Further efforts are needed to make so that we may know more about the relationship between frequency arrangements by the consumers and the way they make their shopping choices. Based on the utility theory, this paper probes into the utility differences between the services provided by the supermarket and the wet market. Then it discusses the essential condition of consumers' utility maximization and explains the frequency difference by comparing their different prices offered by the supermarket and the wet market prices.

INTRODUCTION

Fresh food is generally defined as the primary agricultural products which have not been deeply processed. It includes vegetables, fruits, meat, aquatic products, etc. Chinese consumers used to purchase fresh foods and cook them at home, and the traditional place where they purchase fresh foods is from the wet market. Since the reforming and opening-up policy, more and more new business models from west countries have been introduced into China. Supermarket, as a new fresh food retail model, was introduced into China in the middle of 1990's. From then on, both wet market and supermarket have been coexisting in the market.

Nowadays, people are beginning to have a higher demand for the quality of life, which gradually reveals the drawbacks of wet markets such as lack of sound management mechanism, insecure quality of fresh food and unprotected consumer rights. Meanwhile, both the operating and sanitary conditions of the wet market are far from consumers' satisfaction. By contrast, the supermarket makes up for the shortcomings of the wet market. That is why the number of people purchasing fresh food in supermarkets is proportionately increasing year by year. Under the promotion of the government, there arises a nationwide upsurge of "transforming wet markets to supermarkets." However, it should be noted that, in reality, not all consumers purchase fresh food in supermarkets, and the wet market has not been completely replaced by the supermarket, which adequately justifies the rationality of the existence of the wet market. Therefore, we need to analyze the reason for the coexistence of both the two retail formats from the perspective of their own characteristics and the consumers' demand.

Both the supermarket and the wet market have their own characteristics. Chinese consumers often have their own frequency arrangement at going to one place more often and the other less. Empirical researches have revealed that lots of factors such as income, the quality of fresh food, education, age of consumers, and shopping time, influence Chinese consumers' choice between the supermarket and wet market (Hu & Yu, 2003; He, 2005; Chen, 2006). Specifically, food safety, quality assurance, freshness of fresh food, brand reputation, packing, saving shopping time, and the distance of the consumer's residence from the supermarket are the main factors that attract Chinese consumers to purchase fresh food from the supermarket (Zhou, Lu & Gen, 2003). The degree of shopping convenience and the price of fresh food are the key factors influencing a consumer's decision making (Huang, 2004).

All these empirical researches have disclosed the existence of frequency difference, but they lack explanations on why and how each consumer makes their decision and what the frequency difference means to the consumers. According to existing researches, market demand is the process through which individuals choose their preferred goods and services composition (Samuelson and Nordhaus, 1999). The frequency arrangement of Chinese consumers choosing different fresh food retailing business models is also a process of choosing preferred services composition.

The purpose of this paper is to explain the reasons why Chinese consumers make different frequency arrangement based on the utility theory and existing empirical researches, which may contribute to the consumer behavior analyzing. The research results would likely provide some useful suggestions to the government and the marketers in terms of the realization of the Chinese consumer's welfare maximization.

THE UTILITY DIFFERENCE BETWEEN SUPERMARKET AND WET MARKET

Utility is the subjective enjoyment or usefulness, which people get from consuming goods or services (Samuelson and Nordhaus, 1999). The utility satisfaction, which the fresh food retailing business models bring to the consumer, includes two aspects. On the one hand, the fresh food, which are sold in the supermarket and Wet market, could bring to the consumers the satisfaction of maintaining life and obtaining nutrient substances; on the other hand, the service of the retailing formats will bring to the consumers different utility satisfaction too, which includes the fresh degree, quality safety, variety, packaging, brand reputation, shopping environment, saving shopping time, etc. This paper emphasizes the utility satisfaction of service.

The service of supermarkets and wet markets bring different utility satisfaction to the consumer. The business scale of a supermarket is bigger than the stallholders in the wet market, and its prophase investment (sunk cost) is much more, and its opportunity cost of selling poor-quality fresh food is much higher, so the supermarket is the ideal distribution channel for selling the organic agricultural products, the green agricultural products and the harmless agricultural products. Compared with the wet market, the supermarket has the brand competition advantage. However, the scale of each stallholder in the wet market is relatively smaller, so they have more time to "care" about their goods; meanwhile, the price of fresh food in wet markets is lower, and the velocity of turnover is faster, therefore, the fresh food in the wet market looks fresher. Some empirical researches have proved that the supermarket has the advantages of quality safety, brand credit, shopping environment, and the wet market has the advantages of higher fresh degree and variety (Zhou, 2003; He, 2005; Feng, 2008).

Therefore, from what has been discussed above, it is obvious that that the supermarket could meet the consumer utility of quality safety (this sense of security derives from brand credit) and shopping environment, whereas the wet market could meet the consumer utility of freshness and variety.

THE ESSENTIAL CONDITION OF CONSUMER UTILITY MAXIMIZATION

According to the analysis above, the economic framework used to derive the empirical model assumes that the consumer choice in fresh food reflects the utility function as follows: (1)

$$U(x) = alpha\,0 + alpha\,1 * \Pr ice + alpha\,2 * Freshness + alpha\,3 * Variety + alpha\,4 * Safety + alpha\,5 * Convenienc\,e + alpha\,6 * Environmen\,t$$

It is also assumed that the budget for fresh food in every family (Y) remains unchanged in a certain period, the price of fresh food in the supermarket is P_s, and the price of fresh food in wet market is P_w; moreover, $P_s > P_w$. Meanwhile, every consumer couldn't affect the price alone. Under this condition, the rational consumer will make their total utility ($u(x)$) maximize.

$$\max \quad u(x) = u(f_s, f_w) \tag{2}$$
$$s.t. P \cdot X \leq Y$$

f_s means the frequency of consumer purchasing fresh food in the supermarket during a certain period; f_w means the frequency of consumer purchasing fresh food in the wet market during a certain period; P means the price of fresh food; X means the quantity of fresh food that consumers demand.

Generally, each consumer just chooses one place (the supermarket or the wet market) to purchase the fresh food every time, the marginal utility of the consumer choosing the supermarket is $\partial u / \partial s$, the marginal utility of the consumer choosing the wet market is $\partial u / \partial w$, therefore:

$$\frac{\partial u / \partial s}{\partial u / \partial w} = \frac{P_s}{P_w} \tag{3}$$

This means that the essential condition of consumer utility maximization is the ratio of marginal utility of supermarkets to wet markets equaling the ratio of fresh food price in supermarkets to the price in wet markets.

THE UTILITY EXPLANATION OF CONSUMER'S CHOICE DIFFERENCE

During a certain period, the total quantity of each family's demand for fresh food is X, the budget is Y. So $X \cdot P \leq Y$ or $P \leq Y / X$. P means the highest price acceptable to a consumer. It can be seen from this formula that the highest price that a consumer can accept is proportional to the consumer's budget, when the consumer's total demand for fresh food is unchanged. Therefore, the frequency difference could be explained by the comparison of different price.

The Acceptable Price is Less Than or Equal to P_w

Consumers have no choice but to purchase fresh food in the wet market or plant or breed some by themselves when his /her acceptable price is less than or equal to the price in the supermarket. Due to the restriction of budget, this kind of consumers has to abandon the utility of quality safety and shopping environment which the supermarket could bring them, and turn to pursue the utility maximization of quantity. According to the empirical researches done by Hu & Yu (2003) in Peking, when the consumer's average monthly income is less than RMB￥1000, they just care about the price and they have no way but to choose the lower price site.

The Acceptable Price is Less Than or Equal to p_s and More Than p_w

With consumers' income increasing, the budget that they use to purchase fresh food will be enhanced. At this time, consumers can take an overall consideration of such factors as the utility of quality safety, shopping environment, freshness and variety. They will make a decision between the supermarket and the wet market. Under this circumstance, their frequency arrangement will follow the principle that the ratio of marginal utility of the supermarket to the wet market equals the ratio of fresh food price in the supermarket to the price in the wet market. In other words, the marginal utility which the consumer spends every one dollar in the supermarket or in the wet market is equality, according to $\dfrac{\partial u / \partial c}{p_c} = \dfrac{\partial u / \partial n}{P_n}$ equation.

At this time, the consumer's utility maximization is able to realize.

In fact, the frequency arrangement of every consumer purchasing in the supermarket or in the wet market is different. Here, this difference could be illustrated by the consumer preference difference and the consumption characteristics of fresh food.

Firstly, when the consumer's preference is freshness, or among all the utility satisfaction, the utility of freshness ranks first. According to $\dfrac{\partial u / \partial c}{p_c} = \dfrac{\partial u / \partial n}{P_n}$ equation, the marginal utility of freshness that the consumer spends every one dollar to obtain in the wet market equals the marginal utility of quality safety and shopping environment which consumer spends the same money to obtain from the supermarket. To this kind of consumers, more time to purchase fresh food in the wet market and less to the supermarket will make their utility maximized.

Secondly, since the quality safety of fresh food has both the attributes of search goods and experience goods (Nelson, 1970). Namely, after long-term and repeated consumption, consumers could distinguish the partial quality difference according to their experience, such as the correlation degree between quality with the appearance, the color, the odor and the hardness-softness, as well as the fresh degree, the content of juice, the taste etc. After the long-term experience accumulation, if the consumers hold more knowledge about the quality safety of fresh food than ordinary consumers do, they prefer to choose the wet market to meet their partial utility of quality safety depending on their stronger resolution ability. According to the principle of the marginal utility equality, experienced consumers (older consumers) could satisfy their utility of the freshness, utility of the variety and utility of the partial quality safety by choosing the wet market more. This kind of consumers makes their utility maximal by means of this arrangement. The empirical researches show that age is negatively correlated with "the degree of purchasing in supermarkets" (the regression coefficient is -0.259, P<0.05), the older people prefer to purchase fresh food in Wet market (He, 2005).

Thirdly, with the enhancement of consumers' education level, consumers would pay more attention to the quality safety and the shopping environment. For this kind of consumers, the utility of quality safety and the shopping environment rank first. According to the principle of the marginal utility equality, consumers, with higher education level, prefer to choose the supermarket to make their utility maximization. The empirical researches show that the consumer's education level has positive correlation with "the degree of purchasing in the supermarket" (the regression coefficient is 0.360, P<0.01) (He, 2005). With other variables being equal, the rise of every grade of the consumer education may raise the probability of his/her choosing the supermarket by 74% (Hu, 2003).

Fourthly, when the consumer pays more attention to the shopping convenience, he /she prefers to choose the nearest retail form (site). Therefore, the distribution of different retail forms in a certain region will influence the consumer's decision-making. According to the empirical researches, the distance of the consumer's residence from the supermarket has a great impact on the sales of fresh food in the supermarket (Zhou, Lu & Gen, 2003). When the distance of the habitation to the supermarket reduces one meter, the probability of the consumer purchasing fresh food in the supermarket will raise 0. 3 % (Hu, 2003).

The Acceptable Price is More Than p_s

When the consumers' income gets to a certain extent, namely, their budget for fresh food is more than ordinary consumers, their utility rank is different. With their income increasing, consumers will pay more attention to the quality safety of fresh food and the shopping environment and this kind of utility maximization could be well satisfied from going to the supermarket. Empirical research shows that the average monthly income is more than RMB￥8000, consumers pay almost no attention to the price, they pursue the high quality of fresh food and the convenience and comfort of shopping (Hu & Yu, 2003).

The quality safety of fresh food Means more attributes of credence goods, such as no antibiotic, no hormone, no residual pesticide and no genetically modified component. The cost of the consumer judging these attributes is much higher too. So, in most cases, it is impossible for costumers to judge these attributes of the fresh food. To the high-income consumers, it is a rational choice for them to repose their food safety guarantee on the brand and credit of supermarket.

THE IMPLICATION AND MANAGERIAL SUGGESTIONS

At present, whatever frequency arrangement consumers choose in going to the supermarket or going to the wet market, they have to abandon some utility satisfaction. For example, while consumers get the utility of fresh degree in the wet market, they will have to lose the utility of quality safety and shopping environment at the same time, and vice versa.

With the steady increase of the living standard, consumers in Mainland China are focusing more attention on their life quality and life value, so their demand for the quality safety, fresh degree, variety and shopping environment is becoming higher. In order to upgrade Mainland Chinese consumers' total utility satisfaction level, some methods should be taken.

Supermarket Should Be Encouraged to Connect with Production Base of Fresh Food Directly

The empirical researches show that the proportion of consumers who choose the supermarket is just 62 %, although 76% people believe the fresh food in the supermarket is safer, the proportion of consumers who choose the supermarket is just 62 % (Feng, 2008). It reveals that lots of people's quality safety utility hasn't been satisfied from the supermarket..

The main reason for lots of consumers to choose the wet market to buy fresh food is the higher price of fresh food in the supermarket, which is caused by the intermediate links in circulation. In fact, many supermarkets go not have their own production base; have not built their own supply chain system, and have been purchasing from wholesale market like the stallholders in the wet market. Thus, the supermarket loses its price advantage because of their higher operating cost. In order to make more low-income consumers to satisfy their utility of the quality safety and shopping environment, the supermarket should be encouraged to reduce their intermediate links in circulation, and build their own production bases and supply bases, to reduce the price of fresh food. Meanwhile, the lower price is beneficial to the increased velocity of turnover of fresh food, and finally to the achieved goal of improving the fresh degree.

Strengthen the Fresh Food Quality Monitoring of Supermarket

As is mentioned above, utility is the subjective enjoyment or usefulness. The supermarket possesses the advantages of brand and credit. If the quality problem exists in the supermarket, not only the brand and credit of the supermarket will be affected, but also lots of consumers who pay more attention to the quality safety will have no place to go. So the government should strengthen the quality monitoring of the supermarket, and establish the market competition mechanism of fresh food retail terminal, moreover, the supermarket should concentrate their efforts on their supply chain monitoring and internal quality management.

The consumers in Mainland China have low awareness of quality safety (Feng, 2008). Therefore, in order to enhance the utility satisfaction degree of Chinese consumers in quality safety, the authenticity of quality certification information should be guaranteed, and the propaganda work of food safety knowledge should be strengthened.

Promoting the Retail Formats Reform Reasonably

If the quality safety and shopping environment of the wet market are improved, consumers who choose the wet market would get a total utility upgrade too. This is the original intention that the government promotes the "transformation of the wet market to the supermarket". But the process of "transforming the wet market to the supermarket" should be determined by the market; meanwhile, some measures should be taken to enhance the quality safety level of the wet market.

CONCLUSIONS

There are different utility satisfactions when consumers purchase fresh food. Only if all utility could be met, the consumers' utility maximization will be realized. The supermarket and the wet market have their own advantages, and therefore bring different utility satisfactions to consumers. Consumers have to make their utility maximization by the different frequency arrangement under the condition of budget constraint.

Enhancing the customer utility is very significant to both the supermarket and the wet market, because it is not only a determinant of their benefit maximization, but also a determinant of their competitiveness.

The fresh food retail formats reform is continuing in China. Local governments impel this process. The investments in "transforming the wet market to the supermarket" are mainly used in infrastructure improvement. The enhanced operating cost of the stallholders in the new wet market will finally result in the higher price of fresh food. However, the slower income growth rate will bring about more low-income groups and their utility satisfaction content will decrease gradually. As a result, finding more ways to raise the income of Chinese consumers is the other way to enhance the utility satisfaction of consumers.

This paper explains the consumer's frequency arrangement according to the service utility of the supermarket and the wet market provided to the consumer. As we know from the empirical researches, the service of the supermarket and the wet market provides lots of utility satisfaction, this paper just analyzes parts of them, the others such as the packing, saving shopping time, and varieties are not included. A comprehensive analysis that includes all the factors is the next aim of continuing study. On the other hand, because the consumer behavior is a psychological process, more psychological analytical approaches should be used in future research. At first, a psychometric measuring scale should be designed to measure the consumer's will in choosing fresh food retail format, and the principal component analysis should be used to analyze the factors influencing consumers' selection of the fresh food retail format. Moreover, the structural equation modeling could also be used to validate the utility equation in this study.

Authored by Bin Cui, originally published in *International Journal of China Marketing*, Vol. 2(1), pp. 68-76.

Chapter Seventeen

Global Brands in the Context of China: Insights into Chinese Consumer Decision Making

This paper explores Chinese consumer decision making in relation to ten global brands. The paper uses four constructs (brand familiarity, brand liking, brand trust and knowing a brand's country of origin) to predict brand purchase intent within a sample of Chinese consumers. This research also explores how Chinese consumer self-perceptions of cosmopolitanism, ethnocentrism, global-local identity and identification with a global consumer culture might also influence global brand purchase intent. Regression models were built for all ten global brands, with the hierarchy model providing the strongest evidence. Familiarity, trust and liking generally explained a significant portion of the variance.

INTRODUCTION

The economy of the People's Republic of China (PRC) continues to fascinate and to draw world attention on an almost daily basis. The powerful combination of overall market size, dramatic increases in disposable income (especially in first and second-tier urban cities) and the long-term growth potential of the Chinese economy, make the PRC an exceptionally attractive market for many global firms and their brands (Sheng & Yan, 2011; Yau & Steele, 2000). According to the *Wall Street Journal* (Batson, 2010), China has achieved a gross domestic product (GDP) amounting to $4.758 trillion (estimated by the IMF for 2009). The WSJ expected that China would soon surpass Japan, the world's second largest economy ($5.049 trillion). The IMF also estimated that shift would occur in 2010 since China, they forecasted, would generate $5.745 trillion in 2010 (International Monetary Fund, 2010).

The success of McDonalds (Eckhardt & Houston, 2002; Watson, 2006) and KFC (Liu, 2008) in China have been well documented. Similarly, the significant increase in the number of high net worth individuals within China, when coupled with the cultural tradition that status products support an individual's *mianzi* (or prestige face) and hence become valued expressions of "success," has led many luxury brands to target the PRC as a "must win" market (Degen, 2012). However, as most western commentators note, successful marketing in China demands significant resources, skills and adaptations (Tian & Borges, 2011) – perhaps even a brand new mindset. The recent complicated story of Danone-Wahaha provides a cautionary tale for any business strategist and/or global marketer who thinks that market entry into the PRC is or will be easy.

The research reported here explores Chinese consumer behavior through a focus on ten global brands. The research, part of a three-year global branding project, extended into Asia interests which heretofore targeted consumers living in Central and Eastern Europe (Deli-Grey, Haefner & Rosenbloom, 2012; Rosenblooom & Haefner, 2009). The global branding research sought to identify the strength of global brand trust, global brand familiarity, global brand liking and knowledge of a global brand's country-of-origin (COO) in predicting global brand purchase intent. The research also included five scales measuring consumer attitudes toward (1) global consumer culture, (2) cosmopolitanism, (3) multinational advertising, (4) global-local identities, and (5) ethnocentrism. All five scales were drawn from the extant literature on global brands and have had research supporting their influence on consumer decision-making in a global context. Regression models were built for all ten brands inclusive of the five attitudinal scales to gain insight into the relative contributions of each of these items as independent predictors of global brand purchase intent in Chinese consumers. Regression models are presented that were built for each global brand along with a discussion of the most surprising insights. There were some unexpected findings about Chinese consumer decision making in the data.

CONSUMER BEHAVIOR IN CHINA

As befits the growth of China itself, China-focused consumer behavior research published in English has increased dramatically over the years. Sin & Ho (2001) conducted an early meta-analysis of published consumer research. These researchers reviewed 75 studies on Chinese consumerism and concluded that a wide variety of consumer issues were being researched. Kaigler-Walker, Gilbert & Hu (2010) noted, specifically, that there was extant research on Chinese consumers relative to purchasing motivation (Zhou & Wong, 2008), consumer values (Lee et al., 2004; Tai, 2008), decision making (Fan & Xiao 1998; Hui et al., 2001) and generational and regional differences (Cui & Lui, 2000).

Garner (2005) summarized one of the few large-scale studies published as a book. Garner, a senior strategist at Credit Suisse First Boston, managed a proprietary Chinese consumer lifestyle and spending pattern survey. The survey was conducted in four tier one cities (Beijing, Shanghai, Guangzhou, Shenzhen) and four tier two cities (Shenyang, Chengdu, Xi'an, Wuhan) and included 10 product categories, ranging from automobiles, beverages, electronic and luxury goods through tobacco products and travel services. Garner provides not only category data but also competitive market share data for each product category by city and consumer income levels. Wang (2008) provides a more recent macro-level of view of Chinese consumer behavior, with her focus on key national brands as experienced through the social construction of meaning that domestic advertising firms use to position brands as "local."

The global consulting firm, McKinsey, has been conducting an annual survey of Chinese consumers since 2005. McKinsey uses a stratified sampling plan, which includes approximately 600 cities in which 82% of all urban Chinese consumers live. Furthermore, these same cities are forecast to account for 92% of China's urban GDP by 2015 (Atsmon et. al, 2009). In its most recent Annual Survey (Atsmon, Dixit, Magni & St. Maurice, 2010), McKinsey noted that while the global recession has had some effect on consumer purchasing patterns in China, the combination of government and private-sector incentives has led to very robust retail sales. McKinsey stated that, arguably, the Chinese consumer sector was "the healthiest of any major economy in the world" (Atsmon, Dixit, Magni & St. Maurice, p. 7). Nonetheless, Chinese consumers still continue to embody their own unique mix of characteristics: They are still fundamentally conservative, although there is some behavioral convergence towards behaviors of consumers in more developed economies such as evaluating products beyond mere functionality and trading up for products that deliver greater value and quality. There may even be an emerging hedonic, global youth segment, which McKinsey terms the 'what fits me' group (Annual Survey, 2010).

As a counterpoint to the above, Uncles and He (n.d.) systematically searched for consumer behavior research written in Mandarin between 1985-2004. Their search found over 700 articles on various aspects of Chinese consumer behavior. Their conclusions were: (1) There was a significant body of indigenous literature not recognized by scholars in the West; (2) most research was concerned with consumer economics and understanding consumption functions; and (3) the focus on consumption functions fit well with the rise in disposal consumer income most Chinese have experienced.

BRANDS

Strong brands help firms succeed (Aaker, 1996; de Chernatony & McDonald, 2003). While having a strong consumer franchise is not the only thing firms need for success in their markets, strong brands are often linked with strong brand equity. The global financial crisis of 2008 is an apt reminder that firms with strong brands are buffered from, but not immune from, unexpected market shocks. "Brands have never been more important than they are today. The accelerating rate of turbulent change, the volatility of economics and markets, the relentless progress of technologies and innovation, and increasing market fragmentation have caused the destruction of many companies and products that have failed to develop the lifeline of a strong brand" (Temporal, 2010, p. xiii).

Eckhardt and Bengtsson's (2010) article summarized the 4,000 year-old-history of branding in China, and its long association with Imperial dynasties. This recent article is a strong counterpart to Holt's (2006) history of branding in the late nineteenth century in the United States. Marketers, like every other business professional, must understand and appreciate China's history if they hope to be successful. Ambler and Witzel's (2004) words are well chosen: "The point cannot be emphasized too strongly. In China, history is important if for no other reason, *because the Chinese themselves believe it is*" (p. 39, emphasis in original). "The phenomenon of foreign brands in China appears somewhat different from what is often addressed in research in marketing, because of the complexity of the market situation and cultural characteristics of today's Chinese society and consumer behavior, closely related to the combined experience of generations of Chinese" (Li, 2007, p.11).

There is ongoing academic debate, though, about what constitutes a "global brand." Roberts and Cayla (2009) note that "definitions of global brands are mostly supply side" (p. 350) in that the brand's globalness is defined in terms of number of markets served, size of markets served and the extent to which the brand shares consistent technical specifications across these markets. This mirrors the standard, textbook definition of a global brand (Ghuari & Cateroa, 2010). Roberts and Cayla (2009) also note that while a consumer-centric view of global brands (that is, the process by which consumers categorize brands as "global") is desirable, such a view is still underdeveloped in the marketing literature. This view was supported by Rosenbloom & Haefner (2009), who analyzed multiple, global brand definitions. Their literature review found only one global brand definition that integrated both consumer and producer orientations. In this definition, a global brand was defined as "the multi-market reach of products that are perceived as the same by both consumers and internal constituents" (Johansson and Ronkainen, 2005, p. 340). Steenkamp, Batra and Alden (2003) were very clear that "a brand benefits from consumer perceptions that it is 'global'...only if consumers believe the brand is marketed in multiple countries and is generally recognized as global in these countries" (p. 54).

Country of Origin

All brands have a country-of-origin (COO), yet for global brands, COO is always an issue of marketing strategy concerning whether to highlight it or not. As such, COO has been extensively investigated (Pharr, 2005). Marketing scholars have variously tried to understand how COO affects perceived product value (Cervino, Sanchez & Cubillo, 2005; Hui & Zhou, 2002); brand image and brand equity (Lin & Kao, 2004; Pappu, Quester & Cooksey, 2007). Okechuku (1994) used conjoint analysis to study the effect of COO on product choice in consumers living in Holland, Germany, Canada and the United States and found that COO was one of the two most important attributes in purchase evaluation. Okechuku (1994) found that consumers had a distinct preference for domestic products over foreign ones, especially when the COO was from countries with developing or emerging economies. This finding seems consistent across much of the COO literature—there is a strong domestic preference for many product categories when consumers in developed countries evaluate COO (Watson & Wright, 2000).

Research on Chinese consumers finds a similar pattern: There is a predisposed, strong preference toward domestic products (Cui and Liu, 2001; Li and Gallup, 1995) and foreign products, except for those in luxury product categories, may suffer from the "liability of foreignness" (Peng, 2009; Zaheer, 1995).

H1: The greater the importance of knowing a brand's COO, the greater will be its effect on brand purchase likelihood.

Brand Familiarity

To know a product's COO (Samiee, Shimp, Sharma, 2005), presumes some level of brand familiarity. Brand familiarity creates a feeling in consumers that the brand is "known." This feeling of knowing something about the product begins the transformation process of turning undifferentiated products into brands (Franzen & Moriarty, 2009). Indeed, "familiarity, trust and liking are the three most important drivers of brand loyalty" (Franzen & Moriarty, 2009, pp.310-311).

Brand familiarity reflects "the extent of the consumer's direct and indirect experiences with the brand" (Campbell & Keller, 2003) and directly affects consumer knowledge structures. Consumers who are familiar with a brand have more elaborate, sophisticated brand schemas stored in memory than consumers who are unfamiliar with the brand (Heckler & Childers, 1992; Kent & Allen, 1994; Low & Lamb, 2000). Research has demonstrated that brand familiarity yields more favorable brand evaluation (Janiszewski, 1993; Holden & Vanhuele, 1999). Increased brand familiarity means that consumers will process advertising messages quicker and with less effort because they already "know things" about the brand (Chattopadhyay, 1998).

Consumer familiarity with product categories and brands also may influence COO evaluations. So far, though, this research is inconclusive. Lambert and Jaffe (1998) suggested that consumers already familiar with products from a country used COO marginally in forming brand judgments. Johansson (1989), in contrast, found consumers already familiar with a brand in a product category used COO more fully in their decision making. Phau and Suntornnond (2006) found that while COO does have an effect: "There are only weak associations between product dimensions and country of origin cues particularly for evaluations of unfamiliar brands" (p. 39). Most recently, Ahmed and d'Astous (2008) studied the effect that COO familiarity had on a wide variety of products whose COOs were from 14 different nations. Ahmed and d'Astous (2008) concluded that for their sample of male consumers living in Canada, Morocco and Taiwan "familiarity has a significant and substantial impact on COO evaluations" (p. 96).

H2: Greater familiarity with a global brand increases the likelihood of global brand purchase.

Brand Liking

While brand familiarity is predominantly a cognitive process, brand liking invokes an affective response within consumers. de Houwer (2008) stated, "A core assumption in marketing research is that consumers tend to buy brands and products that they like" (p. 151). Anselmsson, Johansson & Persson (2008) defined brand liking as the "evaluative and global measurement capturing how positive and strong the perceived brand assets are from a consumer perspective" (p. 66). Boutie (1994) extended the concept by noting that brand liking "seeks to build consumers' positive attitude toward a brand based on the belief that it cares about them (or addresses them) as individuals" (p. 4). While intuitively attractive, global brand liking is an underdeveloped area of market research. Few studies of both the general construct of brand trust and/or its relationship to global brands exist. The research reported here contributes to the extant literature on brand liking.

H3: Stronger global brand liking increases the likelihood of global brand purchase intent.

Brand Trust

Trust is an elusive concept (Elliot & Percy, 2007) and can be thought of as an individual characteristic, as a characteristic of interpersonal relations and/or as an institutional attribute (Lewicki & Bunker, 1995). Rotter (1971) defined trust as "a generalized expectancy held by an individual or group that a word, promise, verbal or written statement of another individual or group can be relied on" (p.1). Barney and Hansen (1994) added the idea of hurt and harm when they defined trust as "The mutual confidence that no party to an exchange will exploit another's vulnerabilities" (p. 176). Finally, Bhattacharya, Devinney & Pilluta (1998) highlighted the protective nature of trust when they defined trust as "an expectancy of positive (or nonnegative) outcomes that one can receive based on the expected action of another party in an interaction characterized by uncertainty" (p. 462). Trust thus involves commitment, risk and mutuality. Trust is also a dynamic concept that is always contingent. "The amount of knowledge necessary for trust is somewhere between total knowledge and total ignorance. Given total knowledge there is no need for trust and given total ignorance there is no basis upon which to rationally trust" (McAllister, 1995, p.26).

Delgado-Ballester, Munera-Alemain and Yague-Gullien (2003) defined brand trust as "The confident expectations of the brand's reliability and intentions in situations entailing risk to the consumer" (p. 37). Brand trust has also been defined as "the confidence a consumer develops in the brand's reliability and integrity" (Chatterjee & Chaudhuri, 2005, p.2). Brand trust has been linked with brand loyalty (Lau & Lee, 1999) as well as increased market share and advertising efficiency (Chatterjee & Chaudhuri, 2005).

Of recent interest has been the question of whether brands vary in terms of trust. Romaniuk and Bogomolova (2005) studied this question by controlling for brand size effects when they assessed trust scores of 110 local brands in 13 markets in subjects living in the United Kingdom and Australia. They found little variation in brand trust scores when controlling for market share. They concluded that "trust is more like a 'hygiene' factor in that all brands have to have a certain level of trust to be competitive in the market" (Romaniuk & Bogomolova, 2005, p. 371). If brands do not vary greatly in terms of trust, would the same hold true when consumers were asked to evaluate specifically their trust in a global brand?

H4: Global brand trust increases the likelihood to purchase a global brand.

Ethnocentrism

There is an extensive literature on ethnocentrism primarily because it's a pervasive aspect of all global transactions – not just marketing transactions. Furthermore, consumer ethnocentrism can act as a mediating variable in any COO and global brand evaluation. Ethnocentrism is defined as "the local proclivity of people to view their own group as the center of the universe, to interpret other social units from the perspective of their own group, and to reject persons who are culturally dissimilar while blindingly accepting those what are culturally like themselves" (Shimp & Sharma, 1987, p. 280). Ethnocentrism works unconsciously within individuals, thus making it a powerful, yet unacknowledged, influencer in decision making. Shimp and Sharma (1987) developed the CET scale to measure consumer ethnocentrism and described the psychological and sociological roots of the phenomenon in succeeding research (Sharma, Shimp & Shin, 1995). Consumer ethnocentrism has been more recently termed "domestic country bias" (Balabanis and Diamantopoulos, 2004, p. 80).

Empirical research has identified differences in domestic country bias between consumers living in developed versus developing countries (Batra et al., 2000; Upadhyay & Singh, 2006). The former clearly favored domestic over foreign products, while the latter favored the opposite. Research by Bawa (2004) indicated that contrary to earlier findings that consumers from developing countries were biased toward imported over domestic products, "the label 'made in India' is not a liability. The Indian consumer will not lap up foreign goods merely because of their 'made in' tags" (p.43).

H5: Individuals with strongly held ethnocentric beliefs prefer to buy domestic brands over global brands.

Cosmopolitanism

Another consumer characteristic closely linked with global brands is cosmopolitanism. Cosmopolitanism has its origin in sociology and cultural studies and refers to the fact that some individuals perceive themselves to be more "worldly" and less provincial than others. Skrbis, Kendall and Woodward (2004) suggested that cosmopolitanism is "a conscious openness to the world and to cultural differences" (p. 117). Cleveland and Laroche (2007) included cosmopolitanism as a subscale in their research aimed at developing a composite scale assessing acculturation to global consumer culture. In their confirmation study, their 11-item subscale had a very robust, Cronbach alpha of .906. In their six-country study, cosmopolitanism was a positive predictor of owning a personal portable stereo, CD and DVD players, a television set, a digital camera, a computer, a mobile phone, ATM and computer usage, Web surfing and e-mail, and DVD purchasing. Additionally, cosmopolitanism influenced purchase of a washing machine, a hair dryer, a vacuum, a refrigerator, and a microwave oven (Cleveland, Laroche, & Papadopoulos, 2009).

H6: Individuals with strongly held cosmopolitan values prefer to buy global brands over domestic brands.

Global-Local Identity

As the above discussion of cosmopolitanism indicates, consumers hold many beliefs about themselves. Global-local identity extends the concepts of consumer self-identity. Zhang & Khare (2009) stated that

306

individuals with local identities "have faith in and respect for local traditions and customs, are interested in local events, and recognize the uniqueness of local communities" (p. 525). Individuals with a global identity, in contrast, "believe in the positive effects of globalization, recognize the commonalities rather than dissimilarities among people around the world, and are interested in global events; broadly, being global means identifying with people around the world" (Zhang & Khare, 2009, p. 525). Global-local identities are complex, since individuals can maintain both local and global identities without much cognitive dissonance. In the context of global brands, individuals with local identities would/should prefer local brands; while consumers with global identities would/should prefer global brands.

H7: Individuals with strong local identities prefer to buy local brands over global brands.

Global Consumer Culture

Robertson (1987) defined globalization as "the crystallization of the world as a single space" (p. 38). Robertson's definition fits well within the established conceptualization of globalization as a series of "flows," across transnational boundaries, "of virtually everything that characterizes modern life: flows of capital, commodities, people, knowledge, information, ideas, crime, pollution, diseases, fashions, beliefs, images and so forth" (Tomlinson, 2007, p. 352). These "flows" enable brands to travel the world. Corporate marketing practice supports consumer experiences that "global brands [are] on the center stage. The evidence is everywhere: on the streets, in stores, in the media. Global brands are exerting their power and influence within various domains" (Özsomer & Altaras, 2008, p.1).

This tendency to homogenize markets has resulted in a global consumer culture. A global consumer culture emerges because not only consumers' needs are convergent across national boundaries but also because firms intentionally maintain a consistent global consumer culture positioning strategy in all markets (Alden, Steenkamp, & Batra, 1999). Further, a global consumer culture positioning strategy can have either a local emphasis or a foreign emphasis. A local emphasis is "a strategy that associates the brand with local cultural meanings, reflects the local culture's norms and identities, is portrayed as consumed by local people in the national culture" (Alden, Steenkamp, & Batra, 1999, p.77). A foreign consumer culture position, in contrast, stresses "the brand as symbolic of a specific foreign consumer culture; that is, a brand whose personality, use occasion, and/or user group are associated with a foreign culture" (Alden, Steenkamp, & Batra, 1999, p.77). These two global consumer culture-positioning strategies dovetail with global-local identity discussed above.

H8: Individuals who strongly identify with a global consumer culture will prefer to buy the global brand over the domestic brand.

Exposure to multinational advertising

Closely linked with global consumer culture is exposure to multinational advertising. Consumers must be exposed not only to the global product but also to the global values which the product expresses. Frequently, but not exclusively, this exposure is through advertising (Arnould, 2011). Mertz, He and Alden (2008) note that "advertising cross-culturally creates desires for the advertised products or services – whether affordable or not – and, as such, becomes associated with the inherent symbolism of those offerings" (p. 172) – thereby simultaneously creating and reinforcing a global consumer culture.

H9: Individuals exposed to multinational advertising will be more likely to identify with and buy global brands over domestic brands.

GLOBAL BRAND PURCHASE MODEL

Models of consumer behavior suggest that consumer decision making is very complex (Lavidge-Steiner, 1961; Engel, Kollat & Blackwell, 1973). Hierarchy-of-effects models help simplify information processing as a sequence of perceptual and cognitive processes. AIDA (awareness-interest-desire-action) is one well-known model. As a more specific and nuanced application, Percy and Elliot (2005) have summarized the brand communication process in terms of four stages: Category need-brand awareness-brand attitude-brand purchase intent. To date, though, few researchers have developed a hierarchical model specifically for global brands. The model outlined in Figure 17.1 attempts to fill that gap. Figure 17.1 also summarizes the relational influence of the attitudinal constructs described above (ethnocentrism, cosmopolitanism, global-local identify, global consumer culture and multinational advertising) on global brand purchase intent.

Research Methodology

The objective of this empirical study was to evaluate the relative contribution of each construct presented in Figure 17.1 (country COO, global brand familiarity, global brand liking, global brand trust) as an independent predictor of global brand purchase intent and to determine whether ethnocentrism, cosmopolitanism, global-local identify, global consumer culture and multinational advertising influenced purchase intent as well.

FIGURE 17.1
MODEL SUMMARY

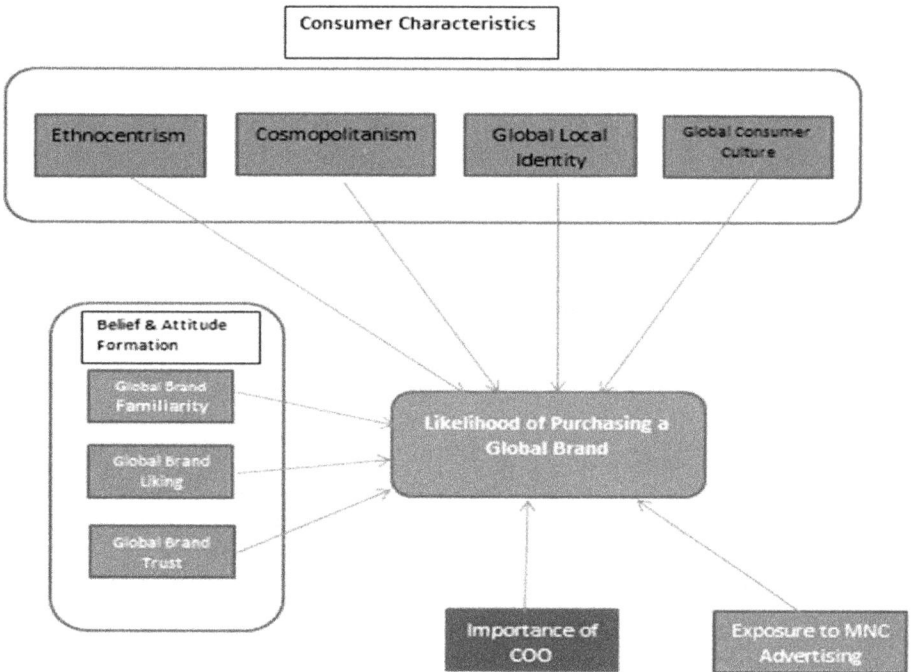

Ten global brands were chosen for this research. Table 17.1 presents the global brands tested. These global brands were chosen to cover a wide variety of product categories (consumer electronics, fashion, banking, personal care products and automobiles). In addition, the global brands chosen included low involvement (Colgate) and high involvement (BMW, Prada) products. Four brands were specifically chosen for their clear COO associations: BMW (Germany), Chanel (France), Haier (China) and Levi's (United States). All global brands were available in the PRC when the research was conducted (March-May 2010).

TABLE 17.1
GLOBAL BRANDS TESTED

Avon	雅芳
BMW	宝马
Chanel	香奈儿
Colgate	高露洁
Haier	海尔
HSBC	汇丰银行
Levi's	李维斯
Prada	Prada 普拉达
Samsung	三星
Zara	Zara

Five point Likert-scales measured each construct. Importance of knowing a brand's COO ranged from "not at all important" to "very important." Global brand familiarity ranged from "not at all familiar" to "very familiar" on a 5-point scale. Global brand trust was scaled "no trust at all" to "total trust." Similarly, liking the brand ranged from "like nothing about the brand" to "like everything about the brand" on a 5-point scale. Finally, likelihood to purchase was a 5- point scale that ranged from "never purchase" to "always purchase." It should be noted that these questions about the brands were phrased with a caveat, "if you were able" to purchase the brand.

Five attitudinal scales were designed to tap various aspects of consumer decision making: ethnocentrism, cosmopolitanism, global-local identity, global consumer culture and awareness of multinational advertising. All the scales used were subsets of previously published and validated survey instruments. Table 17.2 presents the attitudinal items used, and each scale's source, Cronbach alphas, and the factor loading for each item.

TABLE 17.2
SCALES UTILIZED AND ITEM FACTOR LOADINGS

Scales		Item Factor Loading	Cronbach's Alpha
Global Local Identity (Adapted from Zhang & Khare, 2009)			.685
I believe that the local way of life is harmed by globalization.[1]	我觉得本土化的生活正在被全球化所破坏。	.419	
I respect my local traditions.	我尊重自己当地的传统。	.834	
I believe parents should pass along local customs to their children.	我觉得家长们应该把当地民风民俗传承给他们的孩子。	.850	
Cosmopolitanism (Adapted from Cleveland, Laroche, Papadopolous, 2009)			.698
I enjoy exchanging ideas with people from other cultures or countries.	我喜欢与来自异乡不同文化的人们交流意见想法。	.860	
I enjoy being with people from other countries to learn about their views and approaches.	我喜欢从来自异乡的人们那里学习他们的观点和方式。	.712	
I like to observe people from other countries to see what I can learn from them.	我喜欢通过观察来自异乡的人们来看我能从他们那里学到些什么。	.818	
Ethnocentrism (Adapted from Cleveland, Laroche, Papadopolous, 2009)			.819
I do not buy foreign products because it hurts local business and causes unemployment.	我不买外国生产的产品因为这样会伤害当地经济以及导致失业。	.807	
I do not purchase foreign products because it puts people in my home country out of work.	我不买外国生产的产品因为这会使得我国家的人们没有工作。	.859	
I purchase domestic products to prevent other countries from getting rich off of me.	我购买本国国内产品以防止其他国家比我国富裕。	.815	

I buy foreign-made products only when I cannot get a domestically-made product.	我只有当买不到本国国内产品时才会买国外生产的产品。	.742
Openness and desire to emulate GCC (Adapted from Cleveland & Laroche, 2007)		.740
I would like to live like people in the United States do.[2]	我想像在美国生活的人们一样生活。	.353
I think people my age are basically the same around the world. For example, someone who is 20 years old in Russia is basically the same as someone who is 20 years old in the US, Sweden or anywhere else.	我想与我同龄的人们基本上全世界都一样。例如，在俄罗斯一个 20 岁的人基本应该和在美国或瑞典一个 20 岁的人差不多。	.833
I think that my lifestyle is almost the same as that of people in my age-group in other countries.	我认为我的生活方式应该和与我同龄的其他国家的人们的生活方式差不多。	.817
I think my lifestyle is almost the same as that of people in my social class in other countries.	我认为我的生活方式应该和与我一样社会阶层的其他国家的人们的生活方式差不多。	.805
Exposure to MNC advertising (Adapted from Cleveland & Laroche, 2007)		.702
When watching TV, I often see ads for brands that are outside my home country.	当在看电视的时候，我经常收看非我国品牌的广告。	.578
It is quite common to see ads for global brands in the local newspaper.	在当地报纸上经常有全球品牌的广告。	.802
It is quite common to hear ads for global brands on the local radio.	在当地广播里经常可以听到全球品牌的广告。	.814

| Ads for global brands seem to be everywhere. | 好像到处都是全球品牌的广告。 | .814 |

Note. A Principle Components Factor Analysis with Varimax Rotation was utilized for all the scales.

[1] Item was not included in the final scale due to low factor loading.

[2] Item was not included in the final scale due to low factor loading.

Recruitment of Respondents

A four-phase recruitment procedure was utilized for this study.

Phase 1: Selection of key distributors

A personally addressed email was sent to key distributors who have ability to understand both Chinese and English. The key distributors agreed to cooperate in an ongoing global brand study. The key distributors were composed of the Dean of Shanghai Normal University, Shanghai; a faculty member of Jishou University, Hunan; and 10 Chinese for whom researchers have contact information previously. After receiving confirmation from the key distributors, researchers made phone contact with them. During the conversation, researchers explained the purpose of this study and encouraged them to disseminate this information to their acquaintances in China. When researchers sent an English email to the key distributors, it was translated into Chinese and was then distributed to the participants.

Phase 2: Invitation

Two ways of approaching the participants were used: (1) personal invitation by email (in Chinese) from key distributors and (2) a discussion board in the Chinese social network (online community). In terms of personal invitation, each participant received an email inviting him or her to participate in a confidential Global Brand Survey via the web. The message was distributed from the key distributors in order to avoid having it viewed as a junk email. The email included a brief introduction to the survey and a hypertext link contained within the message. When participants clicked the link, their computer's default web browser was directed to surveymonkey.com, an online survey research site, where the complete questionnaire was accessible in Chinese. The email also included additional instructions on how to access the survey by typing in a URL when the browser was not able to launch the survey site appropriately. In the invitation message, participants were assured that the data they provided were transmitted to a secured site, remained confidential, and would be used only for the purposes of this study. The hypertext link could be used only once to access the questionnaire. When the participants attempted to access the site again, a message was provided that they already completed the survey and it was no longer available for access.

The second approach to participants was through Chinese social networks (Online community) that key distributors were engaged in. The members of communities were mainly those who graduated from their college and employed in the various companies. The purpose of the online community is to keep their social network after they graduated from their schools. Within the online community, each key distributor can send a message to every member. The key distributors posted a brief introduction to the survey and a hypertext link in the message. In addition, the key distributors encouraged their friend's family member to participate in this study.

Phase 3: First reminders

Four weeks after the first e-mail message was sent to the participants and after the survey database was checked for the number of participants, a reminder e-mail message was sent to those participants who had not yet responded. This message includes the same information as the first email (short introduction and hypertext link to the web questionnaire) in case the previous e-mail message had not been delivered to the person. The same information was provided in the online community.

Phase 4: Second reminders

Four weeks after the first reminder e-mail, a second reminder message was sent, after the survey database was again checked. Key distributors sent an email reminder to the participants to encourage them to complete the survey. The same information was provided in the online community.

RESULTS

Respondent Profiles

The study sample consisted of 296 Chinese aged 19–60 years, who currently hold Chinese citizenship and reside in the People's Republic of China (See Table 17.3). The majority of the sample was female, 63.2%. Almost 41% had some college or university work, while 55.2% had a bachelor's degree or better. The majority of the sample was not married at 83.8%. Almost 47% were unemployed while 52.7 % were employed part-time or full- time. The average age of the respondents was 24.8 years.

Respondents indicated they did not particularly feel a part of the global consumer culture with an average of 7.9 out of a possible 15 (See Table 17.4). Chinese respondents definitely felt more cosmopolitan and saw global advertising. In terms of their global-local identities, respondents felt more bound by local traditions and felt the local way of life was harmed by globalization. However, they were more ethnocentric having a mean of 7.7 out of 20. There was a disparity between their cosmopolitan views and their more inward leanings in terms of appreciating the local way of life and their more ethnocentric world view.

TABLE 17.3
SAMPLE DEMOGRAPHICS

Demographic	Percentage (Mean)	Frequency
Gender:		
Male	36.8	89
Female	63.2	153
Education:		
High school diploma	3.9	9
Some college/university work	40.9	94
Bachelor's degree	28.3	65
Some graduate work	14.3	33
Master's degree	12.6	29
Marital status:		
Never married	83.8	201
Married	15.4	38
Widow/widower	.4	1
Current Employment Situation:		
Unemployed	46.9	113
Employed part time	37.8	91
Fully employed	14.9	36
Retired	.4	1
Age (mean)	24.8	

TABLE 17.4
SCALE MEANS

Scale	Means
Global Consumer Culture	7.9
Cosmopolitanism	12.5
Multinational Advertising	15.3
Global-Local	8.9
Ethnocentrism	7.7

Note. For global consumer culture, scores can range from 3 to 15. For cosmopolitanism, scores can range from 3 to 15. For multinational advertising, scores can range from 4 to 20. For global-local, scores can range from 2 to 10. For ethnocentrism, scores can range from 4 to 20

Means for Familiarity, Trust, Liking, COO, and Purchase Intent

For familiarity, Chinese respondents indicated the least familiarity with Prada (2.92), Zara (3.04), Avon (3.15), and Levi's (3.21). The greatest level of familiarity was for Haier (4.23), Colgate (4.22), and Samsung (4.10) [See Table 17.5].

Concerning trust, the least trusted global brand was Zara at 2.59. The most trusted global brands were BMW (4.34), Chanel (4.16), Haier (4.08), and Levi's (3.99). For liking, the least liked global brand was Avon at 2.50. The most liked global brands were BMW (4.0), Chanel (3.88), Haier (3.66), and Prada (3.66). For knowing the country-of-origin, respondents felt it was most important for the brands BMW and Haier both at 3.38 and for Chanel at 3.13. The least need-to-know country-of-origin was Avon at 2.26. Finally for purchase intent, the brand most likely to be purchased was Colgate at 4.11. The least likely brand to be purchased was HSBC at 2.23.

Regressions

Separate stepwise multiple regressions were run for the ten brands. The dependent variable was likelihood of purchase of the brand while the independent variables included familiarity with the brand, degree of trust in the brand, degree of liking the brand, and importance of knowing the county-of-origin of the brand. The highest VIF value was 2.3 for trust in Haier with all the remaining VIF values across all the models being below 2.1. All values indicate that multicollinearity was not a problem for any of the models (See Table 17.6).

TABLE 17.5
MEANS FOR FAMILIARITY, TRUST, LIKING, COO, AND PURCHASE INTENT

| Brands | Means | | | | |
	Familiarity	Trust	Liking	COO	Purchase Intent
Avon	3.15	3.00	2.50	2.26	2.79
BMW	3.73	4.34	4.00	3.38	3.18
Chanel	3.55	4.16	3.88	3.13	3.39
Colgate	4.22	3.83	3.46	2.72	4.11
Haier	4.23	4.08	3.66	3.38	3.66
HSBC	3.36	3.79	3.38	2.78	2.23
Levi's	3.21	3.99	3.56	2.72	3.55
Prada	2.92	3.44	3.66	2.90	3.24
Samsung	4.10	3.49	3.15	2.95	3.16
Zara	3.04	2.59	3.36	2.61	3.44

Note. Based on Tukey Kramer multiple comparisons, difference between means greater than .30 were significant $p \leq .05$ for familiarity (See Table 17.5). For trust mean differences greater than .36 were significant $p \leq .05$. For liking, mean differences greater than .37 were significant $p \leq .05$. For strong-weak, mean differences greater than .33 were significant at $p \leq .05$. For COO mean differences greater than .41 was significant at $p \leq .05$. For purchase intent, mean differences greater than .36 were significant at $p \leq .05$.

Most of the models were robust in their predictive ability. The exceptions were BMW with an adjusted R^2 of .122 and HSBC with an adjusted R^2 of .213. The most frequently occurring significant predictor across the ten models was global brand liking (7 times). This confirms H3 that global brand liking increases the likelihood of purchasing global brands. The only brands where brand liking did not occur were BMW, HSBC and Levi's.

TABLE 17.6

CHINESE RESPONDENT REGRESSIONS (FAMILIARITY, TRUST, LIKING, IMPORTANCE OF COO, GLOBAL CONSUMER CULTURE, COSMOPOLITANISM, MULTINATIONAL ADVERTISING, GLOBAL-LOCAL, ETHNOCENTRISM, GENDER, EDUCATION, AND MARTIAL STATUS REGRESSED AGAINST LIKELIHOOD TO BUY)

Model/ Brand	Model Summary				Coefficients (Standardized Betas)			
	F	Sig	R	Adj R^2	Variable(s)	t	Sig	Weight
Avon	32.0	.00	.712	.492	Liking	6.9	.00	.548
					COO	2.6	.00	.208
					Familiarity	2.4	.01	.178
BMW	8.3	.00	.373	.122	Familiarity	3.1	.00	.288
					Global-Local	-2.8	.01	-.257
Chanel	12.7	.00	.520	.250	Liking	3.6	.00	.340
					Familiarity	2.8	.00	.259
					Global-Local	-2.2	.02	-.191
Colgate	20.8	.00	.669	.426	Trust	4.1	.00	.437
					Liking	3.4	.03	.346
					Familiarity	-2.0	.04	-.165
					Cosmo	2.0	.04	.149
Haier	46.4	.00	.755	.558	Liking	5.5	.00	.546
					Global-Local	-3.0	.02	-.199
					Trust	2.1	.03	.214
HSBC	10.1	.00	.486	.213	Trust	4.4	.00	.391
					Global-Local	-2.2	.03	-.194
					Male	2.1	.03	.194
Levi's	20.9	.00	.571	.310	Trust	4.4	.00	.443
					Familiarity	2.0	.04	.206
Prada	21.3	.00	.658	.412	Liking	5.2	.00	.461
					Familiarity	3.4	.00	.303
					Global-Local	-2.1	.03	-.174
Samsung	69.0	.00	.754	.560	Liking	5.4	.00	.500
					Trust	3.3	.00	.310
Zara	33.3	.00	.778	.587	Liking	4.2	.00	.406
					Familiarity	3.7	.00	.276
					Trust	2.2	.02	.214
					Male	-2.0	.03	-.147

Global brand familiarity was a predictor for seven brands, including Avon, BMW, Chanel, Colgate, Levi's, Prada, and Zara. This data would confirm H2, that familiarity with a global brand increases the likelihood of purchase intention. Trust was a significant predictor six times with the exceptions being Avon, BMW, Chanel, and Prada thus giving confirmatory evidence that greater global brand trust increases the likelihood of purchase (H4). COO was a significant predictor for only Avon. Thus, COO did not have an effect on purchase intent. H1 was not confirmed.

For the most part, the attitudinal scales that were used as predictors in the models had limited predictive ability. They appeared in five of the models. Ethnocentrism, desire to emulate global consumer culture, and multinational advertising did not appear as a predictor in any of the models. H5, H8, and H9 were not confirmed. Cosmopolitanism appeared in one model, Colgate, thus not confirming H6.

Global-Local Identity appeared in four models: Chanel, Haier, HSBC, and Prada. When the construct was significant, all weights for Global-Local were negative weight. For Global-Local Identity, the negative loadings indicated that respondents tended to disagree with the three statements in the scale:

- I believe that the local way of life is harmed by globalization.
- I respect my local traditions.
- I believe parents should pass along local customs to their children.
  There was limited support for H7.

The only demographic to appear in the models was gender. Males were more likely than females to have higher purchase intent for HSBC while males were less likely to be interested in the purchase of Zara.

DISCUSSION

As noted above (Table 17.5), Colgate, Haier and Samsung had the highest mean score for global brand familiarity. This is not surprising, since Chinese consumers view all three brands favorably. Colgate, for example, has had a huge impact on Chinese life. Since the brand was introduced in China, it has achieved high penetration rates in Chinese market. The Chinese believe that Colgate was very successful in creating various flavors (such as green tea and honey) and introducing new product design (such as a tub design for children) that helps meet the needs of such domestic products in the Chinese market. In addition, Colgate is positioned as being of high quality and an inexpensive brand. Advertising expenditures are strong for the brand.

Haier is a very interesting brand in that it scored higher on all of the variables (familiarity, trust, liking, COO, and purchase intention). This brand projects a unique image to the Chinese. They see Haier as a representation of China because it is the first global brand from China. In addition, Chinese view Haier as a high quality company.

Samsung is a brand that is seen by most Chinese as limited to the electronics market. For example, many Chinese attributed the image of Samsung mainly to cell phone products, even though Samsung produces various products such as TV, monitors, printer, semi-conductors, etc. Despite of the limited view point of the brand, Chinese see the Samsung brand as user friendly because they find it simpler to input text message in the cell phone. The innovative design of the phone is also more up to date with advanced features.

Table 17.6 supports earlier research (Deli-Grey, Haefner, & Rosenbloom, 2012) that brand liking is the strongest overall predictor of global brand purchase intent. In this regard, these respondents appeared similar to respondents in Hungary and Bulgaria, where similar research was conducted (Rosenbloom, Marcheva, & Haefner, 2011).

For Colgate, HSBC and Levi's, trust was the strongest predictor. One possible explanation for this finding is the hedonic-utilitarian classification of products. Products that emphasize pleasure and affective emotions are hedonic while products that stress functional attributes are utilitarian. Trust can be linked with utilitarian product benefits, while liking is more associated with hedonic products. It seems reasonable to speculate that toothpaste is most valued for its many utilitarian benefits (fresh breath, white teeth, etc.) and that HSBC is a similarly valued for its utilitarian benefits (safety of deposits, security of ATM machines, etc.). Similarly, Levi's, a quintessential American brand, might be valued for its utilitarian benefits as well. In this case, trust equals quality. While more expensive than domestic, Chinese jeans brands, Levi's are noted for their stringent quality control in manufacturing.

Lastly and perhaps the most interesting finding is the absence of most of the attitudinal scales as independent predictors of global brand purchase intent. While the research described in the literature review suggests many interesting conceptual ideas, by and large, respondent orientation towards ethnocentrism (the desire to emulate global consumer culture) and exposure to multinational advertising were not predictors of purchasing these global brands.

Only global-local identity had limited predictive power. Since the loadings in all cases were negative, this finding seems to suggest that this respondent group moderated both traditional Chinese values (many of which are Confucian) and the collective often associated with Chinese culture (Hofstede, 2001).

For the most part, the hierarchy model seemed to have evidence of support with Chinese consumers. Although not every construct appeared in every model as a significant predictor, familiarity, trust and liking generally explained a significant portion of the variance. The sense of the authors is that the Chinese consumers of this study tend to conform with other international consumers more than they differed in the elements that this project reviewed. Familiarity, trust, and liking are the key predictors of purchase intention. It is possible that this merging of consumer decision making is part of the larger notion of a global consumer culture (Lury, 1996) which tends to create more similarities than differences among global consumers. Thus instead of looking for variances between consumers, marketers should be looking for more of the common linkages among them in their strategy development.

Authored by Al Rosenbloom, James Haefner, and Joong-won Lee, originally published in *International Journal of China Marketing*, Vol. 3(1), pp. 20-43.

Chapter Eighteen

A Descriptive Inventory Study of Recent China Marketing Research

This chapter surveys marketing research related to China. It focuses upon marketing journals whose scope covers marketing in Asia and China. One hundred articles selected from seven journals were reviewed and analyzed. The research discovered that academic articles on China marketing published in the last decade or so not only increased in number but also expanded in scope. Although most researchers were Chinese ethnically oriented, non-Chinese scholars and Chinese scholars jointly published a large number of articles (44%). Articles solely written by non-Chinese ethnically oriented scholars were relatively limited. Much research emanated from Hong Kong-based institutions. It is clear that since the role China plays in the world economy has become more important, and since the demand for China marketing research is increasing, current research cannot meet the needs of international business. Therefore, scholars both from China and from all over the world should do more research on China marketing.

INTRODUCTION

Thirty years ago, the economic system of China was a centralized planning system that remained largely closed to international trade, in which the market mechanism played a limited role in the production and consumption process. In the late 1970s and early 1980s, China launched the reform of its economy and its "open to the world" campaign. It is this campaign that brought China into a market-oriented economy, and that created a rapidly growing for-profit sector, and made China a major player in the global economy. As such, the market mechanism has become an important factor in the economic development of China (Tian and Wang, 2003; Tian 2008). Today, no one would deny the importance of China marketing in the world's market, and no one would ignore the increasingly tight connections between China and the rest of the world. China has been roaring into the 21st century with the force of a locomotive and its economy has doubled almost every six years. The great changes that have been made by the Chinese people in every aspect not only impact the domestic market in China but also the international economy (Wu, 2009). Along with the fact that the market-oriented economic system has become the dominant economic force in China, marketing has become one of the hottest subjects discussed in Chinese society, and marketing research has become one of the most rewarding fields for academic study. However, given the fact that the market economic system is relatively new in China, marketing itself as a field of study is still in its initial development stage, and academic marketing research papers, compared with marketing research in Western countries, is not only limited in scope but also in numbers. In addition, due to language constraints much of China marketing research work has not been published in English journals. Current marketing research pertaining to China does not reflect the reality of the Chinese economy, nor does it meet the needs of the business world. Philip Kotler, often called "the father of modern marketing", has written that "China's rapid development of the American-style consumer culture, which is revolutionizing the lives of hundreds of millions of Chinese, will have the potential to reshape the world. As China goes, so goes the world". (Kotler, 2010) This revolutionary development of a consumer market in China has in turn provided opportunities for marketing scholars, whose services should be in demand to help China market their products and services. This article aims to explore the development of marketing research pertaining to the China market by taking an inventory of relevant marketing journals beginning in 1998, when the earliest marketing research papers pertaining to China were posted online.

METHODOLOGY

A list of all marketing journals known to the American marketing association was obtained (AMA, 2010). A search was made of this list for all journals whose titles were linked to marketing in China. There were no such journals. However, the authors were aware of a new journal directly related to marketing in China; whose name is international journal of China marketing (IJCM), and therefore, this journal was chosen. Next, a search was made of the American Marketing Association's comprehensive list for all journals whose titles were associated with marketing in Asia generally, as opposed to marketing in China specifically. The following three journals in that category were identified: Asia Pacific Journal of Marketing and Logistics (APJML), Asian Journal of Marketing (AJM), and Australasian Marketing Journal (AMJ).

In order to find a meaningful sample of journal articles, it was decided to make an online search of these four journals for articles related to China marketing. Eleven articles were found in IJCM, 39 articles were found in APJML, 2 articles were discovered in AJM, and 5 articles were found in AMJ, for a total of 57 articles. Since the authors were not satisfied with a sample number of 57 articles from those four journals, they added three additional journals from the American Marketing Association's comprehensive list that related to international or global marketing.

These three journals were the journal of global marketing (JGM), the journal of international marketing (JIM), and the journal of international consumer marketing (JICM). Nineteen articles were found in JGM, 5 articles were found in JIM, and 19 articles were found in JICM, for a total of 43, bringing the total research sample to 100 articles. Except for the Journal of International Consumer Marketing, the entire table of contents for each journal was searched, starting from the date that the journal articles were posted online, up until the most current issue as of September 20, 2011. The Journal of International Consumer Marketing's table of contents was only searched partially, starting with the most recent issues, because it was felt that earlier issues tended to be more general, theoretical and conceptual, rather than quantitative and practical, as the more recent issues were. The beginning search dates (which were the earliest online publication dates) for journals are listed as follows: AJM (2007), AMJ (June, 1998), APJML (1989), IJCM (November, 2010), JGM (1988), JIM (March, 2005), and JICM (2006).

The abstracts of the one-hundred articles were searched for the following data: authors, authors' affiliations, number of pages of each article, key words, country of the journal's origin, date of publication and whether the research method used was qualitative or quantitative. In addition, an effort was made to categorize each article. After all the abstracts were categorized, a list of sixteen categories had been produced. These categories were narrowed down to five broader categories: 1) advertising, 2) consumer behavior, 3) marketing strategy, 4) theoretical issues, and 5) miscellaneous.

In general, we have (partially) followed the procedure of an earlier survey of journal articles relating to marketing in China by Ouyang et al. (2000). In that research, the authors summarized the work that had been published, the topics covered in the work, and the places the papers have been published. They then identified the individuals and institutions that had contributed to the creation of that particular body of marketing literature.

CONTENTS AND CATEGORIES OF THE ARTICLES

One hundred ninety-five researchers from seventy institutions contributed the one hundred articles selected. Of those 100 articles, 42 were written before 2007, of which 11 were written before 2000, and 58 of the articles were written in 2007 or later. The reader will note the longitudinal increase in the number of articles published. This continues an upward trend in the number of published articles that was noted in earlier research (Ouyang et al., 2000). The earliest article was written in 1988, and the latest article was written in 2011. The average length of the articles (except for the five articles found in JIM, whose abstracts did not include page numbers) was 14.5 pages. There were several types of papers, including concept papers, literature reviews, case studies, qualitative studies and studies using typical quantitative methods. There were seven journals searched. The journals are ranked in Table 1 by the number of articles within them that were related to China marketing.

The Content of the Articles

The researchers studied a broad variety of industries in China: automobiles, books, computers, credit cards, IT (including e-commerce, internet services and telecommunications), food retailing, higher education, internet services, iron and steel, manufacturing, retailing (including hypermarkets and malls), restaurants, sports, tourism, TVs, VCDs and clothing. However, the majority of the articles (65%) did not focus on any one particular industry. The articles were distributed across five categories: 1) advertising 2) consumer behavior, 3) marketing strategy, 4) theoretical issues, and 5) miscellaneous. A verbal description of the content of the articles in each category is given subsequently, Table 18.1 summarizes the content of the one hundred articles examined (Table 18.2 for categories and sub-categories).

Advertising

Eighteen (18%) of the 100 papers in the research sample were related to advertising. Articles related to advertising in China appeared in all seven of the journals chosen for this research. Examples of subjects covered in the advertising category are the influence of culture (La Ferle et al., 2008; Emery and Tian, 2010; La Ferle and Lee, 2003) the influence of English (Hung and Heeler, 1999) on Chinese advertising, governmental regulation of Chinese advertising (Gao, 2007; Gao and Zhang, 2011), and the use of sex appeal in Chinese advertising (Cui and Yang, 2009).

Consumer Behavior

Thirty-nine (39%) of the papers in the research sample dealt with consumer behavior. Articles related to consumer behavior in China appeared in all seven of the journals chosen for this research. Consumer behavior was the most researched topic in the sample journals. Representative subjects investigated in the articles written about consumer behavior in China include the following: Chinese values (Wang et al., 2000; Cheung and Prendergast, 2006; Sun and Wang, 2007; Tai, 2008, Smith et al., 2010), Chinese attitudes (Cui et al., 2008; Li et al., 2009; Sun and Wang, 2010) country of origin effects (Kwok et al., 2006; Oh and Zhang, 2010; Parker et al., 2011; Chao and Arnold, 2005; d'Astous and Li, 2009; Ishiia, 2009; Wong et al., 2008) the influence of children on purchase behavior (MacNeal and Yeh, 1996; MacNeal and Mindy, 1996), sex appeal (Liu et al., 2006; Liu et al., 2010) perception of brand names

(Ang, 1996; Li et al., 2011; Yang et al., 2005), and perception of store image (Chang and Luan, 2010; Hua and Jasper, 2010). From this listing, we can see that country of origin effects produce a large attraction for researchers. Seven (7%) of the 100 articles surveyed concerned this issue.

TABLE 18.1
MARKETING JOURNALS

Journal name		Number Articles	Citations
Asia Pacific journal of marketing and logistics	APJML	39	186
Journal of global marketing	JGM	19	74
Journal of international consumer marketing	JICM	19	72
International journal of China marketing	IJCM	11	1*
Journal of international marketing	JIM	5	50
Australasian marketing journal	AMJ	5	7
Asian journal of marketing	AJM	2	0**
Total		100	390

Source for Citations: Google Scholar.
 *The small number of citations may be due to the late date of IJCM's first issue (2010).
**The two articles used in AJM were not found in Google Scholar.

Marketing Strategy

In the research sample, 24 articles were found (24%) which dealt with marketing strategy. Topics investigated include the following: branding (Ga et al., 2006; Bennet, 2008; Wang et al., 2009; Fu et al., 2009; Bodet, 2010; Chen et al., 2011; Chaoying et al., 2011; Leng and Zhang, 2011), distribution channels (Wing, 1994; Luk et al., 2003; Yi and Jaffe, 2007; Sternquist and W ang, 2010), pricing (Tian et al., 2005; Liu and Tang, 2005; Zhang and Zhou, 2010; Jiang et al., 2011), product positioning (Skallerud and Grønhaug, 2010), and service quality (Prugsamatz and Ofstad, 2006; Gebauer and von Zedtwitz, 2007; Stanworth, 2009). From this, it can be seen that branding was the most popular topic for authors writing about marketing strategy in China.

TABLE 18. 2.
CONTENT OF THE ARTICLES

Category	Number articles	Sub-Category*
		Influence of culture
Advertising	18	Governmental Regulation
		Sex appeal
Consumer Behavior	39	Chinese values
		Chinese attitudes
		Country of origin effects
		Influence of children on purchase behavior
		Sex appeal
		Perception of brand names
		Perception of store image
Marketing Strategy	24	Branding
		Pricing
		Distribution channels
		Product positioning
		Service quality
		Marketing in command and transition economies
		Ancient Chinese theory and real estate marketing
Theory	10	Marketing for foreign-Chinese joint ventures
		Comparison of Indian and Chinese business climates
		Marketing research quantitative & methodological issues
		General articles about China marketing
		Literature survey about China marketing journal articles
Miscellaneous	9	Effects of population aging on marketing in China
		Marketing ethics in China

*There are no subcategories for the theory and miscellaneous category.
Rather, several representative articles are listed.

TABLE 18. 3
AUTHOR'S PUBLICATION CREDITS

Author	Publication Credits	Institution*
Nan Zhou	4	**City University of Hong Kong**
Suk-Ching Ho	3	**Chinese University of Hong Kong**
Geng Cui	3	**Lingnan University (Hong Kong)**
Jianyao Li	3	University of Western Australia
Fang Liu	3	University of Western Australia
19 authors published 2 articles	2	
171 authors published 1 article	1	

*Hong Kong universities are in boldface.

Theoretical Issues

There were 10 articles examined in this study (10%) which have been classified as theoretical. This category includes discussions of different modes of marketing in command and transition economies (Wei, 1995; Logan and McEwan, 2010), principles derived from ancient Chinese history applied to modern real estate marketing (Pheng, 2000), a comparison of the business climates of India and China (Panigrahi et al., 2002), the effects of population aging on marketing in China (Hou, 2011), and theoretical quantitative and methodological issues concerning marketing research in China (Sin and Ho, 2001; Tu, 2011).

Miscellaneous

This final category includes nine articles (9%) found in the research sample that were difficult to categorize, but which nonetheless were of interest. Examples are general articles about marketing in China (Liu, 2007; Thorellia, 1988; Kirpilani and Robinson, 1989; Knowles et al., 1990), a literature survey of articles written about marketing in China (Ouyang et al., 2000), and marketing ethics in China (Walle, 2011; Singh et al., 2007).

CONTRIBUTORS AND THEIR AFFILIATIONS

There were 195 researchers who authored the one hundred articles examined for this paper. There was a good deal of collaboration between western scholars and Chinese scholars. Seventy-eight of the articles had more than one author, and of these 78, western and Chinese researchers jointly authored 34 (44%) of them. The authors of this paper examined each name, and determined whether the name was a western name, or was the Romanization of a Cantonese or Mandarin Chinese name. It was discovered that of the 195 authors who wrote the 100 articles, 111 (57%) of those authors were ethnic Chinese.

Top Contributors

The researchers were ranked using three different methods: publication credits, adjusted publication credits, and number of citations. Tables 3 and 4 used publication credits in order to rank the authors of the one hundred articles that were examined for this paper. Publication credits have been calculated in two ways: by total number of publication credits (Table 18.3), and by adjusted number of publication credits (Table 18.4). If a researcher is listed as an author of an article, that researcher was given a publication credit, no matter whether the author was the sole author, or whether there were co-authors. The total number of publication credits obtained in this fashion equals the author's total publication credits. If the researcher shared the authorship of an article, his adjusted publication credits were determined this way: If there was one other co-author, the researcher received one-half of a publication credit. If there were two other co-authors, the researcher received one-third of a publication credit, and so on. This procedure has been adopted in previous studies (Ouyang et al., 2000). The 195 researchers who wrote the 100 articles were also ranked by citations to their articles by other researchers (Table 18.5). Google Scholar was used in order to find the number of citations to each of the one hundred articles.

It is interesting to note that when the authors are ranked by total publication credits, the top five researchers are all Chinese, and that when the authors are ranked by adjusted publication credits, the top eight include seven Chinese researchers. This apparently indicates that interest in China marketing has not yet become thoroughly globalized. This is backed by the previously noted fact that 111 (57%) of the 195 authors who contributed to the 100 articles are Chinese. As previously mentioned, the researchers were also ranked according to the number of times their articles had been cited by other researchers (Table 18.5). If more than one researcher authored a paper, and the paper was cited once, then each researcher received a citation credit. Thus, no special importance was given to the author whose name was listed first on the paper. An examination of Table 18.5 in order to discover Chinese names reveal that of the top 41 researchers in terms of citations to their articles, 25 (61%) was Chinese. This is an indication of how Chinese researchers of China marketing seem to be dominating the field.

TABLE 18. 4
AUTHOR'S ADJUSTED PUBLICATION CREDITS

Author	Adjusted Publication Credits	Institution
Susan H.C. Tai	2.00	**Hong Kong Polytechnic University**
Zhihong Gao	1.50	Rider University (NJ-USA)
Hongbo Tu	1.33	Wuhan Institute of Technology
Suk-Ching Ho	1.33	**Chinese University of Hong Kong**
Riliang Ou	1.30	Aston Business School (UK)
Nan Zhou	1.25	**City University of Hong Kong**
Carrie La Ferle	1.20	Southern Methodist Univ / Mich State U
Geng Cui	1.17	**Lingnan University (Hong Kong**
187 authors ≤ 1.00	≤ 1.00	

*Hong Kong universities are in boldface.

TABLE 18.5
AUTHOR'S CITATION CREDITS

Author	Citations	Institution*
Allan K. K. Chan	27	**Hong Kong Baptist University**
Cheng-Lu Wang	27	**Hong Kong Baptist University**
Zhen-Xiong Chen	27	**Hong Kong Baptist University**
Zong-Cheng Zheng	27	Zhongshan University (China)
Wei Na Li	23	University of Texas
Mark J. Arnold	21	St. Louis University
Mike C. H. Chao	21	St. Louis University
Nan Zhou	21	**City University of Hong Kong**
Leo Yat Ming Sin	19	**Chinese University of Hong Kong**
Mark Uncles	16	University of South Wales
Simon Kwok	16	University of South Wales
John Fong	15	Macquarie University (Australia)
Lauren A. Swanson	15	**Chinese University of Hong Kong**
Suzan Burton	15	Macquarie University (Australia)
Carrie La Ferle	14	Michigan State U / Southern Methodist U
Swee Hoon Ang	12	National University of Singapore
Fang Liu	12	University of Western Australia
Amy Wong	11	Lingnan University (Hong Kong)
Chui Yim Wong	11	Victoria University (Australia)
Irvine Clarke III	11	James Madison University (USA)
Jamal Al-Khatib	11	University of St. Thomas
Jatinder J. Singh	11	University of Mississippi
Lianxi Zhou	11	University of Guelph (Canada)

Michael J. Polonsky	11	Deakin University (Australia)
Romana Garma	11	Victoria University (Australia)
Scott J. Vitell	11	University of Mississippi
Jie Chen	10	Purdue University (USA)
Lars Ofstad	10	University of Sydney (Australia)
Mindy F. J	10	Texas A&M University (USA)
Sunita Prugsamatz	10	Griffith University (Australia)
Zhilin Yang	10	**City University of Hong Kong**
Kineta Hung	9	**University of Hong Kong**
Stella Yiyan Li	9	**University of Hong Kong**
Steven M. Edwards	9	
Susan H. C. Tai	9	**Hong Kong Polytechnic University**
Brian Murphy	8	Massey University (New Zealand)
Chi Kin (Bennet)	8	**University of Hong Hong**
David K. Tse	8	**University of Hong Hong**
Gerald Yong Ga	8	University of Missouri (USA)
Rongmei Wang	8	Massey University (New Zealand)
Yigang Pan	8	York University (Canada
154 authors 0 – 7	0-7	

*Hong Kong universities are in boldface.

The Researchers' Institutional Affiliations

A look at Table 18.3 (author's publication credits) and Table 18.4 (author's adjusted publication credits) will reveal the institutions associated with the researchers who have done the most China marketing research in our sample of articles. It is notable that of the top five researchers As measured by publication credits, three were affiliated with Hong Kong Universities and also, of the top eight researchers as ranked by adjusted publication credits, four were affiliated with Hong Kong Universities. The Hong Kong institutions have been bolded in Tables 3 and 4 for easy reference. This dominance by Hong Kong institutions continues a trend that was noted in earlier research (Ouyang et al., 2000). The dominance of Hong Kong universities can also be seen by an examination of Table 18.5, which ranks the researchers by citations to their articles. The Hong Kong universities in Table 18.5 have also been bolded for easy reference, demonstrating that of the top 41 researchers listed in Table 18.5, 13 (32%) are affiliated with Hong Kong institutions.

TABLE 18.6
GEOGRAPHICAL DISTRIBUTION OF AUTHORS INSTITUTIONS

Parameter	Hong Kong	PRC	Asian Not PRC Not Hong Kong	European	North American	All Institutions
No. of institutions	7	14	12	7	30	70
Percentage	10	20	17	10	43	100

The data in Table 18.5 may also be examined to determine the distribution of universities between Asia and the W est. W e see that 27 (66%) of the top 41 institutions, as measured by citation credits to their affiliated researchers, are Asian, whereas 14 (34%) of the top 41 institutions are western. It is notable that none of the top 41 institutions are European.

We now turn from examining the 41 institutions listed in Table 5 in order to investigate all of the institutions affiliated with the researchers who wrote the one hundred articles of our sample. Table 18.6 shows the geographical distribution of the seventy institutions whose researchers produced the one hundred articles. The data there show that a small majority (53%) of institutions doing China marketing related research are western universities located either in Europe or North America, while a large minority of such institutions are Asian (47%).

INTERNATIONAL JOURNAL OF CHINA MARKETING

One of the journals used in this study was the International Journal of China Marketing. A special part of this paper will be devoted to this journal, because, as far as is known by the authors, this is the first academic journal in print devoted entirely to marketing in China. The journal was established in the United States in 2010, and was introduced by the renowned marketing scholar Philip Kotler, who has earned the sobriquet "the father of marketing". In the introduction to the inaugural issue, Kotler suggested that the journal could examine "almost all aspects" of marketing in China (Kotler, 2010). Indeed, the scope of IJCMA's publications matches that of the articles found in the other journals used in this research. Subsequently, we will use the same categories which were used to analyze the other journals. W e will sort the relevant articles found in IJCMA into the following categories: advertising, consumer behavior, marketing strategy, and theoretical.

In commentary provided to introduce the third issue, Geoffrey Lantos

333

proclaimed "The notion of a market oriented economy is still brand new in China, while marketing as a field of scholastic study is just in its beginning steps.... "I feel it is an honor to write this commentary on behalf of the editorial board. Like Dr. Philip Kotler and Dr. Ping Zhao, I sincerely hope the International Journal of China Marketing will continue to deliver the highest quality research in the service of those who wish to understand the world of Chinese marketing better" (Lantos, 2011).

It is the authors' considered opinion that IJCM has indeed begun to deliver the highest quality research into the world of China marketing. The subsequent overview will give the reader a taste of the research done so far in the first three issues published to date. It should be noted that the articles in the first two issues were included in the sample of 100 articles studied in this research. The seven articles in the third issue were in press, and not published at the time this paper was written. However, copies of the articles were obtained in advance of their publication. It was decided to discuss these articles, even though they had not been published yet, and even though they were not available for inclusion in the research sample.

Advertising

To date, IJCM has published two articles related to advertising in China. The first article (Emery and Tian, 2010) updated Hofstede's (1980) famous model of cultural variables, related Pollay's (1983) advertising appeals to those variables, and hypothesized that the advertising appeals which appealed to either China's or the United States' salient cultural variables would have the most impact. For example, China is considered very masculine. An advertising appeal of effective would be considered a masculine appeal. Thus, it was hypothesized that an advertisement with an effective appeal should perform better in China than in the United States. Of twenty such hypotheses, only nine were supported, and one was significant in the opposite direction. The authors therefore concluded that it would be unwise to use Hofstede's cultural dimensions as a sole predictor for advertising effectiveness in China. The researchers speculated that for practical use Hofstede's dimensions were either outdated, or too broad, or both. In addition, the authors speculated that the effectiveness of advertising appeals may be moderated by other factors such as age, societal trends, the political-legal environment and product usage.

The second article in IJCM concerning advertising measured changes in brand attitude based upon advertising appeals which mixed rational and emotional appeals (Chaoying et al., 2011). It was hypothesized that customers who predominately processed information cognitively would respond more positively to rational appeals in a mixed-appeal advertisement, and customers who predominately processed information intuitively would more positively respond to emotional appeals in a mixed-appeal advertisement. The authors, having studied an advertisement for a Chinese telecommunication service, concluded that mixing rational and emotional appeals did not hinder effectiveness when those appeals were delivered to a general audience, and that a mixing strategy is a good compromise when trying to attract a population of people which contains those who process both emotionally and rationally.

Consumer Behavior

There were three articles dealing with consumer behavior in the first three issues of IJCM. The first was a case study of an ethnic Chinese restaurant located in the United States (Tian and W ang, 2010). The authors concluded that reliability and value were the primary indicators of satisfaction for foreign customers of ethnic restaurants. The authors failed to corroborate previous research, which suggested that customers' cultural awareness of the ethnic food sold, had positive effects on customer satisfaction. The second article (Li et al., 2011) investigated the attitudes of Chinese peasants towards refrigerator purchases, and ranked the relative importance to these peasants of seven attributes of refrigerators. The refrigerators' brand was discovered to be of the most importance, followed by price, color, structure, power consumption, volume, and cooling capacity. The author concluded that peasant consumer attitudes towards refrigerator attributes varied in different regions and markets, and that therefore, market segmentation was very important. The third article dealing with consumer behavior studied the different attractions to consumers for Chinese supermarkets and Chinese wet markets, the supermarkets being superior in safety and quality, the wet markets being superior in price, convenience and freshness (Cui, 2011).

Marketing Strategy

Articles in IJCM dealing with marketing strategy included research into pricing, product positioning and product development, branding, and service quality. One article examined the propensity for Chinese companies to start price wars (Zhang and Zhou, 2010). The authors conclude that, contrary to much opinion, Chinese businesses are not irrational to fight such wars, but that the rational desire to achieve economies of scales is the motivation behind these wars, and that many Chinese businesses participating in them emerge stronger and more profitable. A second article (Calantone et al., 2011) develops a model whose constructs predict the success of new product launches, and then tests the model using samples from the United States and China. The authors conclude that new product launches in both countries are (generally) governed by the same factors, which are: launch timing, launch execution tactics, resource allocation, marketing activities, distribution channel support, market orientation, and cross- functional integration on launch. A third article describes "Shanzhai" products and branding (Leng and Zhang, 2011), which explains the highly successful marketing strategy employed by small Chinese companies when they imitate the products of large successful brands (and sometimes infringe on the copyright of the more established product's brand name). A fourth article (Shen and W ang, 2011) investigates public satisfaction with education in Beijing, in the context of Chinese education reform.

Theoretical

This category encompasses articles which describe structural or legal aspects of the Chinese economy at a macro-level, or which speculate on the suitability of application of marketing models and methodology to the Chinese context, or which address ethical issues in marketing. One example of research that examines the structure of the Chinese economy is a paper that concluded that China, after the financial crisis of 2008, would surpass the United States in research and development, especially in commercialization of research (Kotler, 2010). Another paper investigating the structure of the Chinese economy and its markets is one that addresses the perennial issue of intellectual property protection (Logan and McEwan, 2010). In this paper, the authors conclude that China should seek a balance between protecting proprietary information and allowing that information to be shared. A third paper which examines the structure of the Chinese economy and its markets is one that looks at the problem of population aging in China (Hou, 2011). This paper warns that the efficiency of the Chinese labor force may be compromised by population aging, as well as the ability of the country's pension system to take care of the nation's elderly.

One paper addresses a marketing model and its applicability in the Chinese context. This paper takes traditional cluster marketing theory and seeks to apply it to the Chinese high-tech industry (Tu, 2011). Another paper also addresses theoretical marketing research issues. This paper argues that traditional anthropological research techniques should be applied to business in China, in order to understand cross-cultural issues in marketing, in order for foreign firms engaged in business there to obtain a competitive advantage (Tian and Borges, 2011).

A final theoretical article involves marketing ethics. This article examined the practice of "cultural tourism" in China (Walle, 2011), and concluded that the traditional marketing focus on the customer was undercutting ethnic communities in China and cheapening their traditions, or unduly creating stress for ethnic people.

DISCUSSION

The findings from this research have impelled the authors to agree with Geoffrey Lantos, who has stated that "The notion of a market oriented economy is still brand new in China, while marketing as a field of scholastic study is just in its beginning steps" (2011). This article has attempted to describe the state of this infant discipline in such a way that readers may ascertain the concerns of researchers in the China marketing field, as well as the characteristics of these researchers and their institutions.

Academic journals have become the primary medium of communicating scholarly knowledge in China marketing, and the number of China marketing-related journals and articles has increased in recent years. However, compared with research covering marketing activity in Western countries, only a handful of journals have covered China marketing issues up to now. The rapid growth of marketing in the Chinese economy makes it increasingly important to gain insight into the relative influence of marketing-related research papers. This research discovers that at this time most interest so far about marketing research related to China is in consumer behavior, although there is a good deal of interest in advertising, marketing strategy, and theoretical issues. As to the research methodologies, the research papers examined in this study mostly tend to be descriptive and content based, although some scholars adopted quantitative research method in their research and the trend of using quantitative method is obvious.

As to the structure of scholars in China marketing research, we can easily see that most authors in the field are Chinese themselves, although much research is jointly collaborative between Chinese and non-Chinese. It is obvious that there is a concentration of scholars doing China marketing in Hong Kong. It is also clear that a small majority of institutions affiliated with China marketing research is located in Europe and North America and that a large minority of such institutions is located in Asia, especially in Honk Kong. The authors of this paper noted that the research conducted by scholars in mainland China is limited; a possible reason could be that most Chinese scholars in China are lack of writing skills in English.

It seems to the authors of this article that several implications flow from the inventory study. One is that the content of China marketing research we analyzed is very broad, but not very deep enough. There are many topics covered in the literature, but few of those topics have been researched thoroughly from different perspectives. There is a need to explore marketing issues in China more deeply by scholars both through qualitative and quantitative methods. Another implication is that professional contacts between China and the west, at both the individual and institutional level, are indispensable prerequisites for doing meaningful marketing research in China. The cultural and language barriers between China and the west are certainly not small. East-west collaboration will help western scholars to dispel the mystery of Chinese markets, and will help Chinese scholars to gain access to advanced marketing research techniques developed in the west.

In the authors' best judgment, China is still virgin territory for researchers, which should entice marketing academicians for years to come. Karl Gerth, Professor of Modern Chinese History at Oxford University, notes that total consumer spending in China of $4 trillion in 2009 is still less than half that of the US, but it has surpassed consumer spending in Japan and is closing in on that of the EU. Gerth points out that it has taken China just a few years to learn what took these consumer countries decades: how to spend. Gerth further points out that China's advertising market has grown by 40% a year over the past two decades and may become the world's largest by 2020. China now has over 2000 newspapers with a total circulation above a billion, the world's ten largest general-circulation magazines, and over 1000 television channels. Advertising in China is now a huge industry, including over 80,000 ad companies that employ over one million people to help build brands. Gerth claims that the consequences are radically transforming China and the world (Gerth, 2011). Such a phenomenon cries for academic investigation into China marketing by trained marketing researchers.

Conclusions

The Chinese national economy has been changed greatly since the 1980s, which has brought China one of the most important and powerful economies in the world. Marketing as a field of study is relatively new in China and marketing research about China, although having improved, cannot meet the demands of the world's business institutions. Scholars from all over the world are definitely encouraged to conduct scientific research on China marketing, moreover, the Chinese scholars in China are encouraged to conduct more research on China marketing and write their research reports and articles in English. The research on China marketing should pay more attentions on theoretical issues along with brand strategies study. We predict that in the near future China marketing research could become a hot research topic for more and more scholars in the academic world.

This study was limited in several ways. The sample of journals was restricted to those marketing journals whose titles focused on marketing in Asia or China. In addition, only articles that were posted online were examined, which may have precluded the inclusion of relevant articles on China marketing. Reasonable suggestions for further research would include an examination of all marketing journals, rather than Asian marketing journals, in order to find related articles. In conjunction with this broadening of the research sample, the chronological scope of the article could be restricted to recent years, perhaps five years, in order to obtain a more recent snapshot of the field.

There were certain restrictions placed on the inclusion of articles within the research sample. For example, articles concerning the behavior of ethnic Chinese consumers living outside of China or Chinese industries located outside of China were excluded. Also excluded were articles about the reaction by non-Chinese consumers to Chinese products consumed in countries other than China. Research into those areas might perhaps be worthwhile. In addition, all articles concerning marketing research into business activity in Hong Kong and Taiwan were excluded. These articles should be worthy of separate investigation. Finally, it is suggested that there is now enough China marketing research available to justify narrowing the scope of research similar to that of this paper. For example, a survey of articles related only to marketing strategy in China, or only related to advertising in China, etc, should perhaps be worthwhile.

Authored by Dan L. Trotter and Tian Guang, originally published in . *African Journal of Business Management*, Vol. 6(17), pp. 5763-5772. Reprinted by permission.

REFERENCES

Aaker, D. (1995). *Building Strong Brands*. 9th edn. New York: Free Press.

Abell, D. F. (1978). Strategic Windows. *Journal of Marketing,* 42 (3), 21-26.

Abernathy, W. and Clark, K. B. (1985). Mapping the Winds of Creative Destruction. *Research Policy,* 14, 3-22.

Ahmed, S. and d'Astous, A. (2008). Antecedents, Moderators and Dimensions of Country-of-origin Evaluations. *International Marketing Review,* 25(1), 75-106.

Ahmed, S. and d'Astous, A. (1996), Country of Origin and Brand Effects: a Multi-dimensional and Multi-attribute Study, *Journal of International Consumer Marketing*, 9(2), 93-115.

Aiken, L. and Stephen G. West. (1991), *Multiple Regression: Testing and Interpreting Interactions*. CA, Thousand Oaks: Sage Publication. Available online: http://books.google.com/books?id=LcWLUyXcmnkCanddq=edition s: ISBN0761907122andhl=zh-CNandsitesec=reviews

Albers-Miller, N. and Stafford, M. (2007). International Services Advertising: An Examination of Variation in Appeal Use for Experiential and Utilitarian Services. *Journal of Child Health Care,* 11 (4), 323-340.

Albers-Miller, N. D. (1996). Designing Cross-Cultural Advertising Research: A Closer Look at Paired Comparisons. *International Marketing Review*, 13(5), 59-76.

Albers-Miller, N. D. and Gelb, B. D. (1996). Business Advertising Appeals as a Mirror of Cultural Dimensions: A Study of Eleven Countries. *Journal of Advertising*, 25(4), 57-71.

Alden, D.L., Steenkamp, J.E.M. and Batra, R. (1999). Brand Positioning Through Advertising in Asia, North America and Europe: The Role of Global Consumer Culture. *Journal of Marketing*, 63(1), 75-87.

Alexandre, Gohin, and Herve Guyomard. (2000). Measuring Market Power for Food Retail Activities: French Evidence. *Journal of Agricultural Economics*, 51,181-195.

Alon, Ilan (2003). *Chinese Economic Transition and International Marketing Strategy*, CA, Santa Barbara: Praeger Publishers.

Alpert, M. I. and Peterson, R. A. (1972). On the Interpretation of Canonical Analysis. *Journal of Marketing Research.* 9 (May), 187.

AMA (2010). September 25) All Marketing Journals, Retrieved September 11, 2011 from http://www.marketingpower.com/Community/ARC/Pages/Research/ Journals/Other/default.aspx

Ambler, T. and Witzel, M. (2003). *Doing Business in China.* 2nd. Ed. London: Routledge.

Anand, J. and Delios.A. (1996). Competing Globally: How Japanese MNCs Have Matched Goals and Strategies in India and China. *Columbia Journal of World Business*, Fall, 50-62.

Anderson, C. (2009). *The Long Tail: Why the Future of Business is Selling Less of More.* Taipei: Commonwealth Publishing Co., Ltd.

Anderson, Chris. (2004). The Long Tail. *Wired Magazine*, 12(10). Available online: http://www.wired.com/wired/archive/12.10/tail.html. Accessed on January 2011.

Andrew, A. (1986). The Effect of Verbal and Visual Components of Advertisements on Brand Attitudes and Attitude toward the Advertisement. *Journal of Consumer Research*, 13 (1), 12-24.

Ang SH (1996). Chinese Consumers' Perception of Alpha-Numeric Brand Names. *Asia Pac. J. Mark. Logist.*, 8(1): 31-47.

Anselmsson, J., Johansson, U. and Persson, N. (2008). The Battle of Brands in the Swedish Market for Consumer Packaged Food: A Cross-Category Examination of Brand Preference and Liking. *Journal of Brand Management*, 16, 63-79.

Arens, W. F. and Bovee, C. L. (1994). *Contemporary Advertising*, 5th edn., Boston: Richard D. Irwin.

Arnold, M.J. and Reynolds, K.E. (2003). Hedonic Shopping Motivations. *Journal of Retailing*, 79, 77-95.

Arnould, E., Price, L. and Zinkhan, G. (2004). *Consumer.* 2nd edn. NY, New York: McGraw Hill.

Atsmon, Y. et al. (2009). *2009 Annual Chinese Consumer Study*. McKinsey Insights China.

Atsmon, Y., Dixit, V., Magni, M. and St-Maurice, I. (2010). China's New Pragmatic Consumers. *McKinsey Quarterly*. Available online: https://www.mckinseyquarterly.com/. Accessed on December 5, 2010 from

Atuahene-Gima, K., Slater, S. F. and Olson, E. M. (2005). The Contingent Value of Responsive and Proactive Market Orientations for New Product Program Performance. *Journal of Product Innovation Management*, 22, 464-482.

Ayers, D., Dahlstrom, R. and Skinner, S. J. (1997). An Exploratory Investigation of Organizational Antecedents to New Product Success. *Journal of Marketing Research*, 34 (1), 107-116.

Babin, B.J., Darden, W.R. and Griffin, M. (1994). Work and/or Fun: Measuring Hedonic and Utilitarian Shopping Value. *Journal of Consumer Research*, 20, 644-656.

Bai, Junhong, and Li, Jing. (2011). Regional Innovation Efficiency in China: the Role of Local Government. *Innovation: Management, Policy, and Practice*, 13 (2), 142 - 153.

Baidu. (2009). *About Baidu*. Available online: http://home.baidu.com/about/milestone/index_1.html. Accessed on Sep 22, 2010.

Bainbridge, W.S. (2007). The Scientific Research Potential of Virtual Worlds. *Science*, 317,472,

Baker, J., Parasuraman, A., Grewal, D. and Voss, G.B. (2002). The Influence of Multiple Store Environment Cues on Perceived Merchandise Aalue and Patronage Intentions. *Journal of Marketing*, 66, 120-141.

Balabanis, G. and Diamantopoulos, A. (2004). Domestic Country Bias, Country-of-origin Effects, and Consumer Ethnocentrism: A Multidimensional Approach. *Journal of the Academy of Marketing Science*, 32(1), 80-95.

Ballard, D.S. and Weigel, D.J. (1999). Communication Process in Marital Commitment: An Integrative Approach," In J. M. Adams and W. H. Jones (ed), *Handbook of Interpersonal Commitment and Relationship Stability*, 407- 424. New York Kluwer Academic/ Plenum Publishers.

Bandura, A. (1997). *Self-efficacy: The Exercise of Control*, New York: Freeman.

Barbara, B. and Gloria, M. (2007). *Social Conventions in Collaborative Virtual Environments*. German National Research Center for Information Technology.

Barney, J. and Hansen, M. (1994). Trustworthiness as a Source of Competitive Advantage. *Strategic Management Journal*, 15(special issue), 175-190.

Barney, J.B. (1986). Strategic Factor Markets: Expectations, Luck, and Business Strategy. *Management Science*, 9 (10), 1231-1241.

Bateson, J. E. G. (1985). Perceived Control and the Service Encounter in *the Service Encounter* by J. A. Czepiel, M. R. Solomon and C. F. Surprenant. (Eds.). MA, Lexington: Lexington Books.

Batra, R. et al. (2000). Effects of Brand Local and Nonlocal Origins on Consumer Attitudes in Developing Countries. *Journal of Consumer Psychology*, 9(2), 83-95.

Batson, A. (2010, January 21). A Second Look at China's GDP Rank. *The Wall Street Journal*. Available online: from http://online.wsj.com/article/. Accessed on November 26, 2010.

Battacharrya, R., Devinney, T. and Pilluta, M. (1998). A Formal Model of Trust Based on Outcomes. *Academy of Management Review*, 23(3), 459-472.

Bawa, A. (2004). Consumer ethnocentrism: CETSCALE Validation and Measurement of Extent. *Vikalpa: The Journal for Decision Makers*, 29(3), 43-57.

Beamish, P.W., Inkpen, A.C. (1998). Japanese Firms and the Decline of Japanese Expatriate. *Journal of World Business*, 33 (1), 35-50.

Belk Russell, and Janeen Costa. (1995). International Tourism: An Assessment and Overview. *Journal of Macromarketing*, 15(2), 33-49.

Bennet D (2008). Brand Loyalty Dynamics - China's Television brands come of age. *Australas. Mark. J.*, 16(2): 39-50.

Bennett, J. and Beith, M. (2007). Alternate Universe. *Newsweekly*, Available online: http://www.newsweek.com/id/32824. Accessed on 15 Nov 2009.

Bennis, W., D. Berlew, E. Schein, and F. I. Steel. (1973), *Interpersonal Dynamics*. 3rd edn. Chicago: Dorsey Press.

Bernard F. (1974). Risk Aversion and the Consumer Choice of Health Insurance Option. *The Review of Economics and Statistics*, 56(2), 209-214.

Bessant, J. and Tidd, J. (2007), *Innovation and Entrepreneurship*. NJ: JohnWiley and Sons.

Bilkey, W.J. and Nes, E. (1982). Country-of-origin effects on product evaluations, *Journal of International Business Studies, Spring/Summer*, 89-99.

Birdwhistell, R.L. (1970). *Kinesics and Context; Essays on Body Motion Communication*, 338. *University of Pennsylvania publications in conduct and communication*. Philadelphia: University of Pennsylvania Press.

Bitner, M. J. (1990). Evaluating Service Encounters: The Effects of Physical Surroundings and Employee Responses. *Journal of Marketing*, 54, 69-82.

Blaxter, L. (2006). *How to research*. 3rd edn. Maidenhead: New York Open University Press.

Bodet G, and Chanavat N (2010). Building global football brand equity: Lessons from the Chinese market. *Asia Pac. J. Mark. Logist.*, 22(1):55-66.

Boer, H. and During, W. E. (2001). Innovation, What Innovation? A Comparison Between Product, Process and Organizational Innovation, *International Journal of Technology Management*, 22 (1-3), 83-107.

Bonner, J.M. and Walker, O. C. Jr. (2004). Selecting Influential Business-to-Business Customers in New Product Development: Relational Embeddedness and Knowledge Heterogeneity Considerations. *Journal of Product Innovation Management*, 21 (3), 155-169.

Bookman, A. (2008). Innovative Models of Aging in Place: Transforming our Communities for an Aging Population. *Community, Work and Family,* 4 (November), 430-431.

Boulding, K. (1956). General Systems Theory: The Skelton of Science, *Management Science,* 2, 197-208.

Boutie, P. (1994). Who will save the brands? *Communication World,* 7, 24-29.

Bowersox, D. et al. (1995). *World Class Logistics: The Challenge of Managing Continuous Change.* Council of Logistics Management.

Bowersox, D. J., Stank, T. P. and Daugherty, P.J. (1999). Lean Launch: Managing Product Introduction Risk Through Response-Based Logistics. *Journal of Product Innovation Management,* 16 (5), 557-568.

Bray, D. and Konsynski, B. (2008). Virtual Worlds: Mutli-Disciplinary Research Opportunities. *The Database for Advanced Information Systems,* 38(4). Available online: http://ssrn.com/abstract=1016485. Accessed on March 7, 2010.

Brennan, D.P. and Lundsten, L. (2000). Impact of large discount stores on small US towns: reasons for shopping and retail strategies. *International Journal of Retail and Distribution,* 28, 155-161.

Brett, A., Martin, B. and Wong, S. (2003). Conclusion Explicitness in Advertising: The Moderating Role of Need for Cognition (NFC) and Argument Quality (AQ) on Persuasion. *Journal of Advertising,* 32 (4), 57-66.

Briley, D. A. and Aaker, J. L. (2006). When does Culture Matter? Effects of Personal Knowledge on the Correction of Culture-based Judgments. *Journal of Marketing Research, 43,* 395-408.

Browne, M. W. and Cudeck, R. (1993). Alternative ways of assessing model fit. in *Testing Structural Equation Models* by K. A. Bollen and J. S. Long. (Eds.), CA, Thousand Oaks: Sage. 136–162.

Busaranon, T., and Chintrakarn, P. (2012). The Relationship Betwen Real Estate Investment Trusts Property Types and Stock Exchange of Thailand Index. *Research Journal of Business Management,* 6(4), 153-158.

Buttery, E. A. and T.K.P. Leung. (1998). The Difference between Chinese and Western Negotiations. *European Journal of Marketing,* 32(3/4), 374-389.

Buttle, F. and Coates, M. (1984). Shopping Motives. *Services Industries Journal,* 4, 71-81.

Calantone RJ, Benedetto CA, and Song M (2011). Expecting Marketing Activities and New Product Launch Execution to Be Different in the U.S. and China: An Empirical Study. *Int. J. China Mark.,* 2(1):

forthcoming.

Calantone, R. J. and Di Benedetto, C. A. (1988). An Integrative Model of the New Product Development Process. *Journal of Product Innovation Management*, 5 (3), 201-215.

Calantone, R. J. and Montoya-Weiss, M. (1994). Product Launch and Follow-On in *Managing New Technology Development* by Souder, W. E. and Sherman, J. D. (Eds.). New York: McGraw-Hill. 217-248.

Calantone, R. J., Di Benedetto, C. A. and Stank, T. P. (2005). Managing the Supply Chain Implications of Launch in *The PDMA Handbook of New Product Development* by Kahn, K. B., Castellion,G., and Griffin, A. (Eds.). 2nd edn. Hoboken, NJ: JohnWiley and Sons. 466-478.

Calantone, R. J., Schmidt, J. B. and Song, M. (1996). Controllable Antecedents of New Product Success: A Cross-National Comparison. *Marketing Science,* 15, 341-358.

Calantone, R.J. and Cooper, R. G. (1979). A Discriminant Model for Identifying Scenarios of Industrial New Product Failure. *Journal of the Academy of Marketing Science,* 7, 163-183.

Calantone, R.J. and Di Benedetto, C. A. (2011). The Effects of Launch Execution and Timing on New Product Performance: An Empirical Study in the U.S. *Journal of the Academy of Marketing Science*, forthcoming.

Carlson, P. (1993). *Media Selection for Information Acquisition and Dissemination: A Study of Manageria Preference*, unpublished doctoral dissertation, University of Minnesota.

Castranova, E, (2001). *Virtual Worlds: A First-Hand Account of Market and Society on the Cyberian Frontier.* CESifo, Working Paper, 618.

Castries, Henride. (2009). Aging and Long – Term Care: Key Challenges in Long – term Care Coverage for Public and Private Systems. *Geneva papers*, 34, 24 – 34.

Castronova, E. (2003). On Virtual Economies. *The International Journal of Computer Game Research*, 3(2). Available online: http://www.gamestudies.org/0302/castronova/. Accessed on June 16, 2009.

Cavusgil, S.T., Kiyak, T. and Yeniyurt, S. (2004). Complementary Approaches to Preliminary Foreign Market Assessment: Country Clustering and Country Ranking, *Industrial Marketing Management*, 33 (7), 607-617.

Central Intelligence Agency (2010). *The World Fact Book*. Retrieved in October 2010 from https://www.cia.gov/library/publications/the-world-factbook/geos/ch.html

Cervino, J., Sanchez, J. and Cubillo, J. (2005). Made an Effect, Competitive Marketing Strategy and Brand Performance: An Empirical Analysis for Spanish Brands. *Journal of American Academy of Business*, 6(2), 237-244.

Chan K. (1995). Information Content of Television Advertising in China. *International Journal of Advertising*, 14 (4), 365-373.

Chan, K. and Cheng H. (2002). One Country, Two Systems: Cultural Values Reflected in Chinese and Hong Kong Television Commercials. *Gazette: The International Journal for Communication Studies*, 64(4), 383-398.

Chaney, I. and Gamble, J. (2008). Retail Store Ownership Influences on Chinese Consumers. *International Business Review*, 17, 170-183.

Chang E, and Luan B (2010). Chinese Consumers' Perception of Hypermarket Store Image. Asia Pac. J. Mark. Logist., 22(4): 512-527. Chao MCH, Arnold MJ (2005). Exploring the Practical Effects of Country of Origin, Animosity, and Price-Quality. *J. Int. Mark.*, 13(2): 114-150.

Chang, K. and Chang, F. (2005). Information Content of Television Advertising in China: An Update. *Asian Journal of Communication*, 15(1), 1-15.

Chaoying T, Jian S, and Ille FR (2011). Information Handling Styles,Advertising and Brand Attitude: A Chinese Brand Case Study. *Int. J.China Mark.*, 2(1): 45-56.

Chatterjee, S. and Chaudhuri, A. (2005). Are trusted brands important? *Marketing Management Journal*, 15(1), 1-16.

Chattopadhyay, A. (1998). When does Comparative Advertising Influence Brand Attitude? The Role of Delay and Market Position. *Psychology and Marketing*, 15(5), 461-75.

Chen G.W. and Sun Gui Ju. (2006). The Food Safety KAP Investigation of Nanjing Consumers. *Journal of China's Public Pealth*, 22, 604-608.

Chen X, Lam LW, and Zou H (2011). Antecedents and Performance Consequences of Integrated Brand Management in China: An Exploratory Study. *J. Glob. Mark.*, 24(2): 167-180.

Chen, Y.F., Brenda, S. (1995). Differences Between International and Domestic Japanese Retailers. *The Service Industries Journal*, 15 (4), 118-134.

Cheng, H. and Schweitzer, J. C. (1996). Cultural Values Reflected in Chinese and U.S.Televisions Commercials. *Journal of Advertising Research,* 36(3), 27-45.

Chesney, T. Chuah, S. andHoffmann, R. (2007). *Virtual World Experimentation: An Exploratory Study*. Available online http://ssrn.com/abstract=1068225. Accessed on March 25, 2010.

Cheung W , and Prendergast G (2006). Exploring the Materialism and Conformity Motivations of Chinese Pirated Product Buyers. *J. Int.Consum. Mark.*, 18(3): 7-31.

Cheung,Wah-Leung and Prendergast, G. P. (2006). Exploring the Materialism and Conformity Motivations of Chinese Pirated Product Buyers. *Journal of International Consumer Marketing*, 18(3), 7-31.

China Advertising Yearbook. (2006). *The Development of China's Advertising Industry.* Beijing: Xinhua Publishing House.

China Association of Advertising. (2009). *China Advertising Year Book,* Beijing, Xinhua News Agency Press.

China National Tourist Office. (2010). *China Tourism Statistics 2009.* Available online: http://www.cnto.org/chinastats_2009ArrivalsByPurpose.asp. Accessed on Aug. 2010.

China Online Marketing. (2011). Available online: http://www.china-online-marketing.com/. Accessed on August 7, 2011.

China Statistic Yearbook. (2009). Available online: http://www.stats.gov.cn/tjsj/ndsj/2009/indexeh.htm. Accessed on June 19, 2010.

Choi, S. and Mattila A. S. (2006). The Role of Disclosure in Variable Hotel Pricing: A Cross-Cultural Comparison of Ccustomers' Fairness Perceptions. *Cornell Hotel and Restaurant Administration Quarterly,* 47 (1), 27-35.

Churchill, G. A., Jr. (1979). A Paradigm for Developing Better Measures of Marketing Constructs. *Journal of Marketing Research,* 16, 64-73.

Clemons, E.K. (2009). The Complex Problem of Monetizing Virtual Electronic Social Networks. *Decision Support Systems,* 48(1), 46-56.

Cleveland, M. and Laroche, M. (2007), Acculturation to the Global Consumer Culture: Scale Development and Research Paradigm. *Journal of Business Research (Special Edition: The Impact of Culture on Marketing Strategy),* 60(3), 249-259.

Cleveland, M., Laroche, M. and Papadopoulos, N. (2009), Cosmopolitanism, Consumer Ethnocentrism, and Materialism: An Eight-country Study of Antecedents and Outcomes," *Journal of International Marketing,* 17, 116-146.

Cooper, J. R. (1998). A Multidimensional Approach to the Adoption of Innovation. *Management Decision,* 36 (8), 493-502.

Cooper, R. G. (1979a). Identifying Industrial New Product Success: Project NewProd. *Industrial Marketing Management,* 8(2), 124-135.

Cooper, R. G. (1983). The Impact of New Product Strategies. *Industrial Marketing Management,* 12, 243-256.

Cooper, R. G. and Kleinschmidt, E. J. (1987). New Products: What Separates Winners From Losers? *Journal of Product Innovation Management*, 4 (3), 169-184.

Cooper, R. G. and Kleinschmidt, E. J. (1990), *New Products: The Key Factors in Success*. IL, Chicago: American Marketing Association.

Cooper, R. G. and Kleinschmidt, E. J. (1993). Major New Products: What Distinguishes the Winners in the Chemical Industry? *Journal of Product Innovation Management*, 10(2), 240-251.

Cooper, R.G. (1979b). The Dimensions of Industrial New Product Success and Failure. *Journal of Marketing*, 43 (2), 93-103.

Cox, A.D., Cox, D. and Anderson, R.D. (2005). Reassessing the pleasures of store shopping. *Journal of Business Research*, 58, 250-259.

Crawford, C. M. (1992). The Hidden Costs of Accelerated Product Development. *Journal of Product Innovation Management*, 9(3), 188-199.

Crawford, C. M. and Di Benedetto, C. A. (2008). *New Products Management*. 9th edn. IL, Burr Ridge: Irwin/McGraw-Hill.

Cui B (2011). The Choice Behavior in Fresh Food Retail Market: A Case Study of Consumers in China. *Int. J. China Mark.*, 2(1):68-76.

Cui G, and Yang X (2009). Responses of Chinese Consumers to Sex Appeals in International Advertising: A Test of Congruency Theory. *J. Glob. Mark.*, 22(3): 229-245.

Cui G, Chan T, and Joy A (2008). Consumers' Attitudes toward Marketing: A Cross-cultural Study of China and Canada. *J. Int. Consum. Mark.*, 20(3-4): 81-93.

Cui, G. (1997). The Different Faces of the Chinese Consumer. *China Business Review*, 24, 34-38.

Cui, G. and Liu, Q (2001). Executive Insights: Emerging Market Segments in a Transition Economy: A Study of Urban Consumers in China. *Journal of International Marketing*, 9(1), 84-106.

Cui, G. and Liu, Q. (2000). Regional Market Segments of China: Opportunities and Barriers in a Big Emerging Market. *Journal of Consumer Marketing*, 17(1), 55-72.

Culter, B. D. and Rajshekhar, G. J. (1992). A Cross-cultural Analysis of the Visual Components of Print Advertising: The United States and the European Community. *Journal of Advertising Research*, 32, 71-80.

d'Astous A, and Li D (2009). Perceptions of countries based on personality traits: a study in China Asia Pac. *J. Mark. Logist.*, 21(4): 475-488.

Daft, R. L. (1978). A Dual-core Model of Organizational Innovation. *Academy of Management Journal*, 21 (2), 193-210.

Daft, R.L. and Lengel, R.H. (1986). Organizational Information Requirements, Media Richness and Structural. *Design Management Science,* 32(5), 554–571.

Damanpour, F. (1987). The Adoption of Technological, Administrative, and Ancillary Innovations: Impact of Organizational Factors. *Journal of Management*, 13 (4), 675-688.

Damanpour, F. (1991). Organizational Innovation: A Meta-analysis of Effects of Determinants and Moderators. *Academy of Management Journal*, 34 (3), 555-590.

David B. (2004). *China's E-Marketing Learns to Drive.* Available online: http://banners.noticiasdot.com/termometro/boletines/docs/consultora s/emarketer/2004/0404/emarketer_300404-2.pdf. Accessed on May 14, 2010.

Davis, F.D., Bagozzi, R.P. and Warshaw, P.R (1989). User Acceptance of Computer Technology: A Comparison of Two Theoretical Models. *Management Science,* 35(8), 982-1003.

Davis, J.P., Steur K. and Pagula Yan, R.A. (2005). Survey Method for Assessing Perceptions of a Game: The Consumer Playtest in Game Design. *Game Studies.* 5(1). Available online: http://www.gamestudies.org. Assessed on July 6, 2009.

Dawar, N. and Parker, P. (1994). Marketing Universals: Consumers' use of Brand Name, Price, Physical Appearance, and Retailer Reputation as Signals of Product Quality. *Journal of Marketing,* 58, 81-95.

Dawson, D., Bloch, P.H. and Ridgway, N.M. (1990). Shopping Motives, Emotional States, and Retail Outcomes. *Journal of Retailing*, 66, 408-427.

de Chernatony L. and McDonald M. (2003). *Creating Powerful Brands.* 3rd edn. Oxford: Butterworth-Heinemann.

de Houwer, J. (2008). Conditioning as a Source of Liking: There is Nothing Simple About It. Ed Wanke (Ed.). *Social Psychology of Consumer Behavior*. New York: Psychological Press.

DeBruyne, M., Moenaert, R., Griffin, A., Hart, S., Hultink, E. J. and Robben, H. S. J. (2002). The Impact of New Product Launch Strategies on Competitive Reaction in Industrial Markets. *Journal of Product Innovation Management, 1*9(2), 159-170.

Degen, R. J. (2012). Opportunity for Luxury Brands in China. *The IUP Journal of Brand Management*, 6(3/4), 75-85.

DeJesus, J. and Tian, R.G., (2004). Cultural Awareness and Consumer Behavior: A Case Study of American Perception of Mexican Food. *High Plains Applied Anthropologist*, 24 (1), 11-21.

DeJesus, Jennifer, and Tian, Robert G. (2004). Cultural Awareness and Consumer Behavior: A Case Study of American Perception of Mexican Food. *High Plains Applied Anthropologist*, 24 (1), 17-29.

Delgado-Ballester, E., Munera-Alemain, J. and Yague-Gullien, M. (2003). Development and Validation of a Brand Trust Scale. *International Journal of Market Research*, 45 (1), 35-53.

Deli-Grey, S., Haefner, J. and Rosenbloom, A. (2012). The Role of Global Brand Familiarity, Trust and Liking in Predicting Global Brand Purchase Intent: a Hungarian–American Comparison. *International Journal of Business and Emerging Markets*, 4(1), 4-27.

Deloitte Development LLC Website. (2010). *Global Powers of Retailing 2010*. Available online: http://www.deloitte.com/view/en_GX/global/industries/consumer-business-transportation/retail/6b79c2cd67b06210VgnVCM200000bb42f00aRCRD.htm. Accessed on Jan 20, 2011.

Deng, Y. and Li Tianzhu. (2010). The Origin of Shanzhai Phenomenon and a Study on Its Openly Innovative Features. *Enterprise Economy*, 1, 21-23.

Dens, N. and De Pelsmacker, P. (2010). Consumer Response to Different Advertising Appeals for New Products: The Moderating Influence of Branding Strategy and Product Category Involvement. *Journal of Brand Management*, 18, 50-65.

Denzin, N. and Lincoln, Y. (1994). *Handbook of Qualitative Research.* CA, Thousand Oaks: Sage.

DeSarbo, W.S., Di Benedetto, C. A., Song, M. and Sinha, I. (2005). Revisiting the Miles and Snow Strategic Framework: Uncovering Relationships Between Strategic Types, Capabilities, Environmental Uncertainty, and Firm Performance. *Strategic Management Journal*, 26(1), 47-74.

Deshpande, R., Farley, J. U. and Webster, F. E. Jr. (1993). Corporate Culture, Customer Orientation, and Innovativeness in Japanese Firms: A Quadrad Analysis. *Journal of Marketing*, 52 (1), 23-36.

Desmarais, F. (2007). Issues in Cross-cultural Studies of Advertising Audiovisual Material. *Prism*, 4(3). Available online: http://www.prismjournal.org/fileadmin/Praxis/Files/Journal_Files/Desmarais.pdf. Accessed on August 2010.

Di Benedetto, C. A. (1999). Identifying the Key Success Factors in New Product Launch. *Journal of Product Innovation Management*, 16(5), 530-544.

Di Benedetto, C. A., Calantone, R. J. and Zhang, C. (2003). International Technology Transfer: Model and Exploratory Study in the People's Republic of China. *International Marketing Review*, 20 (4), 446-462.

351

Di Benedetto, C. A., DeSarbo, W. S. and Song, M. (2008). Strategic Capabilities and Radical Innovation: An Empirical Study in Three Countries. *IEEE Transactions on Engineering Management*, 55 (3), 420-433.

Di Benedetto, C. Anthony. Product Innovation in China: Opportunities and Challenges. *International Journal of China Marketing,* 3(1) 2012.

Dillman, D.A. (1978). *Mail and Telephone Surveys: The Total Design Method.* NY, New York: Wiley.

Ding, J. (2007). Concerns over the Labor Shortage of China Caused by Fertility. *Semimonthly Selected Readings* (in Chinese), 24, 9.

Dodgson, M. and Xue, L. (2009). Editorial: Innovation in China. *Innovation: Management Policy and Practice*, 11 (1), 2-5.

Donabedian, B. (2006). Optimization and Its Alternative in Media Choice: A Model of Reliance on Social Influence Processes. *The Information Society,* 22(2), 121–135.

Doorne, S., Ateljevic, I. and Bai, Z. (2003). Representing Identities Through Tourism: Encounters of Ethnic Minorities in Dali, Yunnan Province, People's Republic of China. *International Journal of Tourism Research*, 5, 1-11.

Douglas, S.P. and Craig, C. S. (1983). Examining Performance of U.S. Multinationals in Foreign Markets. *Journal of International Business Studies*,14 (1), 51-62.

Duan, M. (2009). Analysis on the Impacts of Population Aging on Employment on the Basis of Economics. *The Economic Forum* (in Chinese), 4, 20.

Dyer, J. H. (1996). How Chrysler Created an American Keiretsu. *Harvard Business Review*, 74(8), 42-60.

Dzever, Sam and Quester, Pascale. (1999). Country-of-origin Effects on Purchasing Agents' Product Perceptions: An Australian Perspective, *Industrial Marketing Management*, 28,165-175.

Eckhardt, G. M. and Bengtsson, A. (2010). A Brief history of Branding in China. *Journal of Macromarketing*, 30(3), 210 – 221.

Eckhardt, G. M. and Houston, M. J. (2002). Cultural Paradoxes Reflected in Brand Meaning: McDonald's in Shanghai, China. *Journal of International Marketing*, 10(2), 68-82.

Edson, E. and Stern, B. (2003). Sympathy and Empathy: Emotional Responses to Advertising Dramas. *Journal of Consumer Research,* 29 (4), 566-578.

Elliot, R. and Percy, L. (2007). *Strategic Brand Management*. Oxford: Oxford University Press.

Elliott, G. and Cameron, R. (1994), Consumer Perception of Product Quality and the Country of Origin Effect. *Journal of International Marketing*, 2 (2), 49-62.

Emery C, and Tian K (2010). China Compared with the US: Cultural Differences and the Impacts on Advertising Appeals, *Int. J. China Mark.*, 1(1): 45-59.

Emery, C. R. and Tian, K. R. (2010). China Compared with the US: Cultural Differences and the Impacts on Advertising Appeals. *International Journal of China Marketing*, 1(1), 45-56.

Emery, C. R. and Tian, R. G. (2002a). *A Review of Empirical Research on Advertising in China from 1992-2001*. Research Manuscript 2002-3, Lander University, Greenwood, SC.

Emery, C. R. and Tian, R. G. (2002b). Cross-cultural Issues in Internet Marketing. *Journal of American Academy of Business*, 12 (2), 217-225.

Emery, C. R. and Tian, R. G. (2003). The Effect of Cultural Differences on the Effectiveness of Advertising Appeals: A Comparison between China and the U.S. *Journal of Transformation in Business and Economics*, 2(3). 48-59.

Engardio, P. and Dexter Roberts. (2004). The China Price. *BusinessWeek*, 3911 (December 6), 102.

Engel, J., Kollat, D. and Blackwell, R. (1973). *Consumer Behavior*. 2nd edn. New York: Holt, Rinehart and Winston.

Erica Mina Okada. (2005). Justification Effects on Consumer Choice of Hedonic and Utilitarian Goods. *Journal of Marketing Research*, 42(1). 43-53.

Fan, J.X. and Xiao, J.J. (1998). Consumer Decision-making Styles of Young-adult Chinese. *Journal of Consumer Affairs*, 32(2), 275-94.

Feng Zhong Ze, and Li Qing Jiang. (2008). The Agricultural Production Quality Safety Cognition of Consumer and the Analysis of Influencing Factors, *Journal of China's Rural Economy*, 1, 25-27.

Feng, B., Liu, C., Shi, Y., and Jiang, H. (2010). *Measurement of Real Estate Buble in China: An Overview of Direct Test Models Since 2003*. International conference on E-Business and E-Government, (2934-2937). Guangzhou.

Feng, Kui. (2007). The Value of Cluster Marketing: Based on Shengzhou Neckties Industry. *Commercial Research* (in Chinese), 57, 99-101.

Fernandez, D. R., Carlson, D. S., Stepina, L. P. and Nicholson, J. D. (1997). Hofstede's Country Classification 25 Years Later. *The Journal of Social Psychology*, 17, 21-18.

Ferry, D.L.K., Sawyer, C.Tand Sawyer, J.E. (2001). Measuring Facts of Media Richness. *Journal of Computer Information Systems*, 41, 69–78.

Fisher, Caroline (2012). China's Future in the World Marketplace. *International Journal of China Marketing,* 2(2).

Fisher, R. (2005). Gender Differences in Responses to Emotional Advertising: The Effect of the Presence of Others. *Advances in Consumer Research*, 31 (4), 850-858.

Fishman, Ted C. (2005) China, Inc. Scribner, 2006, 368 pages.

Fisk, George. (1973). Criteria for a Theory of Responsible Consumption. *Journal of Marketing*, 37(April): 24-31.

Fisk, George. (1982). Editor's Working Definition of Macromarketing. *Journal of Macromarketing*, Spring, 3-4.

Flint-Goor, A. and Liebermann Y. (1996). Message Strategy by Product-class Type: A. Matching Model. *Journal of Research in Marketing*, 13, 237- 249.

Fortune 500 Website. (2010). Available online: http://money.cnn.com/magazines/fortune/fortune500/2010/. Accessed on Jan 20, 2011.

Franzen, G. and Moriarty, S. (2009). *The Science and Art of Branding.* Armonk: M.E. Sharpe.

Fraser, D. and Raynor, M. (1996). The Power of Parity. *Forecast*, May/June, 8-12.

Fryxell, G.E. et al. (2004). Successful Localization Programs in China: An Important Element in Strategy Implementation. *Journal of World Business*, 39, 268-282.

Fteschrin, M. and Lattermann, C. (2008). User Acceptance of Virtual World. *Journal of Electronic Commerce*, 9 (3), 231-242.

Fu G, Saunders J, and Ou R (2009). Brand Extensions in Emerging Markets: Theory Development and Testing in China. *J. Glob. Mark.*, 22(3): 217-228.

Ga Y, Pan Y, Tse DK, and Yim CKB (2006). Market Share Performance of Foreign and Domestic Brands in China. J. Int. Mark., 14(2): 32-51. Gao Z (2007). An In-Depth Examination Of China's Advertising Regulation System. *Asia Pac. J. Mark. Logist.*, 19(3): 307-323.

Gadiesh, O., Leung, P. and Vestring, T. (2007). The Battle for China's Good Enough Market. *Harvard Business Review*, 85, 81-89.

Gang, Chen. (2011). Sustainable Development of Eco-Cultural Tourism in Remote Regions: Lessons Learned from Southwest China. *International Journal of Business Anthropology*, 2 (1), 121-35.

Gao Wang. (2005).The Model Estimation of the Random Coefficients of Conjoint Analysis.*Quantitative andTechnical Economics*, 32, (07), 96-107.

Gao Z, and Zhang H (2011). A Comparative Study Of Chinese And US Consumers' Attitudes Toward Advertising Regulation. *Asia Pac. J. Mark. Logist.*, 23(1): 72-90.

Gao, Q. (2010). China Internet Population Hits 420 Million. *China Daily,* July 15, 2010.

Gao, X. (2011). *Study on China Real Estate Price Bubble: Will it Burst Soon?* 2011 International Conference on Management and Service Science. Wuhan.

Garner, J. (2005). *The Rise of the Chinese Consumer: Theory and Evidence*. West Sussex, UK: John Wiley and Sons Ltd.

Gassenheimer, J. B. and Calantone, R. J. (1994). Managing Economic Dependence and Relational Activities Within a Competitive Channel Environment. *Journal of Business Research*, 29(3), 189-197.

Gassenheimer, J. B., Calantone, R. J. and Scully, J. I. (1994). Supplier Involvement and Dealer Satisfaction: Implications for Enhancing Channel Relationships. *Journal of Business and Industrial Marketing,* 10(2), 7-19.

Gatignon, H. and Xuereb, J.-M. (1997). Strategic Orientation of the Firm and New Product Performance. *Journal of Marketing Research,* 34 (1), 77-90.

Gebauer H, and von Zedtwitz M (2007). Differences in orientations between W estern European and Chinese service organizations. *Asia Pac. J. Mark. Logist.*, 19(4): 363-379.

Gerth K (2011). As China Goes, *So Goes the W orld: How Chinese. Consumers Are Transforming Everything*. New York: Hill & Wang.

Gerth, Karl (2010). As China Goes, *So Goes the World: How Chinese Consumers Are Transforming Everything*. New York: Hill and Wang.

Geuens, M. and De Pelsmacker, P. (1997). Product Category Involvement and the Reaction of Polish and Belgian Consumers to Different Types of Advertising Appeals. *European Advances in Consumer Research*, 3, 33-41.

Ghauri, P. and Cateroa, P. (2010). *International Marketing.* 3rd Edn. London: McGraw Hill.

Gierl, H. and Praxmarer, S. (2007). The Effects of a Value-oriented Advertising Strategy on Brand Attitude. *Der Markt,* 46 (4), 148-156.

Goldhaber, M. H. (1997). The Attention Economy and the Net. *First Monday.* (2)4. Available online: http://firstmonday.org/htbin/cgiwrap/bin/ojs/index.php/fm/article/vie w/519/440. Accessed in September 2011.

355

Green P, Rao V. (1971). Conjoint Measurement for Quantifying Judgmental Data. *Journal of Marketing Research,* 08, (03), 355-363.

Green P, Srinivasan V. (1978). Conjoint Analysis in Consumer Research: Issues and Outlook. *Journal of Consumer Research*, 5, (2), 103-123.

Green P, Srinivasan V. (1990) Conjoint Analysis in Marketing: New Developments with Implications for Research and Practice. *Journal of Marketing*, 54, (04), 3-19.

Green P, Wind Y. (1975). New Way to Measure Consumers' Judgments. *Harvard Business Review,* 53, (04), 107-120.

Griffin, A. (1992). Evaluating QFD's Use in U.S. Firms as a Process for Developing Products. *Journal of Product Innovation Management,* 9(3), 171-182.

Griffin, A. (1995). Modeling and Measuring Product Development Cycle Time Across Industries. *Marketing Science Institute Report.* MA, Cambridge: Marketing Science Institute. 95-117.

Griffin, A. and Hauser, J. R. (1992). Patterns of Communication Among Marketing, Engineering, and Manufacturing: A Comparison Between Two New Product Teams. *Management Science,* 38 (3), 360-373.

Griffin, A. and Hauser, J. R. (1993). The Voice of the Customer. *Marketing Science,* 12 (1), 1-27.

Griffin, A. and Page, A. L. (1993). An Interim Report on Measuring Product Development Success and Failure. *Journal of Product Innovation Management*, 10(4), 291-308.

Guangdong Statistical Yearbook. (2009). Available online: http://www.gdstats.gov.cn/tjnj/table/10/e104.htm. Accessed on Mar 23, 2010.

Guiltinan, J. P. (1999). Launch Strategy, Launch Tactics, and Demand Outcomes. *Journal of Product Innovation Management*, 16 (5), 509-529.

Guo, Y. and Barnes, S. (2007). Why People Buy Virtual Items in Virtual Worlds with Real Money. *The Data Base for Advances in Information Systems*, 38(4), 69-76.

Guoqun Fu, and Xueying Tong. (2003). How Do Brand Price and Place of Origin Influence Consumers' Choices to Purchase. *Journal of Management Sciences in China*, 06(06), 79-84.

Gupta, A.K. and Wilemon, D. L. (1986). The Credibility-Cooperation Connection at the RandD-Marketing Interface. *Journal of Product Innovation Management,* 5(1), 20-31.

Gupta, A.K., Raj. S. P. and Wilemon, D. L. (1986). A Model for Studying RandD-Marketing Interface in the Product Innovation Process. *Journal of Marketing,* 50(2), 7-17.

Gustin, S. (2010). *Now the No. 2 Economy, What's Ahead for China?* Available online: http://www.dailyfinance.com/story/China-number-two-whats-ahead/19595235/. Accessed on Aug. 2010.

Hair, Jr., Joseph, F. anderson, R. E., Tatham, R. L. and Black, W. C. (1998). *Multivariate Data Analysis.* 5th edn. NJ, Upper Saddle River: Prentice Hall.

Hall, E. T. (1976), *Beyond Culture.* New York: Anchor Press-Doubleday.

Haytko, L.H. and Baker, J. (2004). It's all at the Mall: Exploring Adolescent Girls' experiences. *Journal of Retailing,* 80, 67-83.

Haywood, K. Michael. (1990). Revising and Implementing the Marketing Concept as it Applies to Tourism. *Tourism Management,* 1990, 195-205.

He Jun, Ji Yue Qing, and Wu Hao Jie. (2005). Consumer Behavior Mode of Fresh Food——Comparison of Supermarket and Free Market of Agricultural Products. *Journal of China Agricultural University (Social sciences edition)*, 3, 67-71.

Heath, R. and Feldwick, P. (2007). Fifty Years Using the Wrong Model of Advertising. *International Journal of Market Research,* 50 (1), 29-59.

Heckler, S. and Childers, T. (1992). The Role of Expectancy and Memory in for Verbal and Visual Information: What is Incongruency? *Journal of Consumer Research,* 18, 475-92.

Heim, K. (1997). Foreign Ventures in China Urged to Localize Faster. *In Asian Wall Street Journal.* 12 Dec 1997.

Hemp, P. (2006). Avatar-based Marketing. *Harvard Business Review,* 84(6), 48-57.

Henderson, David R. (1997). What Are Price Wars Good For? Absolutely Nothing. *Fortune*, 135 (9), 156.

Henley, J. and Nyaw M.K. (1986). Introducing Market Forces into Managerial Decision-Making in Chinese Industrial Enterprises. *Journal of Management Studies,* 23(6), 635-656.

Herbig, Paul. (1998). *Handbook of cross-cultural marketing.* New York: The International Business Press.

Herzberg, F. (1966). *Work and the Nature of Man.* OH, Cleveland: World Publishing.

Hill, T. (1989). *Manufacturing Strategy.* IL, Homewood: Irwin Publishing.

Hofstede G (1980). *Culture's Consequences: International Differences in Work-Related Value.* CA, Beverly Hills Sage Publications.

Hofstede, G. (1984). The Cultural Relativity of the Quality of Life Concept. *Academy of Management Review*, 9(3), 381-393.

Hofstede, G. (1991). *Cultures and Organizations: Software of the Mind.* London: McGraw-Hill Book Company.

Hofstede, G. (2001). *Culture's Consequence: Comparing Values, Behaviors, Institutions and Organization Across Nations*. London: Sage Publications.

Holden, S. and Vanhuele, M. (1999). Know the Name, Forget the Exposure: Brand Familiarity Versus Memory of Exposure Context. *Psychology and Marketing*, 16 (6), 479-496.

Holsapple, C.W., Pakath R. and Sasidharan, S.A. (2005). Website Interface Design Framework for the Cognitively Impaired: A Study in the Context of Alzheimer's Disease. *Journal of Electronic Commerce Research*, 6(4), 291-303.

Hong, J. W., Muderrisoglu, A. and Zinkhan, G. M. (1987). Cultural Differences and Advertising Expression: A Comparative Content Analysis of Japanese and U.S. Magazine Advertising. *Journal of Advertising,* 16 (1), 55-62, 68.

Horn, Sierk A. and Cross, Adam R. (2009). Japanese Management at a Crossroads? The Changing Role of China in the Transformation of Corporate Japan. *Asia Pacific Business Review*, 15(3), 285-308.

Hornikx, J.M.A. and O'Keefe, D.J. (2009). Adapting Consumer Advertising Appeals to Cultural Values: A Meta-analytic Review of Effects on Persuasiveness and Ad Liking in Beck, C.S. (ed.), *Communication Yearbook* 33, New York : Lawrence Erlbaum. 38-71.

Hou L (2011). Challenges and Opportunities: The Impacts of Population Aging on Marketing in China and the Chinese Economy. *Int. J. China Mark.*, 1(2): 70-80.

Hovgaard, A. and Hansen, E. (2004). Innovativeness in the Forest Products Industry. *Forest Products Journal*, 54 (1), 26-33.

Hsinchun, C., Sven T. and Fu, T.J. (2008). *Cyber Extremism in Web 2.0: An Exploratory Study of International Jihadist Groups*. IEEE International Conference on Intelligence and Security Informatics.

Hu Ding Huan, Yu Hai Feng, and T. Reardon. (2003). The Fresh Food Management of Chinese Supermarket and the Purchase Behavior. *Journal of China's Rural Economy,* 8, 13-14.

Huang Zu Hui, Zhou Jie Hong, and Jin Shao sh. (2004). Wet Market Transform to Supermarket and the Purchase Behavior Analysis of Agriculture Product. *Journal of Zhejiang Academic Journal*, 5, 88.

Huddleston, P., Whipple, J., Mattick, R.N. and Lee, S.J. (2009). Customer Satisfaction in Food Retailing: Comparing Specialty and Conventional Grocery Stores. *International Journal of Retail and Distribution Management,* 37(1), 63-80.

Hui, A. Y., et al. (2001). An Investigation of Decision-making Styles of Consumers in China. *The Journal of Consumer Affairs*, 35, 226-345.

Hui, M. and Zhou, L. (2002). Linking Product Evaluations and Purchase Intention for Country-of-origin Effects. *Journal of Global Marketing*, 15(3/4), 95-101.

Huixin Ke, and Paul. Frostier. (1994).the Conjoint Analysis in Marketing Research. *The Mathematical Statistics and Management*, 4, (6), 23-25.

Hultink, E. J. and Robben, H. S. J. (1995). Measuring New Product Success: The Difference That Time Perspective Makes. *Journal of Product Innovation Management,* 12(5), 392-405.

Hultink, E. J. and Robben, H. S. J. (1999). Launch Strategy and New Product Performance: An Empirical Examination in the Netherlands. *Journal of Product Innovation Management*, 16(6), 545-556.

Hultink, E. J., Griffin, A., Hart, S. and Robben, H. S. J. (1997). Industrial New Product Launch Strategies and Product Development Performance. *Journal of Product Innovation Management*, 14, 243-257.

Hultink, E. J., Griffin, A., Robben, H. S.J. and Hart, S. (1998). In Search of Generic Launch Strategies for New Products. *International Journal of Research in Marketing*, 15, 269-285.

Hultink, E. J., Hart, S., Robben, H. S. J. and Griffin, A. (1999). New Consumer Product Launch: Strategies and Performance. *Journal of Strategic Marketing*, 7(3), 153-174.

Hultink, E. J., Hart, S., Robben, H. S. J. and Griffin, A. (2000). Launch Decisions and New Product Success: An Empirical Comparison of Consumer and Industrial Products. *Journal of Product Innovation Management,* 17(1), 5-23.

Hung K, Heeler RM (1999). Language and Its Effects on Advertising Modality: The Case of Chinese and English. *Australas. Mark. J.*, 7(2): 7-14.

Hussain, A. and Rivers, P.A. (2009). Confronting the Challenges of Long – term Health Care Crisis in the United States. *Journal of Health Finance,* Winter, 73.

INSEAD. *The Global Innovation Index 2011*. Available online: www.globalinnovationindex.org.

International Monetary Fund. (2010, October). World Economic and Financial Surveys: World Economic Outlook Database. Available online: http://www.imf.org/external/pubs/ft/weo/2010/02/weodata/weoselser.aspx?a=1andc=001,505andt=2. Accessed on January 5, 2011.

International Trade Center. Available online: http://www.trademap.org/tradestat/Bilateral_TS.aspxV. Accessed on Feb, 2011

IResearch. (2009). *Survey Report on Chinese Netizens' Online Shopping Influence Factors and Decision-making Model 2009* (2009 年中国网民购买决策影响力研究报告).

Ishiia K (2009). Nationalistic Sentiments of Chinese Consumers: The Effects and Determinants of Animosity and Consumer Ethnocentrism. J. Int. Consum. Mark., 21(4): 299-308.

Itagaki, H. (2009). Competitiveness, Localization and Japanese Companies in China: Realities and Alternate Approaches. *Asia Pacific Business Review*, 15(3), 451-462.

Jaeger, P. T. and Thompson, K. M. (2003). E-government Around the World: Lessons, Challenges, and Future Directions. *Government Information Quarterly*, 20, 389–394.

Jamison, David J. (1999). Masks Without Meanings: Notes on the Processes, Consumption, and Exchange in the context of First World-Third World Tourism" *Journal of Macromarketing*, 19 (June), 8-19.

Janaina de Moura Engracia Giraldi, and Ana Akemi Ikeda. (2009). An Application of the Personification Approach in the Country Image Study, *Brazilian Business Review*, 6 (2), 132-146.

Janiszewski, C. (1993). Preattentive mere exposure effects. *Journal of Consumer Research,* 20 (3), 376-92.

Jassawalla, A. R. and Sashittal, H. C. (1998). An Examination of Collaboration in High-Technology New Product Development Processes. *Journal of Product Innovation Management,* 15(3), 237-254.

Jaworski, B.J. and Kohli, A. K. (1993). Market Orientation: Antecedents and Consequences. *Journal of Marketing,* 57 (3), 53-71.

Jefferson, G. H., Rawski, T. G. and Zheng, Y. (1992). Growth, Efficiency, and Convergence in China's State and Collective Industry. *Economic Development and Cultural Change,* 40 (1), 239-266.

Jiang J, Chou T, and Tao X (2011). The Impact of Price Discount, Product Complementarity and Relational Investment on Customer Loyalty: Empirical Evidence from China's Telecommunications Industry. *Asian J. Mark.*, 5: 1-16.

Joffre Swait, and Wiktor Adamowicz. (2001). The Influence of Task Complexity on Consumer Choice: A Latent Class Model of Decision Strategy Switching. 28, 135-148.

Johansson, J. and Ronkainen, I. (2003). Global Brands? Does Familiarity Breed Contempt? in. Jain, S. (Ed.). *Handbook of Research in International Marketing*. Cheltenham: Edward Elgar Publishing.

Johansson, J.K. (1989). Determinants and Effects of the Use of 'Made in' Labels. *International Marketing Review*, 6(1), 47-58.

Johansson, J.K., Ronkainnen, I.A.and Czinkota, M.R. (1994), Negative Country-of-origin Effects: the Case of Russia, *Journal of International Business Studies*, 25, 157-76.

John, J. Watson and Katrina Wright. (2000), Consumer Ethnocentrism and Attitudes toward Domestic and Foreign Products, *European Journal of Marketing,* 34 (9/10), 1149-1166.

Johnson, W. H. A. and Weiss, J. W. (2008). A Stage Model of Education and Innovation Type in China, the Paradox of the Dragon. *Journal of Technology Management in China*, 3 (1), 66-81.

Jordan, Ann T. (2003). *Business Anthropology*, IL, Prospect Heights: Waveland Press.

Kahai, S.S. and Cooper, R.B. (2003). Exploring the Core Concepts of Media Richness Theory: The Impact of Cue Multiplicity and Feedback Immediacy on Decision Quality. *Journal of Management Information Systems,* 20(1), 263–300.

Kaigler-Walker, K., Gilbert, Z. and Hu, H. (2010). Domains of Chinese Women's Perception of Appearance and Use of Fashion Products: Conceptualization and Scale Development. *Journal of Global Business,* 4(1), 27-35.

Kajima, K. (1978), *Direct Foreign Investment A Japanese Model of Multinational Business Operations,* London: Croom Helm.

Kalwani, M. U. and Narayandas, N. (1995). Long-Term Manufacturer-Supplier Relationships: Do They Pay Off for Supplier Firms? *Journal of Marketing*, 59(1), 1-16.

Kano, N., N. Seraku, F. Takahashi, and S. Tsuji. (1984). Attractive Quality and Must-Be Quality. *Hinshitsu*, 14(2).

Kaocong Tian, Jixue Wei, and Yanrong Zhou. (2003). the Application of Conjoint Analysis in the Management of Hospitals. *Chinese Journal of Hospital Statistics*, 08, (03), 98-103.

Katherine, L. N. R. T. Rust, and V. A. Zeithaml. (2001). What Drives Customer Equity? *Marketing Management*, 10 (1): 20-25.

Katz, D. (1960). The Functional Approach to the Study of Attitudes. *Public Opinion Quarterly,* 24, 163-204.

Keller, K. (1998). S*trategic Brand Management.* NJ, Upper Saddle River : Prentice Hall.

Kent, R. and Allen, C. (1994). Competitive Consumer Interference Effects for Consumer Memory in Advertising: The Role of Brand Familiarity. *Journal of Marketing*, 58, 97-105.

Kiecker, P. and Hartman, C. L. (1993). Purchase Pal Use: Why Others Choose to Shop with Others in *Marketing Theory and Application* by R. Varadarajan and B. Jaworski. (Eds.). IL, Chicago: American Marketing Association. 378-384.

Killick, E. (2008). Creating Community: Land Titling, Education, and Settlement Formation Among the Asheninka of Peruvian Anmazonia. *The Journal of Latin American and Caribbean Anthropology*, 13, 22-47.

Kim, K.H., Park, J.Y. Kim, D.Y., Moon, H.I. and Chun, H.C. (2002). E-lifestyle and Motives to Use Online Games. *Irish Marketing Review*, 15(2), 71-77.

Kim, W. C. and Mauborgne, R. (1999). Creating New Market Space: A Systematic Approach to Value Innovation Can Help Companies Break Free from the Competitive Pack. *Harvard Business Review*, (January-February), 83-93.

Kirpilani V, and Robinson W R (1989). The China Market and Lessons from Successful Exporters. *J. Glob. Mark.*, 2(4): 81-98.

Kleinschmidt, E. J. and Cooper, R. G. (1991). The Impact of Product Innovativeness on Performance. *Journal of Product Innovation Management*, 8(4), 240-251.

Knight, G. A. and Calantone, R. J. (2000), A Flexible Model of Consumer Country-of Origin Perceptions - a Cross-Cultural Investigation. *International Marketing Review*, 17 (2). 127-145.

Knight, K. E. (1967). A Descriptive Model of the Intra-firm Innovation Process, *The Journal of Business*, 40 (4), 478-496.

Knowles LL, Mathur I, and Jai-Sheng C (1990). Chinese Perspectives on Joint Ventures for Marketing in China. J. Glob. Mark., 3(1): 33-54. Kotler P (2010). The Importance of China Marketing. *Int. J. China Mark.*, 1(1): 14-16.

Kobayashi-Hillary, M. (2007). *Building a Future with Brics: The Next Decade for Offshoring.* NY, New York: Springer.

Kohli, A. K. and Jaworski, B.J. (1990). Market Orientation: The Construct, Research Propositions, and Managerial Implications. *Journal of Marketing,* 54 (2), 1-18.

Kopp, R. (1999). The Rice-paper Ceiling in Japanese Companies: Why It Exists and Persists i*n Japanese multinationals abroad: individual and organizational learning.* S.L. Beechler and A. Bird (ed.). New York: Oxford University Press. 107-128.

Kotler, P. (2010), China Marketing, Marketing China: A Relatively New But Fast Growing Field of Study. *International Journal of China Marketing,*1(1).

Kotler, Philip. (2003). *Marketing Management.* Shanghai: Shanghai People's Publishing House.

Kotler, Philip. (2010). The Importance of China Marketing. *International Journal of China Marketing*, 1(1).

Kozhevnikov, M. (2007). Cognitive Styles in the Context of Modern Psychology: Toward an Integrated Framework of Cognitive Style. *Psychological bulletin,* 133 (3), 464-481.

Kumar, N., Stern, L. W. and Anderson, J.C. (1993). Conducting Interorganizational Research Using Key Informants. *Academy of Management Journal*, 36, 1633-1651.

Kumar, R. and Best, M. L. (2006). Impact and Sustainability of E-Government Services in Developing Countries: Lessons Learned from Tamil Nadu, India, *The Information Society*, 22 (1), 1-12.

Kune, J. B. (2009). Population Aging and the Affluent Society: The Case of the Netherlands. *Pensions*, 14, (4), 231-241.

Kurlantzick, Joshua (2002). Making it in China._*U.S. News and World Report*, 10/07/2002, 44.

Kvale, S, (1996). *Interviews: An Introduction to Qualitative Research Interviewing*. CA, Thousand Oaks:Sage.

Kwok S, Uncles M, and Huang Y (2006). Brand Preferences And Brand Choices Among Urban Chinese Consumers: An Investigation Of Country-Of-Origin Effects. *Asia Pac. J. Mark. Logist.*, 18(3): 163-172.

La Barbera, P., Weingard, P. and Yorkston, E. (1998). Matching the Message to the Mind: Advertising Imagery and Consumer Processing Styles. *Journal of Advertising Research,* 38 (5), 29-41.

La Ferle C, and Lee W N (2003). Attitudes Toward Advertising - A Comparative Study of Consumers in China, Taiwan, South Korea and the United States. *J. Int. Consum. Mark.*, 15(2): 5-23.

La Ferle C, Edwards SM, and Li W N (2008). Culture, Attitudes, and Media Patterns in China, Taiwan, and the U.S.: Balancing Standardization and Localization Decisions. *J. Glob. Mark.*, 21(3): 191-205.

Lan, Wen Qiao. (2006). Regional Marketing of Enterprise Cluster: Incentive and Road. *Journal of Beijing Institute of Finance and Commerce Management* (in Chinese), 22(2), 39-41.

Langerak, F., Hultink,E. J. and Robben, H. S. J. (2004). The Impact of Market Orientation, Product Advantage, and Launch Proficiency on New Product Performance and Organizational Performance. *Journal of Product Innovation Management,* 21(2), 79-94.

Lantos GP (2011). Consumer Behavior in Action: Real-Life Managerial Applications. *Int. J. China Mark.*, 2(1): forthcoming.

Larry, L. Carter, Jr, (2002). *Consumer Attitudes Toward Cross-border Brand Alliances: Adding a Consideration of Country of Origin Fit* , unpublished thesis ,Virginia Polytechnic Institute and State University.

Lavidge, R. and Steiner, G. (1961) A Model for Ppredictive Measurement of
    Advertising Effectiveness, *Journal of Marketing*, 61, 59–62.
Lee, D. Y.. and P. L. Dawes. (2006). Guanxi, Trust, and Long-Term
    Orientation in Chinese Business Markets. *Journal of International
    Marketing*, 13(2),28-56.
Lee, Dong-Jin, M. Joseph Sirgy, Val Larsen, and Newell D. Wright. (2002).
    Developing a Subjective Measure of Consumer Well Being. *Journal
    of Macromarketing*, 22 (2), 158-169.
Lee, J. and Lee, W. (2007). Country of Origin and Brand Familiarity in
    Consumer Product Evaluation: The Strategic Brand Alliance
    Perspective. *American Academy of Advertising and Korean
    Advertising Society*, Asia Pacific Conference, Seoul, Korea.
    Available online:
    http://advertising.utexas.edu/sp/groups/public/@commadvfac/docum
    ents/. Accessed on 6/3/09.
Lee, J. S., et al. (2004). Changing Roles and Values of Female Consumers in
    China. *Business Horizons*, May/June, 17-22.
Lee, Y. and O'Connor, G. C. (2003). The Impact of Communication Strategy
    on Launching New Products: The Moderating Role of Product
    Innovativeness. *Journal of Product Innovation Management*, 20(1),
    4-21.
Leedy, P.O., and Ormrod, J.E. (2005). *Practical Research: Planning and
    design.* 8th ed. Upper Saddle River, NJ: Pearson Prentice Hall.
Leimster, J.M., Pascal, S. and Helmut, K. (2004). *Success Factors of Virtual
    Communities from the Perspective of Members and Operators: An
    Empirical Study.* 37th Hawai International Conference on System
    Sciences.
Leng X, and Zhang M (2011). Shanzhai as a W eak Brand in Contemporary
    China Marketing. *Int. J. China Mark.*, 1(2): 81-94.
Leng, Xionghui. (2010). The Promotion Strategy of Marketing
    Communication Effects-Based on Involvement. *China* Business, 2,
    32-33.
Lew, Alan A. (1987). The History, Policies and Social Impact of
    International Tourism in the People's Republic of China. *Asian
    Profile*, 15(2),117-128.
Lewicki, R.J. and Bunker, B.B. (1995). Trust in Relationships: A Model of
    Trust Development and Decline in *Conflict, Cooperation and Justice*
    by B.B. Bunker and J.Z. Rubin. (Eds.). San Francisco: Jossey-Bass.
    133-173.
Li B, Tu H, and Li B (2011). Demand Attributes and Market Segmentation:
    An Evaluation of Refrigerator Purchase Behavior in Rural China. *Int.
    J. China Mark.*, 1(2): 13-33.

Li J, Mizerski D, Lee A, and Liu F (2009). The Relationship Between Attitude And Behavior: An Empirical Study In China. *Asia Pac. J. Mark. Logist.*, 21(2): 232-242.

Li Q, W ang X, and Yang Z (2011). The Effects of Corporate-Brand Credibility, Perceived Corporate-Brand Origin, and Self-Image Congruence on Purchase Intention: Evidence From China's Auto Industry. *J. Glob. Mark.*, 24(1): 58-68.

Li, C. (2007). *Brand Culture and Consumption: Chinese Consumers and theForeign Brands.* Available online: www.cerdi.org/uploads/sfCmsContent/html/253/LI_Chen.pdf. Accessed on 1/7/2011.

Li, D. and Gallup, A. (1995). In Search of the Chinese Consumer. *The China Business Review*, September-October, 19-22.

Li, F. and Wang, Y. (2006). Chinese Retailing Industry in the Form of Physical Stores in *The Development of the Retailing Industry in China (1981-2005)* by F. Li and G.Wang. (Eds.). Beijing: Social Science Literature Publishing House. 149-168.

Li, F., Zhou, N., Nicholls, J.A.F., Zhuang, G. and Kranendonk, C. (2004). Interlinear or Inscription? A Comparative Study of Chinese and American Mall Shoppers' behavior. *Journal of Consumer Marketing,* 21, 51-61.

Li, G., Zhao, L.L. (2007). 广州：日本人眼中的底特律 (Guangzhou Equals to Detroit: From a Japanese Perspective). *In Guangzhou Daily.* 3 May 2007, A2

Li, H, Daugherty T. and Biocca, F. (2003). The Role of Virtual Experience in Consumer Learning. *Journal of Consumer Psychology*, 13(4), 395-408.

Li, H. and Zhang, Y. (2007). The Role of Manager's Political Networking and Functional Experience in New Venture Performance: Evidence from China's Transition Economy. *Strategic Management Journal,* 28, 791-804.

Li, Q. (2010). (a, b, c, d). The Forthcoming of the Grey Tide - Pondering over the Population Aging in China. *Information on Scientific and Technical Resources* (in Chinese),10, 233.

Liang, K. and L. Jacobs. (1995). China's advertising agencies: Problems and relations. *International Journal of Advertising*, 13(3), 205-212.

Lilien, G. L. and Yoon, E. (1990). The Timing of Competitive Market Entry: An Exploratory Study of New Industrial Practices. *Management Science,* 36(5), 1633-1651.

Lillis, M. and Tian, R. (2010). Cultural Issues in Business World: An Anthropological Perspective, *Journal of Social Science*, 6 (1), 99-112.

Lillis, Michae,l and Robert Guang Tian. (2010). Cultural Issues in Business World: An Anthropological Perspective. *Journal of Social Science.* 6 (1), 99-112.

Lin, C. and Kao, D. (2004). The Impacts of Country-of-origin on Brand Equity. *Journal of American Academy of Business, Cambridge*, 5, 37-40.

Lin, M.Y. and Chang, L.H. (2003). Determinants of Habitual Behavior for National and Leading Brands in China. *Journal of Products and Brand Management*, 12, 94-104.

Linden Lab. (2010). *Second Life Security Bulletin.* Accessed 12 June 2010.

Liu F, Li J, and Cheng H (2006). Sex Appeal Advertising: Gender Differences In Chinese Consumers' Responses. *Asia Pac. J. Mark. Logist.*, 18(1): 19-28.

Liu K (2007). China, Emerging markets, Regional marketing, Retail trade, World economy. *Asia Pac. J. Mark. Logist.*, 19(4): 398-412.

Liu MT, Shi G, and Wong A (2010). How Physical Attractiveness and Endorser-Product Match-up Guide Selection of a Female Athlete Endorser in China. *J. Int. Consum. Mark.*, 22(2): 169-181.

Liu Y, and Tang F (2005). An Empirical Analysis on Pricing Patterns in China's Online Book Market. *J. Int. Consum. Mark.*, 18(1-2): 117-136.

Liu, Hen jiang, and Ji Xiang Chen. (2005 a). Dynamism and Competitive Advantage: The Development Logic of Industrial Clusters. *Chinese Soft Science* (in Chinese), 2005(2), 125-130.

Liu, Hen Jiang, and Ji Xiang Chen. (2005 b). The Development Research of China Industrial Cluster Based on the Dynamism. *Economic Geography* (in Chinese), 25(5):607-611.

Liu, K. (2007). Unfolding the Post-transition Era: The Landscape and Mindscape of China's Retail Industry after 2004. *Asia Pacific Journal of Marketing and Logistics*, 19, 398-412.

Liu, Lanjian, and Si Chunlin. (2010). Lower Market Destroys: The Case about Shanzhai Handset. *Technical Economy and Management Research*, 3, 46-49.

Liu, W. (2008). *KFC in China: Secret Recipe for Success.* Singapore: Wiley and Sons.

Logan RK, and McEwan D (2010). The Emerging of New Business Culture: A Few Key Issues Pertain to Open Economy and Marketing. *Int. J. China Mark.*, 1(1): 73-84.

Lovelock, C. H. (1983). Classifying Services to Gain Strategic Marketing Insights. *Journal of Marketing,* 47, 8-24.

Low, G. and Lamb, C. (2000). The Measurement and Dimensionality of Brand Associations. *Journal of Product and Brand Management,* 9(6), 350-68.

Lowry, P.B, Robert, T.L. Romano, N.C., Cheney, P.D. and Hightower, R.T. (2006). The Impact of Group Size and Social Presence on Small-Group Communication. *Small Group Research,* 37(3), 631-661.

Lu, Taihong. (2005). *Consumer Behavior.* Beijing: Higher Education Press.

Luce, Turkey. (1964). Simultaneous Conjoint Measurement: A New Type of Fundamental Measurement. *Journal of Mathematical Psychology*, 1, (09), 1-27.

Luga Lake Mosou Cultural Development Association. Available online: http://mosuoproject.org/. Accessed on March 2011.

Luk STK, Li ELY, Ye W , and Xue Y (2003). Characteristics of Chinese Wholesalers' Marketing Behavior: A Functional Approach. *J. Glob. Mark.*, 16(1-2): 71-95.

Luo Y. (2003). Industrial Dynamics and Managerial Networking in an Emerging Market: The Case of China. *Strategic Management Journal* , 24 (13), 1315-1327.

Luo, Gangyi. (2009). An Analysis of Advantages and Strategies of Shanzhai Marketing. *China Business*. 10, 90-91.

Lury, C. (1996). *Consumer Culture*. NK, Brunswick: Rutgers University Press.

Lv, You Ping. (2005). Competitiveness of Clusters of Zhejiang Based on Cooperative Marketing. *Business Economics and Management* (in Chinese), 8, 47-56.

Lyn, P. (2008). Second Life: The Seventh Face of the Library. *Electronic Library and Information Systems*, 42(1), 232- 242.

MacCallum, R.C., Browne, M.W. and Sugawara, H., M. (1996). Power Analysis and Determination of Sample Size for Covariance Structure Modeling. *Psychological Methods*, 1 (2), 130-49.

MacKenzie, S. and Lutz, R. (1982). Monitoring Advertising Effectiveness: A Structural Equation Analysis of the Mediating Role of Attitude Toward the Ad. Working Paper No. 117, *Centre for Marketing Studies*, UCLA, Los Angeles, CA.

MacNeal JU, and Mindy FJ (1996). Children's Influence on Chinese Families' Newfound Leisure Time and Its Marketing Implications. *Asia Pac. J. Mark. Logist.*, 8(3): 32-57.

Maestas, N. and Zissimopoulos, J. (2010). How Longer Work Lives Ease the Crunch of Population Aging. *Journal of Economic Prospective*, 24 (1), Winter, 139- 160.

Maheswaran, D. (1994), Promoting Country-of-origin as a Stereotype: Effects of Consumer Expertise and Attribute Strength on Product Evaluations, *Journal of Consumer Research*, 21, 354-65.

Mai, L.W. and Zhao, H. (2004). The Characteristics of Supermarket Shoppers in Beijing. *International Journal of Retail and Distribution Management,* 32, 56-62.

Maidique, M. and Zirger, B. J. (1984). A Study of Success and Failure in Product Innovation: The Case of the U.S. Electronics Industry. *IEEE Transactions on Engineering Management*, EM-31 (4), 192-203.

Malhotra, N.K. (1996). *Marketing Research: An Applied Orientation.* 2nd edn. NJ, Upper Saddle River: Prentice-Hall.

Mantel, S. and Kardes, F. (1999). The Role of Direction of Comparison, Attribute-based Processing, and Attitude-based Processing in Consumer Preference. *Journal of Consumer Research,* 25 (March), 335–52.

Mariampolski, H. (2001). *Qualitative Market Research.* CA, Thousand Oaks: Sage.

Markus, M.L. (1994). Electronic Mail as the Medium of Managerial Choice. *Organization Science*, 5(4), 502-527.

Martin, I. M. and Eroglu, S. (1993). Measuring a Multi-dimensional Construct: Country Image, *Journal of Business Research*, 28 (3), 191-210

Matsunaga. (2000). *The Changing Face of Japanese Retail: Working in a Chain Store.* London and New York: Routledge.

McAllister, D. (1995). Affect- and Cognition-based Trust as Foundations for Interpersonal Cooperation in Organizations. *Academy of Management Review*, 38(1), 24-59.

McGoldrick, P.J. and Ho, S.L. (1992). International Position: Japanese Department Stores in Hong Kong. *European Journal of Marketing,* 26(9), 61-73.

Menon, A., Bharadwaj, S.G. and Howell, R. (1996). The Quality and Effectiveness of Marketing Strategy: Effects of Functional and Dysfunctional Conflict in Interorganizational Relationships. *Journal of the Academy of Marketing Science,* 24, 299-313.

Messinger, P.R., Stroulia, E., Lyons, K., Bone, M., Niud, R.H., Smirnova, K. and Perelgute, S. (2009). Virtual Worlds-Past, Present and Future: New Direction in Social Computing. *Decision Support Systems*, 47(3), 204-228.

Michael J. Barone, Anthony D. Miyazaki, and Kimberly A. Taylor. (2000). The Influence of Cause-elated Marketing on Consumer Choice: Does One Good Turn Deserve Another? *Journal of the Academy of Marketing Science*, 28(2), 248-262.

Millson, M. R., Raj, S.P. and Wilemon, D. (1992). A Survey of Major Approaches for Accelerating New Product Development. *Journal of Product Innovation Management,* 9(1), 53-69.

Ministry of International Trade and Industry Website. (1997). *Highlights of The 6th Basic Survey of Overseas Business activities of Japanese companies (Definite Report).* Available online: http://www.miti.go.jp/intro-e/a225101e.html. Accessed on March 1, 2008.

Mintu, A.T., Calantone, R. J. and Gassenheimer, J. B. (1994). Towards Improving Cross-Cultural Research: Extending Churchill's Research Paradigm. *Journal of International Consumer Marketing,* 7(2), 5-23.

Monga, A. B. and John, D. R. (2007). Cultural Differences in Brand Extension Evaluation: The Influence of Analytic Versus Holistic Thinking. *Journal of Consumer Research, 33,* 529-536.

Montoya-Weiss, M. M. and Calantone, R. J. (1994). Determinants of New Product Performance: A Review and Meta-Analysis. *Journal of Product Innovation Management,* 11(5), 397-418.

Mooij, M. de (2004). *Consumer Behavior and Culture,* London, UK: SAGE.

Moore, D., Harris, W. and Chen, H. (1995). Affect Intensity: An Individual Difference Response to Advertising Appeals. *Journal of Consumer Research,* 22 (2), 154– 64.

Moorman, C. and Slotegraaf, R. J. (1999). The Contingency Value of Complementary Capabilities in Product Development. *Journal of Marketing Research,* 36 (2), 239-257.

Morgan, R.M. and Hunt, S.D. (1994). The Commitment-Trust Theory of Relationship Marketing. *Journal of Marketing,* 58 (3), 20-38.

Morrison, Allistar. (1989). *Tourism and Hospitality Marketing.* NY, Albany: Delmar.

Mortensen, L. and Nicholas, G. (2010). Riding the Tourism Train?: Navigating Intellectual Property Heritage and Community Based Approaches to Cultural Tourism. *Anthropology News*, 51, 11-12.

Mu, J. Peng, G. and MacLachlan, D.L. (2009). Effect of Risk Management on NPD Performance. *Technovation,* 29 (3), 170–180.

Mu, Ming. and Juan Wang. (2007). Regional Clusters of SMEs Tourism Marketing and Its Applicability. *Learning and Practice* (in Chinese), 2, 46-47.

Mu, R. and Fan, Y. (2011). Framework for Building National Innovation Capacity in China. *Journal of Chinese Economic and Business Studies*, 9(4), 317-327.

Myers, M. B., Calantone, R. J., Page, T. J., Jr. and Taylor, C. R. (2000). An Application of Multiple-Group Causal Models in Assessing Cross-

Cultural Measurement Equivalence. *Journal of International Marketing,* 8 (4), 108-121.

Narver, J. C., Slater, S. F. and MacLachlan, D. L. (2004). Responsive and Proactive Market Orientation and New-Product Success. *Journal of Product Innovation Management*, 21(5), 334-347.

Narver, J.C. and Slater, S.F. (1990).The Effect of a Market Orientation on Business Profitability. *Journal of Marketing,* 54 (4), 80-93.

Nass, C. and Moon, Y. (2000). Machines and Mindlessness: Social Responses to Computers. *Journal of Social Issues,* 56(1), 81-103.

Nelson, M. R. and Paek, H. J. (2005). Cross-cultural Differences in Sexual Advertising Content in a Transnational Women's magazine. *Sex Roles*, 53, 371-384.

Nelson, P. (1970). Information and Consumer Behavior, *Journal of Political Economy*, 78, 311-329.

Netemeyer, R., Durvasula, S. and Lichtenstein, D. (1991). A Cross-national Assessment of the Reliability and Validity of the CETSCALE. *Journal of Marketing Research*, 28, 320-327.

Nguyen, Tho D. (2009). Place Development: Attributes and Business Customer Satisfaction in Tien Giabg Province Vietnam. *Journal of Macromarketing*, 29 December, 384-391.

Nick G. (2007). *Entropia's Virtual World Comes to China.* Available online: http://techcrunch.com/tag/entropia-universe/. Accessed on August 17, 2010.

Norman, D. N. (1998). *The Design of Everyday Things.* New York: Doubleday. Available online: http://katsvision.com/canm606/session_3/03_norman_01.pdf. Assessed on May 27, 2009.

Norton, J., Parry, M. E. and Song, M. (1994). Integrating RandD and Marketing: A Comparison of Practices in the Japanese and American Chemical Industries. *IEEE Transactions on Engineering Management,* 41(1), 5-20.

O'reilly T. (2005). *What is web 2.0.* Available online: http://www.oreillynet.com/pub/a/oreilly/tim/news/2005/09/30/what-is-web- 20.html. Accessed on March 5, 2010.

Oates, B.J. (2006). *Researching Information Systems and Computing.* CA, Thousand Oaks: Sage.

Oh L, and Zhang Y (2010). Understanding Chinese Users' Preference for Domestic over Foreign Internet Services. *J. Int. Consum. Mark.*, 22(3): 227-243.

Okechuku, C. (1994). The Importance of Product Country of Origin: A Conjoint Analysis of the USA, Canada, Germany, and the Netherlands. *European Journal of Marketing*, 28(4), 5-19.

Oliver, R.L. (1997). *Satisfaction: A Behavioral Perspective on the Consumer.* New York: McGraw Hill.

Olshansky, S.J. (2009). Future Trends in Human Longevity: Implications for Investments, Pension and the Global Economy. *Pensions,* 14, (3), 149-163.

Olson, E. M., Walker, O.C., Jr. and Ruekert, R. W. (1995). Organizing for Effective New Product Development: The Moderating Role of Product Innovativeness. *Journal of Marketing*, 59 (1), 48-62.

Ondrejka, C.R. (2006). Escaping the Gilded Cage: User Created Content and Building the Metaverse. in *The State of Play: Law, Games, and Virtual Worlds* by Balkin J.M. and Noveck, B.S. (Eds.). New York: New York University Press.

Ou, W.M., Abratt, R. and Dion, P. (2006). The Influence of Retailer Reputation on Store Patronage. *Journal of Retailing and Consumer Services*, 13, 221-230.

Ouyang M, Zhou D, and Zhou N (2000). Twenty Years of Research on Marketing in China. *J. Glob. Mark.*, 14(1-2): 187-201.

Özsomer, A. and Altares, S. (2008), Global Brand Purchase Likelihood: A Critical Synthesis and Integrated Conceptual Framework. *Journal of International Marketing*, 16(4), 1-28.

Padsakoff, P. and Organ, D. (1986). Self-Reports in Organizational Research: Problem and Prospects, *Journal of Management,* 12 (4), 531-544.

Page, R. and Aaron, B. (2005). Age-Related Differences in Responses to Emotional Advertisements. *Journal of Consumer Research*, 32, 343-354.

Paliwoda, Stanley J. and John K. Ryans (2008). *International Business vs. International Marketing.* UK, Cheltenham: Edward Elgar Publishing.

Panigrahi B, Ede FO, and Calcich S (2002). American Executives' Perceptions of The Business Climate of The Two Emerging Markets of India and China. *Asia Pac. J. Mark. Logist.*, 14(1): 40-58.

Panitz, B. (2000). A Promising Future. *Restaurant USA: The Magazine of the National Restaurant Association*, 20(2), 13-18.

Papadopoulos, N. and Heslop, L. A. (1990). A Comparative Image Analysis of Domestic Versus Imported Products, *International Journal of Research in Marketing*, 7, 283-294.

Papadopoulos, N. and Heslop, L. A. (1993). *Product and Country Images: Impact and Role in International, Marketing.* New York: Haworth Press.

Pappu, R., Quester, P. and Cooksey, R. (2006). Country Image and Consumer-based Brand Equity: Relationships and Implications for International Marketing. *Journal of International Business Studies*, 38, 726-745.

371

Parasuraman, A., L. L. Berry, and V. A. Zeithaml. (1991). Understanding Customer Expectations of Service. *Sloan Management Review*, 52(3), 39-48.

Parasuraman, A., V. A. Zeithaml, and L. L. Berry. (1985). A Conceptual Model of Service Quality and Its Implications for Future Research. *Journal of Marketing*, Fall, 41-50.

Parker RS, Haytco DL, and Hermans CM (2011). Ethnocentrism and Its Effect on the Chinese Consumer: A Threat to Foreign Goods? *J. Glob. Mark.*, 24(1): 4-17.

Parry, M. E. and Song, M. (1994), Identifying New Product Success in China. *Journal of Product Innovation Management*, 11(1), 15-30.

Peltier, J. and Schibrowsky, J. (1994). Need for Cognition, Advertisement Viewing Time and Memory for Advertising Stimuli. *Advertising Consumer Research*, 21(1), 244-50.

Peng, M. W. (2009). *Global Business*. OH, Mason: South-Western Cengage Learning.

Percy, L. and Rossiter, J. (2006). A Model of Brand Awareness and Brand Attitude

Peter, R., Mark, B. Aukje, T. and Marcia, L. (2008). *Face to Face with White Rabbit-Sharing Ideas in Second Life*. New Zealand: Victoria University of Wellington

Petersen, K., Handfield, R. B. and Ragatz, G.L. (2003). A Model of Supplier Integration into New Product Development. *Journal of Product Innovation Management*, 29 (4), 284-299.

Petty, R. E., Cacioppo, J. T. and Schumaun, D. (1983). Central and Peripheral Routes to Advertising Effectiveness: The Moderating Role of Involvement. *Journal of Consumer Research*, 10 (2), 135-146.

Petty, R.E., J.T.Cacipoop, and D.Schumann. (1983). Central and Peripheral Routes to Advertising Effectiveness: The Moderating Role of Involvement. *Journal of Consumer Research*. 10, 135-146.

Pharr, J. (2005). Synthesizing Country-of-origin Research from the Last Decade: Is the Concept still Salient in an Era of Global Brands? *Journal of Marketing: Theory and Practice,* 13 (4), 34-45

Phau, I. and Suntornnond, V. (2006). Dimensions of Consumer Knowledge and its Impacts on Country of Origin Effects among Australia Consumers: A Case of Fast-consuming Product. *Journal of Consumer Marketing,* 23 (1), 34-42.

Pheng LS (2000). Chinese Business Principles (770-221 B.C.): Relevance For Real Estate Marketing And Management. *Asia Pac. J. Mark. Logist.*, 12(1): 17-36.

Phillips, L. (1981). Assessing Measurement Error in Key Informant Reports: A Methodological Note on Organizational Analysis in Marketing. *Journal of Marketing Research,* 18, 395-415.

Pillsbury, R. (1998). *No Foreign Food: The American Diet in Time and Place.* CO, Boulder: Westview Press.

Podoshen, J.S., Li, L. and Zhang, J. (2011). Materialism and Conspicuous Consumption in China: A Cross Cultural Examination. *International Journal of Consumer Studies*, 35, 17-25.

Podsakoff, P.M. and Organ, D. (1986). Self-Reports in Organizational Research: Problems and Prospects. *Journal of Management,* 12, 531-543.

Pollay RW (1983). "Measuring The Cultural Values Manifest In Advertising." in Leigh J H, Martin CR Jr., (Eds.). *Current Issues and Research in Advertising.* Ann Arbor: Graduate School of Business, Division of Research, University of Michigan, 72-92.

Pollay, R. W. (1983). Measuring the Cultural Values Manifest in Advertising. in *Current Issues and Research in Advertising* by J. H. Leigh and C. R. Martin, Jr.. (Eds.). Ann Arbor: Graduate School of Business, Division of Research, University of Michigan. 72-92.

Pollay, R. W. and Gallagher, K. (1990). Advertising and Cultural Values: Reflections in the Distorted Mirror. *International Journal of Advertising*, 9, 359-372.

Pooler, J. (2003). Why We Shop: Emotional Rewards and Retail Strategies. CT, Westport: Praeger.

Porter, M. E. (1980), *Competitive Strategy.* New York: Free Press.

Porter, M. E. (1986). *Competition in Global Industries.* Boston: Harvard Business School Press.

Porter, Michael E. (1990). *Competitive Advantage of Nations* (in Chinese). Beijing: CITIC Publishing House.

Powers, P.J. (2000). Reports on Foreign Supermarkets Woes are Misleading. *China Business Review,* 27, 54.

Prugsamatz S, and Ofstad L (2006). The Influence Of Explicit And Implicit Service Promises On Chinese Students' Expectations Of Overseas Universities. *Asia Pac. J. Mark. Logist.*, 18(2): 129-145.

Pucik, V. (1999). When Performance Does Not Matter: Human Resource Management in Japanese Owned U.S. Affiliates in *Japanese Multinationals Abroad: Individual and Organizational Learning by* S.L. Beechler and A. Bird. (Eds.). New York: Oxford University Press. 169–188.

Purcell, P. J. (2007). Pension Sponsorship and Participation. *Journal of Pension Planning and Compliance*, 24(4), 45-46.

Purcell, P. J. (2009). Older Workers: Employment and Retirement Trends.

Journal of Deferred Compensation, 5, 98- 99.

Puto, C. P. and Wells, W. D. (1984). Informational and Transformational Advertising: The Differential Effects of Time. *Advances in Consumer Research.* 11, 638-643.

Qi, F. (2005). Building a New Pension Mode with Chinese Characteristics. *Economic Issues Inquiry* (in Chinese), 2, 59.

Ramya Neelamegham and Dipark Jain. (1999). Consumer Choice Process for Experience Goods: An Econometric Model and Analysis. *Journal of Marketing Research*, 36(3), 373-386.

Rao, Akshay R., Mark E. Bergen, and Scott Davis. (2000). How to Fight a Price War. *Harvard Business Review*, 78 (2), 107-117.

Rappa, M. (2009). *Business Models on the Web.* Available online: http://digitalenterprise.org/models/models.pdf. Accessed on April 10, 2009.

Ratchford, B. (1987). New Insights about the FCB Grid. *Journal of Advertising Research*, 27 (4), 24-38.

Reeves, B. and Nass, C.I. (1996). *The Media Equation: How People Treat Computers, Television and New Media Real People and Places.* CA, Stanford: CSLI Publications.

Ren, L., Xue, G. and Krabbendam, K. (2010). Sustainable Competitive Advantage and Marketing Innovation within Firms: A Pragmatic Approach for Chinese Firms. *Management Research Review*, 33 (1), 79-89.

Resnik A. and Stern B. (1977). An Analysis of Information Content in Television Advertising. *Journal of Marketing*, 41 (1), 50-53.

Ritzer, George. (2000), *The McDonaldization of Society.* CA, Thousand Oaks, Pine Forge Press.

Ritzer, George. (2007), *The Globalization of Nothing 2.* CA, Thousand Oaks, Pine Forge Press.

Roberts, J.and Cayla, J. (2009). Global Branding. in *The SAGE Handbook of International Marketing* by Kotabe, M. and Helsen, K. (Eds.). CA, Thousand Oaks: Sage.346-360.

Robertson, R. (1987). Globalization and Societal Modernization: A Note on Japan and Japanese Religion. *Sociological Analysis,* 47, 35-42.

Rodrigues, C. (2001). *International Management: A Cultural Approach.* Cincinnati, OH: South-Western College Publishing.

Rojas, D S. and Turner, E. (2011). Spam and Pop Tarts? Joint Response to Anthropology and Tourism. *Anthropology News*, V 52b # 4.

Romaniuk, J. and Bogomolova, S. (2005). Variation in Brand Trust Scores. *Journal of Targeting, Measurement and Analysis for Marketing*, 13(4), 363-373.

Rosenbloom, A. and Haefner, J. (2009). Country-of-origin Effects and Global Brand Trust: A First Look. *Journal of Global Marketing,* 22(4), 267-278.

Rosenbloom, A., Marcheva, A. and Haefner, J. (2011). Global Brand Perceptions of Bulgarian Consumers: Some Contemporary Insights in *Mechanisms for Managing the Development of Socio-economic Systems* by Martyakova, E. (Eds.). Donetsk, Ukraine: DVNZ Don NTU, 269-276.

Roth, M. and Romeo, J. (1992). Matching Product Category and Country Image Perceptions: A Framework for Managing Country of Origin Effects. *Journal of International Business Studies*, 23(3), 477-497.

Rothwell, R. (1972). *Factors for Success in Industrial Innovation from SAPPHO. A Comparative Study of Success and Failure in Industrial Innovation*. Brighton, Sussex: S.P.R.U.

Rotter, J. (1971). Generalized Expectancies for Interpersonal Trust. *American Psychologist*, 35, 1-7.

Rowley, J., Baregheh, A. and Sambrook, S. (2011). Towards an Innovation-type Mapping Tool. *Management Decision*, 49 (1), 73-86.

Rowley, T., Behrens, D. and Karckhardt, D. (2000). Redundant Governance Structures: An Analysis of Structural and Relational Embeddedness in the Steel and Semiconductor Industries. *Strategic Management Journal,* 21(3), 369-386.

Ruan, Shitao. (2009). Advantages and Disadvantages of "Shanzhai-Star" Being Spokesperson. *Advertiser Market Watch*, 9, 139.

Rubera, G. and Kirca, A. H. (2012). Firm Innovativeness and its Performance Outcomes: A Meta-analytic Review and Theoretical Integration. *Journal of Marketing*, 76(3), 130-147.

Ruekert, R. W. and Walker, O.C. (1987b). Marketing's Interaction with Other Functional Units: A Conceptual Framework and Empirical Evidence. *Journal of Marketing,* 51 (1), 1-19.

Ruekert, R.W. and Walker, O. C. (1987a). Interactions Between Marketing and Rand Departments in Implementing Different Business Strategies. *Strategic Management Journal*, 8, 233-248.

Ruiz, S. and Sicilia, M. (2004). The Impact of Cognitive and/or Affective Processing Styles on Consumer Response to Advertising Appeals. *Journal of Business Research*, 57 (6): 657- 664.

Rust, R.T., Lemon, K.N. and Zeithaml, V.A. (2004). *Return on Marketing: Using Customer Equity to focus marketing strategy. Journal of Marketing, 68(1), 109-127.*

Ruyter, K. and Scholl, N. (1998). Positioning Qualitative Market Research: Reflections from Theory and Practice. *Qualitative Market Research,* 1, 7-14.

Salter, D., Evans, N. and Forney, D. (1997). Test-retest of the Myers—Briggs Type Indicator: An Examination of Dominant Function. *Educational Psychology Measurement*, 57 (4), 590-597.

Samiee, S. and Jeong, I. (1994). Cross-cultural Research in Advertising: Assessment Methodologies. *Journal of the Academy of Marketing Science*, 22, 205-217.

Samiee, S., Shimp, T. and Sharma, S. (2005). Brand *Origin* Recognition Accuracy: Its Antecedents and Consumers' cognitive Limitations. *Journal of International Business Studies*, 36 (4), 379-397.

Samuelson, Paul A. and William D. Nordhaus. (1999). *Economics.* 6th edn.Translator: Chen Xiao (tr. （1999., Hua xia Publishing House, 62-65.

Saxon, Mike (2006). *An American's Guide To Doing Business In China: Negotiating Contracts And Agreements*. MA, Avon: Adams Media.

Schaefer, A.D., Hermans, C.M. and Parker, R. S. (2004). A Cross-cultural Exploration of Materialism in Adolescents. *International Journal of Consumer Studies, 28, 399-411.*

Scherbina, A., and Schlusche, B. (2012). Asset Bubbles: An Application to Residential Real Estate. *European Financial Management*, 18(3), 464-491.

Schermerhorn, J. R., Jr. and Nyaw, M.K. (1991). Managerial Leadership in Chinese Industrial Enterprises in *Organization and Management in China 1979-1990* by Shenkar, O. (Eds.). London: M. E. Sharpe, 9-21.

Schwartz, H. M. and S. M. Davis. (1981). Matching Corporate Culture and Business Strategy. *Organizational Dynamics*, 59, 91-98.

Second Life Users. (2010). Available online: http://dwellonit.taterunino.net/sl-statistical-charts/. Accessed on June 15, 2010.

Second Life. (2010). *Explore Second Life Through Our Destination Guide*. Available online: www.secondlife.com. Accessed on June 24, 2010.

Sekaran, U. (1983). Methodological and Theoretical Issues and Advancements in Cross-Cultural Research. *Journal of International Business Studies, 14* (4), 61-73.

Senguder, T. (2000). Effects of Values and Culture on International Consumer Satisfaction. *Journal of American Academy of Business, Cambridge, 12* (1), 96-103.

Senguder, Turan. (2007). Cross-National Customer Satisfaction Judgment in Turkey and the United States. in *Perspectives in Consumer Behavior: An Anthropological Approach* by S. Demirdjian, T. Senguder, and R. Tian (Eds.). Fort Worth, TX: Fellows Press of America. 63-75.

Sharma, S., Shimp, T. and Shin, J. (1995). Consumer Ethnocentrism: A Test of Antecedents and Moderators. *Journal of the Academy of Marketing Science*, 23(1), 26-37.

Shavitt, S. and Zhang, J. (2004). Advertising and culture. *Encyclopedia of Applied psychology,* 47-51.

Shen Y, and Wang X (2011). Citizen Satisfaction with Educational Services: The Marketing Implications of Public Administration. *Int. J. China Mark.*, 2(1): 77-91.

Sheng, S. and Yan, M. (2011). China vs. the United States: Market Connections and Trade Relations. *International Journal of China Marketing*, 2(1), 45-56.

Sheng, Y. S. and Mullen, M. R. (2011). A Hybrid Model for Export Market Opportunity Analysis. *International Marketing Review*, 28(2), 163-182.

Sherman, J. D., Souder, W. E. and Jenssen, S. A. (2000). Differential Effects of the Primary Forms of Cross-Functional Integration on Product Development Cycle Time. *Journal of Product Innovation Management,* 17(4), 257-267.

Shimp, T. A. and Sharma, S. (1987) .Consumer Ethnocentrism: Construction and Validation of the CETSCALE. *Journal of Marketing* Research, 24, 280-289.

Silverstein, B. (2009). Ethnic Food Brands: A Guide to the World on a Shelf. Available online: http://www.brandchannel.com/features_effect.asp?pf_id=477. Accessed On Aug, 2010.

Simonazzi, A. (2009). Care Regimes and National Employment Models. *Cambridge Journal of Economics*, 33, 211 – 232.

Sin LYM, and Ho S (2001). An Assessment Of Theoretical And Methodological Development In Consumer Research On Greater China: 1979-1997. *Asia Pac. J. Mark. Logist.*, 13(1): 3-42.

Sin, L. Y. M. and Ho, S. C. (2001). An Assessment of Theoretical and Methodological Development in Consumer Research on Greater China: 1979–1997. *Asia Pacific Journal of Marketing and Logistics*, 13(1), 3–42.

Singh JJ, Vitell SJ, Al-Khatib J, and Clarke IC (2007). The Role of Moral Intensity and Personal Moral Philosophies in the Ethical Decision Making of Marketers: A Cross-Cultural Comparison of China and the United States. *J. Int. Mark.*, 15(2): 86-112.

Sinohotelguide.com. (2000). *Attraction and Sightseeing in Kunming: Yunan Nationalities Villages*. Available online: http://www.sinohotelguide.com/kunming/tour/sight/nantion.html. Accessed on March, 2011.

Skallerud K, and Grønhaug K (2010). Chinese Food Retailers' Positioning Strategies And The Influence On Their Buying Behaviour. *Asia Pac. J. Mark. Logist.*, 22(2): 196-209.

Skrbis, Z., Kendall, G. and Woodward, I. (2004). Locating Cosmopolitanism: Between Humanist Ideal and Grounded Social Category. *Theory and Society,* 21, 115–129.

Slater, Charles C. (1979) *Macro-Marketing Distributive Processes From a Societal Perspective* Boulder Colorado: Graduate School of Business Administration.

Slater, Charles C. and Jenkins, Dorothy (1979) Systems Approach To Comparative Macromarketing in *Macro-Marketing: New Steps In The Learning Curve* by George Fisk and Robert Nason (Eds.). Boulder Colorado: Graduate School of Business.

Smith JR, Liu S, Liesch P, and Callois C (2010). The Role Of Behavioral, Normative, And Control Beliefs In The Consumption Of Australian Products And Services By Chinese Consumers. *Australas. Mark. J.,*18(4): 206-213.

Sojka, J. and Giese, J. (1997). Thinking and/or Feeling: An Examination of Interaction between Processing Styles. *Advertising Consumer Research.* 24, 438-442.

Solomon, Michael R. (2004). *Consumer Behavior: Buying, Having and Being.* 6th edn. NJ, Upper Saddle River: Prentice Hall.

Song, M. and Montoya-Weiss, M. M. (1998). Critical Development Activities for Really New Versus Incremental Products. *Journal of Product Innovation Management,* 15(2), 124-135.

Song, M. and Parry, M. E. (1994). The Dimensions of Industrial New Product Success and Failure in State Enterprises in the People's Republic of China. *Journal of Product Innovation Management,* 11(2), 105-118.

Song, M. and Parry, M. E. (1996). What Separates Japanese New Product Winners From Losers. *Journal of Product Innovation Management,* 13 (3), 1-14.

Song, M. and Parry, M. E. (1997a). The Determinants of Japanese New Product Successes. *Journal of Marketing Research,* 34 (1), 64-76.

Song, M. and Parry, M. E. (1997b). A Cross-National Comparative Study of New Product Development Processes: Japan and the United States. *Journal of Marketing,* 61 (2), 1-18.

Song, M., Montoya-Weiss, M. M. and Schmidt, J. B. (1997). Antecedents and Consequences of Cross-Functional Cooperation: A Comparison of RandD, Manufacturing, and Marketing Perspectives. *Journal of Product Innovation Management,* 14(1), 35-47.

Song, Yan and Yin Lu. (2010). Research on "Shanzhai" Pattern Based on "Segment Zero"-A Case of the Development of "Shanzhai" Mobile Telephone. *Rand D Management*.6, 39-46.

Spiggle, S. (1994). Analysis and Interpretation of Qualitative Data in Consumer Research. *Journal of Consumer Behavior*, 21, 491-503.

Spreng, R.A., Mackenzie, S. B. and Olshasky, R. W. (1996). A Reexamination for the Determinants of Consumer Satisfaction. *Journal of Marketing,* 60 (3), 15-32.

Stanworth JO (2009). Developers And Terminators In Hypermarkets' Relationships W ith Chinese Customers. *Asia Pac. J. Mark. Logist.*, 21(2): 280-293.

Steenkamp, J-E., Batra, R. and Alden, D. (2003). How Perceived Brand Globalness Creates Brand Value. *Journal of International Business Studies,* 34 (1), 53-65.

Steiger, J. H. (1989). EzPATH: *Causal Modeling .* IL, Evanston: SYSTAT.

Sternquist B, and Wang L (2010). Buying Committees In The Chinese Retail Industry. Asia *Pac. J. Mark. Logist.*, 22(4): 492-511.

Stewart, D. and Love, W. (1968). A General Canonical Correlation Index. *Psychological Bulletin*, 70, 160-163.

St-Maurice I., Sussmuth-Dyckerhoff, C. and Tsai H. (2008). What's New with the Chinese Consumer. *The McKinsey Quarterly*, 45, October, 1-8.

Stuart, B. and Brand, J.M. (2008). Value in Virtual Worlds: An Axiological Approach. *Journal of Electronic Commerce Research,* 9(3): 195-206.

Sun J, and Wang X (2007). Personal Global Connectivity and Consumer Behavior. *J. Int. Consum. Mark.*, 19(3): 103-119.

Sun S, and Wang Y (2010). Familiarity, Beliefs, Attitudes, and Consumer Responses Toward Online Advertising in China and the United States. *J. Glob. Mark.*, 23(2): 127-138.

Sun, S. (2007). On Cross-cultural Pragmatic Failure in English Advertisements Translated from Chinese, *Sino-US English Teaching*, 4(6), 60-65.

Sundar, S.S. and Nass, C.I. (2000). Source Orientation in Human-Computer Interaction: Programmer, Networker, Or Independent Social Actor"? *Communication Research*, 27(6): 683-703.

Sunderland, P. and R. M. Denny. (2007). *Doing Anthropology in Consumer Research*. CA, Walnut Creek: Left Coast Press.

Swike, E., Thompson, S. and Vasquez, C. (2008). Piracy in China. *Business Horizons*, 51(6), 493-500.

Swink, M. (2002). Product Development – Faster, On-Time. *Research-Technology Management* 45 (4), 50-58.

Syring, D. (2009). La Vida Matizada: Time Sense, Everyday Rhythms, and Globalized Ideas of Work. *Anthropology and Humanism,* 34, 119-34.

Tai SHC (2008). Relationship Between The Personal Values And Shopping Orientation Of Chinese Consumers. *Asia Pac. J. Mark. Logist.,* 20(4): 381-395.

Tai, S. H. (2008). Relationship between the Personal Values and Shopping Orientation of Chinese Consumers. *Asia Pacific Journal of Marketing,* 20(4), 381-395.

Tai, S.H.C. (2005). Shopping Style of Working Chinese Females. *Journal of Retailing and Consumer Services,* 12, 191-203.

Talamasca, A. (2008). *Second Life Addiction: Do You Have a Problem?* Available online http://www.secondlifeinsider.com/2006/10/13/sl-addiction-do-you-have-aproblem. Accessed on 12 Jun 2008.

Tang, E.P., Chan, R.Y.K. and Tai, S.H.C. (2001). Emotional Influence of Environmental Cues on Chinese Consumers in a Leisure Service Setting. *Journal of International Consumer Marketing,* 14, 67-87.

Taniguchi, T. (2005). A Cold Peace: The Changing Security Equation in Northeast Asia. *Orbis,* 49 (3), 445–457.

Tao, Yonghou. (2010). Formation Mechanism of Shanzhai Model and Its Implications to Organizational Innovation. *China Soft Science,* 11,123-143.

Tauber, E. M. (1972). Why do People Shop? *Journal of Marketing,* 36, 46-49.

Tavassoli, N. and Han, J. 2001. Auditory and Visual Brand Identifiers in Chinese and English. *Journal of International Marketing,* Vol 1(2), 13-28.

Taylor, B. (1999). Japanese Management Style in China? Production Practices in Japanese Manufacturing Plants. *New Technology, Work and Employment,* 14(2), 129-142.

Temporal, P. (2010). *Advanced Brand Management: Managing Brands in a Changing World.* 2nd edn. Singapore: John Wiley and Sons.

Terpstra, V. and Sarathy, R. (2001). *International Marketing,* 8th ed, IL, Chicago: Dryden Press.

The Guangzhou Japanese CCI Website. (2010). Available online http://gz.nicchu.com/guest/index.php. Accessed on Jan 29th, 2011

The State Council, People's Republic of China. Available online: www.gov.cn/jrzg/2006-02/09/content 183787.htm.

Thoelke, J. M., Hultink, E. J. and Robben, H. S. J. (2001). Launching New Product Features: A Multiple Case Examination. *Journal of Product Innovation Management,* 18(1), 3-14.

Thomas Reardon and Julio A. Berdegue. (2002). The Rapid Rise of Supermarket in Latin America: Challenges and Opportunities for

De-elopement. *Development Policy Review,* 371-388.

Thomlinson, John. (1991). *Cultural imperialism: a critical introduction.* MD, Baltimore: Johns Hopkins University Press.

Thompson, C.J. (1997). Interpreting Consumers: A Hermeneutical Framework for Deriving Marketing Insights from the Texts of Consumers' Consumption Stories. *Journal of Marketing Research,* 34, 438-455.

Thorellia HB (1988). What Can Third W orld Countries Learn from China? *J. Glob. Mark.,* 1(1-2): 69-84.

Tian G (2008). *A Critique of Pan-Market,* TX, Fort W orth: Fellows Press of America.

Tian K, and Borges L (2011). Cross-Cultural Issues in Marketing Communications: An Anthropological Perspective of International Business. *Int. J. China Mark.,* 2(1): forthcoming.

Tian RG, and Wang CH (2002). "China National Economies." in Pendergast, Sara, and Tom Pendergast (Eds.) W orldmark Encyclopedia of National Economies. 4 vols. MI, Farmington Hills: Gale Group.

Tian RG, and Wang CH (2010). Cross-Cultural Customer Satisfaction at a Chinese Restaurant: The Implications to China Foodservice Marketing. *Int. J. China Mark.,* 1(1): 60-72.

Tian Z, He Y, Zhao C, and Yi G (2005). The Pricing Behavior of Firms In The Chinese Iron And Steel Industry. *Asia Pac. J. Mark. Logist.,* 17(3): 67-88.

Tian, Guang (2008). *A Critique of Pan-Market.* TX, Fort Worth: Fellows Press of America.

Tian, Guang and Trotter, Dan. (2012) Key Issues In Cross-Cultural Business Communication: Anthropological Approaches To International Business. *African Journal of Business Management,* 6 (22), 6456-6464.

Tian, K. and Borges, L. (2011). Cross-Cultural Issues in Marketing Communications: An Anthropological Perspective of International Business. *International Journal of China Marketing,* 2(1), 110-126.

Tian, R. G. (2000). The Implications of Rights to Culture in Trans-national Marketing: An Anthropological Perspective. *High Plains Applied Anthropologist,* 20(2), 135-145.

Tian, R. G. and Camilla Wang (2002). China National Economies, in *Worldmark Encyclopedia of National Economies* by Pendergast Sara and Tom Pendergast. (Eds.) MI, Farmington Hills: Gale Group.

Tian, Robert G. (2001). Cultural Awareness of the Consumers at a Chinese Restaurant: An Anthropological Descriptive Analysis. *Journal of Food Products Marketing,* 7(1/2), 111-130.

Tian, Robert G. (2002 a). Marketing in the 21st Century: Cross-cultural Issues, *The Journal of the Association of Marketing Educators*, 5(3), 70-77.

Tian, Robert G. (2002 b) Anthropological Approaches to Marketing: The New Practices in the 21st Century. *Practicing Anthropology,* 24(1), Spring 39-40.

Tian, Robert G. and Camilla H. Wang. (2010). Cross-Cultural Customer Satisfaction at a Chinese Restaurant: The Implications to China Foodservice Marketing. *International Journal of China Marketing*, 1(1), 60-72.

Tian, Robert Guang and Camilla Hong Wang (2002). "China National Economies." in Pendergast, Sara, and Tom Pendergast (Eds.) *Worldmark Encyclopedia of National Economies*. 4 vols. MI, Farmington Hills: Gale Group.

Tomás, J. and G. Arias. (1998). A Relationship Marketing Approach to Guanxi. *European Journal of Marketing.* 32(1/2), 145-156.

Tomlinson, J. (2007). Cultural Globalization in *The Blackwell Companion to Globalization* by G. Ritzer (Eds). MA, Madden, MA: Blackwell Publishing. 352-366.

Towner, S. J. (1994). Four Ways to Accelerate New Product Development. *Long Range Planning,* 27(2), 57-65.

Travel China Guide. (2011).Bai Nationality. Available online: http://www.travelchinaguide.com/intro/nationality/bai/. Accessed on March 2011.

Trend Hunter World (2010). *Asian Fast Food Booms: China Restaurant Industry Remains a Huge Growth Opportunity*. Available online: http://www.trendhunter.com/trends/yumbrands. Accessed on August 2010.

Trott, P. (2005). *Innovation Management and New Product Development.* Harlow: Prentice-Hall.

Dan L. Trotter and Tian Guang. (2012). A Descriptive Inventory Study of Recent China Marketing Research. *African Journal of Business Management,* Vol. 6(17), pp. 5763-5772.

Troy, L. C., Hirunyawipada, T. and Paswan, A. K. (2008). Cross-Functional Integration and New Product Success: An Empirical Investigation of the Findings. *Journal of Marketing.* 72(6), 132-145.

Troy, L. C., Hirunyawipada, T. and Paswan, A. K. (2008). Cross-Functional Integration and New Product Success: An Empirical Investigation of the Findings. *Journal of Marketing.* 72(6), 132-145.

Tsang, A.S.L, Zhuang, G., Li, F. and Zhou, N. (2003). A Comparison of Shopping Behavior in Xi'an and Hong Kong Malls: Utilitarian

Versus Non-utilitarian Shoppers. *Journal of International Consumer Marketing*, 16, 29-46.

Tse, D.K., Belk, R.W, and Zhou, N. (1989). Becoming a Consumer Society: A Longitudinal and Cross-cultural Content Analysis of Print Ads from Hong Kong, The People's Republic China, and Taiwan. *Journal of Consumer Research*, 15, 452-472.

Tu H (2011). Cluster Marketing Models and Strategies: The Implications Thereof in the Chinese High-Tech Industry. *Int. J. China Mark.*, 1(2):34-44.

Tushman M.L. and Anderson, P. (1986). Technological Discontinuities and Organizational Environments. *Administrative Science Quarterly*, 31, 439-465.

Uncles M. and He, T. (n.d.). A Window on Consumer Behaviour Research in China. Available online: http://smib.vuw.ac.nz:8081/WWW/ANZMAC2006/documents/Uncl es_Mark.pdf. Accessed on 12/6/2010.

Uncles, M.D. and Kwok, S. (2009). Patterns of Store Patronage in Urban China. *Journal of Business Research*, 62, 68-81.

Upadhyay, Y. and Singh, S. (2006). Preference for Domestic Goods: A Study of Consumer Ethnocentrism. *The Journal of Business Perspective*, 10(3), 59-68.

Urban, G. L. and Hauser, J. R. (1993) *Design and Marketing of New Products*. 2nd edn., NJ, Englewood Cliffs: Prentice-Hall.

US-China Business Council. (2002). Gansu province. *China Business Review*, 29, 17-23.

Vedrashko, I. (2006). *Advertising in Computer Games.* MA, Cambridge: Massachusetts Institute of Technology.

Vic, K. (2007). *Watch out Second Life: China Launches Virtual Universe with Seven Million Souls.* Available online: http://www.guardian.co.uk/world/2007/jun/02/china.web2.0. Accessed on 2 June 2007.

Vili, L. (2007). *Second Life Moves to China, Becomes Family Friendly?* Available online: http://virtual-economy.org/blog/second_life_moves_to_china_bec.

Walle AH (2011). Marketing Equitable Ethnic Cultural Tourism in China. *Int. J. China Mark.*, 1(2): 57-69.

Walle, Alf H. (2010) *The Equitable Cultural Tourism Handbook.* NC, Charlotte: Information Age Publications.

Wang CL, Chen ZX, Chan AKK, and Zheng ZC (2000). The Influence of Hedonic Values on Consumer Behaviors. *J. Glob. Mark.*, 14(1-2):169-186.

Wang XH, Linyang Z, and Liu NR (2009). The Impacts of Brand Personality and Congruity on Purchase Intention: Evidence From the Chinese Mainland's Automobile Market. *J. Glob. Mark.*, 22(3): 199-215.

Wang, C.L., Siu, N.Y.M. and Hui, A.S.Y. (2004). Consumer Decision-making Style on Domestic and Important Brand Clothing. *European Journal of Marketing*, 38, 239-252.

Wang, G., Li, F. and Liu, X. (2008). The Development of the Retailing Industry in China: 1981-2005. *Journal of Marketing Channel*, 15, 145-166.

Wang, G., Li, F. and Lu, Q. (2006). An Empirical Study of Customer Satisfaction of Chained Hyper-markets in China: Based on Nationwide Survey Data of 20 Chained Hyper-markets. *Management World*, 6, 101-110.

Wang, H., and Wang, K. (2012). What is Unique About Chinese Real Estate Markets? *Journal of Real Estate Research*, 34(3), 275-289.

Wang, J. (2006). On China's Population Aging. *The Financial Field* (in Chinese), 1, 238.

Wang, J. (2008). *Brand New China: Advertising, Media, and Commercial Culture.* MA, Cambridge: Harvard University Press

Wang, Ji Chi (2001).*Corporate Cluster and Regional Development*(in Chinese). Peking: Peking University Press, 239.

Wang, Lili and Sheng Dong. (2007). More Perspectives on "Shanzhai" Phenomenon. *Advertising Grand Integrated.* 9th Version, 136.

Wang, S., Chan, S., and Xu, B. (2012). The Estimation and Determinants of the Price Elasticity of Housing Supply: Evidence from China. *Journal of Real Estate Research*, 34(2), 311-344.

Wang, S.G. (2009). Foreign Retailers in Post-WTO China: Stories of Success and Setbacks. *Asia Pacific Business Review,* 15(1), 59-77.

Wang, Z.M., Takao S. (1994). The Patterns of Human Resource *Management*: Eight Cases of Chinese-Japanese Joint Ventures and Two Cases of Wholly Japanese Ventures. *Journal of Managerial Psychology*, 9 (4), 12-22.

Wang, Z.Q. and Zhang, J. (2005). Surviving the Cycle. *China Daily*, 8, August, 3.

Watson, J. and Wright, K. (2000). Consumer Ethnocentrism and Attitudes Toward Domestic and Foreign Products. *European Journal of Marketing*, 34(9/10), 1149-1166.

Watson, James. (1990). McDonald's in Hong Kong: Consumerism, Dietary Change, and the Rise of a Children's Culture in *Golden Arches East: McDonald's in East Asia* by James L. Watson (Eds.). Stanford: Stanford University Press. 78-109.

Watson. E. (2006). *Golden Arches East: McDonald's in East Asia.* Palo Alto: Stanford University Press.

Wei S (1995). The New Features of Marketing Environment in The People's Republic of China. *Asia Pac. J. Mark. Logist.*, 7(3): 20-35. Wing CCK (1994). Distribution Reform and Retail Structure in China: An Empirical Analysis of Entries and Exits of Enterprises. *Asia Pac. J. Mark. Logist.*, 6(3): 3-25.

Wei, L. and Williams, M. (2007). *Innovations and Technology Research Laboratory.* Sydney, NSW, Australia: University of Technology Press.

Wei, Shou Hua (2002). Dynamics of Competition in Clusters with Reference to a Case. *China Industrial Economy* (in Chinese), 175(10): 27-34.

Westbrook, R. A. and Black, W. C. (1985). A Motivation-based Shopper Typology. *Journal of Retailing*, 61, 78-103.

Westbrook, R. A. and Reilly, M. D. (1983). Value Perception Disparity: An Alternative to the Disconfirmation of Expectation Theory of Consumer Satisfaction in *Advances of Consumer Research* by Bagozzi, R. P. and Tybout, A. M. (Eds). MI, Ann Arbor: Association of Consumer Research, 256-261.

Wittink D.R., Vriens M. and Burhenne W. (1994). Commercial Use of Conjoint Analysis in Europe: Results and Critical Reflections. *International Journal of Research in Marketing,* 11(1), 41-52.

Wong CY, Polonsky MJ, and Garma R (2008). The Impact Of Consumer Ethnocentrism And Country Of Origin Sub-Components For High Involvement Products On Young Chinese Consumers' Product Assessments. *Asia Pac. J. Mark. Logist.*, 20(4): 455-478.

Wong, A. and Dean, A. (2009). Enhancing Value for Chinese Shoppers: The Contribution of Store and Customer Characteristics. *Journal of Retailing and Consumer Sciences*, 16, 123-134.

Wong, G.K. and Yu, L. (2002). Income and Social Inequality in China: Impact on Consumption and Shopping Patterns. *International Journal of Social Economics*, 29, 370-384.

Wong, G.K. and Yu, L. (2003). Consumers' Perception of Store Image of Joint Venture Shopping Centers: First-tier Versus Second-tier Cities in China. *Journal of Retailing and Consumer Services*, 10, 61-70.

Wong, H.W. (1999). *Japanese Bosses, Chinese Workers: Power and Control in a Hong Kong Megastore,* England, Curzon Press.

Wong, M. andHendry, C. (1999). Comparing International Human Resource Management Practices between Yaohan and Jusco in Hong Kong. *Asia Pacific Business Review,* 6 (1), 104-122.

World Health Organization. (2007). Global Age – Friendly Cities, A Guide. *WHO Press,* 5.

Wu Z (2009). *China in the World Economy*. New York: Routledge.

Wu, J. and Liu, D. (2007). The Effect of Trust and Enjoyment on Intention to Play Online Games. *Journal of Electronic Commerce Research*, 8(4): 128-140.

Wu, J., Li, P.T. and Rao, S. (2009). Why They Enjoy Virtual Game Worlds? An Empirical Investigation. *Journal of Electronic Commerce Research*, 9(3), 219-230.

Wu, Xianying (2004). 跨国公司本土化策略的主要障碍及对策研究 (Research on Obstacles and Countermeasures of Localization Decision of MNC). *Forum on Science and Technology in China,* 6, 20-22.

Wu, Y. (2011). Innovation and Economic Growth in China: Evidence at the Provincial Level. *Journal of the Asia Pacific Economy*, 16(2), 129-142.

Wu, Zhongming (2009). *China in the World Economy*. New York: Routledge.

Xia, Ya Ming and Lina Chen. (2007)Wuhan China Optical Valley of Regional Branding. *Contemporary Economics*(in Chinese), 1, 14.

Xiao, G. and Kim, J. (2009). The Investigation of Chinese Consumer Values, Consumption Values, Life Satisfaction, and Consumption Behavior. *Psychology and Marketing*, 26, 610-624.

Xiaoqun He and Shaojie Chen.(2000). The Application of Conjoint Analysis in the Inquiry of Apartments. *Statistical Research,* 10 (12), 10-14.

Xinhua (2009). *Regulation on Revitalisation of Electronic Information Industry*. Available online: http://news.xinhuanet.com/fortune/2009-04/15/content_11191634.htm. accessed on: September 10, 2010.

Xinhua News Agency (2009). *China Aims for 3.3 Trillion Yuan Restaurant Industry by 2013.* Available online: http://news.xinhuanet.com/english/2009-01/26/content_10722259.htm. Accessed on August 2010.

Xu, Hongming. (2009). Adivon: Shanzhai Brands' Shanzhai Marketing. *New Marketing.* (2009)1, 44-46.

Xu, Q., Li, H., Hui, E., and Chen, Z. (2010). Evaluating the Real Estate Market by Confidence Index in China: A Case Study of Shenzhen. *International Journal of Housing Markets and Anlysis*, 3(4), 327-350.

Yan R. (1994). To Reach China's Consumers, Adapt to Guo Qing. *Harvard Business Review*, September-October 1994, 66-67.

Yang Z, Zhou N, and Chen J (2005). Brand Choice of Older Chinese Consumers. *J. Int. Consum. Mark.*, 17(4): 65-81.

Yang, D., Fryxell, G. E. and Sie, A. K. Y. (2008). Anti-piracy Effectiveness and Managerial Confidence: Insights from Multinationals in China. *Journal of World Business*, 43(3), 321-339.

Yang, Y. (2008). The Perfection of the Employment and Population Policies of China under the Condition of Population Aging . *The Finance of*

China (in Chinese), 7, 46.

Yang, Z.L., Zhou, N. and Chen J. (2005). Brand Choice of Older Chinese Consumers. *Journal of International Consumer Marketing*, 17, 65-81.

Yau, O.H.M. and Steele, H.C. (2000). *China Business: Challenges in the 21st Century*. Hong Kong: The Chinese University Press.

Yee, N. (2009). *The Norrathian Scrolls: A Study of Ever Quest*. Available online: http://www.nickyee. com/eqt/report.html. Accessed on March 21, 2009.

Yi L, and Jaffe, ED (2007). Economic development and channel evolution in The People's Republic of China. *Asia Pac. J. Mark. Logist*., 19(1): 22-39.

Yin, Lu, and LI Tianzhu. (2010). Study on the General Disciplinarian of Shanzhai Phenomena and Its Policy Suggestion. *Studies in Science of Science,* 3, 321-328.

Yin, R.K. (2003). *Case Study Research: Design and Methods*. 3rd edn. CA, Thousand Oaks: Sage.

Yohogi, Toshiyuki. (2007), 小売業国際化プロセス*(Retail Internationalization Process),* Tokyo: Yuhikaku.

Yu, LiAnne, Cynthia Chan, and Christopher Ireland (2006). *China's New Culture of Cool: Understanding the World's Fastest-Growing Market*. CA, Berkeley: New Riders Press.

Zaheer S. (1995). Overcoming the Liability of Foreignness. *Academy of Management Journal*, 38 (2), 341-360.

Zahra, S. J. and Covin, J. G. (1993). Business Strategy, Technology Policy and Firm Performance. *Strategic Management Journal* 14, 451-478.

Zaltman, G., Duncanand, R. and Holbek, J. (1973). *Innovations and Organizations*, New York: Wiley.

Zang,Y. and J.P. Neelankavil. (1997). The Influence of Culture on Advertising Effectiveness in China and the USA: Cross-cultural Study._*European Journal of Marketing*, 31(2), 134-149.

Zeithaml, A. Parasuraman and L. L. Berry (1990). *Delivering Quality Service: Balancing Customer Perceptions and Expectations*. New York: The Free Press.

Zhan,W. and Renwei, H. (2003),What Will the World Gain from China in Twenty Years? *The China Business Review*, 30 (2), 36-39.

Zhang ZJ, and Zhou D (2010). The Art of Price W ar: A Perspective From China. *Int. J. China Mark.*, 1(1): 17-30

Zhang, A., Zhang, Y. and Zhao, R. (2003). A Study of the RandD Efficiency and Productivity of Chinese Firms, *Journal of Comparative Economics*, 31 (3), 443-464.

Zhang, J. (2004). *Cultural Values Reflected in Chinese Advertisements: Self-construal and Persuasion Implications*, unpublished doctoral dissertation, University of Illinois at Urbana-Champaign.

Zhang, J. and Shavitt, S. (2003). Cultural Values in Advertisements to the Chinese X-generation: Promoting Modernity and Individualism. *Journal of Advertising, 32*(1), 23-33.

Zhang, N. (2009)The Influence of the Population Aging on the Labor Resources of China. *The Economy of North China* (in Chinese), 8, 10.

Zhang, Shu. (2005). *Make A Company Localized or Personalized: A Case Study of A Japanese Electric Subsidiary in Shanghai*, unpublished master thesis, the University of Hong Kong.

Zhang, X., Grigoriou, N. and Li, L. (2008). The Myth of China as a Single Market: The Influence of Personal Value Differences on Buying Decisions. *International Journal of Market Research*, 50, 377-402.

Zhang, Y. and Khare, A. (2009). The Impact of Accessible Identities on the Evaluation of Global Versus Local Products. *Journal of Consumer Research*, 36, 524-537.

Zhao, X. and F. Shen (1995). Audience Rreaction to Commercial Advertising in China in the 1980s. *International Journal of Advertising*. 14(4), 374-390.

Zhe Xu, Tingting Fang, Wenping Su. (2004). the Application of the Method of Combination Analysis in the Research on Consumers' Preference of Product Attributes. *Quantifiably Economic and Technologically Economic Research*, 12, (11), 138-149.

Zheng, Guangguan and Xuemei Chen.(2006).The Cluster Marketing Formation and Development of Exploration .*Commercial Economics Review*(in Chinese), 24(7),78-80.

Zhou Ling-qiang and Huang Zhu-hui. (2004). Sustainable Development of Rural Tourism in China: Challenges and Policies. *Economic Geography*, 4, 4.

Zhou Ying Heng, Lu Ling Xiao, and Geng Xian Hui.(2003). The Change of the Fresh Food Purchasing Channels and its Trend: An Investigation on Why Consumers in Nan Jing Select Supermarkets. *Journal of Chinese Distribution Economics, 4*, 14~17.

Zhou, L. and Wong, A (2008). Exploring the Influence of Product Conspicuousness and Social Compliance on Purchasing Motives of Young Chinese Consumers for Foreign Brands. *Journal of Consumer Behaviour*, 7, 470-483.

Zhu, Jianrong. (2003). Marketing Management of SME Clusters. *Journal of Beijing Technology and Business University (Social Science)* (in Chinese), 18(4), 26.

Zhu, K., Kraemer, K. and Xu, S. (2006). The Process of Innovation Assimilation by Firms in Different Countries: A Technology Diffusion Perspective. *Management Science*, 52 (10), 1557-1576.

Zhu, Y. and Warner, M. (2000). An Emerging Model of Employment Relations in China: A Divergent Path From the Japanese? *International business review*, 9, 345–361.

Zimmer, L. (2007). How Viable is Virtual Commerce? - Businesses That Understand the Potential of Second Life are Finding Real-World Commercial Opportunities in the Virtual Space, *Manhasset*, 6(1), 44-48.

Zinkhan, George M. (1994). International Advertising: A Research Agenda. *Journal of Advertising,* 23(1), 11-16.

Zirger, B. J. and Maidique, M. A. (1990). A Model of New Product Development: An Empirical Test. *Management Science,* 36(7), 867-883.

CONTRIBUTORS

C. Anthony Di Benedetto, Temple Univ./Technische Universiteit Endhoven
Roger J. Calantone, Michigan State University
Bin Cui, Yangzhou University
Lizhu Daivs, California State University, Fresno
James Haefner, Univesity of St. Francis
Nanch Hodges, University of North Carolina at Greensboro
Liping Hou, Southwestern University of Fiance and Economics
Franics R. Ille, Interatnional University of Monaco
Joong-won, Lee, California State University
Xionghui Leng, East China Jiaotong University
Baoku Li, Lianing Technical Univerity
Hao-Fan Mo, Jinwen University of Science and Technology
Jeseph Peyrefitte, Univeristy of Southern mississippi
Al Rosenblook, Dominican University
Gajendra Sharma, Lianing Technical University
Shirley Ye Sheng, Barry Univeristy
Michael Song, University of Missouri – Kansas City
Jian Sun, Graduate University of the Chinese Academy of Sciences
Chaoying Tang, Graduate University of the Chinese Academy of Sciences
Robert Guang Tian, Medaille College
Hongbo Tu, Wh Han Institute of Technology
Huang Wang, The University of Hong Kong
Camilla Hong Wang, Medaille College
Lijuan Wang, Lianing Technical University
Roman Wong, Barry University
Wong Ming Wong, Shantou University
Alf H. Walle, Shandong University of Science and Technology
Z. John Zhang, The Wharton School University of Pennsylvania
Mingyan Zhang, Nanchang University
Dongsheng Zhou, China-Europe International Business School

INDEX